Old World History
Grade 6

LAIDLAW HISTORY SERIES

Builders of America, Grade 4
American History, Grade 5
Old World History, Grade 6
United States History, Grade 7
United States History, Grade 8

Old World History
Grade 6

Rt. Rev. Msgr. Edmund J. Goebel, Ph.D.
Superintendent of Schools, Archdiocese of Milwaukee

Sister Mary Richardine, B.V.M.
Associate Secretary, Elementary School Department
National Catholic Educational Association
Washington, D.C.

John E. O'Loughlin, Ph.D.
History Department, Emmanuel College
Boston, Massachusetts

Consultant: Very Rev. Msgr. James Clyne, Ph.D.
Superintendent, Elementary Schools   *Archdiocese of Los Angeles*

LAIDLAW BROTHERS · PUBLISHERS
A Division of Doubleday & Company, Inc.

River Forest, Illinois

Summit, New Jersey   Palo Alto, California   Dallas, Texas   Atlanta, Georgia

ACKNOWLEDGMENTS

The authors especially wish to acknowledge the contribution made to THE LAIDLAW HISTORY SERIES by the late Rt. Rev. Msgr. Thomas J. Quigley, formerly Superintendent of Schools, Diocese of Pittsburgh, and co-author of OUR OLD WORLD BACKGROUND.

Grateful acknowledgment is also made to the following for their assistance in reviewing the manuscript and for their consultation:

Rev. Martin P. Harney, S.J.
Professor of History
Boston College
Boston, Massachusetts

Sister Mary Donalda, B.V.M.
Acting Chairman of the History Department
Mundelein College
Chicago, Illinois

Sister Mary Reynoldine, O.P.
Associate Professor Library Science
Rosary College, River Forest, Illinois
Editor of the National Catholic Book List

ILLUSTRATIONS

The maps for this book were prepared by George Armstrong. Other art work was drawn by George Armstrong, James Buckley, Raymon Naylor, and Marion Pahl.

Sources for photographs used in this book are acknowledged on page 384.

Contents

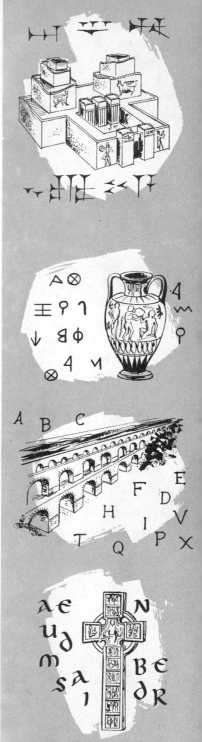

Unit *1 — Early Civilizations*

CHAPTER

1. Prehistoric Times 11
2. Peoples of the Ancient East 19

Unit *2 — The Ancient Greeks*

CHAPTER

3. The Civilization of Greece 43
4. The Glories of Greece 57

Unit *3 — The Story of Rome*

CHAPTER

5. Early Rome and the Republic 73
6. Rome Gains an Empire 87

Unit *4 — Growth of the Church*

CHAPTER

7. The Christian Era Begins 105
8. The Barbarian Invasions 115
9. The Rise of a New Religion 125
10. Europe Becomes Christian 131

Unit **5 — *The Early Middle Ages***

CHAPTER

11. A New Empire in the West 149

12. A New Political System 159

13. When Knighthood Was in Flower 169

14. The Church in the Middle Ages 181

Unit **6 — *Early England***

CHAPTER

15. England's Early History 199

16. The Normans in England 213

17. England in the Late Middle Ages 221

Unit **7 — *European Nations Develop***

CHAPTER

18. France Becomes a Nation 239

19. Two Nations: Spain and Portugal 253

20. Other Lands Become Nations 261

21. Wars to Rescue the Holy Land 275

Unit **8 — *The Late Middle Ages***

CHAPTER

22. Monks and Cathedrals 293

23. Schools and Culture in the Middle Ages 305

24. The Growth of Towns and Trade 315

Unit 9 – The Age of Change

CHAPTER

25. A New Age of the Arts and Learning   333

26. Protestant Revolution and Catholic Reformation . .   347

27. Europeans Begin to Explore the World   361

Glossary   373

Index   379

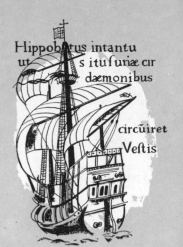

Hippobatus intantu
ut s itufunæ cir
daemonibus

circuiret
Veftis

Maps for You to Use

Ancient Egypt and the Near East   8
Ancient Egypt   20
The Ancient Near East   26
Ancient Greece   40
Alexander's Empire, 323 B.C.   65
The Italian Peninsula   70
The Roman Empire   93
Europe During Early Christian Times   102
The Holy Land   112
The Barbarian Migrations   116
Moslem Conquests   127
Saxon England   139
Charlemagne's Empire, 800 A.D.   146
Division of Charlemagne's Empire   157
The British Isles   196
Invasions of the Northmen   206
Western Europe at the Time of the Crusades   236
France   245
The Iberian Peninsula   254
The Holy Roman Empire   262
Medieval Italy   270
Movement of the Slavs   273
The Eastern Roman Empire   276
The Holy Land   280
Europe in the Late Middle Ages   290
Medieval Universities   306
Europe in an Age of Change   330
Trade Routes to the East   362
Routes of the Explorers   367

UNIT 1
Early Civilizations

(PREHISTORY — 500 B.C.)

CHAPTER

1. Prehistoric Times
2. Peoples of the Ancient East

ANCIENT EGYPT AND THE NEAR EAST

—— THE PERSIAN EMPIRE ABOUT 500 B.C.

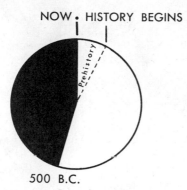

NOW • HISTORY BEGINS

Prehistory

500 B.C.

INTRODUCTION

Scientists believe that man had lived on the earth for many thousands of years before he invented writing. During that time he began, gradually, to learn to use his abilities to improve his ways of living, but his progress was very, very slow. Thousands of years passed as he learned how to make and to use crude tools and weapons, how to use fire, how to tame wild animals, and how to farm.

At last, in certain parts of the world, man began to progress more rapidly. He settled along the shores of warm seas or in fertile river valleys. These locations provided him with good soil, fresh water, and some protection from outside enemies. It was here that man began to achieve *civilization*. He learned to trade, or exchange, goods and ideas with others. He learned to live in groups under some form of government. He learned to use metals, and he learned to write.

The part of man's story from his creation until he learned to write is called *prehistory*. As soon as he learned to write and to keep written records of what he did, *history* began. In this unit we are first going to read about man's life during prehistory. Then we shall read about the very early history of man.

We shall learn how prehistoric man made his first slow advances and how, later, he began to make more rapid progress in using his abilities to improve his ways of living. Then we shall learn about some of the earliest civilizations in man's history —where they developed and how. We shall see that some of the ideas and discoveries of these very early civilizations are still being made use of today.

1

Prehistoric Times

THE OLD STONE AGE

The Clues. The time before writing was invented is called *prehistoric* time. To know how men lived in that period requires real detective work. It means studying every possible clue. The clues are the many kinds of remains left by men of long ago.

The scientist who is interested in finding the clues from prehistoric time is called an *archaeologist* (är'-kĕ·ŏl'ŏ·jĭst). An archaeologist must be a good detective. For example, an archaeologist may decide to explore a cave. On first sight he may see nothing more than a huge pile of dirt in a corner of the cave. The dirt may cover a heap of rubbish. By carefully clearing away the dirt and examining the rubbish, the scientist may uncover many important clues. He may find the bones of animals or birds that once had been

used for food. He may find stone arrowheads which would tell us that the men living in this cave during prehistoric time were hunters who used the bow and arrow.

*　　*　　*　　*　　*

If you have watched a detective solve a mystery on a TV program, tell how he made use of clues in the same way as an archaeologist.

*　　*　　*　　*　　*

Early Tools and Arts. Stones were among the earliest tools and weapons used by man. The first tools and weapons were rough and crude, since man used the stones just as he found them. The period when stones were used without being shaped or sharpened is called the *Old Stone Age.*

The women of prehistoric time made rough clothing by sewing to-

11

In prehistoric times, hunting was not a sport—it was a necessity. Man used the animals he killed for food and clothing. Often, he made spoons, needles, and fishhooks from the bones.

gether the skins of wild animals. This kind of clothing gave their men protection from the cold and from the rough branches of the forest as they went hunting. In addition to hunting animals, the men also searched for nuts, berries, fruits, and roots in order to feed their families.

Man drew pictures on the cave walls and many of these drawings may still be seen today. This was the earliest attempt at art. Such pictures were later developed into the earliest form of writing.

This ability of early man to draw and paint should be no surprise to us because man has many gifts which animals do not have. As you know, man is made in "the image and likeness of God." Even after Adam and Eve disobeyed God and were driven from the Garden of Eden man did not lose these gifts but used them to improve his life in many ways.

God's Gifts to Man. The mind of man is one of the most wonderful gifts of God. The mind enabled early man to think about events as they happened. The mind enabled him to remember other similar events. He could then plan new ways to escape danger and trouble. This gave man a great advantage in the struggle with his animal enemies, even though some of them were huge and powerful.

Speech is another wonderful gift of God. A person making a discovery or an improvement was able to tell his friends and neighbors about it. In turn, they could use the new way that made work easier. In this way knowledge was spread.

Each man has a remarkable pair of natural tools—his hands. They are far more skillful than the paws of any wild animal. The hands are capable of doing various types of work. They were of great value to early man in fashioning and using stone tools and weapons. Early man had another advantage in that he walked upright leaving his hands free for work.

* * * * *

Of all the gifts God gave to man, which one truly set him apart from the wild animals?

* * * * *

THE NEW STONE AGE

Improvement and Change. As the years passed, man slowly—very slowly—made many improvements in the stones that he used for tools and weapons. He learned to sharpen the stones and to shape them to fit his needs. Wooden handles were sometimes added. With the sharpened tools man could do better work. This change brought about another period which is called the *New Stone Age*. By the time man reached the New Stone Age, the clues show us that he had improved his living conditions in many other ways.

Lake Dwellers. During the summer of 1921 there was little rain in Switzerland. The waters of Lake Geneva sank to a very low level and revealed an interesting set of clues about man in the New Stone Age.

As the water level sank there appeared many wooden posts. These had served as supports for houses built out over the water. The prehistoric people of this area had built their homes on piers.

Other people in the New Stone Age lived in tents. You probably

In England, a prehistoric tribal monument— Stonehenge — still stands. The 40-ton rocks were positioned without the aid of machinery.

To escape from enemies and savage animals, some prehistoric men built their houses atop posts sunk deep into lake mud. What other reasons may have led men to become "lake dwellers?"

have seen pictures of the wigwams of North American Indians. The Indians were still living under New Stone Age conditions when the first European explorers and missionary priests arrived in America about 1500 years after the birth of Christ.

Freedom from Want. All the clues of the New Stone Age tell us that man had tamed, or domesticated, many animals. We know that during this period horses, dogs, cattle, sheep, and goats became the servants of man.

Cattle, for example, were a great help to early man. They supplied man with milk and meat for food. The skin could be used for clothing, for bed covering, and for tents. The horns and bones made good tools and weapons.

Man was constantly searching for animals to help him with his heavy work. The horse and oxen were found to be very helpful in pulling a plow or in carrying a heavy burden. In dry countries the camel was used and in cold lands the reindeer. In some countries man even tamed the elephant to be a beast of burden.

Man discovered how to grind certain wild grains into flour in order to make a coarse bread. Finding bread a nourishing food, man soon settled down to plant and care for the grain used in making bread. That is how farming began.

At first man probably broke the ground for planting with a sharp stick or even a sharp stone or shell. Later he may have used a sharp deerhorn or some animal's tooth fastened to a long stick. These were

14

the first crude plows. The next important step was to train animals to pull the plows. With his crops and his cattle and sheep, man became less of a hunter and more of a farmer.

With his increased food supply, man looked for some means of storing the grain after it ripened. Pottery came to be used for this purpose. Someone had discovered that clay would harden in the heat of the sun or of a fire. As man's skill improved, the clay was worked into various shapes and forms to make pottery that was beautiful as well as useful. A vast amount of pottery has been found in places where families of the New Stone Age lived.

The Use of Fire. We do not know how man first learned about fire. We do know that in the beginning fire was rarely used and was carefully guarded. In some places where men did not know about the true God, fire was worshiped as a god.

Sometime before prehistoric man entered the New Stone Age, he discovered the use of fire. In time, he found that fire helped him in a number of ways. Man cooked his food over a fire. Fire gave man warmth. It helped him bake his pottery. It gave him protection from wild animals because animals are afraid of fire.

* * * * *

How has fire helped man to preserve and store food?

* * * * *

New Stone Age man took steps toward becoming modern man. He moved out of the caves into simple houses. He learned to make threads for weaving cloth from flax and sheep's wool. He used fire as a weapon, a source of comfort, and as a means of cooking food and baking pottery.

Early Government. At this early period mankind lived together in families which consisted of more than father, mother, and children. The family included grandparents, aunts, uncles, and cousins. All lived together and worked together. As time went on and the number of families increased, groups of families joined to form clans or tribes. These clans and tribes used the old family ways of government in establishing their community life. There was a chief and council of elders who governed a tribe, much like the father and older members ruled a family.

THE AGE OF METALS

More Rapid Progress. There are no clues to indicate where or how man first discovered metals. Yet, he soon realized that metal was superior to stone for weapons and tools. While the period in which man used stone tools is called the Stone Age, the period in which he began to use metal tools is sometimes called the *Age of Metals.*

The first metal used by man was probably copper. Long after discovering copper man learned to mix it with tin and produce bronze, a harder metal. Next, man found that iron was a stronger metal than bronze. We say that people lived in the *Bronze Age* and then the *Iron Age* as these metals came to be the principal ones used.

* * * * *

Prehistoric man found many other uses for metal besides making tools and weapons. Can you think of some of them?

* * * * *

The Invention of Writing. It was probably over 3000 years before the birth of Christ that man learned how to write. Writing was very helpful in spreading new ideas. The best information we have as to how man lived is contained in his writings on paper, in clay, or carved in stone.

Early Metal Implements

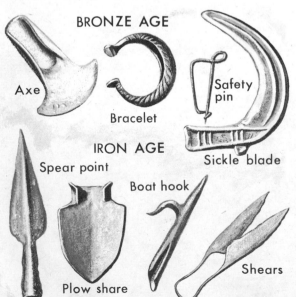

BRONZE AGE

Axe

Bracelet

Safety pin

Sickle blade

IRON AGE

Spear point

Boat hook

Plow share

Shears

These written records tell us how these early peoples improved their farms, built their homes and temples, and defended their lands against invaders. Some records describe religious beliefs, others explain laws and governments.

By the time man learned to write, he already had a large number of unwritten stories and songs which told of his earlier history. These had been passed along by word of mouth from one generation to another. When the songs were written down, it was difficult to separate what was true from what was made up. In spite of this, the stories and songs tell us a great deal about the life of man in the period before recorded history began.

In the case of the Hebrews, God revealed the chief events in their past history to Moses, one of their greatest leaders. Moses wrote down this story in five books, which form the first five books of the Old Testament in the Bible.

* * * * *

What are some of the ways your life would be different if man had not learned to write?

* * * * *

Summing Up. Certain scientists called archaeologists have pieced together a story of the earliest times

This primitive artist may have believed that his paintings of reindeer, bison, and other animals would bring him luck in hunting.

by using clues found in caves, villages, and burial mounds of prehistoric man. Pieces of tools, weapons, pottery, and jewelry each tell a story.

The archaeologists tell us that the changes in early man's way of life have taken a long time. During many thousands of years, man must have constantly struggled to use his God-given talents in order to make his life better. Through the centuries man's talents led him to discover how to speak and to write, how to use fire and metals, how to farm, and how to govern himself. By developing the gifts which God had given him, early man discovered and worked out many things important to our lives today.

FOR BETTER UNDERSTANDING

Checking Up

1. If you were an archaeologist where would you search for clues to the past?

2. What are some of the clues that tell us about man in the Old Stone Age?

3. What natural objects did man first use for tools?

4. What improvements brought about the New Stone Age?

5. Tell how man increased his food supply during the New Stone Age.

6. How did the gift of fire help man?

7. What advantages did man gain by using metals?

8. What are prehistoric times?

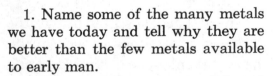

Yesterday and Today

1. Name some of the many metals we have today and tell why they are better than the few metals available to early man.

2. Is your diet more varied and healthful than that of early man? Explain your answer.

3. How did the way of life of the Indians that lived in your part of the country when the first Europeans arrived resemble the living conditions of prehistoric man?

Terms

Define: domesticated animals, pottery, archaeologist, Lake Dwellers, flint, bronze, Iron Age.

Interesting Things to Do

1. Most boys and girls are fond of animals. You might make a report tracing the history of the horse or the dog from prehistoric times to the present.

2. Visit a museum or library near your school that has tools or pictures of tools used by prehistoric man. You could then present an oral report to the class about man's development of the wheel or the boat.

3. A scrap book can help to make history more exciting. The class can decide to keep individual scrapbooks or to have one scrapbook for the entire class with each pupil making contributions. You may include pictures from magazines, postcards, photographs; you may draw maps or charts about the period of history you are studying. To begin your scrapbook make a report about the daily life of an Egyptian merchant. Use your classroom or library encyclopedia to help you. Draw colorful pictures to illustrate your report.

2

Peoples of the Ancient East

EGYPT, LAND ALONG THE NILE

Gift of the Nile. Egypt was one of the earliest countries to develop an important civilization. There the people made great gains in agriculture, architecture, business, government, and science. Many of these improvements have been of great value to us.

There are several reasons why the Egyptians made such an early start on the road to civilized living. The nature of the land reveals one of the reasons. Egypt had a fertile river valley set in the midst of a great desert area. If you look at the map on page 20, you will see that the Nile River rises in east-central Africa and flows northward to the Mediterranean Sea. Each year as the snows melt in the mountains near the sources of the Nile, its waters rise. As the rising waters flow northward, the Nile overflows its banks and floods the land of Egypt along both sides of the river.

These flood waters carry a rich mud, or silt, which is left on the land when the waters recede. This rich black soil, fresh each year, makes the land very fertile. If this flood did not happen regularly, Egypt would become a desert since there is little rainfall. The country is so dependent on this annual flood that an early historian called Egypt *the gift of the Nile.*

More Land, More Food. The Egyptians wanted to increase the area of their fertile land in order to grow more food. They needed more land than just the land near the river which was flooded every year. So they dug ditches to carry the flood waters into a wider area. Then they built dikes to hold the water on the land. By this skillful system

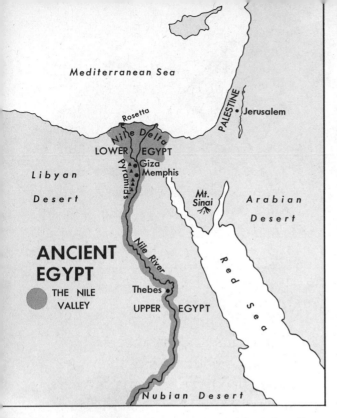

ANCIENT EGYPT

● THE NILE VALLEY

Mediterranean Sea

Rosetta

Nile Delta

LOWER EGYPT

Giza

Memphis

Pyramids

Libyan Desert

PALESTINE · Jerusalem

Mt. Sinai

Arabian Desert

Nile River

Red Sea

Thebes ●

UPPER EGYPT

Nubian Desert

Even today modern Egypt depends upon the waters of the Nile. In 1960 a great dam was started at *Aswan* on the upper Nile River. When the dam is completed much of Egypt will be supplied with a more regular flow of water. The storing of flood waters for release during the dry seasons will permit the Egyptians to enlarge their irrigated farming area and increase their food supply.

*　　*　　*　　*　　*

Can you name two large dams in the U.S. which supply water for irrigation projects and tell what states these dams are in?

*　　*　　*　　*　　*

Egyptian Government. At one period in its history Egypt was divided into two kingdoms. At a very early date, about 3,400 years before Christ, these two kingdoms were united into one nation. In the whole land of Egypt there were then no barriers to stop people from visiting one another. This meant that people could tell each other about new ideas they had and improvements they made. Egyptian civilization, therefore, developed at a more rapid rate than before. The Nile River furnished the main avenue for travel, for news, and for business in the days when roads were few.

called *irrigation* (ĭr′ĭ·gā′shŭn), the Egyptians were able to increase their food supplies.

With the increased supplies of grain and other foods, living became easier in Egypt. Life was rather easy in the Nile Valley. The climate was warm and the skies were always blue. The people had no worries about adequate shelter from the cold or snow. There was little danger of invading enemies because the desert on both sides of the valley gave protection. When a people do not have to worry about the threat of hunger, cold, and war, they have time to develop a great civilization. So it was with the Egyptians.

20

The united kingdom of Egypt was governed by a ruler called a *Pharaoh* (fâr'ō). The Pharaoh held great power over the land and the people. The nobles helped him govern. Usually the nobles were men who owned large areas of land. In addition, there were many freemen most of whom were engaged in business or commerce. The freemen had little to say about their government.

The number of slaves in ancient Egypt was very large. These slaves were forced to do the hard work. Many of them were mistreated and poorly fed. They labored long hours in the heat of the sun taking care of the estates of the great nobles. Slaves were also used in the building of the great monuments and temples. Some of these slaves had been captured in war. Some were people who had been sold into slavery. You probably remember the Bible story of Joseph, who was sold into slavery by his brothers.

* * * * *

Why, do you suppose, were there so many slaves in ancient Egypt?

* * * * *

WHAT THE EGYPTIANS WERE LIKE

Egyptian Monuments. The Pharaohs left a group of monuments that are called the *pyramids* (pǐr'à·mǐdz), many of which were built about 3000 years before Christ. The pyramids are huge structures. The largest pyramid is 760 feet on each of its four sides. The pyramids were one of the Seven Wonders of the Ancient World.

The Great Pyramid at *Giza* (gē'zà) with its temples and other buildings covers thirteen acres of ground. A Greek historian claimed that it took 100,000 men twenty years to build this pyramid. The pyramids at Giza are actually tombs and form a royal cemetery. The Pharaohs wanted to show their great power, so they built these elaborate tombs for themselves and their families.

Desert sands have blunted the features of the Great Sphinx at Giza which bears the face of the Pharaoh who built it about 4,800 years ago.

The burial chamber was located near the center of the pyramid. The entrance to the passageway which led to the burial place of a Pharaoh was usually a secret. This entrance was placed high up on the pyramid and carefully sealed. This was to prevent robbers from stealing the precious ornaments and articles which were placed in the tomb.

The Mummies. The Egyptians believed that the soul of a man did not die with the body. For this reason the nobles and rich men tried to preserve the body from destruction. After death the body was very carefully embalmed with spices and oils. Then it was wrapped in several layers of linen cloth. Next the body was placed in a casket, or case, that was shaped and painted to look like a man. Such an embalmed body is known as a *mummy*. Many of these mummies still exist. Some of them have been brought to this country. Perhaps you live near a museum which has one of these mummies.

The Egyptians tried to live honest and upright lives. They followed a rule of life which was very similar to the Ten Commandments. Egyptians believed that after death each man's soul was weighed to find out whether his good deeds were greater than his bad ones.

* * * * *

Does our knowing about the Egyptian belief in a life after death help us to understand the Egyptians' desire to live honest and upright lives?

* * * * *

Archaeologists discovered the tomb of King Tutankhamen in 1922. A gold mask inset with jewels covered the face of the mummy. The paintings on the wall were symbolic of the Pharaoh's life.

Many Egyptians believed that there was only one God, but most of them thought there were many gods. There was great confusion in their minds because they had no one to lead them to the true God.

Egyptian Writing. More important than the pyramids was the Egyptian invention of writing. At first the Egyptians wrote out their messages by drawing a different picture for each word. Later each picture represented a syllable. Such picture writing is called *hieroglyphic* (hī′ĕr·ŏ·glĭf′ĭk) writing. The Egyptians eventually reduced these pictures to an alphabet of twenty-four symbols, or letters.

The Egyptians invented a writing material called *papyrus* (pȧ·pī′rŭs). From the word papyrus we get our word *paper*. The papyrus plant was a reed which grew along the banks of the Nile River. These reeds were split lengthwise into thin strips. The strips were laid close together to form a layer. Then another layer was placed crosswise on this. After several layers were so made, the whole was soaked in water and then pressed tightly together. This formed a sheet of writing material which could be used like paper.

To write on papyrus the Egyptian writer, or scribe, used an ink made from water, soot, and the gum of

Hieroglyphics

Egyptian script

Greek

The Greek inscription on the Rosetta Stone provided a key to ancient Egyptian writing.

certain vegetables. For a pen he used a pointed reed slit at the end.

Rediscovering Hieroglyphics. After thousands of years hieroglyphic writing was no longer used. Finally there was no one alive who could read the hieroglyphics. Many attempts were made by scholars to find some clue to this ancient Egyptian writing, but none were successful.

In the year 1799, as the soldiers of Napoleon were digging trenches near the town of Rosetta at one of the mouths of the Nile River, they found a stone slab with three kinds of writing on it. The first inscription was in hieroglyphics. The second was in a later Egyptian script, which no one could read either. The third was in the Greek language, which many scholars could read.

Guessing that the three inscriptions contained the same message, a French scholar worked for a long time to decipher the hieroglyphics on the Rosetta Stone. In 1822, he announced that he had worked out the alphabet of the ancient Egyptians and could read the hieroglyphics. This provided the key to all other Egyptian writings.

EGYPTIAN LEARNING

Contributions to Science. Because the Nile River washed away all boundary markers each year, the Egyptians invented a method of surveying the land. By this method they were able to tell where the boundaries should be after the waters receded. This led them to the development of *geometry* (a Greek word meaning *earth measure*).

In constructing the pyramids and their great temples, it was necessary for the Egyptians to have exact measurements. They were able to make such measurements because they had developed the study of arithmetic in all its branches. They had even discovered how to find the area of a circle.

The Egyptians were faced with the difficulty of knowing when to expect the annual overflow of the Nile River. They began to study the position of the stars in the sky at night. They watched the changes in the path of the sun and the moon. This led to the beginnings of the science of *astronomy* (a Greek word meaning *star arrangement*). From this study they worked out a calendar with a year of 365 days divided into twelve months.

When the Egyptians noticed that Sirius, the Dog Star, appeared after having been invisible for some time, they knew that the Nile would soon flood. They based their calendar on this event.

Egyptian Trade. Very early in their history the Egyptians built boats in order to send their goods up and down the Nile River. Later they built sturdier boats and dared to sail out into the Mediterranean Sea. They built a canal between the Nile and the Red Sea in order that they might travel to the lands bordering that body of water.

The Egyptian merchants carried many products of their country to other lands. These products included grains, leather, pottery, linen, and cotton cloth. In trade the merchants received ivory, gold, ostrich feathers, spices, gems, perfumes, oils, and rugs, which the Egyptians did not have.

The Egyptian merchants exchanged ideas as well as goods in the lands they visited.

* * * * *

Why was trade as important in the advancement of ancient Egypt as was the discovery of writing and the development of science?

* * * * *

THE LAND BETWEEN TWO RIVERS

Babylonia. The Egyptians were not the only people to become civilized at a very early period. If you look at the map on page 26, you will find the land called *Mesopotamia* (měs′ổ·pổ·tā′mǐ·à), a Greek word meaning *between the rivers*.

Notice that the Arabian Desert and the northern part of the Red Sea lie between Mesopotamia and Egypt. While civilization was developing in Egypt, several very early civilizations developed in Mesopotamia. The greatest of these societies was *Babylon*, and that part of Mesopotamia where it developed was called *Babylonia*.

You have read that Egypt depended upon the Nile River. Mesopotamia was favored with two rivers, the *Tigris* (tī′grǐs) and the *Euphrates* (ū·frā′tēz). These rivers flowed southward from mountains near the Black Sea into the Persian Gulf.

Like the Nile, these rivers carried and deposited rich earth when they overflowed their banks each spring. This made the land between the two rivers very fertile. As in Egypt, there was little rain in the Tigris-Euphrates Valley. Like the Egyptians, the Babylonians developed a system of irrigation.

The Tigris and Euphrates pro-

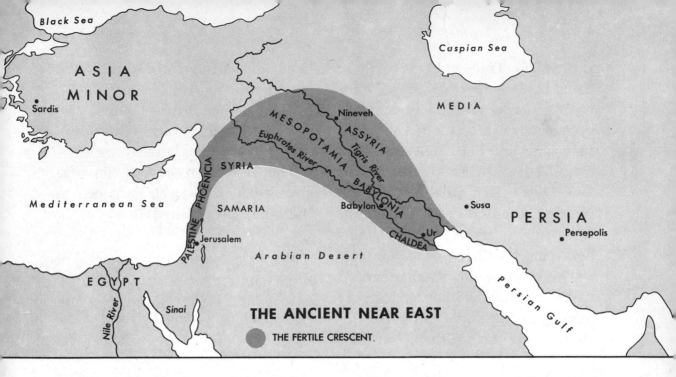

Black Sea

Caspian Sea

ASIA MINOR

MEDIA

Sardis

MESOPOTAMIA

Nineveh

ASSYRIA

Euphrates River

Tigris River

BABYLONIA

SYRIA

Mediterranean Sea

SAMARIA

Babylon

Susa

PERSIA

PHOENICIA

PALESTINE

Jerusalem

CHALDEA

Ur

Persepolis

Arabian Desert

EGYPT

Sinai

Nile River

Persian Gulf

THE ANCIENT NEAR EAST

THE FERTILE CRESCENT

vided avenues of travel for ships. So it was natural that many of the Babylonians should become merchants. As merchants the people living in the Tigris-Euphrates Valley came into contact with other peoples who lived beyond their valley.

Babylonian Buildings. Because there was very little stone or wood for building, the Babylonians learned to use a plentiful material— clay. They shaped clay into bricks of various sizes and hardened the bricks by baking them either in the sun or over a fire. The Babylonians learned to decorate bricks with color and with enamel.

The brick buildings of Babylonia have not lasted like the stone monuments of Egypt. Clay buildings that are deserted or not used for many years crumble. After the winds have blown sand into them, the ruins look like large mounds or low hills. By digging into these mounds archaeologists have found many clues that tell us how the people of Babylonia lived.

Although the Babylonians had to depend on brick rather than stone, they were able to construct many large temples and palaces. To the Babylonians these buildings looked so tall that they seemed to try to reach into the clouds.

The Babylonians were able to construct tall buildings by placing one story on top of another and making each story smaller than the one beneath it. On the outside there was a continuous incline, or ramp, connecting the various floors. The Tower of Babel, which is mentioned in the Bible, was one of these buildings. One of the later kings of Babylonia planted flowers, shrubs, and trees on each of the floors of one of these great buildings. These terraces became known as the *Hanging Gardens of Babylon* and were counted as one of the Seven Wonders of the Ancient World.

*   *   *   *   *

What buildings in our modern cities may have been inspired by the tall buildings of ancient Babylon?

*   *   *   *   *

Babylonian Writing. In order to write, an ancient Babylonian took soft clay and molded it into a flat tablet with rounded edges. Then the writer, or scribe, using a square-tipped stick, or reed, wrote by pressing a corner of this stick into the soft clay. The reed made a symbol, or sign, which was shaped like a wedge. The Babylonian writing is called *cuneiform* (kŭ·nē′ĭ·fôrm) which is a Latin word meaning *wedge-shaped*. By combining some of the nearly 600 wedge-shaped symbols in the Babylonian alphabet the scribe could write out the words of his message.

When the writing was finished, the tablet was placed in a clay case or envelope. Then it was baked until quite hard. Thousands of these clay tablets have been found in the ruined cities of Babylonia. Some of the kings had gathered them into large libraries.

Business in Babylonia. Many of the clay tablets which have been found show us how the Babylonians carried on their business and trade. Merchants sent out their bills in the form of clay tablets. It was very valuable to have clay business contracts. No changes could be made in the business agreement, for it would be very easy to tell if anyone had made such changes.

As trade became more important the Babylonians organized banks to handle money matters. They were the world's first bankers. Merchants

The Tower of Babel was a pyramid-like temple of brick similar to the one below. The Babylonians called these buildings *ziggurats*.

This is a replica of the black stone column on which Hammurabi's Code was inscribed.

of Babylon became more skillful in arithmetic than the Egyptians. As their trade grew, the Babylonians found it inconvenient to guess at the size or weight of the goods they bought or sold. So they invented a system of weights and measures. Among the weights were the pound and the ounce.

The Babylonians counted by twelves. It is from them that we borrowed such measures as the dozen and the foot. They divided the year into months, weeks, and days. They divided the hour into sixty minutes and the minute into sixty seconds as we do.

Religion in Babylon. Babylonian priests lived in the temples. They believed that their great god *Marduk* (mär′dŏŏk) ruled all the other gods including the gods of the sun, the moon, and the stars. Although the Babylonian priests studied the stars like the Egyptians in order to make a calendar, the Babylonians believed Marduk told the stars what was going to happen. Then by observing the stars the priests claimed they could see into the future. Today we call such beliefs *astrology* (ăs·trŏl′ȯ·jĭ). There are some people today who still believe in the very ancient practice of astrology.

Beginning of Good Laws. About four thousand years ago (2,000 years before Christ) a great and wise king ruled over the Babylonians. His name was *Hammurabi* (häm′ŏŏ·rä′bė). When he began to rule he found that different parts of his country had different laws. Sometimes the laws in one part of the country allowed people to do certain things which were not allowed by the laws in other parts. The laws issued by later kings were often exactly opposite to those made by earlier kings. It was difficult for the people to obey laws which were so confusing. Many people had been punished unjustly.

Hammurabi collected all the laws and improved them. He had them carved on a huge block of stone so that all his people might know them. This was the first time in the history of the world that all the laws of a people had been collected and put in written form.

* * * * *

Why would it not be convenient to carve today's laws on stone and set them up in public places for you to read?

* * * * *

TWO MIGHTY PEOPLES

A Bold, Fierce People. The Babylonians were not so well situated to prevent invasion as were the Egyptians. The Babylonians were protected on the west by the Arabian Desert and on the south by the Persian Gulf. They had, however, no natural protection on the north and east.

Just to the north of Babylonia was a small kingdom called *Assyria* (ă·sĭr′ĭ·à). The Assyrians were a bold, fierce people who loved war. They increased the size of their army until they were stronger than any of their neighbors. They armed their soldiers with iron weapons and with bows and arrows. The Assyrians were among the first people to use horses and chariots in warfare. They had whole companies armed with slings; some of these were trained to hurl fireballs into a city. They also used huge battering rams to make a breach in the walls of a city. Other nations are remembered for spreading new ideas and improved working methods. The Assyrians are remembered for spreading fear and destruction.

Assyrian palaces were "guarded" by sculptures like the one below. This winged bull with a human head was supposed to ward off evil.

Conquerors of Babylonia. The Assyrians conquered all the peoples about them. About 1600 years before Christ, they invaded Babylonia and conquered that nation. The Assyrians made slaves of the people. They leveled the great city of Babylon to the ground. They made their own city of *Nineveh* (nĭn′ĕ·vĕ) the capital of their new empire. The Assyrians grew powerful enough to invade and capture Egypt.

Conquerors of the Assyrians. Over the years the Assyrians had waged so many bloody wars that most of their men had been killed in battle. Their army then came to be made up of men from the conquered nations. These men, naturally, were unwilling to fight and die for their hated conqueror. This weakness of the Assyrians gave another people an opportunity to challenge their power.

The challengers were called the *Chaldeans* (kăl·dē′ănz), whose land was south of the Euphrates River on the Persian Gulf. They defeated the Assyrians and destroyed Nineveh 612 years before Christ. One of the Chaldean kings, *Nebuchadnezzar* (nĕb′ů·kăd·nĕz′ẽr), rebuilt the city of Babylon. The Chaldeans restored the civilized ways of the Babylonians. For a while there was peace in the valley between the two rivers.

The Chaldeans, however, were not content to rest. They turned to conquer the peoples to the west of them. In your Bible history you will read how they captured Jerusalem 586 years before Christ and took the Jewish people as captives into Babylon.

Years passed and the Chaldeans in turn grew weak. The *Persians* invaded the Tigris-Euphrates Valley from the north and overcame the Chaldeans 538 years before the birth of Christ.

THE EMPIRE OF THE PERSIANS

A Mighty Empire. The Persians lived along the northern shore of the Persian Gulf. Joining forces with their kinsmen the *Medes*, the Persians came to rule the entire area between the Persian Gulf on the south, the Caspian Sea and Black Sea on the north, and the Mediterranean Sea on the west. Under the leadership of three of their kings, they conquered every country between India and Egypt. They even added Egypt to their empire 525 years before Christ was born. They tried to invade Europe, but were driven back by the Greeks.

The architecture of King Darius's royal palace at Persepolis showed influences of the previous inhabitants of the Tigris-Euphrates Valley—the Chaldeans, the Babylonians, and the Assyrians. Today, near modern Iran, only the ruins remain of the once-magnificent capital city.

The Great King. By 521 years before Christ the Persian Empire under *Darius* (dȧ·rī′ŭs) *the Great*, was the largest territory which the world had yet seen governed by one ruler. *The Great King*, as the Persians called their rulers, had a difficult problem in controlling so many peoples and such a large empire.

Darius the Great solved these difficulties in a number of ways. One way was that he created a secret service force in each part of the empire. These men were known as *the eyes and ears* of the emperor. Through his system of spies Darius in his capital at *Susa* knew what was happening in every part of the empire.

In order to make travel easier and speedier within the empire, the Great King, Darius, built a system of roads. These connected the great cities of the empire. The most important of these was known as the *Royal Road*. It extended from the capital at Susa in the east to Sardis at the western end of Asia Minor. The road covered a distance equal to about half the width of the United States, over 1500 miles. Along the route were bridges and ferries to hasten couriers as they carried messages to and from the Great King. Inns where the couriers could obtain fresh horses were built along the route. At these inns other travelers could secure food, rest, and protection at night.

A Period of Peace. Although a Persian boy was not taught to read or write, he was trained "to ride, to shoot with the bow, and to speak the truth." Truthfulness was a virtue that all Persians tried to acquire.

*   *   *   *   *

How are the aims or purposes of your education like those of the Persian boy?

*   *   *   *   *

31

Persian rule brought two hundred years of peace to the war-weary peoples of western Asia. With peace business revived and cities grew prosperous again. People turned their attention to better ways of living. The best in the older civilizations was revived and the whole of the great Persian Empire benefited. Under the Great King, *Xerxes* (zûrk′sēz), a beautiful new capital city was built at *Persepolis* (pēr·sĕp′ȯ·lĭs). This city was the symbol of Persian peace and prosperity.

EARLY TRADERS

The Fertile Crescent. If you look at the map on page 26, you will see a semicircle of fertile land reaching through the desert from the Mediterranean Sea on the north and west up to the Tigris-Euphrates River Valley on the south. This area, which is often called the *Fertile Crescent*, attracted tribes from the less fertile mountain and desert districts.

Along the Mediterranean between the Nile and Tigris-Euphrates river valleys, there developed two nations, the *Phoenician* (fė·nĭsh′ăn) and the *Hebrew*, that have made important contributions to our civilization. Neither nation was very large. Being located between Egypt and the powerful peoples of the Tigris-Euphrates Valley, both were constantly being invaded.

A farm family of ancient times works its fields in an area of the Fertile Crescent. Note that the mud brick buildings of the town in the background resemble some of our modern buildings.

The Phoenician Fleet. Phoenicia was a small strip of territory running along the eastern end of the Mediterranean Sea for a distance of about two hundred miles. The mountains of Lebanon formed a natural boundary on the east. No part of the country was more than thirty-five miles from the sea. The people, therefore, turned to the sea to make a living. They became skilled sailors and traveled all over the Mediterranean. They even ventured out into the Atlantic Ocean as far as the British Isles.

The Phoenicians traded with all the peoples of the Mediterranean world. To these lands the Phoenicians carried the civilized ideas of Egypt, Babylonia, and Persia.

The Alphabet. The Phoenicians developed a new and simplified alphabet which had twenty-two letters. The alphabet was the most valuable gift the Phoenicians made to civilization. The nations of the Mediterranean area adopted this alphabet and suited it to their own needs. Many of the letters in the words you are now reading came from the Phoenician alphabet.

* * * * *

Why was the Phoenician alphabet an important advancement over other kinds of writing?

* * * * *

THE HEBREWS

The Bible. On the road between Egypt and Babylonia there lived a shepherd people, the Hebrews, who were neighbors of the Phoenicians. The Hebrews lived mostly in the mountain valleys along the Jordan River from the Sea of Galilee on the north to the Dead Sea on the south.

The Hebrews kept valuable records of their own history. These records are contained in a collection of forty-five books which form the Old Testament of the Bible. You are probably familiar with the story of the Hebrew people from your study of Bible history.

The Bible is the most important book in the whole world. It is much more than a history of the Jewish people. It contains the word of God, usually spoken through His prophets. We find in the Old Testament the promises that God made to His chosen people. We find the directions which God gave for a good life. There are also beautiful poems and thrilling stories. Many people read at least a chapter of the Bible every day as a spiritual exercise.

Neighbors of the Hebrews. *Abraham*, the founder of the Hebrew race, originally came from the city of *Ur* in Chaldea, which is near the Euphrates River, close to the Persian Gulf. He left the land between the two rivers at about the time that Hammurabi ruled there.

Joseph, the great-grandson of Abraham, was sold as a slave into Egypt. In time, Joseph became a chief adviser to the Pharaoh. When Joseph's father, *Jacob*, and his family were threatened by famine, Joseph invited the Hebrews to Egypt. There they lived happily until a new group of Pharaohs came into power and made slaves of them. *Moses* then led the twelve tribes of Hebrews out of Egypt about 1200 years before Christ. After wandering in the desert for forty years the Hebrews settled in the land called *Palestine*.

* * * * *

Do you know what two modern countries occupy the ancient land of Palestine?

* * * * *

Sometime later *Saul* united the twelve tribes of the Hebrews into one kingdom. About 1,000 years before Christ, Saul was followed as king by *David*, who was both a brave warrior and a singer of beautiful songs. The songs David sang are the Psalms of the Bible, which often appear in the prayers and ceremonies of the Church.

When *Solomon*, the son of David, became king, he began to build a great temple in Jerusalem. The Phoenicians sent skilled workmen to help with the building. Their ships brought many of the precious and beautiful objects with which Solomon decorated the Temple of the Lord.

After the death of Solomon the kingdom of the Hebrews divided into two parts. Ten tribes rebelled and set up the kingdom of *Israel* in the northern section of the land. *Samaria* (sȧ·mâr′ĭ·ȧ) was the capital of Israel. The two tribes that remained in the south continued as the kingdom of *Judea*. Jerusalem remained their capital.

The kingdom of Israel along with the city of Samaria was destroyed by *Sargon* (sär′gŏn), the king of Assyria, 722 years before Christ and the ten tribes were carried into slavery.

Nebuchadnezzar, a Chaldean king, destroyed the city of Jerusalem and the kingdom of Judea 586 years before Christ. Nebuchadnezzar forced the people of Judea to go to Babylon as slaves.

When the Persians conquered Babylon they permitted the Jews to return to Jerusalem. The Persian king even helped in the rebuilding of the Temple, which was completed about 516 years before Christ.

King Solomon used millions of dollars worth of gold and silver in building the Temple of the Lord. The temple, which was a dream of Solomon's father, took eight years to build.

Faithful to God. All the nations that were neighbors of the Hebrews were pagan and worshiped many gods in several different forms. The Hebrews, however, kept their belief in the one true God. It was not easy to hold to this belief when all the neighboring nations believed otherwise. To keep the Hebrews strong in their faith, God sent them great prophets from time to time to remind them there was but one God.

The Great Promise. Because of the loyalty of the Jewish people to Him, God promised that He would

Michelangelo's statue of Moses, the man to whom God gave the Ten Commandments, is in the Church of St. Peter in Chains, Rome.

The Hebrews had already received the Ten Commandments from God. These Commandments furnished them with a rule of life. This rule showed how God expected them to live nobly and righteously in order to be worthy of the Saviour. Throughout the Old Testament we find many noble and wonderful ideas about the way in which men should live.

Sometimes a king of Israel became unjust and oppressed his people. The prophets were not afraid to remind the king that he must treat his people with justice. They also reminded the king of his duty to help the poor of the kingdom.

Because God is just and kind He required His people to practice justice and kindness. This led the Hebrews to realize that all men are equal in the sight of God. When Christ, the Redeemer, came on earth He explained this very clearly. You probably remember the Gospel story of the lawyer who asked Christ, "Master, which is the great commandment of the law?" Jesus answered, "Thou shalt love the Lord thy God with thy whole heart and with thy whole soul and with thy whole mind: Thou shalt love thy neighbor as thyself." This was very different from the cruel practices of the Assyrians.

send a *Messias*, or Saviour for mankind, who would be born of the house of David. Many prophets foretold events about the birth, life, and death of Christ the Saviour. Wherever the Jewish people went they told the other nations of the Saviour who would come and lead all men to the Kingdom of God.

Summing Up. Early Egypt holds an important place in the history of the world. Some of the first steps toward civilization were taken there along the Nile River. In another river valley in Mesopotamia, man also developed a series of great civilizations—Babylonian, Assyrian, Chaldean, and Persian.

From the Egyptians and the peoples of Mesopotamia—particularly the Babylonians and Persians—have come the sciences of geometry and astronomy, the advancement of trade, the development of law, and the beginnings of orderly government. In addition, these peoples developed calendars, systems of weights and measures, and the art of writing. They have given to us a great heritage of land improvement through irrigation, and the great monuments of their past still exist to inform and inspire us.

The peoples of the Fertile Crescent have provided us with a great heritage. To the Phoenicians we owe our alphabet and the spread of civilized ideas to many lands. To the Hebrews we owe our understanding of the One True God and His plan for us. This knowledge is revealed to us in the Old Testament of the Bible and in God's gift of His Son Jesus Christ to the Hebrews as the Saviour of all men.

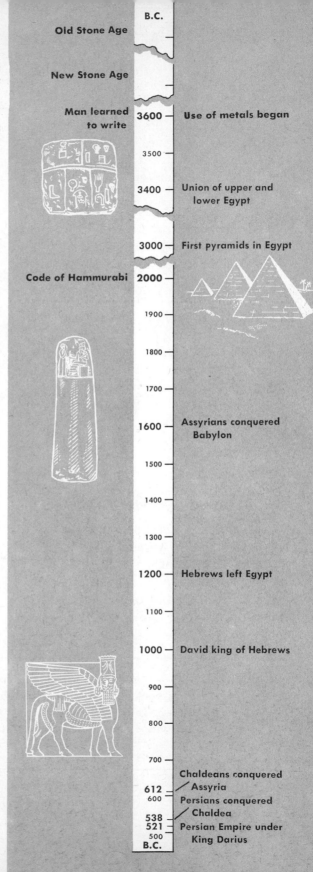

Old Stone Age

New Stone Age

Man learned to write — 3600 B.C. — Use of metals began

3500

3400 — Union of upper and lower Egypt

3000 — First pyramids in Egypt

Code of Hammurabi — 2000

1900

1800

1700

1600 — Assyrians conquered Babylon

1500

1400

1300

1200 — Hebrews left Egypt

1100

1000 — David king of Hebrews

900

800

700

612 — Chaldeans conquered Assyria

600 — Persians conquered Chaldea

538

521 — Persian Empire under King Darius

500 B.C.

FOR BETTER UNDERSTANDING

Checking Up

1. How did the Egyptians secure and use their slaves?

2. How did the Rosetta Stone provide the master clue to Egyptian writings?

3. Define hieroglyphic writing and cuneiform writing.

4. What advances did the Egyptians make in science and arithmetic?

5. What improvements were made by the Babylonians to aid their business and trading activities?

6. What were some of the ways used by the Great Kings of Persia to govern their mighty empire?

7. Describe the developments made by the Assyrians in methods of warfare.

8. Why should we remember Hammurabi?

Yesterday and Today

1. What different countries make up the Fertile Crescent today? Is the life of the peoples who live in these countries very much like or very much different from that of the peoples who lived there long ago?

2. What great ideas did we get from the early Hebrews? Do you feel that these ideas affect your way of living and thinking today? If so, how?

Persons, Places, and Terms

Identify: Darius, Abraham, Joseph, Moses, Saul, David, Solomon, Xerxes, Nebuchadnezzar, Sargon.

Locate: Mesopotamia, Nineveh, Samaria, Nile River.

Define: Bible, pyramid, irrigation, mummies, astrology, astronomy, cuneiform, Royal Road.

Interesting Things to Do

1. Read again in your Bible History the stories of Abraham, Joseph, Moses, David, and Solomon. Notice how their lives were connected with the other peoples of the ancient East.

2. Make a model of the pyramids from clay, soap, or cardboard.

3. Look for pictures and stories about early Egyptians and see what you can find concerning their everyday ways of living and working. Make drawings and reports for your scrapbook.

You will probably notice the letters B.C. and A.D. after the dates listed in this book. The letters B.C. mean *before Christ*. The letters A.D. come from two Latin words, *anno Domini*, which mean *in the year of Our Lord*. You can see that we date the events of history from the birth of Christ, which was the most important event in all history.

UNDERSTANDING THE UNIT

For Discussion

1. Why did a great change take place in the life of early man when he turned from hunting to farming and herding for his main food supply?

2. What was the most important discovery of early man? Give several reasons to support your choice.

3. Why did the Egyptians and Babylonians use different materials for writing?

4. Why is the Bible the most important book in the whole world?

For You to Answer

1. Tell how Stone Age man progressed in making clothing, providing shelter, increasing the food supply, and improving tools and weapons.

2. What is the great gift of the ancient Hebrews to our civilization?

3. What improvements in transportation were made by the Persians?

4. How did the ancient Egyptians and Babylonians carry on farming with little rainfall?

Linking Geography with History

1. How did such factors as climate, rainfall, temperature, etc., affect the way people in the ancient East lived and made a living? Include Egypt, Babylonia, and Phoenicia in your report.

2. Tell how rivers served early man as important highways.

3. How did natural boundaries (mountain ranges, deserts, bodies of water) help Egypt to develop an important civilization?

4. What were the natural boundaries of the Persian Empire?

5. Show how the location of a nation can affect its history, using Judea and Israel as your examples.

Interesting Things to Do

1. Make a list of the peoples mentioned in Unit One and their contributions to civilization.

2. Two of the Seven Wonders of the Ancient World were mentioned in Unit One. Make a report to the class about them.

Books to Read

Brindze, Ruth, *The Story of Our Calendar*.

Coe, Frederick, *Graven with Flint*.

Cottrell, Leonard, *Land of the Pharaohs*.

Gere, Frances K., *Boy of Babylon*.

Hartman, Gertrude, *In Bible Days*.

Kjelgaard, Jim, *Fire-Hunter*.

Quennell, Marjorie and Charles, *Everyday Life in the New Stone Age*.

Russell, Solveig P., *A is for Apple and Why*.

Worm, Piet, *Stories from the Old Testament*.

UNIT 2

The Ancient Greeks

(800 B.C. — 300 B.C.)

CHAPTER

3. The Civilization of Greece
4. The Glories of Greece

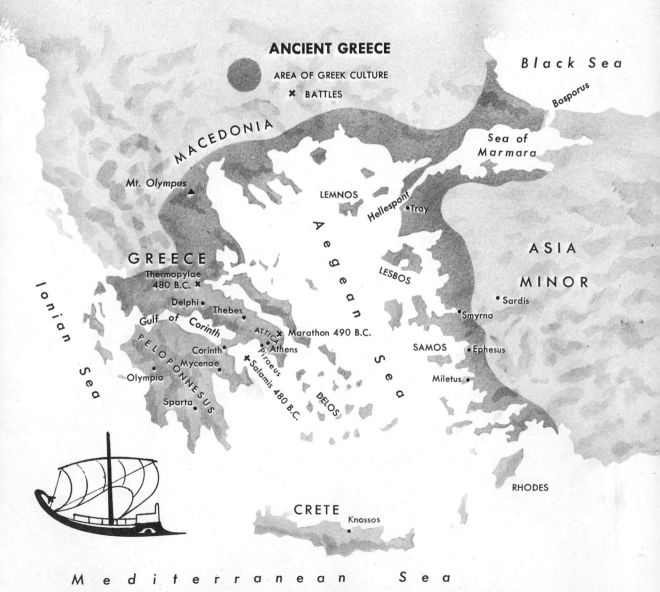

ANCIENT GREECE

AREA OF GREEK CULTURE

✕ BATTLES

Black Sea

Bosporus

MACEDONIA

Sea of Marmara

Mt. Olympus

LEMNOS

Hellespont • Troy

Aegean Sea

ASIA

MINOR

GREECE

Thermopylae 480 B.C. ✕

LESBOS

• Sardis

Delphi •

Thebes •

• Smyrna

Gulf of Corinth

ATTICA ✕ Marathon 490 B.C.

SAMOS

• Ephesus

P E L O P O N N E S U S

Corinth •

• Athens

Mycenae •

Piraeus

Olympia •

✝ Salamis 480 B.C.

Miletus •

Sparta •

DELOS

Ionian Sea

RHODES

CRETE

Knossos

M e d i t e r r a n e a n   S e a

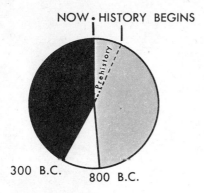

NOW • HISTORY BEGINS

Prehistory

300 B.C.   800 B.C.

INTRODUCTION

Long after the rise of early civilizations in Asia and Africa, a people who became known as Greeks developed a new civilization in the southeastern part of Europe. Their land came to be called Greece.

Although the Greeks made use of many ideas which they obtained from other peoples, they also developed new ideas of their own. Stimulated by their intense interest in new ideas, and driven by their enthusiastic desire to learn, the Greeks built a civilization which was quite advanced.

As they searched for knowledge, the Greeks came to understand and to appreciate beauty. Their homes, their temples, and their cities illustrated this love of beauty. As a result, the vases, the statues, and the buildings of the ancient Greeks are still admired and copied today.

In ancient Greece, a number of small independent communities called *city-states* grew up. In one of these city-states, *Athens*, a form of democratic government developed. Leaders were chosen and important decisions were made by a vote of the citizens. While the democracy of Athens was quite different from our democracy today, the idea that the people should be free to govern themselves came to us from the Greeks of Athens.

In this unit you will read about the Greek people and about the remarkable civilization that they built. You will learn that they established a number of colonies in lands across the seas. Then you will discover how their ideas about learning, about beauty, and about freedom came to influence the areas around the Mediterranean Sea and the lands in the East.

3

The Civilization of Greece

THE LAND OF GREECE

Home of the Hellenes. The area which we call *Greece* is a peninsula which juts out from the mainland of Europe.

You can see the home of the Greeks if you look at the map on page 40. The ancient Greeks believed they were all descended from a common ancestor named *Hellen* (hĕl′ĕn). They called their land *Hellas* and they called themselves *Hellenes.*

The earliest of the Greeks began to move south into the Hellenic peninsula about the year 2000 B.C. They were a shepherd folk looking for a fertile pasture land. This land of Greece was already inhabited and as the Greek tribes moved farther southward the original tribes living there were obliged to flee. The natives that remained were forced to become slaves. As the Grecian tribes settled in the land their way of life gradually changed. Many of these changes were due to the nature of the country in which they had settled.

What Greece Was Like. The peninsula of Greece is not very large. It is not quite so large as our state of Maine or our state of South Carolina. Rugged mountains crisscross the land in all directions. Because of this the country is divided into many small valleys and plains. In ancient times only difficult mountain paths connected the valleys and plains. There are no great rivers like the Nile or the Tigris and Euphrates to help unify people. The coastline is rugged; deep inlets of water dot the shore and great stretches of land reach into the sea.

An Outdoor People. The mountains and the sea had important

CANAANITE-PHOENICIAN	EARLY GREEK	LATER GREEK	LATIN	ENGLISH
ⴽ Ⴟ	Λ	Λ	A	A
𝟗 ⅁	S Ƨ	B	B	B
⅂	⅂	Γ	C G	C,G
◁ ◭	Δ	Δ	D	D
ⴺ ⴺ	ⴺ	Ⱑ	E	E
Y	Y	Ⲩ	F V	F,U,V, W,Y
⏤ ⏥	I	I		Z
Ⱨ Ⱨ	𝟠	𝟠	H	H
⊗	⊗	⊗		(Th)
⇂	⟩	⟩	I	I, J

The alphabet used in the Fertile Crescent is reflected in the writing we use today. Read across to see how our alphabet developed.

effects on the people. It helped make them strong, rugged, self reliant, and independent. The climate was mild even in winter and the people stayed out of doors nearly all the time. They worked out of doors. Their markets were in the open air. Their games, their plays, even their religious ceremonies were held under the open sky.

*   *   *   *   *

Why should mountains, sea, and mild climate tend to make a people self-reliant and independent?

*   *   *   *   *

The soil of Hellas was poor and it was difficult to grow enough wheat and barley to feed an increasing population. There was no opportunity to develop irrigation as in Egypt and Babylonia. Yet olive trees and grape vines prospered on the hilly slopes. Shepherds were able to keep large flocks on the uplands. Fish were plentiful in the sea.

A Seafaring People. No part of Greece was more than fifty miles from the sea. So it was natural that many of the Greeks should become sailors.

It was easy to make a voyage from Greece across the Aegean Sea to Asia Minor. There were islands all the way to protect the ships. The people called these islands *the stepping stones* to the great ports and trading centers of Asia Minor.

Learning from Others. Whenever the Greeks traveled to other lands, their alert minds carefully observed how the people worked and lived. On their return to Greece the traders explained these new ideas to their friends and neighbors. As a result the Greeks began to improve their own ways of living. In many material ways the Greeks soon equaled and later surpassed other peoples.

The most valuable gift which the Greeks received from another people was the alphabet of the Phoenicians. As usual the Greeks made improvements. They gave vowel sounds to the existing letters of the Phoenician alphabet. The alphabet of the Greeks is similar to our alphabet of today.

GOVERNMENT IN GREECE

The City-States. The other nations that we have studied united many states into one large kingdom. The Greeks did not follow this plan. The people of each Greek state remained completely independent of one another partly because of the mountain ranges and the difficulties of travel. The Greek love of freedom was also responsible for this independence.

Each of these states was usually composed of a city and the neighboring countryside. The city ruled the state and so they were called city-states.

Each city had its own laws, its own army, and often its own gods. The city was usually built around a hill which had a fortress, or citadel, at the top. In time the fortress-hill included most of the temples. This area was usually called an *acropolis* (ȧ·krŏp′ȯ·lĭs). Acropolis comes from two Greek words meaning *highest city*. Below the acropolis on the level ground was the market place.

* * * * *

What public places and buildings fill the same purpose for us as the buildings on the acropolis served for the ancient Greeks?

* * * * *

City-State Before Country. The people of each city-state loved their city more than they loved the land of Hellas, or Greece. They did not even think of Greece as their country. They did not want their city-state to join other city-states in forming a nation. They thought it was far better to keep their city absolutely free. Usually the people of one city-state were jealous of those of another. Wars were thus very common.

The ruins of the ancient Acropolis stand 200 feet above the city of Athens. The Parthenon, a temple built in honor of the goddess Athena, occupies the highest point on the Acropolis.

GREEK COLONIES ON DISTANT SHORES

Trading Posts Established. The Greeks saw that the Phoenicians, in order to help their own trade, had established colonies in various parts of the Mediterranean world. So the Greeks began to establish trading posts. Many of these posts grew into prosperous cities that were larger than their parent cities. Each colony was independent of the parent city-state, but had ties of origin, language, and religion.

Reasons for Emigrating. The reasons why the Greeks were willing to leave their homeland were much like those of our ancestors who left their homeland to come to America.

Greek men often left their homes early in the day to meet in the market place for a discussion. Women and girls seldom went out.

The Greek sailors found that the soil was very fertile and land was plentiful in many far-off places. This was good news for the people of the city-states. Their land was poor, their population was growing large. Here was a new bread basket.

* * * * *

Can you imagine why the Greeks called their new colonies bread baskets?

* * * * *

There were other reasons for emmigration. Many Greeks, who were farmers with large debts, were eager for debt-free land. Others that were landless and poor looked for the chance to begin a new life.

The supply of metal at home was not sufficient to meet all the demands for metalwork. Many Greeks went to other lands in search of the gold, silver, copper, and tin which they needed.

Some of the Greek people did not like the government in their own city-state. This was especially true whenever a tyrant, or dictator, seized control of the government. In the new lands those who left the land of Hellas could be free and decide the way their cities were to be ruled.

SPARTA, THE MILITARY STATE

Continually at War. In southern Greece in an area called *Peloponnesus* (pĕl'ŏ·pŏ·nē'sŭs), which you can see on the map on page 40, was the city-state, *Sparta*. The Spartans were continually at war with their neighbors.

In the Peloponnesian Wars, Sparta conquered each of the neighboring states and made the people slaves. The slaves outnumbered the Spartans and it was necessary for Sparta to keep a large standing army at all times.

In Sparta when a baby was born, if it was strong and healthy, it was allowed to live. If it appeared to be weak or crippled the child was left on a mountain side to die. This was a cruel practice, but the Spartans had no interest in any child that might be weak and sickly. Today we provide hospitals for the care of crippled children and help them to live happy and useful lives.

Spartan Training. When a boy was seven years of age, he was taken from his mother and sent to a camp with other boys. A group of boys was placed in the care of a Spartan warrior.

The chief purpose of this training was to develop strong, rugged

In Sparta, where education was almost entirely physical, boys grew to manhood in fine physical condition, but few could read or write.

bodies. The boys wore the same scant clothing in winter and summer. They wore neither shoes nor hats. They were forced to bathe in the river every day in the year.

The only food they were given was black bean soup and a little coarse bread. Most of the time the boys were hungry and they were urged to steal the extra food they needed. If they were caught they were whipped. They were not punished for stealing, but because they were not smart enough to steal without being caught. This was considered good training for war.

Sparta Over All. The Spartan boys spent several hours each day exercising in the gymnasium. They practiced running, wrestling, and riding. They became skilled in the use of the spear as well as the bow and arrow.

Spartans did not consider reading and writing necessary. Boys were taught the legends of great heroes of the past. They were also taught music so that they could sing the warlike songs of Sparta as they went into battle.

The Spartan boy learned to practice self-control even when in great pain. For instance, the Spartans thought it was good training to give each boy a severe whipping in public once a year. A Spartan boy would rather die than cry for mercy during this test.

* * * * *

Do you agree with the Spartan method of training boys?

* * * * *

Military Strength Only. When a youth reached the age of twenty he officially entered the army for a term of forty years. With such a large and well-trained army Sparta was able to make all the other city-states of southern Greece fear its power. The Spartans were so confident of their military strength that they built no walls around their city.

Sparta was successful in its attempt to produce strong, healthy bodies. Yet little attention was given by the Spartans to the proper training of the soul or the mind.

There was no democracy and very little personal freedom in Sparta. A Spartan was willing to give up his property, wife, children, and even his life for the good of Sparta. Spartans thought that all the people should be servants of the state. In our country we believe that the state should be the servant of the people.

ATHENS, HOME OF GOOD CITIZENS

The Violet Crown. The greatest of the Greek city-states was *Athens*. It was situated on the peninsula of *Attica* (ăt'ĭ·ká), which you can see if you turn to the map on page 40.

At Athens the sky is clear nearly every day of the year. The nearby Aegean Sea is bright blue in color. The brilliant sunlight makes the colors of the countryside bright and beautiful. At times a purple mist gathers in the mountains and hills surrounding Athens. This mist was called *the violet crown* of Athens.

Athens itself was not on the coast, but it had a good port a few miles away. The Athenians built many ships as more and more people turned to the sea to make a living. In time Athens became as strong on the sea as Sparta was on land.

Athens Loses Its King. Our word *democracy* comes from two Greek words meaning *the rule of the people*. The Athenians were the first people to develop a democratic government. Athens, like the other city-states of Greece, had been ruled by a king. The king never had great power and a council of nobles, or rich men, always had to approve all laws.

The nobles began to weaken the power of the king and finally ruled without a king after 750 B.C. At the same time the nobles began to oppress the poor citizens. Many of the poor farmers could not pay their debts and were forced to sell themselves or their children into slavery.

Athenian Reformers. In time the position of the common people grew worse. Finally in the year 621 B.C. *Draco* (drā′kō), one of the nobles, or rulers, of Athens wrote down all the laws. Although the laws were still harsh, the poor people at least knew what they said.

A freeman of Athens discusses a recommendation made by the Council. All freemen had the right to speak and to vote in the Assembly.

About thirty years later, in 594 B.C., a noble named *Solon* (sō′lŏn) was selected to improve the laws. He was a wise and learned man who was well known as a poet. The new laws of Solon prevented any Athenian from being sold into slavery because of debts. Those who were already slaves because of their debts were made freemen again.

Solon made the government more democratic. All citizens were given the right to vote in the *Assembly*, a council of freemen that made the laws. All freemen had equal rights in the courts. Solon's code of laws

49

was so good that many of his ideas are still used today.

How the People Governed. Under Solon's laws the freemen of Athens were interested in their government. Every man was considered to be qualified for every position in the government. Most of the officials were chosen by lot as we draw straws in our games to see who plays first. Every citizen could suggest a law to the Assembly, but a Council of 500 Citizens made most of the recommendations.

Athens was not a perfect democracy. There were more slaves than freemen in Athens. These slaves had no rights and could not vote. There also lived in Athens a large number of people who had come from other sections of Greece or from foreign lands. These people were never permitted to become citizens of Athens, to vote, or to participate in the government. The government of Athens was, however, more democratic than any other up to that time.

EDUCATION IN ATHENS

Athenian Boys. For several hours each day Athenian boys went to the gymnasium. There they were taught to dance, swim, run, jump, wrestle, box, and ride. Every boy was taught to throw the spear and to use the bow. These were the weapons he would have to use in time of war.

Athenian boys spent several hours a day at the home of their teacher learning to read, write, and draw. The pupils in Athens wrote on tablets made of wood and covered with wax. A sharp-pointed tool, called a *stylus* (stī'lŭs), was used to scratch the letters into the soft wax.

Music had an important place in the education of the Athenian boy. He was expected to be able to sing the battle songs of his people and the songs about Greek heroes. The boy learned to play at least one musical instrument and to recite many beautiful poems.

Athenian boys studied arithmetic, geography, and history. All the subjects in the Athenian schools were planned to educate the boys to be good and useful citizens. The Athenians believed that only an educated people could preserve democracy and the blessings of liberty. Today we in the United States believe this, and that is why boys and girls are obliged to go to school.

The Oath of Good Citizenship. The young Athenian became a citizen at the age of eighteen. In a solemn ceremony he was given a spear and a shield, the weapons of war. In the presence of all the freemen of Athens the new citizen took the oath of good citizenship.

After taking the oath of citizenship the Athenian boy entered the army for two years. At the end of his military service he was allowed to vote. He then took an active part in the government of his city.

* * * * *

At what age do citizens in your state become eligible to vote in all elections?

* * * * *

Athenian Girls. The girls in ancient Athens never went to school. At home they were trained by their mothers to cook, to spin, and to weave. A girl was seldom taught to

THE ATHENIAN OATH OF GOOD CITIZENSHIP

We will never bring disgrace to our city by any dishonest or cowardly act. We will fight both alone and with our companions for the ideals and sacred things. We will revere and obey the laws of the city. We will always try to encourage the sense of civic duty in others. In every way we will strive to pass on to our sons a city greater and better than it was when our fathers passed it on to us.

read or write. Sometimes she was taught a form of dancing in order that she might take part in the religious festivals. The Athenian girl rarely went outside her own home except to attend religious exercises. In Greece girls were not considered to be important.

BONDS OF UNION AMONG THE GREEKS

Greek Language. Although the city-states were not united under one government the people of Greece had several things in common. The people in different areas of Greece spoke different dialects of the Greek language, but they could all understand one another. All people who were not Greeks were called *barbarians*, that is, foreigners.

* * * * *

Is language an important bond of union in the United States today?

* * * * *

Greek Literature. The boys of Sparta and of Athens learned many of the same poems. Most of these poems told interesting stories about the early heroes of the Greek race. Before these poems were written down around 700 B.C. they had been passed on by word of mouth from father to son. Most of the poems had been put into the form of poetry which made them easier to remember and recite. Parts of these stories had some truth in them. Other parts were not true at all. Such stories are called *legends*, or *myths*.

The Great Poems. The most interesting Greek legends were those told by the great poet *Homer*, who lived around 850 B.C. Even today we are thrilled with the exciting adventures told by Homer in the poems the *Iliad* (ĭl′ĭ·ăd) and the *Odyssey* (ŏd′ĭ·sĭ).

The Greeks considered these mythical poems as sacred literature. The Athenians had the poems engraved on wooden tablets which were kept in the temple of the goddess Athena on the Acropolis. The stories are religious in that they tell how the Greeks believed that their pagan gods rewarded and punished men. Many of the tales in the *Iliad* and *Odyssey* tell of many cruel and harsh things the gods were supposed to have done. The poems also tell many interesting tales about the bravery and daring of the Greeks who lived in ancient times.

According to the legend by Homer, when this huge wooden horse appeared before the gates of Troy, the unsuspecting Trojans brought it inside the city walls. That evening, the horse released its cargo of Greek soldiers who opened the city gates to the waiting Greek army.

The *Iliad* tells the story of the *Trojan* (trō′jăn) *War*. This was a war fought between the Greeks and the Trojans. The Trojans lived in the city of *Troy* near the coast in Asia Minor. A Trojan prince had stolen Helen, the beautiful wife of a Greek king, and the Greeks joined together to war against the Trojans. The war lasted ten long years.

At last the Greeks won by a trick. Pretending to give up they boarded their ships and made ready to sail back to Greece. Before going they left a large wooden horse just outside the walls of Troy. This, they said, was a gift to the Trojans.

When the Trojans saw the horse they believed it to be a gift and took it inside their city walls.

In the night Greek soldiers crept from their hiding place inside the horse and opened the gates of Troy. Outside the rest of the Greeks who had come back under the cover of darkness were waiting. The Greek soldiers then killed the Trojans and burned the city. This ended the Trojan War.

The *Odyssey* tells how *Odysseus* (ŏ·dĭs′ūs), one of the Greek kings, journeyed home after the burning of Troy. For ten years Odysseus and his followers wandered about the earth trying to find their way home. During this time they had all sorts of trouble and many thrilling adventures.

* * * * *

With what other legends similar to the Iliad *and* Odyssey *are you familiar?*

* * * * *

Based on Truth. A German-American merchant named *Heinrich Schliemann*, who was greatly interested in these stories, believed that there was a great deal of truth in the *Iliad*. In 1870 Schliemann gathered an expedition together and sailed to the spot in Asia Minor where the Trojan War was supposed to have taken place. There he found a small hill although the rest of the countryside was completely level. This hill, or mound, was about 100 feet high and covered with fragments of rock and rubbish.

Slowly and carefully Schliemann dug into the hill. He began to find many clues of various types. He finally discovered the remains of nine cities. Each one had been built on top of the ruins of an earlier one. The sixth city down from the top was the Troy of Homer's poem. The city had been destroyed by fire around 1200 B.C. The remains showed that Troy existed just as Homer had described it in the *Iliad*.

THE RELIGION OF THE GREEKS

Greek Gods and Goddesses. The Greeks worshiped many gods. They believed that the gods lived on *Mount Olympus* (ṓ·lĭm′pŭs), the highest mountain in Greece. The Romans later worshiped many of the same gods using different names for them.

The Olympic Games. Processions, dances, plays, and great sport festivals were held to honor the gods. The most famous of these festivals, the *Olympic Games*, was held every four years in honor of *Zeus* (zōōs). To the Greeks, Zeus was the *Father of the Gods*. The games took place on the plain of Olympia near the western coast of Greece. To these games, which lasted five days, came Greeks from Athens, Sparta, and the other city-states. Many made the long journey from the Greek colonies overseas. If two Greek states were at war a truce was made in order that no Greek would be hindered from going to Olympia either as a contestant or as a spectator.

The early contests were held in running. Wrestling, spear-throwing, and jumping were added. Later even boxing, horse racing, and chariot racing were added to the exciting contests. Poets, artists, and

Contestants in the Greek Olympic Games competed in foot races, boxing, jumping, wrestling, and throwing the javelin and discus. The modern Olympics, which are still held every four years, include a number of new sporting events. Can you name some of them?

orators finally came to take part in the program.

The Wreath of Victory. The highest honor a Greek could achieve was to win a prize in an Olympic contest. The prize, a wreath of wild olive leaves cut from a sacred olive tree, seems of little value to us. To the Greeks it was their most important reward, or honor. The winner of an Olympic contest was held in high esteem for the rest of his life. This was especially true if a man could win the *pentathlon* (pĕn·tăth′lŏn)—a series of five events. These were running, jumping, wrestling, discus throwing, and javelin throwing.

Modern Olympic Games. The Olympic Games have been revived in modern times on a world-wide scale. The modern series was first held at Athens in 1896 and athletes from all over the world were invited to compete. Since that time the Olympics have been held every four years. They have been held in many different countries including the United States. Twice in modern times a world war has prevented them from being held.

Many new contests have been added since the days of the Greeks. Athletes now compete in swimming, skiing, bobsledding, and other athletic events. For each modern Olympics, a torch is lighted at Athens and sent to the country where the games are being held.

* * * * *

Today women take part in the Olympic Games. Why would this have seemed strange to the ancient Greeks?

* * * * *

Someday you may have the opportunity to compete in or watch the Olympic Games. Today even when the Olympic Games are held far away we can see them on television from our own homes.

Summing Up. Out of the natural isolation of mountain-separated valleys and plains, the early Greeks developed fiercely independent city-states. A warm climate and a closeness to the sea also made the Greeks an active outdoor people who became great traders.

As each city-state progressed it developed its own unique form of government. Athens was the first to develop a democratic form of government. Sparta followed the ideals of a military dictatorship.

The Greeks, even with their different forms of government, shared a common heritage in language, literature, and religion. This was particularly expressed in the celebration of the Olympic Games.

FOR BETTER UNDERSTANDING

 Checking Up

1. Explain what was meant by a city-state in ancient Greece.

2. Why did the Greeks establish so many colonies?

3. Describe the training of a Spartan boy.

4. Tell how the people governed themselves in Athens.

5. What important work did Draco and Solon perform?

6. What duties were expected of an Athenian citizen?

7. Tell the story of the *Iliad*.

8. Describe the purpose and tell about some of the events of the ancient Olympic Games.

 Yesterday and Today

1. Are there any towns in your state with Greek names? If so, do you know why they are so named?

2. Only Greeks could compete in the early Olympic Games. Name some of the countries which sent athletes to the last International Olympics?

3. Compare the reasons why the Greeks founded new colonies with the reasons that have caused millions of Europeans to come to America. Would the same reasons encourage Americans to found new colonies in Antarctica or on the moon?

 Persons, Places, and Terms

Identify: Draco, Solon, Homer, Zeus, Schliemann.

Locate: Troy, Olympia, Mt. Olympus, Athens, Sparta.

Define: acropolis, democracy, oath, stylus, colony.

Interesting Things to Do

1. Write on the chalkboard the good citizenship oath of the Athenian youths. Make it a class project to recite it daily for a week.

2. Find some pictures of the early Olympic Games for your scrapbook and for the bulletin board. Also, find pictures and stories of the present-day Olympics. Several nations have issued stamps in honor of recent Olympics. Perhaps someone in the class has a stamp collection and can bring these Olympic stamps to school.

3. You can have a pleasant story hour if each pupil finds a story about a Greek god or goddess and tells it to the class. Begin by looking up some of those gods who were supposed to have lived atop Mt. Olympus. Among them are *Apollo, Athena, Hephaestus, Hermes, Poseidon,* and *Zeus.* Other names which may lead to interesting tales are *Atlas, Perseus, Hercules, Demeter, Bellerophon,* and *Pan.*

4. You may have been surprised that music was a major part of the training of a Greek boy. How many patriotic songs and poems do you know that help to develop bravery, courage, and loyalty? Perhaps each member of the class could learn at least one such poem, and recite it at a school assembly, or to the class.

4

The Glories of Greece

THE BRAVE DEFENSE OF GREECE

The Threat of Persia. The kings of Persia always looked for more lands to conquer. The prosperous Greek colonies in Asia Minor along the Aegean Sea attracted them. With their large army the Persians easily conquered all the Greek colonies in that area by 500 B.C.

In the fight to preserve their freedom the Greeks in Asia Minor were helped by several cities in Hellas. Athens especially gave strong support to the colonies. The Athenians felt that the growing threat of Persian power should be stopped. Darius the Great, king of Persia, became angry with the Athenians because they had helped their Greek kinsmen in Asia Minor. He decided that the Athenians should be punished. It took Darius a long time to prepare an expedition against Greece.

* * * * *

The Greeks felt it was time to stop the advance of Persian power. In our day what nations have we felt must be stopped from taking over more countries?

* * * * *

The Battle of Marathon. Early in the summer of 490 B.C. a large fleet carried Darius' army across the Aegean to the coast of Hellas. Here the Persians landed and set up a camp on the plain of *Marathon* about twenty-four miles northeast of Athens.

Throughout Greece there was great fear of the Persians. The Athenians immediately took steps to save their city. They sent *Pheidippides* (fī·dĭp′ĭ·dēz), a swift runner, to Sparta to ask for help. The Spartans had to wait until their season of religious festivals was over. They believed that it would be unlucky to start on a journey before that time.

Not being able to wait for the Spartans, the Athenian generals and *Callimachus* (kă·lĭm′á·kŭs), the leader of the battle forces, met as a council of war. The council adopted the plan of the general *Miltiades* (mĭl·tī′á·dēz) which was to march to Marathon and attack the Persians before they could do any harm.

Early on the day of battle Callimachus arranged his troops in three divisions. There was a middle group and a right and left wing. The middle was made up of few men. The right and left wings were composed of many well-armed men.

When the battle began on the plain at Marathon, the Persians charged the advancing Greeks. The main body of Persians broke through the weak center of the Greek battle line. The strong right and left wings of the Greek battle force held back the wings of the Persian line. Then the two wings of the Greek battle line closed like a pincers on the exposed center of the advancing Persian line.

The Greeks swiftly defeated the advancing center of the Persian battle force. The remainder of King Darius' army fell back in confusion and after much trouble got aboard their ships to sail quickly back to Asia Minor. Six thousand Persians lay dead on the battlefield: only one hundred and ninety-two Athenians lost their lives in this great battle for freedom.

Pheidippides had fought all day in the battle; however, he was sent to bring the glad news to Athens. He ran the entire twenty-four miles to the city. As he reached the market place he gasped the word, "Victory," to the waiting crowd. Then he fell to the ground and died.

An Uneasy Truce. The Persians were determined to conquer Greece. The Greeks knew that the Persians would return. Both sides prepared for the next invasion.

Xerxes, the son and successor to King Darius, sent his soldiers into Greece by the land route ten years after Marathon. He built a bridge to help his mighty army cross the Hellespont. His fleet followed along the shore and kept in touch with the army. As Xerxes crossed from Asia into Europe in 480 B.C., he expected that his forces would conquer all of Hellas.

Defeat of the Persians. At *Thermopylae* (thẽr·mŏp′ĭ·lē), a mountain pass in north central Greece, the Persians were delayed by a small but brave band of Spartans. Under the leadership of their king,

Leonidas (lē·ŏn′ĭ·dăs), the Spartans resisted the Persians. These Greeks, however, were betrayed to the enemy who was led over a secret mountain trail behind them.

When Xerxes reached Athens he found the city deserted. The women and children had been sent to nearby islands and the Athenian soldiers had taken to their ships. Xerxes burned the city, but this was no real victory. In a naval battle which took place in the straits between the island of *Salamis* (săl′a·mĭs) and the mainland, the Athenian navy defeated the mighty fleet of Persia.

This victory in 480 B.C. was due to the leadership of *Themistocles* (thē·mĭs′tŏ·klēz), who had urged the Athenians to build a navy and led them to victory.

Never again did the Persians seriously threaten the Greeks. The Battle of Salamis was one of the most important battles of the world. It meant that the Greeks would be free to pass on their love of freedom and ideas of democracy to other peoples.

The jealous Spartans did not want the Athenians to rebuild the walls which the Persians had torn down when they burned the city. Themistocles had a plan; while he went to Sparta to discuss peace, the entire population of Athens—men,

The simple tools with which the Athenians worked made the rebuilding of the walls a remarkable feat.

women, and children—rebuilt the walls. They not only rebuilt the walls of the city but extended the walls along both sides of the road from Athens to its port of *Piraeus* (pī·rē′ŭs). Themistocles' trick made it possible for Athens to protect itself and thus secure time to regain its strength.

* * * * *

In what way did Themistocles' trick prove that the ability to think is as important as the ability to fight?

* * * * *

59

THE GOLDEN AGE OF GREECE

Athens Gains Glory. About thirty years after the rebuilding of its walls, the people of Athens chose *Pericles* (pĕr'ĭ·klēz) as their leader. Pericles was so trusted that the people kept him in office for thirty years. This period is called the *Age of Pericles* or the *Golden Age of Greece*. During this time (460-429 B.C.) Athens reached its greatest development in building, in art, and in military strength.

The Athenians were always afraid that the Persians might attempt another invasion of Greece. The Greek city-states on the Aegean islands and in Asia Minor were even more afraid. They entered into an alliance with Athens called the *Delian League.* Athens was to maintain her large navy in order to protect the other Greek cities. They, in turn, would help pay for the support of the navy. Soon two hundred and fifty cities were paying taxes into the treasury of the League on the island of *Delos* (dē'lŏs).

With a powerful Athenian navy on patrol no Persian ship dared enter the Aegean Sea. Trade between the Greek cities revived and the most prosperous city of all was Athens with its port of Piraeus.

The Acropolis. All this wealth and prosperity helped the Athenians rebuild their city. The Acropolis was no longer needed as a fort, or place of protection. The people of Athens set to work to make the Acropolis the most beautiful place in the world. Here the Athenians erected beautiful new temples, altars, and statues. All this beauty was to pay honor to their gods. The people were thankful that they had been successful against the Persians.

Honor to Athena. The chief temple on the Acropolis was the *Parthenon* (pär'thĕ·nŏn) built in honor of *Athena,* the virgin goddess and patroness of Athens. The Parthenon was made of white marble and had a wide porch on all four sides. The roof was held up by graceful columns also made of clear white marble. Above these columns was a border of beautifully carved marble. The carved figures were painted in brilliant colors. The Parthenon was

Greek architecture, which is copied even today, is noted for its use of (1) Doric, (2) Ionic, and (3) Corinthian columns.

The world's only reproduction of the Athenian Parthenon is located in Nashville, Tennessee. This modern Parthenon contains casts of many of the sculptures from the original temple.

so beautiful that people still use it as a model for public buildings.

* * * * *

Can you name any buildings in your community or in your state capital or in our nation's capital that are copies of Greek buildings?

* * * * *

The Great Sculptor. There were two beautiful statues of Athena on the Acropolis. One of these was inside the Parthenon. It stood forty feet high or about seven times as high as a grown man. This beautiful statue was the work of *Phidias* (fĭd′ĭ·ăs), who lived from about 500 to 430 B.C.

Outside the Parthenon, inside the entrance gate to the Acropolis, was another statue of Athena. It was twice as high as the one inside the Parthenon and this, too, was fash-

ioned by Phidias. This great statue was made of bronze. Sailors returning home could see the helmet which Athena wore as they entered the harbor of Piraeus. Then they knew they were really home.

The Theater. On one side of the Acropolis hill Pericles built a theater. The people sat on benches on the slope of the hill. The theater was open to the blue Athenian sky and was so large that it could seat all the freemen of Athens at one time. Pericles thought that the people could learn from the plays. He even gave free seats to the poor.

The theater formed part of the Athenians' religion. The plays were offered in honor of the gods. These plays were given twice a year, at the spring festival and again at midwinter. Poets competed to see whose play would be performed. *Aeschylus* (ĕs′kĭ·lŭs) who lived from 525 to 456 B.C., *Sophocles* (sŏf′ô·klēz) who lived from about 496 to 406 B.C., and *Euripides* (ů·rĭp′ĭ·dēz) who lived in Athens until 408 B.C., all wrote *tragedies*. These plays were about the great Greek heros and gods. *Aristophanes* (ăr̂ĭs·tŏf′à·nēz) who lived from about 448 to about 380 B.C. was the great writer of *comedy* which also developed out of the worship of the gods. His plays are remembered for their satire on Athenian political life.

The Great Writers. In addition to plays, the ancient Greeks left many other books. Some of their writers wrote beautiful poetry. Others wrote the first histories and geographies. *Thucydides* (thů·sĭd′ĭ·dēz), who lived from about 471 to 400 B.C., wrote part of the history of the Peloponnesian Wars (431-404 B.C.) —wars between Athens and Sparta. You will read about these wars later in this chapter. The other great historian of ancient Greece was *Herodotus* (hĕ·rŏd′ô·tŭs), who lived from about 484 to about 425 B.C. He was the first historical writer of note and is called the *Father of History*. He wrote the story of the wars between Greece and Persia (500–479 B.C.). He has furnished us with what we know about those wars.

The Greeks had a popular story-teller. He was *Aesop* (ē′sŏp) who lived from 620 to 560 B.C. Aesop was the author of a great many stories in which the chief characters are animals that talk and act like human beings. These tales, known as *Aesop's Fables*, were popular with the ancient Greeks just as they are popular with boys and girls today.

Lovers of Wisdom. The most famous of the Greek writers and thinkers were the *philosophers*. A philosopher, according to the original meaning of the word, is a *lover of wisdom*.

The chief Greek philosophers were *Socrates* (sŏk′rà·tēz), *Plato* (plā′tō), and *Aristotle* (ăr̂ĭs·tŏt′l). Socrates (470?–399 B.C.) was the first great Athenian philosopher. Although he left no writings we know his thoughts through the writings of his pupil Plato, who lived from 427 to 347 B.C.

Plato lived more than 2,000 years ago and we still believe much of what he said about life. He was one of the world's greatest thinkers and one of the best writers that ever lived.

Plato's greatest pupil was Aristotle (384–322 B.C.), who also became a great thinker and teacher. Many people think that Aristotle was one of the greatest teachers the world has ever known. Aristotle was the founder of such sciences as logic, psychology, biology, and politics. He studied the constitutions of many of the city-states in Greece. From his writings we have learned much of what we know of early Greek government.

So great was the wisdom of these Greek philosophers that some of the most important writers of the Catholic Church like *St. Augustine*, bishop of Hippo, and *St. Thomas Aquinas* have followed their teachings.

The Greatest Orator. There were many great orators in Athens although none became more famous than *Demosthenes* (dē·mŏs′thē·nēz), who lived from about 385 to 322 B.C. As a boy he stuttered and stammered so much that he could scarcely be understood.

Therefore, Demosthenes went to the beach every day, put a handful of pebbles in his mouth, and spoke against the roaring waves of the sea. He kept this up until he was able to speak clearly. Then he went into the Assembly and made wonderful speeches. By long study and practice he became the greatest orator of his time.

*　*　*　*　*

Why was it so important for a Greek citizen to be able to speak well in public? Is this ability still important?

*　*　*　*　*

ALEXANDER THE GREAT

The Suicide of Hellas. The Greeks never learned to unite their city-states into one country. Fear of the Persians led them to work together for a while. When the danger of a Persian invasion grew less the rivalries of the various city-states began again. Athens and Sparta were especially jealous of each other.

Athens had turned the Delian League into her own empire. The treasury was moved from the island of Delos to the Acropolis in Athens. The taxes from the members of the League were used to rebuild Athens and beautify the Acropolis. The members of the Delian League were allowed to trade only with Athens and each other. The citizens of the city-states of the Athenian empire weren't allowed to decide many local issues for themselves. They often had to have their legal hearings in Athens before Athenian judges.

63

Encouraged by the general unrest in the Athenian empire, Sparta and her allies declared war on Athens. For nearly thirty years (431-404 B.C.) the Peloponnesian Wars raged. Both sides finally grew weak. Then a series of disasters overtook the Athenians. Many of their ships were captured and destroyed at a port in Asia Minor. A great plague swept through the overcrowded, refugee-filled Athens. Thousands died. Sparta, as a result, was able to overpower Athens and win the war.

For a time after 404 B.C. Sparta was the leader of all Greece. Then another city-state, *Thebes* (thēbz), grew strong and took over Hellenic leadership. By 350 B.C. all the Greek city-states were weakened by their constant wars with one another.

*   *   *   *   *

How might the history of Greece have been happier if the city-states had worked together rather than having been jealous of each other?

*   *   *   *   *

Philip, the King. North of the Greek city-states was the large kingdom of Macedonia, or Macedon. *Philip* (382–336 B.C.), the king of Macedonia, had united these northern kinsmen of the Greeks into one nation. When he realized how weak the Greek city-states were, he set out to capture them one by one. The Greek cities would not unite although Demosthenes warned them of the danger in a series of speeches called *Philippics*, which were directed against Philip. Philip was soon master of all Greece.

Philip dreamed of conquering the rest of the known world. To do this he needed the help of the Greeks. In order to get their help Philip threatened them with great harm if they did not join him. He knew, of course, how the Greeks hated the Persians so he did not have to threaten very hard. Philip did not live to carry out his plan of attacking Persia. At the very time that the Greeks were getting ready to make war against Persia Philip was killed.

The Young King. Upon the death of Philip in 336 B.C. his son, *Alexander* (356–323 B.C.), became king of Macedonia and of all the conquered lands. Alexander was only twenty years old at the time, yet he had been trained to become a leader of his people.

Alexander was well educated. In fact, he had had the best teachers his father could secure for him. One of these was the philosopher Aristotle, who was brought to Macedonia to teach the young prince.

From Aristotle Alexander learned to love Greek art and literature and gained a great respect for knowledge.

Alexander and His Empire. Alexander decided to carry out his father's plan to make war upon Persia. He collected a large army of Greeks and led it across the Hellespont into Asia Minor. City after city and country after country came under the rule of Alexander. He freed the Greek city-states of Asia Minor. He captured the remainder of Asia Minor, Phoenicia, Judea, and Egypt. Alexander then marched into the very heart of the Persian Empire. After a great battle Persian power was broken. Alexander pursued the defeated Persian king, *Darius III*, and stopped his pursuit only when Darius' body was delivered to him. By now the young Macedonian king was known as *Alexander the Great*.

He was still not satisfied and looked around for new worlds to conquer. He marched his armies as far east as India. Because of great hardships his Greek soldiers refused to go any farther. He then returned to Babylon where he became ill and

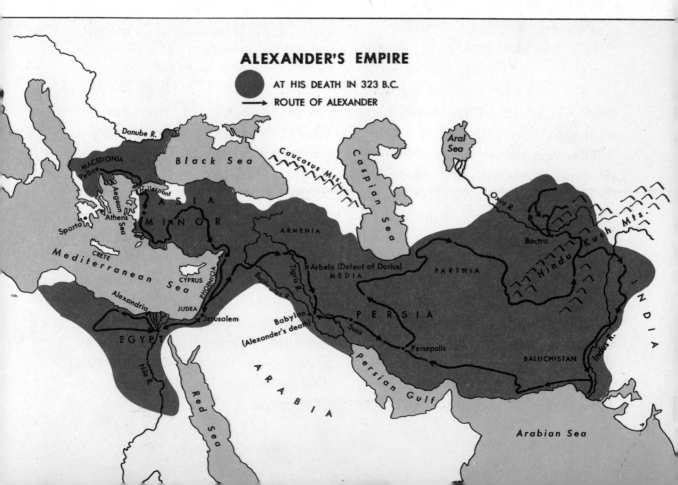

ALEXANDER'S EMPIRE

AT HIS DEATH IN 323 B.C.

ROUTE OF ALEXANDER

According to legend, Alexander the Great selected a site near the mouth of the Nile River and sketched plans for a city in the soil. Of all the cities Alexander built, this one—Alexandria—became the most famous.

died. At the time of his death Alexander was thirty-three years old.

The Spread of Greek Culture. Alexander attempted to blend the Greek and Oriental civilizations. Thereby a large part of the Eastern world learned about Greek art, Greek science, and Greek literature.

Alexander built seventy cities throughout his vast empire. Each of these followed the plan of a Greek city. The most famous of these was *Alexandria* in Egypt. Here was built the great lighthouse that became famous as one of the

Seven Wonders of the Ancient World. Here, too, was built a great university with libraries and museums. The University of Alexandria became one of the most famous centers of learning in the ancient world. In time it became the home of many great Christian scholars. In this way the best of Greek civilization was preserved for future generations. To give one example, the earliest Greek language copy we have of the Old Testament was found in the library at Alexandria.

Alexander's empire fell apart after his death. However, Alexander had accomplished a great feat. Greek civilization, which he so greatly admired, continued to spread throughout the Eastern world. The Greek love for beauty, freedom, truth, and learning was passed on to other peoples.

Summing Up. The ancient Greeks were threatened by the armies of the mighty Persian Empire. The Greeks, united under the leadership of Athens, defeated this menace to their freedom. After the Greek victory over Persia, Athens grew to be powerful and wealthy as the head of the Delian League. While this Athenian prominence did not last long, it did produce some of the greatest philosophers, writers, artists, and political leaders the world has ever known.

After the Peloponnesian War the greatly weakened city-states came under the domination of Philip, king of Macedonia. Philip's son, Alexander the Great, led the Greek legions to conquer the entire eastern Mediterranean world from Asia Minor to Egypt and India. Alexander introduced Greek ideas and culture to the civilized world and so passed on this valuable heritage to us.

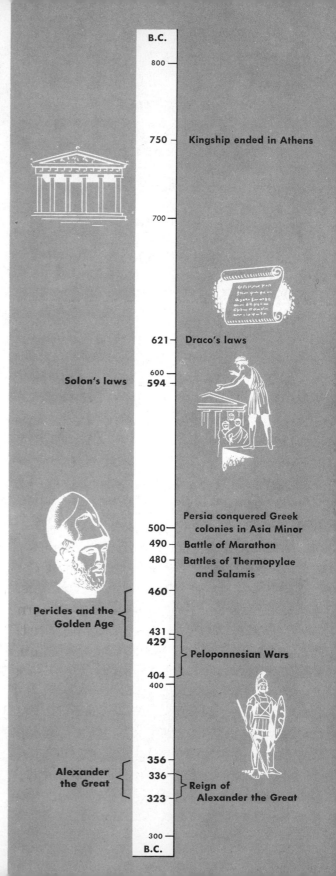

B.C.

800

750 — Kingship ended in Athens

700

621 — Draco's laws

Solon's laws 600
594

Persia conquered Greek
500 — colonies in Asia Minor
490 — Battle of Marathon
480 — Battles of Thermopylae
and Salamis

460

Pericles and the
Golden Age

431
429
Peloponnesian Wars

404
400

Alexander 356
the Great 336
Reign of
323 — Alexander the Great

300
B.C.

FOR BETTER UNDERSTANDING

Checking Up

1. What were the causes of the Persian attacks on the Greeks?

2. Describe how Xerxes prepared for the invasion of Greece.

3. Explain why we consider the battle of Salamis to be important.

4. Describe the plans of Pericles to safeguard and improve the city of Athens.

5. What were some of the chief buildings and statues on the Acropolis in Athens?

6. Describe the theater at Athens.

7. Explain what is meant by the *Suicide of Hellas.*

8. How did Philip of Macedon become the leader of all the Greeks?

9. Why does Alexander deserve to be called *the Great?*

Yesterday and Today

1. There may be some buildings in your community that have copied some features of the buildings on the Athenian Acropolis. Make a list of these and tell the type of Grecian column used.

2. The Athenian boy was trained to become a good and useful citizen. Make a list of the ways in which you can become a good citizen.

3. Does your community have a plan such as Pericles had for Athens? If so, describe the efforts made in your city or town to improve its appearance and to have beautiful and useful parks, libraries, schools, and churches.

Persons, Places, and Terms

Identify: Miltiades, Xerxes, Demosthenes, Philip, Alexander, Pheidippides, Plato, Aristotle, Sophocles, Euripides, Socrates, Thucydides.

Locate: Thermopylae, Piraeus, Asia Minor, Macedonia, Alexandria, Salamis.

Define: patroness, philosopher, gymnasium, despot, culture.

Interesting Things to Do

1. Read some of *Aesop's Fables* and report on them to the class.

2. Write a letter as if you were a soldier in the army of Alexander. Describe to a friend back in Athens, the places you have visited, the different things you have seen as well as the character of Alexander's leadership.

3. In your scrapbook place some pictures of ancient Athens. You probably can also find pictures of buildings in this country that have been built in the Greek style.

UNDERSTANDING THE UNIT

For Discussion

1. How did the Greeks make good use of their natural resources?

2. Would you prefer to have lived in ancient Athens or Sparta? Why?

3. Show why the Greeks considered themselves to be one people. Also, tell why they failed to unite.

4. Did the Olympic Games help to unite the Greek people? Do they serve a peaceful purpose today?

5. What were the chief cultural and artistic contributions of the Greeks to our civilization?

For You to Answer

1. How was Sparta different from most of the other Greek city-states?

2. How did the early Greek mariners and traders help to spread civilization?

3. Why was Philip of Macedonia able to conquer the Greek city-states?

4. What were some of the results of Alexander's conquests?

5. Name two great poems studied and learned by the ancient Greeks.

6. Tell what famous ancient Greek philosophers influenced some of the Church's most important writers and teachers.

7. Identify the following dates and tell why they were important in Greek history: 621 B.C., 490 B.C., 480 B.C., 323 B.C.

Linking Geography with History

1. Rivers were important to Egypt and Babylonia, but seas became important for the Greeks. What seas were sailed by Greek mariners and what distant lands could they visit by sea?

2. Study the map showing Alexander's empire. Find the same area in your geography book or on the globe in your classroom. Make a list of the present-day countries that are included in the area of Alexander's empire.

3. How did the location of Alexandria help to make it an important city?

Interesting Things to Do

1. Find the original meaning of these words and compare it with the present meaning: *gymnasium, oracle, marathon, barbarian.*

2. Your local library, and certainly the encyclopedia, will have many pictures of Greek objects which you can study in order to write a story to put in your scrapbook.

Books to Read

Benson, Sally, *Stories of the Gods and Heroes.*

Braymer, Marjorie, *The Walls of Windy Troy.*

Church, Alfred, *Iliad for Boys and Girls; Odyssey for Boys and Girls.*

Colum, Padraic, *Golden Fleece.*

Gianakoulis, Theodore, *Land and People of Greece.*

Robinson, Cyril E., *Everyday Life in Ancient Greece.*

UNIT 3
The Story of Rome

(800 B.C. — BIRTH OF CHRIST)

CHAPTER

5. Early Rome and the Republic
6. Rome Gains an Empire

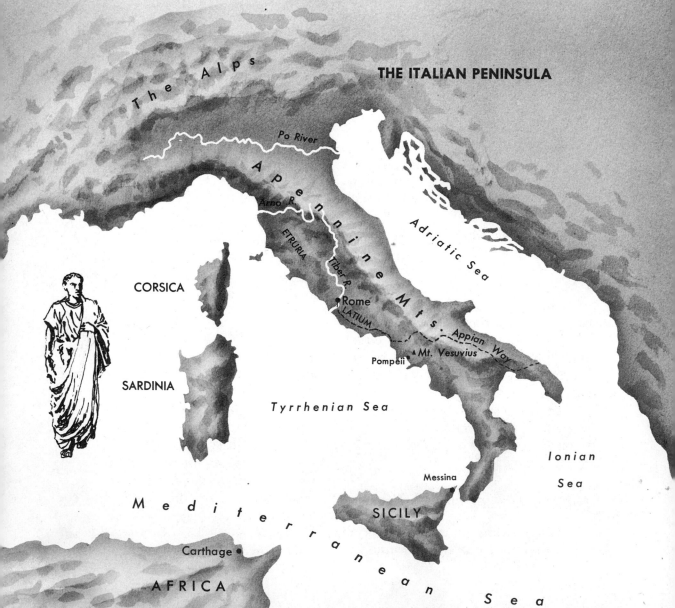

THE ITALIAN PENINSULA

The Alps

Po River

Apennine

Arno R.

ETRURIA

Tiber R.

Adriatic Sea

Rome
LATIUM

Appian Way

Pompeii   ▲ Mt. Vesuvius

CORSICA

SARDINIA

Tyrrhenian Sea

Ionian Sea

Messina

SICILY

Mediterranean Sea

Carthage •

AFRICA

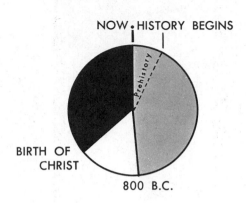

NOW • HISTORY BEGINS

Prehistory

BIRTH OF
CHRIST

800 B.C.

INTRODUCTION

West of the country of Greece, extending out into the Mediterranean Sea, lies the peninsula of Italy. At about the same time that city-states were being formed in Greece, a small farming village was founded in central Italy by wandering tribes.

Rome, as the village was called, grew to be the center of a powerful republic which dominated the Mediterranean world. Later, it became the head of an extensive empire which stretched from the Persian Gulf to the Atlantic Ocean, and from Egypt to Britain.

Although the Romans built their empire by the use of military force, they governed it skillfully. Citizens of other cities and countries within the empire were permitted to become Roman citizens. Throughout the empire there was a standard code of laws, a Roman government, and a common language. Roads were built which connected all parts of the empire, and trade and travel were encouraged. Roman soldiers, recruited from every section of the empire, spread Roman ideas and culture from one end of the empire to the other.

As you read this unit, you will see that the Romans had great admiration for the civilization of the Greeks, and adopted many of their ideas. However, the Romans developed ideas of their own, especially those dealing with law, justice, and government.

By combining the ideas of the Greeks with their own ideas, the Romans built a new civilization which they carried throughout their extensive empire. As a result, Greek culture was preserved and, together with the ideas and the contributions of the Romans, it became a part of the culture of much of western Europe.

5

Early Rome and the Republic

THE LAND OF ITALY

Greater Greece. There is a land located to the west of Greece which today we call Italy. The Greeks liked the region so well that they founded a great many colonies in southern Italy. This area they called *Greater Greece.* Here the Greeks first came in contact with a remarkable people, the Romans.

This homeland of the Romans is a peninsula jutting out into the Mediterranean Sea. By looking at the map on page 70 you can see that the peninsula of Italy, shaped like a boot, almost divides the Mediterranean Sea into two parts.

Italy has two mountain ranges of importance. The mighty *Alps,* on the north, keep out the cold winter winds. This protective fence gives Italy a mild, pleasant climate. The *Apennines* (ăp′ĕ·nīnz) *Mountains* run along the east coast of Italy.

The western side of the country is a wide plain. Most of the ports are, therefore, on the west coast.

This great plain of Italy was important for the people. They were able to raise more grain at home than the Greeks could. The high areas near the mountains were well suited for the olive trees and grape vines which the farmers cultivated. There was plenty of room for large flocks of sheep to graze.

The great plain was important in another way. There were no natural barriers to keep the people divided into small states as in Greece.

If you look at the map on page 70, you will see that west of Italy are two large islands, *Corsica* (kôr′sĭ·kȧ) and *Sardinia* (sär-dĭn′ĭ·ȧ). To the south is another island, *Sicily* (sĭs′ĭ·lĭ). This island was very important to Italy since it

The Appian Way, an ancient Roman highway, was begun in 312 B.C. Today, more than 2,000 years later, chariot wheel grooves can be seen on some parts of the road which are still in use.

almost forms a land bridge across the Mediterranean Sea to the north coast of Africa.

Rome. If ever a city was destined for greatness by its location, it was the city of Rome, which was located near the center of Italy.

* * * * *

What great cities in our country owe their importance to their location on lakes, rivers, or oceans?

* * * . * *

Rome was located on the Tiber River about twelve miles upstream from the sea. The city was built around seven hills. Just south of Rome was the plain of *Latium* (lā'shǐ·ŭm). There lived a people who called themselves *Latins* (lăt'- ĭnz), who had moved into Italy from the north about 1500 B.C. The Latins were farm and shepherd folk. After the Latin tribes made Rome their capital, around 700 B.C., they became known as Romans.

Many stories and legends were told by the Latins about the founding of Rome. One tale was about *Aeneas* (ĕ·nē′ăs), who with his family escaped from the burning city of Troy. Aeneas supposedly settled in Latium and became the father of the Latin people.

Another legend tells of twin brothers, *Romulus* (rŏm′ū·lŭs) and *Remus* (rē′mŭs). They had supposedly founded a city on the hills near the Tiber River in 753 B.C. As a result of a quarrel Romulus killed Remus and called the city *Rome* in his own honor.

ORIGINS OF ROMAN CULTURE

Rome's Neighbors. The neighbors of the Romans north of the Tiber River were the *Etruscans* (ĕ·trŭs′kănz). These people had come into Italy from Asia Minor about 1000 B.C. We wish we knew more about the Etruscan people, but no one has yet discovered a key to their writing. From the remains found in their cities, however, we know that the Etruscans were skilled at building aqueducts, bridges, canals, and roads. The Romans were quick to imitate and master these skills.

Later the Romans studied the Etruscan methods in pottery making, painting, astronomy, and medicine. In addition, Rome's first lessons in collecting and training an army to carry on warfare came from the Etruscans.

The Greeks. The Greek colonists of southern Italy and Sicily sailed up the Tiber River to trade with the Romans. From them the

The foot soldiers formed the backbone of the Etruscan forces. Spears and axes were used both for throwing and for striking.

Roman farmers and shepherds learned new ways of trading. The Romans learned to measure and to weigh articles which they bought and sold as well as the use of money. The Romans also followed the Greek's example in making ships and sailing the seas.

The Latin Language. As a result of trading with the Greeks, the Latins began to use the Greek alphabet. Then as they conquered the lands about them, the Romans taught the Latin language to other peoples.

The Romans used their alphabet not only to write but to count. Roman numerals are actually letters of the alphabet put together in certain combinations.

The Vestal Virgins spent ten years learning their duties, ten as priestesses, and ten teaching the new maidens.

*   *   *   *   *

You have probably learned some of the Roman numerals. Can you give the Roman numerals for 16, 8, and 3?

*   *   *   *   *

Roman Religion. Both Greeks and Romans worshiped the same gods. The names they each gave to the gods, however, were frequently different.

Of all the gods the Romans especially honored *Vesta*, the goddess of the hearth and home. In Rome there was a temple in honor of Vesta. In this temple a fire burned continually. Six beautiful maidens called *Vestal Virgins* were chosen to spend all their time in the service of this goddess. The Vestal Virgins were accorded great honor because they kept the sacred fire, which the Romans believed was a protection against national disaster. The cult of Vesta had begun in primitive times as the worship of fire.

The Kings of Rome. In the early days of the city of Rome, an Etruscan ruler had led his army across the Tiber River. He had driven out the Roman chiefs and set himself up as the king of the Romans. For the next two hundred and fifty years Rome was ruled by Etruscan kings.

Some of these Etruscan kings helped to improve the city of Rome. They drained the near-by swamps and constructed a sewerage system for the city. They built a protective wall around the seven hills. They even built boat docks along the Tiber River in order to encourage trade.

Even after the Etruscans lost their power, their achievements remained to help make Rome a great power.

Unfortunately some of the Etruscan rulers were cruel men. This was especially true of one king, *Tarquin* (tär'kwĭn) *the Proud*. He became so unjust that the people drove him from the city about 510 B.C.

THE ROMAN REPUBLIC

What Is a Republic? After the Romans had driven out their last king, they set up a republic in the year 509 B.C. The word *republic* comes from a Latin word which means *public things* or *public affairs*. In a republic the people elect their chief officials. These officials in turn decide on the course of the government, or public affairs. The government of our country is a republic.

The Consuls. In the republic the Romans had as their chief officials two *consuls*. They were each elected for terms of one year. There were two consuls in order that one man might not have all the power in his own hands. The Romans thought that each consul could watch the other and keep him from getting too much power. In addition to their other duties, the consuls had charge of the Roman army.

Cincinnatus (his name means "curly-haired") was one of the early heroes of Rome. He served as dictator of Rome twice, both times in answer to a summons from the senate.

The Roman Dictator. The Romans used to choose a dictator in time of war or crisis. This one man then had all the power in Rome. Even the consuls had to obey him. However, no man could be a dictator for more than six months at a time.

* * * * *

Why do you suppose the Romans did not want any one man to secure control of the government for too long a time?

* * * * *

The Romans loved to tell about an emergency when *Cincinnatus* (sĭn′sĭ·nā′tŭs) was called to be dictator. Enemies were marching on Rome and the army could not stop them. The messengers from Rome found Cincinnatus plowing a field. When he read the message, Cincinnatus left his plow and oxen, hurried to Rome, got together a new army, and defeated the enemy in a single day. Then he came home and finished his plowing. The story may not be true, but it shows that the Romans liked a man who dropped everything to help his country.

The Noble Families. The earliest settlers of Rome, or *the first families*, as they might be called, had become the nobles of the city. They were called *patricians* (pȧ·trĭsh′ ănz). Only patricians could be elected to the chief offices of the government.

The Romans had a senate, or group of elders, which made the laws, declared war, and made treaties. It was the senate that really ruled Rome. Naturally, all the senators were patricians.

The members of the senate were men of superior ability and strong influence in the state. Many of the Roman senators were famous for their oratory. Can you name any of these orators?

The Common People. The people who settled in Rome later than the patrician families were called *plebeians* (plĕ·bē'yănz). The word plebeian comes from a Latin word meaning *the common people*. The plebeians were freemen, but had few privileges. They were the owners of the small farms and the workmen of the city.

The plebeians could not hold public office, they could not be priests, and they could not marry into a patrician family. They were forced to serve in the army without pay. They were also obliged to pay taxes, even though they could not vote. If a plebeian went off to war, he might find on his return that his farm or business was in debt. To pay the debt he might have to borrow money from the patricians.

The Uphill Fight. The plebeians were constantly trying to better their position. They began a struggle to secure equality with the patricians. This struggle went on in Rome for about two hundred years.

Early Rome acquired much of its wealth from the farm produce and the sheep raised by the plebeians whose lands lay in the nearby countryside. Some plebeians worked on lands owned by upper-class patricians; others were fortunate enough to own their own land.

The first victory of the plebeians was secured by a strike. The patricians needed troops to fight a war and promised that all plebeian debtors would be released from prison if the plebeians would fight. When the war was over, the patrician senate refused to fulfill its promise. So the plebeians left Rome and settled on a hill about three miles away.

To win the plebeians back to Rome, the patricians gave them a part in the government. The plebeians were allowed to elect some of their own members to the office of *tribune* (trĭb´ūn). The tribunes were permitted to have a place just outside the door of the senate. If the senate tried to pass a law that was unfavorable to the people, a tribune could shout, *Veto*, which is Latin for *I forbid*. Then the senate could not pass the law.

* * * * *

The veto power is used by our President in the United States. Can you explain how this use is like the old Roman veto and how it differs from it?

* * * * *

The plebeians next demanded written laws. You remember that in ancient Babylon, and later in Athens, the laws were written

Tribunes had the special duty of protecting the plebeians and seeing that they received justice in the law courts.

down. In Rome the laws were carved on twelve tablets about 450 B.C. Then the tablets were set up in the *Forum* (fō´rŭm), the market place of Rome. There all the citizens could read them. These laws applied to patrician and plebeian alike. All citizens in Rome were then equal before the law.

Gradually the plebeians gained other rights. They were permitted to marry patricians. At last a law was passed which said that at least one of the Roman consuls must be a plebeian. After that plebeians were permitted to become senators, priests, and generals. The plebeians gained rights equal to those of the patricians about 300 B.C.

Roman Character. Rome did not become great simply because of its laws, its armies, or its language. Its laws were great and its armies were great and its language was noble because of the character of its people.

The Romans were a simple, frugal, honest people who were not afraid of hard work. They showed their loyalty to their city in many practical ways. They were very proud to be Romans and were careful not to commit any dishonorable act.

The character of the Romans was developed by their family life. The father insisted on strict obedience, honesty, and hard work from the members of the family. These virtues were then practiced in the life of the city.

ROMAN CONQUESTS

Master of Italy. Rome needed protection from its neighbors, especially from the Etruscans who lived just north of Rome. Rome was often attacked by the Italian tribes of west central Italy, the *Samnites* (săm′nĭtz). After many long and bitter wars, these neighboring peo-

The Roman Forum was the center of Roman legal and public affairs. Many of the ancient columns and arches still stand to suggest the grandeur of this gathering place of ancient Rome.

ples were brought under the control of Rome. Then the Roman armies conquered the Greek cities of southern Italy. Rome became master throughout the entire peninsula of Italy by 265 B.C.

The Romans adopted a wise policy in governing conquered tribes and states. These peoples were admitted to many of the privileges of Roman citizens. Rome gave them full protection against all enemies. Each city was permitted to govern itself in local matters. In turn the cities were to let Rome handle their relations with other countries and to regulate trade. This policy made the cities of Italy loyal to Rome.

A series of roads was built connecting the great cities of Italy with Rome. In this way troops could quickly be sent against any city that might decide to revolt. The Romans also drained swamps, dug tunnels through mountains, and built bridges across rivers. The Roman highways were so well built that some of them are still in use today.

Rival of Rome. Roman expansion into southern Italy brought Rome into conflict with another great power of the Mediterranean area, *Carthage* (kär′thĭj). Carthage had a favorable location in North Africa. If you look at the map on page 70, you will see the location of this city that had been founded in about 850 B.C. by the Phoenicians, as a colony for trading purposes. It had become the most powerful and prosperous city in the whole Mediterranean world.

Carthage in turn had established other trading colonies in many important places. It controlled the lands along the coast of North Africa and most of Spain. The islands of Corsica and Sardinia were under the rule of Carthage, as well as the western half of the island of Sicily. The Carthaginians held the Strait of Gibraltar and permitted no ship to enter or leave the Mediterranean Sea without their permission.

Wars with Carthage. With Sicily as a base, Carthage could cut off Roman trade with many Mediterranean lands. So when Carthage sent an army against one of the Greek cities in Sicily in 265 B.C., Rome declared war. That war and the following wars with Carthage were called *Punic* (pū′nĭk) *Wars*, after the Latin name for the Phoenician founders of Carthage. By the end of the First Punic War in 241 B.C., Rome had driven the Carthaginians from Sicily, Corsica, and Sardinia.

After more than twenty years of peace, war again broke out between

Rome and Carthage in 218 B.C. During the Second Punic War, the Carthaginian general *Hannibal* (hăn′ĭ·băl) set out from Spain with a huge army and invaded Italy from the north. He performed the mighty task of crossing the Alps, but he lost half his army in this difficult venture.

Hannibal defeated the Romans in several battles but was never able to crush them completely. Hannibal remained in Italy fifteen years. However, when a Roman

Hannibal's plans to invade Italy included the use of war elephants. Can you imagine the reaction of the Romans, who had never seen elephants, when these huge creatures lumbered into sight?

army crossed over to North Africa and threatened the city of Carthage, Hannibal was called home to protect the city. The Romans captured Carthage and sent Hannibal into exile in the year 211 B.C. Carthage was spared being destroyed, but was placed under a very strict treaty that limited its freedom.

Peace lasted over fifty years, but the Romans grew jealous of Carthage's recovery as a center of trade. So Rome began the Third Punic War in 149 B.C. The war ended when Rome completely destroyed the city of Carthage. The city was burned to the ground in 146 B.C. The land was plowed up and sown with salt so that nothing could ever grow there.

Master of the Mediterranean. With the fall of Carthage, Rome became master of the western half of the Mediterranean world. All the possessions of Carthage became Roman provinces.

Rome had extended its influence to the countries of the East during the period of the Carthaginian struggle. The empire of Alexander the Great had broken up into several parts after his death in 323 B.C. Rome had gained control of Macedonia, Greece, Syria, and Egypt by the time Carthage was destroyed. All Mediterranean lands were included within the Roman domain, or had become allies of Rome, by the year 146 B.C.

* * * * *

Why do you suppose that some countries became allies of Rome?

* * * * *

Summing Up. The Romans, like the Greeks, began as a simple shepherd and farm folk settling in a new land. They developed their civilization through contact with others. Part of the heritage which the Romans received was the alphabet and the religion of the Greeks. Much of the Romans' knowledge of the practical arts, such as the art of building, came from the Etruscans.

Rome ended its domination by the Etruscans when Tarquin the Proud was expelled in 510 B.C. Then Rome went on to establish a new form of government, the republic. In the growth of the republic, the plebeians struggled for two centuries to secure their rights from the ruling class. They were finally successful.

In time Rome became the master of Italy, which was easily united into one country because of its great plain. Then after defeating Carthage, her great rival, Rome gained control of the whole Mediterranean world by the year 146 B.C.

FOR BETTER UNDERSTANDING

 Checking Up

1. Tell how natural conditions made it possible for Rome to dominate Italy.

2. What important arts and devices did the Romans learn from their Etruscan and Greek neighbors?

3. What is a republic?

4. What were the official duties of the Roman consuls?

5. Tell how the plebeians, over the centuries, secured equality with the patricians.

6. Describe the character of the Roman people during the early days of the republic.

7. What was the main cause of the rivalry between Rome and Carthage?

8. Describe the career of Hannibal.

9. What new territories did Rome acquire after the Punic Wars?

 Yesterday and Today

1. In your arithmetic book, dictionary, or encyclopedia, look up the Roman system of numbers. Write the following important dates of Roman history in Roman numerals, and identify each date: 509 B.C., 265 B.C.

2. Ask your teacher to spell out on the chalkboard the Latin names for the Roman numbers from one to ten.

Then make a list of common English words that are formed from these Latin words.

3. Compare Cincinnatus with some present-day rulers who are called *dictators*. Be sure to tell how these men differ from Cincinnatus.

Persons, Places, and Terms

Identify: Aeneas, Romulus, Tarquin, Cincinnatus.

Locate: Alps, Apennines, Corsica, Sardinia, Sicily, Rome, Latium, Carthage.

Define: Greater Greece, aqueducts, Etruscans, Vestal Virgin, republic, consul, dictator, patrician, plebeian, senate, tribune.

Interesting Things to Do

1. Read some of the stories of early Rome, and report on them to the class. You will like the stories of "Horatio at the Bridge" and "Cornelia and Her Jewels."

2. You might organize your room as a republic. You would need to elect officers, assign duties, and set up some rules, or laws, to follow.

3. Find pictures of the Vestal Virgins, of Carthage, and of Hannibal for your scrapbook.

6

Rome Gains an Empire

THE REPUBLIC DECLINES

The Provinces. The lands conquered by Rome were called provinces and were placed under the control of a governor, who was sent by the senate. The native peoples had no part in the government nor any of the privileges of Roman citizens. The natives were often treated harshly by the governors and were forced to pay heavy taxes to Rome. The taxes were collected by a group of men called *publicans* (pŭb′lĭ-kănz). You probably have read about the publicans in one of the Gospel stories.

As you might imagine, the Romans were not well liked by the people of the provinces. It was necessary to keep a large Roman army in the provinces to prevent revolts by these peoples.

In addition, the long wars had brought about many changes at home for the Romans. Thousands of the finest young Romans had been killed in the wars. Others had been in the army so long that they did not know how to earn a living as civilians.

Great wealth poured into Rome from the provinces and from the booty of war. Some of the Romans became so wealthy that they lived like kings. The virtues that had helped to make Rome great— honesty, simple living, and hard work—began to disappear.

No Work. At the same time a large number of the Romans were becoming poorer and poorer. The small farmers had lost everything they owned since they had been kept busy fighting in many wars over the years. While they were away from home they could not care for their farms. These plebeians then had to borrow from the wealthy in order to live. If the farmers were unable to pay their debts, they lost their farms to the wealthy, who already had more land than they could use. Then the men who had lost their farms went to Rome and the other big cities of Italy to find work. Since they could find no work to do, Rome became filled with large numbers of men and their families who were also without homes.

The situation at Rome was made worse by the presence of thousands of slaves. These slaves were men and women who had been captured during the many wars. There were so many slaves that they could be bought for very little money. An ordinary family could afford to have three or four slaves, and the very wealthy had hundreds of slaves.

* * * * *

Our own country once had slaves, and we fought a great war to rid ourselves of slavery. Why is slavery bad for a country?

* * * * *

Food for Votes. As citizens the many poor and unemployed who had moved to Rome still had the right to vote. So the generals and other rich men who wanted to get

Table manners, as we know them, were practically nonexistent at the elaborate dinners given by wealthy Romans. Slaves served these dinners on costly dishes of gold and silver.

Charioteers, urged on by shouting spectators, skid around a turn of the racing arena. Despite the fact that chariot racing was dangerous, many young men risked their lives for this sport. In return, they received immense salaries and became the pampered heroes of Roman society.

the votes of the unemployed men gave them free grain for bread. In this way even the poor were able to live without working. Many of the wealthy even entertained the poor with free games and shows. Often these contests were exciting boxing matches and chariot races. Sometimes there were fights between men and wild beasts.

This idle mob helped to destroy the republic. They were no longer interested in the affairs of the government. They voted for the man who provided them with the most free food or the most exciting entertainment. Therefore, only the wealthy, or those whom they supported, could afford to run for public office.

The Efforts to Reform. By the year 130 B.C. the common people of Rome had begun to lose their rights in the government as well as their chance to find work. The senate was controlled by the rich patricians, who cared little for the poor except to buy their votes. Yet, men came into prominence who tried to restore the republic to its original ways. Among these were the *Gracchi* (grăk'ī), two brothers, who as members of a noble Roman family took up the cause of the poor against the rich. The older brother, *Tiberius Gracchus* (tī·bẹr'ĭ·ŭs grăk' ŭs), was elected tribune. He had a law passed to break up large sections of public lands into small farms. This would make many families self-supporting again. Before Tiberius could carry out this plan he was killed by a mob of angry senators in the year 133 B.C.

Ten years later *Gaius* (gā'yŭs), the younger brother of Tiberius Gracchus, was elected tribune. He took up the work started by his older brother and tried to carry out his plans. Gaius wanted the government to build roads and public buildings and so permit the unemployed to earn a living. However, Gaius was killed by a mob in 121 B.C.

From the story of these brothers you can see that Rome had changed a great deal. In the old days people obeyed the laws and honored their leaders. Now the power in Rome went to those who could get a large section of the mob to follow them. Soon various mobs began to fight one another and Rome was left without any real government.

A NEW POWER IN ROME

A Young Noble. In the midst of all this confusion at Rome, a young patrician attracted favorable attention. He was *Julius Caesar* (sē'zẽr), who was born about 102 B.C. He became popular by the usual methods of free shows, games, and athletic contests for the people. He was elected consul, the highest office in Rome. Caesar knew that the bad conditions in Rome would have to be corrected. He also knew that his term as consul was far too short to be able to correct the centuries of wrong doing. Caesar realized that he needed an army to protect himself, or he would be murdered like the Gracchi.

The General. When his term as consul came to an end, Caesar had himself appointed governor of the province of *Gaul* (gôl), which was located north of the Po River in what is now northern Italy and southern France. Caesar had an army which he trained into a mighty force. He himself endured all the hardships of his soldiers, and because of his popularity they were ready to follow him anywhere. Caesar led his army through what is now northern France and Belgium and even crossed over into England. He extended the boundary of the Roman state up to the river Rhine in what is now modern Germany.

Leader of Rome. Caesar returned to Rome at the head of a conquering army. His popularity had increased to such an extent that the people made him dictator for ten years. Later they made him dictator for life. They offered him a crown, but this he refused. Caesar knew

Julius Caesar was a great soldier. With the aid of his army, he extended the boundaries of the Roman Empire.

that the Romans did not like the idea of having a king. He did not need the title of king. He had all the power of a king without the title. Rome was then ruled by one man—Julius Caesar.

Caesar did accept the title of *imperator* (ĭm′pĕ·rā′tôr), which meant *commander* or *general*. From this title we get the word *emperor*, which was the title given to the successors of Julius Caesar.

REFORMS OF JULIUS CAESAR

Reorganized city government in Italy

Started public building program

Improved living conditions for the poor

Encouraged colonization

Introduced a new calendar system

Caesar was obliged to fight other wars in the East and always returned to Rome as a conquering hero. He had many plans to improve the conditions in Rome and throughout the empire. He wanted to send colonies of poor Romans into the provinces. He tried to encourage the farmers so that Italy might produce enough grain to feed the people of the cities. He started a program of public building to reduce the number of unemployed and at the same time improve the city of Rome.

Julius Caesar changed and corrected the calendar. He introduced the idea of leap year—an extra day every four years. He divided the year into twelve months. One of the months he renamed for himself—July. The calendar as changed by Julius Caesar is the calendar we use today, but with later corrections made by Pope Gregory XIII.

Caesar's Death. Caesar was not able to carry out his program completely. There were many people who did not like to see him become so powerful. There were others who wanted to be rid of the dictator who had destroyed the republic even though he was trying to help Rome. In the year 44 B.C., a group of men stabbed him to death as he entered the Senate House.

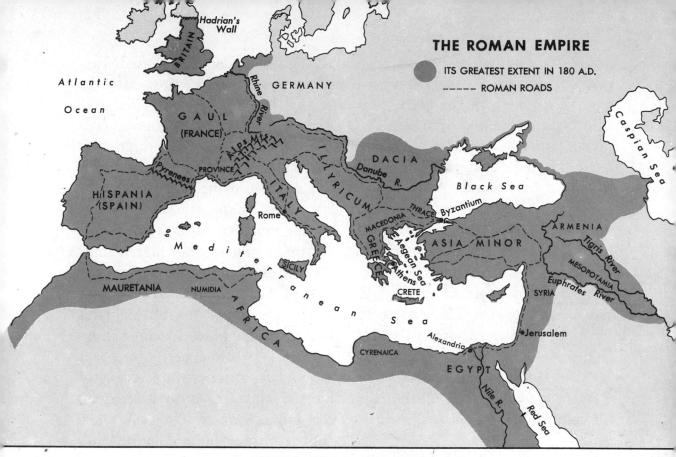

THE ROMAN EMPIRE

ITS GREATEST EXTENT IN 180 A.D.

----- ROMAN ROADS

A NEW ERA OF PEACE

A Fight for Power. After the death of Julius Caesar, the people had difficulty in deciding upon a new ruler. Caesar had adopted his grandnephew *Octavius* (ŏk·tā′vĭ·ŭs) and had made him his heir, but Octavius was only eighteen years old at the time of Caesar's death. In addition, Octavius had to defeat *Brutus* (brōō′tŭs), one of Caesar's murderers, and *Mark Antony*, the most powerful general in the Roman world, in order to become master of Rome. Thirteen years after Caesar's death, Octavius be-

came master of Rome and all its possessions after defeating all his enemies.

Octavius, like Julius Caesar before him, refused to become a king. He kept all the offices of the republic and was elected to most of them. Like his uncle, he accepted the title of *emperor*. He also received several new titles. One of these was *princeps*, or prince, which meant *first citizen*.

The most important title he received was *Augustus* (ô·gŭs′tŭs). This Latin word means *majestic* or *grand.* It had never before been given to any man. It had been used only in speaking of the gods. This title became the one by which Octavius was generally known. It is from this title that the month of *August* got its name.

Sole Ruler. After 27 B.C., Augustus was the sole ruler of the vast Roman Empire. Fortunately for the empire, he was a just and wise ruler. Two hundred years of peace and greatness followed. The people of the empire lived happily under Roman law and order. This period is called Rome's *Golden Age* or the *Pax Romana*, which means the *Peace of Rome* or *Roman Peace.*

The Roman poet Vergil reads his poem, the *Aeneid,* to Augustus. Vergil dedicated the work to Augustus because he felt that the emperor was a descendant of the poem's hero.

Augustus ruled the Roman Empire for over forty years after he became the sole ruler. This gave him an opportunity to improve conditions thoughout the empire. He sent capable and honest governors to rule the provinces. He had a census taken of the empire and gave the provinces a fairer tax system.

Athens had reached her highest degree of civilization during the Age of Pericles, after the Persian Wars. The long rule of Augustus had a similar place in the history of Rome. It was a period of peace after a long series of wars. Augustus himself encouraged artists, architects, and writers. He gave them support from the public treasury and showered them with honors.

Augustus made Rome a city of great beauty as Pericles had done at Athens. A new Forum, a new theater, and many splendid temples were erected at Rome. In fact, Augustus made the city so beautiful that it is said, "He found a city built of brick and left it built of marble."

*　　*　　*　　*　　*

What other great men in history can you name who did great things for their people?

*　　*　　*　　*　　*

OUR DEBT TO ROME

We are Rome's Heirs. The world we live in would be vastly different if the Romans had not made their contributions to civilization. Rome made a lasting impression on the vast empire which she governed. We in America are heirs of the great Roman civilization, which was developed long before our land was discovered.

Spread of Greek Civilization. Most conquering armies destroy a civilization that is strange to them. The Romans, however, did not destroy the civilization of the Greeks because it was a civilization they admired.

After Rome conquered Greece between 197-163 B.C., thousands of Greeks were brought back to Rome as slaves. A large number of these were so well educated that many Roman boys had Greek tutors or were sent to schools where the teachers were Greeks. In this way the Romans were taught to admire and preserve the civilization of their teachers even though the teachers were their slaves.

As the Romans developed their own civilization they borrowed many ideas from the Greeks in religion, architecture, language, and literature. They permitted the Greek university at Alexandria in Egypt to continue. One of the great scholars at Alexandria in the days of the Roman Empire was *Ptolemy* (tŏl'ĕ·mĭ). He was a student of astronomy and geography. His studies and his maps were used by Columbus in preparing for the first voyage to America over 1,000 years later.

Buildings and Bridges. We have already seen that the Romans had a remarkable system of good roads. They were also skilled in erecting buildings.

Many of the buildings built by the Romans are still standing today, and a few are still in use. Others are partially in ruins but they provide enough clues to indicate what the buildings were like originally.

Roman Gifts to Man

1. The republic as a form of government
2. A system of law
3. The Latin language
4. The spread of Greek ideas
5. The spread of Christianity
6. Greater freedom for women
7. Beautiful buildings and statues
8. Use of the dome in building
9. Use of the arch in amphitheatres, aqueducts, and bridges
10. A network of concrete roads

In southern Italy the town of *Pompeii* (pŏm·pā′yė) was completely covered by ashes, soot, and lava when the volcano of *Mount Vesuvius* (vė·sū′vĭ·ŭs) erupted in the year 79 A.D. Archaeologists have excavated the town in our own day, and we have a complete picture of what a Roman town was like.

In Rome. The center of public life in Rome was the Forum. This was originally the market place, but later was used by the citizens as a gathering place, as well as for public meetings. Here speakers addressed the people from a mounted platform called the *rostrum* (rŏs′trŭm). Around the Forum were some of the chief temples of Rome and the Senate House.

The Romans learned how to use the arch, and they used it in many of their buildings. Fourteen *aqueducts* (ăk′wė·dŭkts) were constructed to bring pure water from the hills to Rome. These consisted of a series of arches which supported the channel that carried the water over high and low places into the city. These aqueducts were so well built that some of them are still standing.

The arch was also prominent in the amphitheaters, which were used like our stadiums of today. The most famous of these amphitheaters is the *Colosseum* (kŏl′ŏ·sē′ŭm) at Rome, which could seat 50,000 people at the games and shows. The use of the arch may also be seen in the triumphal arches, which conquering emperors erected at Rome in honor of their victories.

The Romans developed the arch into the dome to give a new feature to their buildings. The *Pantheon* (păn′thė·ŏn), a temple which Augustus erected to all the gods, is the best example of this construction. The building with the largest dome in the modern world is also located in Rome. It is St. Peter's Church.

* * * * * *

What famous building in our own country's capital has a dome?

* * * * * *

The Romans had another type of large building which was called a *basilica* (bȧ·sĭl′ĭ·kȧ). It was similar to certain of the Greek buildings except that the columns were on the inside instead of on the outside.

The basilica, a large airy structure, was used both for courtrooms and for stores. The Christians found the basilica very suitable for churches. Today some of the great Catholic churches throughout the world are called basilicas.

Langúage and Literature. Latin was the language spoken in business and government throughout the Roman Empire. From London to Babylon men of different races could talk to one another by using Latin. At the time that Christ founded His Church, Latin was the language which could be understood in all the countries of the civilized world. After St. Peter became Bishop of Rome, it was natural that the ceremonies of the Church and the writings of the popes should be in the Latin language.

The people of Italy, Rumania, France, Spain, and Portugal today speak languages which developed from Latin. More than half the people in the Western Hemisphere speak one of the *Romance languages.*

* * * * *

Why do you suppose French, Italian, Spanish, and Portuguese are called Romance languages?

* * * * *

South of the Rio Grande River, which forms the border between the United States and Mexico, all the land is called *Latin America.* These Central and South American countries are called Latin America because they speak Portuguese or

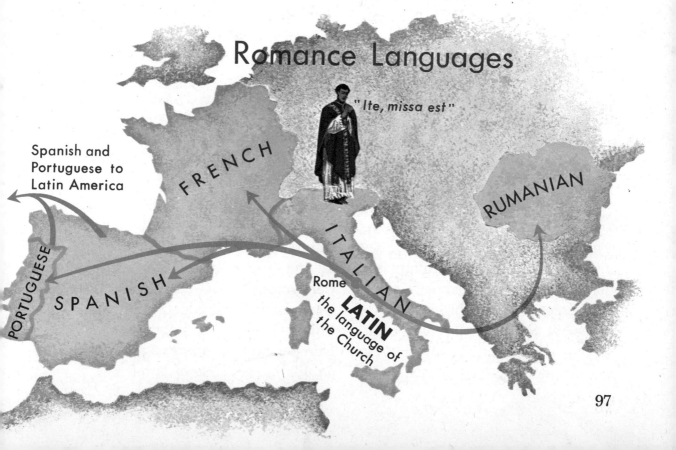

Romance Languages

"Ite, missa est"

Spanish and Portuguese to Latin America

FRENCH

RUMANIAN

ITALIAN

PORTUGUESE

SPANISH

Rome
LATIN
the language of
the Church

Spanish, which are Latin or Romance languages. Even our English language would be very different if we had not taken thousands of words from the Latin.

The literature of the Romans is still read and studied in our schools and colleges. Julius Caesar wrote a valuable account of his campaigns in Gaul and Britain. This is perhaps the best-known Latin book today. *Cicero* (sĭs'ẽr·ō), the great orator who lived at the time of Caesar, is studied by men who wish to become good speakers. The Romans also produced a great epic poem like Homer's *Iliad*. It is *The Aeneid* (ė·nē'ĭd) written by *Vergil* (vur'jĭl), who was a friend of the Emperor Augustus. *The Aeneid* tells the story of Aeneas, who escaped from Troy and after many adventures founded the city of Rome. There are many other Romans who wrote histories, poems, stories, and plays.

Orderly Government. There were many different races and nations within the Roman Empire. The Romans gave the empire a good government for several centuries. They showed the world that many nations could be united under a single government. And the world has never lost the hope that once again nations might unite and live in peace under one government.

The Roman people had a great respect for law. They also believed that the laws should be just.

* * * * *

One of the ideas which the Romans developed in their laws was that a man is considered innocent until he has been proven guilty. Is the idea accepted as a basis of law in our country?

* * * * *

One of the Christian emperors who ruled the empire long after the time of Augustus was called *Justinian* (jŭs·tĭn'ĭ·ăn). He performed a very important service for the world. He thought that the Roman laws that had developed through the centuries were confusing to the ordinary people. So he had a group of well-educated men collect all the Roman laws. They studied the laws and then arranged them in good order. This new collection of Roman laws was called the *Justinian Code*, or the *Body of Civil Law*. It was published in the year 534 A.D., and became the law for the entire empire. It was so good that many of the European nations which were later formed out of the Roman Empire retained the Justinian Code. Even today, laws in Europe and the Americas are based on Justinian's code of laws.

Summing Up. The Roman Republic fell into decay and the Roman Empire came to take its place. The decline of the Republic was caused by the great number of wars that introduced slavery as a general practice, gained great riches for the few, and left the great mass of people without property or jobs. These conditions, accompanied by a loss of the moral and spiritual values which had helped Rome to become great, made the Republic subject to the wealthy, who could buy the street mob's votes.

Efforts for reform such as those of the Gracchi brothers were doomed to failure because of the opposition of the corrupt patricians. Finally, through military might and popular appeal, Julius Caesar came to be the dictator of Rome and instituted many reforms. After Caesar was slain, Octavius became the new dictator, or emperor. Octavius, who took the imperial title Augustus, gave the new empire stable government. With good government the Romans brought peace and prosperity to the world and in so doing were able to perfect their many gifts of architecture, law, and government. They preserved the Greek heritage in literature and the arts which they passed on through the nations of Western Europe.

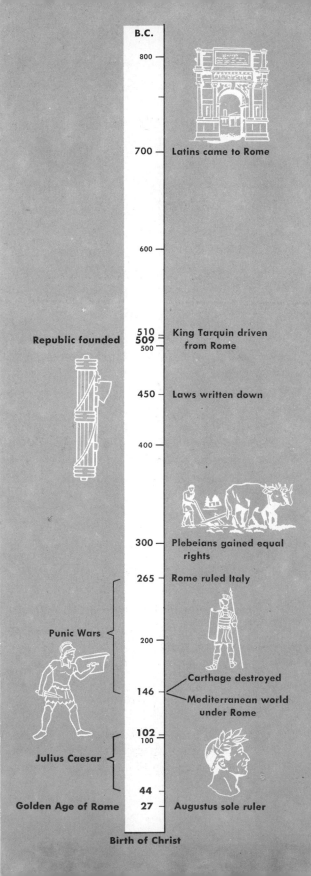

B.C.

800

700 — Latins came to Rome

600

Republic founded

510
509 — King Tarquin driven from Rome
500

450 — Laws written down

400

300 — Plebeians gained equal rights

265 — Rome ruled Italy

Punic Wars

200

Carthage destroyed
146 — Mediterranean world under Rome

Julius Caesar

102
100

44

Golden Age of Rome   27 — Augustus sole ruler

Birth of Christ

FOR BETTER UNDERSTANDING

 Checking Up

1. Describe how the Romans ruled their provinces.

2. What changes took place among the Romans after the Empire had brought them great wealth?

3. Who were Tiberius and Gaius Gracchus? Tell why they were slain.

4. List the steps by which Julius Caesar rose to supreme power in Rome.

5. Describe how Augustus gave the empire a good government.

6. Show how the Romans helped to preserve as well as to spread the culture and learning of ancient Greece.

7. List some of the Roman contributions to architecture.

8. Why has Latin always been an important language?

9. In what way did Justinian make an important contribution to our civilization of today?

 Yesterday and Today

1. Compare the American policy of extending citizenship to all our territories and possessions with that of the Romans in extending citizenship to their provinces.

2. Compare the athletic and recreational facilities in your community with those in ancient Rome. Which would you prefer?

3. Show the influence of Roman buildings on our architecture by naming some buildings in your community or state capital or our nation's capital that were inspired by Roman models.

Persons, Places, and Terms

Identify: Tiberius Gracchus, Gaius Gracchus, Julius Caesar, Augustus Caesar, Brutus, Mark Antony, Ptolemy, Cicero, Vergil, Justinian.

Locate: Po River, Rhine River, Pompeii, Gaul, Alexandria.

Define: publican, emperor, province, *Pax Romana*, Forum, rostrum, Colosseum, amphitheater, Pantheon, basilica.

Interesting Things to Do

1. Roman roads ran from the great capital city to all parts of the Empire. Try to find out how far an average Roman traveler was able to go in a day.

2. Read about Julius Caesar in your library books and encyclopedias, then write a report about him for your scrapbook.

3. A committee of the class can make a picture display of Roman houses and furnishings. Another committee group can prepare a report to explain the photographs and drawings in the display.

4. You might prepare a display for your bulletin board that would show influences of the ancient Romans on our life in America. Use sketches, pictures, photographs, and newspaper stories that are related to this theme.

UNDERSTANDING THE UNIT

  For Discussion

1. Tell why the Romans of the period of the republic provided for a dictator.

2. What factors hindered Julius Caesar from carrying out his reforms? How did these factors affect Augustus?

3. Tell why the following dates were important in the history of Rome: 450 B.C., 146 B.C., 44 B.C., 27 B.C.

 For You to Answer

1. What were the chief officials of the Roman republic called, and what were their duties?

2. Describe how the plebeians secured a position of equality with the patricians in Rome.

3. What were the conditions in the Roman Republic that the Gracchi brothers tried to correct?

4. Make a list of the accomplishments of Julius Caesar.

 Linking Geography and History

1. How did the location of the mountain ranges in Italy affect the lives of the Latin people. Compare this with the effect that the mountains of Greece had on the development of its people.

2. Using your text and other reference aids, draw a map of the Roman Republic. Then, using colors, show the expansion of Rome into an empire:
   a. In red, color the area of Roman territory in 133 B.C.
   b. In blue, color the areas under Roman rule at the time of Caesar's death in 44 B.C.
   c. In green, color the Roman Empire at its greatest extent, 180 A.D.

Interesting Things to Do

1. You might draw some pictures of important Roman landmarks such as the Pantheon or the Colosseum, or you might draw a plan of a typical Roman house. These pictures could be posted on the bulletin board or put in your scrapbook.

2. The class might invite someone who has traveled or lived in Italy to visit your school and talk about the country and show pictures.

Books to Read

Coolidge, Olivia, *Roman People*.
Duggan, Alfred, *Children of the Wolf*.
Foster, Genevieve, *Augustus Caesar's World*.
Gale, Elizabeth, *Julia Valeria*.
Gunther, John, *Julius Caesar*.
Lawrence, Isabelle, *Gift of the Golden Cup*.
Merrell, Leigh, *Prisoners of Hannibal*.
Snedeker, Caroline, *White Isle*.
Sutcliff, Rosemary, *The Silver Branch*.

UNIT 4
Growth of the Church

(BIRTH OF CHRIST — 800 A.D.)

CHAPTER

7. The Christian Era Begins
8. The Barbarian Invasions
9. The Rise of a New Religion
10. Europe Becomes Christian

EUROPE DURING EARLY CHRISTIAN TIMES

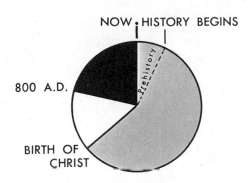

NOW • HISTORY BEGINS

Prehistory

800 A.D.

BIRTH OF
CHRIST

INTRODUCTION

During the reign of Augustus Caesar, while the Roman Empire was at its height, an event took place which had been foretold by Hebrew prophets long before. Jesus Christ, our Redeemer, was born in Bethlehem. This was the most important event in all history. Christ's birth, His life on earth, and His teachings have influenced the lives of men ever since.

While Christ lived on earth, He lived the perfect life, taught men how God expected them to live, and established His Church. After He ascended into Heaven, His followers, the Apostles, carried on the mission of teaching all men Christ's way of life.

As you read the chapters in this unit you will see that for a time the early Christians suffered persecutions at the hands of the Romans. Despite the many inhuman punishments inflicted upon Christians, the Church attracted converts, grew in strength, and set out to convert and to civilize the peoples of Europe.

In the meantime, the power of Rome had declined. Weakened by troubles from within and by attacks from without, the Western Roman Empire had fallen before invading barbarian tribes by the year 476 A.D.

After the Roman Empire had collapsed, the Church suffered numerous attacks by barbarian tribes and Moslem forces. The invasions and attacks failed to halt the growth of the Church or the continuance of its work. The Church not only taught the truths of God to the peoples of Europe, but it also helped to bring civilization to them. In so doing, it was instrumental in preserving the achievements of the ancient world for future generations.

103

7

The Christian Era Begins

THE LIFE OF CHRIST

Fulfillment of Prophecy. Judea, the land of the Jews (now modern Israel), was under the control of the Romans at the time of Christ's birth. *King Herod*, who came from a nearby country, ruled Judea for the Romans from the capital at Jerusalem. The prophets had foretold that when a stranger became the ruler of Jerusalem the Jews could expect the Messias.

The Roman Emperor Augustus's decree that a census of all peoples of the empire should be taken, helped to fulfill a number of prophecies about the birth of Christ. As St. Joseph and the Blessed Virgin Mary were descended from King David, it was necessary for them to journey from their home in Nazareth to Bethlehem, the city of David, in order to be enrolled in the Roman census. There in a stable in which Joseph and Mary had sought refuge for the night, Jesus Christ the Son of God was born. These details had been foretold in the writings of the prophet *Isaias*.

Christ's Earthly Life. Jesus, as you know, spent the early part of His life at Nazareth. He was obedient to Joseph and Mary. The Holy Family had a happy life together, even though they were very poor.

When He was about thirty years of age, Jesus began His public life. He preached to the Jews and gathered about Him a band of faithful apostles and disciples. During His earthly ministry, Jesus worked many miracles as proof that He was the Son of God.

Christ, through his teachings, made many enemies. They succeeded in having Him sentenced to death on false charges. Then Jesus was nailed to a cross and suffered death on the day we call *Good Friday*. Three days later, on the first Easter Day, He arose from the dead giving final proof that He was God.

For forty days after His Resurrection, Christ remained on earth preparing His apostles and disciples for the task of spreading His teachings to the whole world. Then He ascended into heaven, after commanding His followers to teach the whole world what He had taught them. Before He left, Christ promised that He would send the Holy Spirit to guide His followers and remain with them always.

* * * * *

In what ways is the Holy Spirit present in and guiding the Church today?

* * * * *

CHRIST FOUNDS THE CHURCH

Descent of The Spirit. The history of the Church began with the first Pentecost, which was ten days after the Ascension of Our Lord. On that day the Holy Spirit descended upon the apostles, who were filled with great courage and began at once to preach the *gospel*, or *good news*, of Christ to the people of Jerusalem. Three thousand converts were won to the Church that very day.

Head of the Church. As Christ selected His apostles, it was clear that *St. Peter* was their leader. In fact, Jesus changed Peter's name from *Simon* to *Peter,* a Latin word that means *rock*. Christ said to him, "Thou art *Peter* (the rock) and upon this rock I will build My Church."

Peter lived near the banks of the Jordan River and was by trade a fisherman. He was brought to Jesus

Christ attracted large groups of people wherever He went. When word reached them that Christ was in the area, young and old alike traveled great distances to hear Him preach.

by his brother Andrew. Later, Jesus called upon both Peter and Andrew to become "fishers of men." Peter, along with the other apostles, traveled far and wide to spread the gospel of Christ.

After preaching in many cities of the Near East, Peter went to the most important city in the world—Rome the capital of the Roman Empire. He became the Bishop of Rome. Peter's presence made Rome the capital of the new Church of Christ. Since that time the Bishops of Rome have been the heads of the Church. They have the title of *pope*. This is a late Latin word that means *father*. The pope serves as a loving father for the whole Church. We often call the pope the *Holy Father*.

St. Peter died as a martyr, probably in 64 A.D. Peter was crucified as was Christ. However, Peter asked to be crucified upside down since he did not feel worthy to die in the same manner as Christ.

The Great Preacher. The greatest preacher of the early Church was *St. Paul*. When he first came to Jerusalem, he was known as *Saul of Tarsus*. He became one of the chief persecutors of the Christians, as the followers of Christ were called. Saul was present at the death of *St. Stephen*, the first martyr.

God, however, called Saul to be a great apostle. After his baptism he became known as Paul. As Paul he earned the title *Apostle of the Gentiles*. This means that he preached the gospel of Christ to the people who were not Jews.

Paul was a man of great energy and was filled with a great love for God. He, in turn, stirred the converts to great love and enthusiasm for Christ. Paul founded churches in many cities of the Roman Empire. He wrote many letters to these churches while he journeyed throughout the Mediterranean area. These letters are among the Epistles which are read daily at Mass. St. Peter, St. James, and St. John also wrote Epistles.

St. Paul went to Rome where he suffered martyrdom about 67 A.D. He was beheaded because he, as a Roman citizen, could not be crucified like Our Lord or St. Peter.

Universal Church. The apostles at first preached only to the Jews in Judea and the neighboring countries. Then they began, as Christ had told them, to "go and teach all nations." The apostles journeyed from Jerusalem to all parts of the Roman Empire. From the very earliest days the religion of Christ was *catholic*, which means *universal*.

THE CHURCH GROWS

The Persecutions. During the lifetime of the apostles, the twelve chosen companions of Christ, the Church grew to a remarkable extent. It grew so rapidly that it aroused the hatred and hostility of the Romans.

The Christians would not go to the temples and worship the pagan gods of Rome. Many of the emperors after Augustus wished to be worshiped as gods, but the Christians said that there was only one true God. So the emperors began to persecute the Christians. There were ten serious persecutions in all. The first was under the cruel emperor, Nero, who reigned from 54 to 68 A.D. During his reign both St. Peter and St. Paul suffered martyrdom. The many Christians that were martyred faced death with courage and even joy. The apostles themselves had given the example of willingness to die for Christ. All of the apostles died as martyrs except St. John and even he suffered many tortures.

The Romans thought that they could make the Christians give up their religion. They inflicted the Christians with inhuman punishments. For example, they threw Christians to wild animals in the Colosseum to amuse the mob. There were almost as many different punishments as there were martyrs.

The Catacombs. During the worst of the persecutions, the Christians took refuge in passageways and rooms which were hollowed out under the city of Rome. In these underground rooms, called *catacombs* (kăt′a·kōmz), the Christians buried their dead as was the Roman custom. During the persecutions

the Christians also worshiped there; the priest said Mass, and the faithful received Holy Communion.

In the catacombs the priest usually said Mass over the tomb of a martyr. In our churches today, in the center of each altar, is an altar stone which contains the relics of a martyr.

Martyrs. The Christians continued to grow in numbers in spite of the persecutions. As the Roman people saw that the Christians were ready to suffer torture and even death for their belief in God, these pagans came to realize that Christianity was the true religion. "The blood of the martyrs is the seed of the Church" became a famous saying.

* * * * *

Can you remember the names of any early Christian martyrs?

* * * * *

Teachings of Jesus. The teachings of Christ attracted people to His Church. Christ had the message of hope for all the peoples conquered by the Romans and for those who had been made slaves. This message was "Come to me you who are heavily burdened and I will refresh you." Our Lord taught that all human beings were equal in the sight of God. The slave was equal to his master, the wife to her husband, and no race was better than another. This belief in the equality of all men is the basis of our modern democracy.

In pagan times, women were considered to be inferior creatures. Their fathers or their husbands had absolute control over them. Christ taught that women had the same rights and privileges as men. The followers of Christ then gave women a respect and understanding that

Persecution of the Christians did not stop the spread of the religion. Instead, many Romans came to respect Christians for the courage and devotion they displayed in the face of death.

was new to the world. The honor paid to the Blessed Mother also brought a new respect for womanhood.

Christ made it clear that He came to save all men. He commanded men to, "Love thy neighbor as thyself." The whole human race should be considered as one's neighbors, is what Jesus meant by this commandment. Thus from the beginning of the Church, the faithful have given help to the needy and consideration to the problems of all men.

The peoples of the ancient world had always been cruel in dealing with their foes. However, Christ commanded, "Love your enemies, do good to them that hate you . . . so that you may be children of your Father in heaven."

Christ, during his life on earth and in his teachings, had given a great deal of attention to the poor and oppressed. Yet, many of the proud and noble Romans were attracted to His Church. Army leaders, businessmen, and advisers of the emperors, as well as common people and slaves, became Christians.

The Church Grows. The teachings of Christ and His Church had an important influence on the lives of those who became Christians. The

To escape persecution by Roman emperors, early Christians met for worship in the catacombs beneath Rome. Some catacombs were so complete that they were almost like underground cities.

converts were inspired to lead pure and holy lives. As you know, the good example that the early Christians gave to their neighbors and fellow workers was one of the main reasons for the rapid growth of the Church.

In several practical ways the Roman Empire itself helped the spread of Christianity. First, all the peoples of the known world were united under the rule of Rome in a land that was at peace. This meant that it was easier for the apostles to spread the teachings of Christ, since there were no wars to prevent them from going where they wished. Second, the great network of Roman roads provided quick, safe travel. Third, the common use of the Greek and Latin languages by all the peoples of the Roman Empire made it easier for Christians to spread the gospel.

Freedom for the Church. The worst persecution of the Church began while *Diocletian* (dī′ö·klē′shăn) was Roman Emperor. This persecution lasted from 303 to 311 A.D. However, a later emperor, *Constantine* (kŏn′stăn·tīn), was friendly to the Christians. His mother, *St. Helena*, was a Christian and is famous because she discovered the True Cross of Christ at Jerusalem.

By the time the last of the heirs of Augustus died, the person who controlled the strongest Roman legions usually became emperor. So Constantine had to wage war with a rival for the throne.

In the year 312 A.D., as Constantine and his forces approached Rome, the forces of *Maxentius* (măk·sĕn′shĭ·ŭs), Constantine's rival, blocked the way at the *Milvian* (mĭl′vĭ·ăn) *Bridge* on the Tiber River. Before the battle began, a cross in the sky appeared to Constantine. On the cross was written, *In this sign conquer*. Constantine immediately placed a cross on each standard of his legions.

Although outnumbered three to one, Constantine's legions won the battle. Constantine did not immediately become a Christian, but the next year, 313 A.D., he issued a law that gave the Christians permission to practice their religion freely. This was called the *Edict of Milan*. The Christians were then able to worship openly.

By 395 A.D., the Roman emperors made Christianity the religion of the state. As a result, the pagan temples were closed or were taken over by the Christians. All of the festivals in honor of the pagan gods, including the Olympic Games, were abolished.

THE CHURCH'S ORGANIZATION

The Apostles. Christ Himself ordained the organization of the Church when He chose twelve apostles and seventy-two disciples. To the apostles He gave full powers to administer all the sacraments. The apostles were the first bishops of the Church. In turn, they consecrated other bishops and left these bishops as leaders in the chief cities of the empire. Later, as the Church grew, a group of towns and cities called a *diocese* (dĭ'ō·sēs) was put under the charge of a bishop.

As the Church continued to grow, groups of dioceses were formed to make up *provinces*. Each province

THE HOLY LAND

was governed by an archbishop, who was the leader of the bishops in the various dioceses that made up his province. The bishops of *Jerusalem, Antioch* (ăn'tĭ·ŏk), *Constantinople* (kŏn'stăn·t'n·ō' p'l), and *Alexandria* were known as *patriarchs* (pā'trĭ·ärks), a title which they have even today. The head of the whole Church, was St. Peter. Today his successors, the Bishops of Rome still head the Church.

In the early days the bishops were assisted by priests and deacons. Priests, ordained by bishops, were to say Mass and administer most of the sacraments. The deacons had charge of the charitable duties of the Church. They visited the sick and gave food and clothing to the poor.

The Church borrowed several ideas from the Roman Empire. For instance, a diocese was formed along the lines of a district, or a division, of the empire. The Christians began to build their churches in the form of the Roman basilicas. The vestments which the priest wears at Mass are developments of two Roman garments— the *toga* (tō'gȧ) and the *tunic* (tū'nĭk).

The First Church Council. After Constantine freed the Church from persecution, the Church began the practice of holding councils of bishops to discuss problems. They were held under the leadership of the pope. The first of the councils was held in the year 325 A.D. at the town of *Nicaea* (nĭ·sē′à) in Asia Minor.

One of the reasons that the council met was to discuss the fact that some people denied that Christ was God. The council declared that the Church believed and taught that Jesus Christ was really and truly God. The council further said that Christ was not only God but was equal with God the Father.

The council wrote a profession of faith for all true Christians, which stated these beliefs along with other Christian truths. This profession is known as the *Nicene Creed*.

* * * * *

Does the Church still hold councils of its bishops?

* * * * *

Summing Up. Jesus Christ the Son of God fulfilled the promises which God had made through the Hebrew prophets. Jesus Christ was indeed the Saviour of mankind, as His life and death show.

During His lifetime Christ called twelve men to be His apostles and He made St. Peter, who became Bishop of Rome, the head of the

The Edict of Milan was an important achievement of the Emperor Constantine.

apostles. After He ascended into heaven, Christ sent the Holy Spirit to fill His apostles with love and enthusiasm of God. After this the Church grew so rapidly that it soon spread all over the Roman Empire. The Romans, however, were afraid of the Christians, so they persecuted them.

Through divine intervention, Constantine became the Roman Emperor and in 313 A.D. issued the Edict of Milan, which allowed freedom of worship to the Christians. By 395 A.D. the Church was free.

FOR BETTER UNDERSTANDING

 Checking Up

1. How did Christ make it clear that St. Peter was to be the visible head of the Church?

2. Tell about the missionary work and writings of St. Paul.

3. Why did the Roman emperors persecute the Christians?

4. For what purposes did the Christians use the catacombs?

5. Why did the Catholic Church attract so many people during its early days in the Roman Empire?

6. How did the teachings of Christ and His Church affect the lives of the people who became Christians?

7. What was the importance of the Council of Nicaea?

8. Tell why each of the following dates is important: 54 A.D., 313 A.D., 325 A.D., 395 A.D.

 Yesterday and Today

1. Look up the First Amendment to the Constitution of the United States and compare its intent with that of the Edict of Milan.

2. Name some countries where in recent times members of the church have suffered persecution because of their faith.

3. List some present-day evidences of the universal, or world-wide, nature of the Catholic Church. The membership of the College of Cardinals and the missionary activities of the Church would be a good place to start.

 Persons, Places, and Terms

Identify: Herod, St. Peter, St. Paul, St. Stephen, Nero, Diocletian, Constantine, Maxentius.

Locate: Jerusalem, Bethlehem, Nazareth, Rome, Antioch, Constantinople, Alexandria, Nicaea.

Define: Messias, census, prophecy, gospel, convert, catholic, martyr, persecution, catacomb, diocese, bishop, patriarch, priest, deacon, Nicene Creed.

Interesting Things to Do

1. Our Lord often taught by using parables. Read one of these parables aloud, and then explain its meaning to the class.

2. The class could prepare a *Book of Martyrs* for your scrapbook. Each member of the class could select a different martyr and prepare a short paper telling about his or her martyrdom. There is a list, naming early Roman martyrs, in the Canon of the Mass that you might use.

8

The Barbarian Invasions

THE WEAKNESS OF THE ROMAN EMPIRE

Division of the Empire. For about three hundred years after the time of Augustus, the Roman Empire remained strong and powerful. Yet, it was hard for the emperor living at Rome to keep closely in touch with the eastern part of the Mediterranean world. Large armies had to be kept there to hold back the various enemies who tried to invade the empire.

When Constantine became emperor in 312 A.D., he wanted to strengthen his hold over this eastern territory. He, therefore, decided to build a new capital in the East. The new capital was named *Constantinople*, that is, *the city of Constantine.*

Constantinople was located on the narrow channel of water which forms the passage for ships going from the Mediterranean to the Black Sea. The leading land routes between Asia and Europe passed the location where Constantine built his eastern capital. You can see what a wonderful location Constantinople had by looking at the map on page 116. Quite naturally, the city then became a very important trading center. The modern city of Constantinople is called *Istanbul* (ĭs′tăn·bōōl′) and is located in Turkey.

During his lifetime Constantine ruled the entire Roman Empire from his new capital. After his death in 337 A.D., the empire was divided between Constantine's two sons. The part of the old empire which had its capital at Constantinople became known as the Eastern Roman Empire. The other part was known as the Western Roman Empire and was ruled from Rome.

The Western Empire Declines. Many weaknesses had developed within the Western Empire. Some of the emperors were weak leaders.

Many of the Romans had lost the virtues which made their country great. They had become greedy and lazy. They were too lazy either to work or to fight. Those Romans who were wealthy preferred to live in extreme luxury. They looked upon work as something which only slaves should do. The poor were also unwilling to work, preferring to live on public handouts.

*   *   *   *   *

In contrast to the Romans of the empire, why do we consider the worker and his work to have dignity?

*   *   *   *   *

As time went on, the fields of Italy were left idle. Italy then did not produce enough grain for the people of the cities. The emperors had to bring grain from distant parts of the empire. This was given to the people without charge. It was an expensive method of feeding the idle mob in the city of Rome in order to keep them from rioting. Such a policy meant that taxes increased and became a great burden on those who were earning money.

The Roman, or Latin, people declined in numbers. This meant that the emperors had difficulty finding Romans for their armies. The emperors came to depend on the barbarian peoples who lived outside the empire. They brought thousands of these barbarians to Rome as slaves to do the work in the city and on the farms. Later several barbarian tribes were permitted to come into the empire and settle down. Soon the Roman legions were made up almost entirely of barbarians. Some of the barbarian leaders became Roman generals, and some became the chief advisers of the emperors. Without realizing what they were doing, the Romans had permitted these outsiders to take over the chief governmental offices in the empire.

THE RACES OF EUROPE

Barbarian Peoples. Near the river Rhine Caesar had found tribes of the *Teutonic* (tŭ·tŏn'ĭk) race. These Teutonic tribes lived among rough mountains, dense forests, and swamplands in what is now Germany and Austria. The Rhine and the *Danube* (dăn'ūb) rivers formed a natural boundary between the Teutons, or Germans, and the Roman Empire. A great wall and a series of forts were erected by the Romans in order to keep these tribes from entering the empire.

The tribes which Julius Caesar had conquered in Gaul and Britain

This Teutonic chief might be urging his warriors to invade Rome. The striking of weapons against their shields was the warriors' method of indicating their approval.

were called *Celts* (sĕlts). It is these tribes who were the ancestors of the modern English–speaking peoples.

The *Slavic* (släv′ĭk) tribes lived to the east of Italy between the Adriatic Sea and the Danube River as well as to the north and east of the Teutonic tribes. These peoples had a type of tribal organization similar to both the Teutons and Celts.

All these tribes were half-civilized and were constantly trying to invade the Roman Empire, because they were attracted by its warm climate and rich lands.

The Teutons. The Romans have left us some vivid descriptions of the Teutons, who were very tall and seemed like giants to the shorter Latin peoples. The Teutons had fair skin, blond hair, and fierce blue eyes. Living outdoors most of the time in a cold climate had made them very hardy and strong.

They lived in small villages. Their houses were thatched huts. Their food was simple. They ate mostly fish, meat, fruit, vegetables, grains, milk, and cheese. The clothing of these barbaric tribesmen was usually made from the skins of animals or from a rough woolen or linen cloth.

These people were very warlike. In fact, the warriors left most of the everyday work to the old men and the women.

*   *   *   *   *

How would the life of a Teutonic tribesman compare with that of an early American Indian?

*   *   *   *   *

These tribesmen had many good qualities. They were brave and courageous. They were always true to their word. They treated women with great respect, and their family life was superior to that of the Romans during the time of the empire.

Before the Christian missionaries taught the German tribes about the true God, these barbarians worshiped many gods and goddesses. The chief of these gods was *Woden* (wō′d'n). His wife was *Frigga* (frĭg′gä). *Thor* (thôr), the son of Woden, was the god of thunder, and another son, *Tiu* (tē′ōō), was the god of war.

The days of our week have come from the names of these four gods. Wednesday is Woden's day; Friday is Frigga's day; Thursday is Thor's day; and Tuesday is Tiu's day.

Government of the Teutons. The Teutonic tribesmen had no written laws, yet they had a great respect for the customs and unwritten rules of their tribes.

At the head of each tribe was a

118

chief who was chosen by the warriors. When the tribe was at peace, the chief acted as judge and settled minor disputes. In matters of more importance he discussed affairs with the warriors in an assembly. Then a vote was taken. If the warriors agreed to the chief's suggestions, they clashed their spears or swords against their shields. This was their method of voting.

* * * * *

How does our way of electing our leaders resemble that of the Teutonic tribes?

* * * * *

THE EMPIRE STRUGGLES AGAINST THE BARBARIANS

A Fierce People. All of these peoples—Teutons, Celts, and Slavs—might have made a peaceful settlement with the Romans. These tribes, who lived along the border of the empire, had become partly civilized. However, a new and different people entered Europe from the east.

These were the fierce *Huns* (hŭnz), who came from central Asia. Coming on horseback, they appeared suddenly in great numbers. Wherever they went, they threw fear into all who saw them.

According to writers of the time, they were terrible–looking creatures. The Huns' faces were made ugly by deep gashes, which had been cut into them when they were babies. The Huns were short; their noses were flat; their eyes were small, black, and deep set. Their dark hair was long and straggly.

A Defeat in the East. Directly in the path of the advancing Huns were the *Gothic* (gŏth'ĭk) tribes. Look on page 116 and you will see the location of the homes of these peoples on the map. The *East*

Their terrible appearance, coupled with their savage behavior, made the Huns a fearsome and feared tribe. Early records indicate that the Huns literally spent their lives on horseback.

Goths, or *Ostrogoths* (ŏs′trṓ·gŏths), surrendered to the Huns. The *West Goths*, or *Visigoths* (vĭz′ĭ·gŏths), fled before them. The Visigoth chieftains begged the Emperor *Valens* (vā′lĕnz) at Constantinople to permit them to cross the lower Danube River into the Eastern Empire.

Valens made an agreement with the Visigoths. They were to furnish him with warriors, and he would supply food to the Visigoths. When the emperor failed to keep his promises the Visigoths rebelled. If you turn to page 116 you will be able to locate *Adrianople* (ā′drĭ·ăn–ō′p'l), where in the year 378 A.D. the Visigoths defeated Valens and his army. This battle opened up all of Greece to the northern tribesmen.

Later, the entire Visigoth nation under their leader *Alaric* (ăl′á·rĭk) began to move again. They crossed through Greece and marched north around the Adriatic Sea into Italy. In 410 A.D. they captured and sacked the city of Rome. Many of the treasures of the city were destroyed or stolen. The Visigoths finally moved on into Spain where they settled in a fertile, pleasant area.

The Scourge of God. The Huns then moved into the territory north of the Danube which had been vacated by the Visigoths. Under *Attila* (ăt′ĭ·là) they marched into Gaul in 451 A.D.

The invading barbarians frequently established their new homes in the midst of the ruins of the cities that they had destroyed.

For three years Attila and his Huns burned and ravaged the towns in Gaul and Italy. Attila thus earned the name, *Scourge of God*. He finally advanced toward Rome, and as he did so *Pope St. Leo* went out to meet him. Attila was impressed by the dignity of the pope and agreed not to attack Rome.

Shortly thereafter, in 453, Attila died and his followers were forced back to the east. They were no longer a threat to Europe, and they disappeared from recorded history.

FALL OF THE WESTERN ROMAN EMPIRE

Roman Power Is Broken. Shortly after the Huns returned to Asia, many of the Teutonic tribes began to seize great sections of the Roman Empire. The power of Rome over her Western Empire was broken. The emperor at Rome had to depend almost entirely on Teutonic soldiers to defend Rome itself. In the year 476 A.D. the legions at Rome deposed the last of the Roman Emperors *Augustulus*, meaning *little Augustus*. They then proclaimed one of their generals, a Teuton named *Odoacer* (ō′dô·ā′sēr), as king. A barbarian then ruled from the throne of the Caesars. Odoacer did little, however, to re-establish Roman power.

More Invasions. The invasions continued for another hundred years. The *Vandals* (văn′dălz) crossed the Rhine from Germany. They journeyed across Gaul and Spain and established a Vandal kingdom in North Africa.

The *Angles* (ăng′g'lz), *Saxons* (săk′s'nz), and *Jutes* (jōōts) moved into Celtic Britain from the northwest coast of continental Europe. Look at the map on page 116 and you will see the route the *Franks* (frăngks) and *Burgundians* (bûr·gŭn′dĭ·ănz) took as they crossed the Rhine into Gaul where they, too, established kingdoms. There was still another invasion of Italy. This time a tribe of long-bearded men, called *Lombards* (lŏm′bärdz), settled in northern Italy. The region where they settled is today still called *Lombardy*.

AFTER THE INVASIONS

The Eastern Empire. Rome, the proud and ancient capital of the Western Empire, had fallen into the hands of the barbarians. Constantinople, the newer capital of the Eastern Empire, escaped capture and looting. For a time the great emperor of the East, *Justinian*, who ruled from 527 to 565, even won back Italy and the Vandal kingdom in North Africa. Justinian's victory was, however, not of long duration.

For a thousand years after the fall of Rome, the Eastern capital remained a large, rich, and beautiful city. Here thousands of people came to trade their wares. Silk, rugs, spices, glass, and many other products from Asia were bought and sold in Constantinople. Constantinople continued to be a city of splendid churches, palaces, amphitheaters, aqueducts, and paved roads. There men continued to read and study, and Greek learning was preserved.

In the West. During the invasions of the barbarians, and for many years afterwards, Europe was in a state of great disorder. Vast numbers of people were turned out of their homes. Instead of working for a living, many became robbers and took by force what they wanted. There was much less business and trade than under the empire. Travel became difficult because roads and bridges were no longer kept in repair.

Whole cities were reduced to ruins. The barbarians did not understand civilized ways of living, so they destroyed paintings, statues, furniture, pottery, and buildings. Many libraries were also destroyed. In this way a great deal of knowledge about such subjects as history, geography, mathematics, and astronomy was lost forever.

Instead of being ruled by Roman law, both the conquered peoples and their conquerors, the barbarians, usually followed the tribal customs

It is not hard to see why Constantinople was one of the finest cities in the world. The architecture of this area and period (500-600), with its domed buildings, is called *Byzantine*.

of the barbarians. So for a long time much of what the Romans had achieved seemed to be lost.

The Church Survives. The mighty empire of the Romans had been destroyed. The Catholic Church with its capital at Rome, however, continued to survive. Goths, Huns, and Vandals had attacked or threatened the city of Rome, but the Church continued to elect successors of St. Peter as Bishops of Rome. Not only did the Church survive; it set out to convert and to civilize the barbarian tribes.

A Mixture of Peoples. Gradually, throughout the lands of the old empire, the barbarians and the civilized peoples settled down to peaceful living. They traded with one another, and they intermarried. In France, Spain, Portugal, and Italy, the barbarians adopted the dress, the language, the customs, and even the laws of the Romans.

This mixture of the civilized Romans and the barbaric Teutons, Slavs, and Celts had many good results. The invaders brought new strength and new life into Europe. They brought with them the spirit of liberty and they revived the love of the virtue of courage. These peoples became the ancestors of the founders of many of the present-day nations of Europe. This means that they are also our ancestors and the ancestors of many peoples in the Americas.

* * * * *

How were the barbarian invasions of the Roman Empire similar to, yet different from, the migration of millions of people to the New World in the last century?

* * * * *

Summing Up. After Constantine's death, the Roman Empire was divided with one emperor ruling the West from Rome and the other ruling the East from Constantinople. The divided empire existed for several hundred years. Finally, because of weak leaders, the many slaves who took work from the people, the decadence of the very rich, and the idle plebeians who preferred not to work but to be entertained, the Western Empire fell to barbarian invasions from the north and east. All of the great culture of Rome seemed lost, as the hordes of killing and destroying Teutons, Goths, and Huns overran Italy and the western provinces. Yet, the Eastern Empire with its capital at Constantinople remained as a great center of culture and learning. The Church also survived to convert the barbarians and bring peace and light to the world.

FOR BETTER UNDERSTANDING

Checking Up

1. Why was Constantinople an important city from its beginnings?

2. Describe the weaknesses of the Western Roman Empire.

3. Who were the chief tribal peoples of Europe and where were their homes?

4. Describe the customs of the Teutonic people.

5. Describe the Huns and their effect on the empire and on the other peoples of Europe.

6. Describe general conditions in the West after the barbarian invasions.

7. How was the Catholic Church affected by the invasions?

8. Identify each of the following dates, and tell why it is important: 337 A.D., 378 A.D., 410 A.D., 453 A.D., 476 A.D.

Yesterday and Today

1. Tell how the following countries or sections of countries owe their names to the tribes that settled there: Lombardy, Burgundy, Germany, Yugoslavia.

2. What is the largest city in your state? Compare the reasons for its growth with the factors that contributed to the growth of Rome and Constantinople.

3. Is our nation faced with any problems similar to those of the Roman Empire in its last days?

Persons, Places, and Terms

Identify: Valens, Alaric, Attila, Pope St. Leo, Augustulus, Odoacer, Justinian.

Locate: Constantinople, Rhine River, Danube River, Gaul, Britain, Adrianople.

Define: customs, migrations, Thor, Huns, Goths, Vandals.

Interesting Things to Do

1. Look up Istanbul in an encyclopedia, and prepare a report for the class on the present importance of the city.

2. Draw a map of Europe, and show where each of the barbarian tribes finally settled. You can put the map in your scrapbook.

9

The Rise of a New Religion

A RELIGION FOUNDED BY MAN

The Prophet's Land. If you turn to the map on page 127 you will be able to locate *Arabia*, the great desert region near the Red Sea, which is located between the Tigris-Euphrates Valley and Egypt. The Arabian people were mostly wandering shepherds, who were savage in their behavior and pagan in their religion.

Mecca (měk′å), a city of Arabia, was a trading center near the Red Sea. Caravans carrying goods between the West and Far East usually passed there. The Arab peoples considered Mecca a holy city, for located there was the temple called the *Kaaba* (kä′bå). This temple contained a black stone, believed to be a *meteorite* (mē′tĕ·ēr·ĭt), which had fallen from the sky. The Arabs considered this stone sacred. Around the Kaaba were 360 idols, one for each day of the year in the ancient Arabian calendar. These idols were also worshiped by many Arabs.

The Prophet's Early Life. About the time the barbarian invasions were reaching their peak in Western Europe, *Mohammed* (mǒ·hăm′ĕd) was born in the year 570 A.D. at Mecca.

Mohammed, as he grew to manhood, became a camel driver. Later he married a wealthy widow and became a merchant. He then traveled on long journeys from place to place in charge of his wife's camel caravans. On his journeys he met many shepherds and traders. Some of them were Christians and some were Jews. From them he learned many things about the Christian and Jewish religions—about the One God.

Mohammed came to believe that there was only one God, and he believed the name for God was *Allah* (ăl'ä). Mohammed claimed that the angel Gabriel had appeared and revealed many new ideas to him. Mohammed became convinced that he was the chosen prophet of God. Mohammed denied that Christ was God and said that Moses and Christ were only prophets of the true God. Mohammed claimed that he was the greatest of the prophets.

Mohammed Leaves Mecca. Mohammed began to preach his new religion at Mecca, but he gained very few converts. The people of Mecca expelled Mohammed and his small band of followers from the city in 622. The little group fled to *Medina* (mĕ·dē'nä), a nearby Arabian city. This flight is known as the *Hegira* (hĕ·jī'rä). The Mohammedans date their calendar from the Hegira, as we date ours from the birth of Christ.

In Medina, he attracted many followers, and after about eight years he gained control of the city. With his followers he returned to Mecca and captured that city. Then he made Mecca the center of *Islam* (ĭs'läm), which is the name he gave his new religion. Many western peoples call the religion *Mohammedanism* (mō·hăm'ĕ·dăn·ĭz'm).

The Holy Book. After the death of Mohammed, his sayings were collected in a book called the *Koran* (kō·răn'). It is the holy book of the followers of Mohammed, whom he called *Moslems* (mŏz'lĕmz).

Mohammed's flight from Mecca took place on July 16, 622. His safe arrival in Medina, about two months later, marked the turning point in the prophet's career.

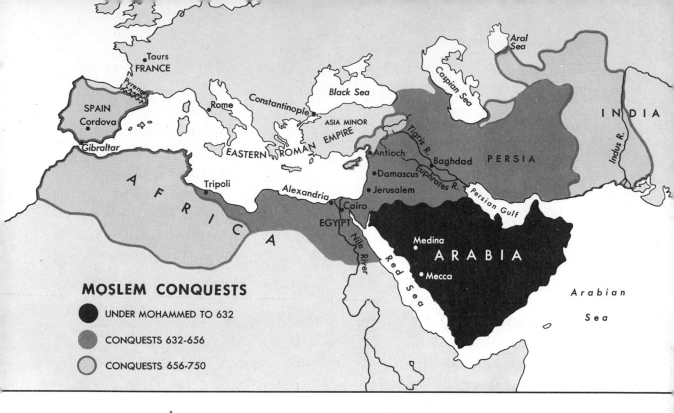

MOSLEM CONQUESTS

- ● UNDER MOHAMMED TO 632
- ● CONQUESTS 632-656
- ○ CONQUESTS 656-750

The *Koran* contains the laws for being a good Moslem. Prayer and fasting are encouraged, as well as the giving of alms to the poor. In the *Koran*, Mohammed urged all faithful followers to make at least one visit to Mecca during their lifetime.

The Moslem faith is summed up in a very short creed: "There is no God but Allah, and Mohammed is His Prophet." This creed is sung five times each day from the high tower of every Moslem *mosque* (mŏsk), or church.

* * * * *

The Koran is the holy book of the Moslems. What is the holy book of the Christians? Is there any similarity between the two books?

* * * * *

MOHAMMEDAN CONQUESTS

Out of Asia. The desert tribes of Arabia were soon converted to Islam, and these war-like peoples readily found a way to combine their love of fighting with their new religion. Mohammed taught that any man who died battling to extend his religion would go to paradise. This teaching made the shepherd followers of Mohammed eager to fight for their religion. In the name of Allah, they set out to conquer the world. If you look at the map on page 127 you will be able to locate the conquests of these armies. They conquered all of Arabia, and then all the countries of western Asia. These hordes attempted to cross over into Europe, at Constantinople, but the armies of the Eastern Empire prevented them from advancing in that direction.

The Mohammedans then turned and captured Egypt, as well as the great Christian centers of Jerusalem and Antioch. Next the Moslem armies conquered all of North Africa.

*   *   *   *   *

Do you feel that the missionary methods used by St. Peter and St. Paul were better than the war-like methods used to spread the Moslem faith? If so, why?

*   *   *˙   *   *

Nearly 100 years after Mohammed's Hegira, these armies crossed over into Spain at Gibraltar and de-stroyed the kingdom of the Visigoths. The Moslem armies next crossed the *Pyrenees* (pǐr′ė·nēz) into France, and it seemed as if they would conquer all Europe.

A Great Battle. On the northern side of the Pyrenees were the Franks. The Franks, like the Visigoths and the other invaders of the Roman Empire, were beginning to settle down and found new civilized kingdoms. The Franks, who had become Christians, rose up to defend Europe against this invader.

Near the city of *Tours* (tŏor) in the year 732 A.D., the Franks defeated the Moslems. This battle stopped the Moslem advance into Western Europe, and Europe remained Christian.

The man who had led the Franks to victory at Tours was *Charles*, the mayor of the palace of the Frankish kings at *Cologne* (kǒ·lōn′). The victory over the Moslems made him very famous. Because of his bravery and boldness in fighting the enemy, he was called *Charles Martel* (mär–tĕl′) or *Charles the Hammer.*

MOSLEM CIVILIZATION

New Ideas. The Moslems brought about many changes in the lands which they conquered, particularly in Spain. They introduced Arabian ideas and customs. For instance, they introduced Arabic numerals. Europeans found that these numerals were easier to use than the Roman numerals. Today in your arithmetic you use the Arabic numerals which are 1, 2, 3, 4, 5, 6, 7, 8, 9, and 0.

The Arabic and North African Moslems brought to Europe many new products from the East. Among these were fine steel weapons, tapestries, muslin, silk, carpets, and a heavy cloth used in making tents. They also taught the people of Europe to raise and to use many new foodstuffs—rice, sugar cane, peaches, melons, apricots, oranges, and lemons. The Moslems introduced into Europe several kinds of fine sheep and the swift Arabian horse.

A New City. The city that became the center of Moslem civilization in the East was built at *Baghdad* (băg′dăd) on the Tigris River, near the ruins of Babylon. Most of the caravan routes of the East went through this city, which became very wealthy and powerful. Perhaps you have read some stories of Baghdad in the collection of tales that is called *One Thousand and One Nights*, or more commonly the *Arabian Nights*. Among the best known of these tales are "Ali Baba and the Forty Thieves," "Aladdin and His Wonderful Lamp," and "Sinbad the Sailor."

The Arabs also established a high type of civilization in Persia, Palestine, North Africa, and Spain. They studied the Greek philosophers, Plato and Aristotle, advanced the science of medicine, and created many great works of art and literature, as well as many beautiful buildings. In doing so they passed on many very fine methods and ideas that have enriched our world of today.

*   *   *   *   *

Just as our ancestors in Western Europe learned from the Moslems, what are some of the things that we can learn from other civilizations that are different from ours?

*   *   *   *   *

Summing Up. Out of Mecca in the Arabian Desert, came Mohammed, who founded a new religion which he called Islam. After the death of Mohammed, his followers carried Islam into Asia Minor, North Africa, and Spain. The advance of Moslem armies threatened to engulf all of Europe. It was the Franks, under Charles Martel, who defeated these armies and saved Europe for Christianity. The Moslems, in time, developed very advanced civilizations in Persia, Egypt, and Spain. The Moslems brought many new ideas to the people they had conquered. We benefit today from many of their discoveries.

FOR BETTER UNDERSTANDING

 Checking Up

1. What were the chief religious ideas of Mohammed?

2. What is contained in the *Koran?*

3. List the religious obligations of a Moslem.

4. How did the Moslems extend their religion?

5. Explain why it was important that the Mohammedans lost the Battle of Tours.

6. What were the important Moslem contributions to civilization?

7. Identify each of the following dates and tell its importance: 570 A.D., 622 A.D., 732 A.D.

Yesterday and Today

1. Make a study of the historic city of Baghdad, and report to the class on its present importance.

2. Mohammed learned much from people that he met in his travels to the market places of the Near East. How many different ways do we have of learning about the other peoples of the world?

3. Make a list of present-day countries that have very large Moslem populations. Explain why there are no North or South American or Western European nations (with the exception of Albania) on your list.

Persons, Places, and Terms

Identify: Mohammed, Charles Martel.

Locate: Arabia, Mecca, Medina, Gibraltar, Pyrenees, Tours, Baghdad, Persia.

Define: Kaaba, meteorite, caravan, Allah, *Koran*, Hegira, mosque. Islam, Moslem.

Interesting Things to Do

1. Draw a map showing the spread of Islam. Be sure to show the location of Mecca, Medina, Baghdad, Constantinople, and Tours.

2. Write a short biography of Mohammed for your scrapbook.

3. Have a story hour. A member of the class or your teacher can read stories from *One Thousand and One Nights.*

4. Find pictures for the class bulletin board that will show what life is like today in Mohammedan countries. Include pictures of mosques, bazaars, and the various types of dress.

5. If you are interested in horses, you will like to read about Arabian horses and their influence on the important strains, or types, of horses in our country today. Your encyclopedia will help you to get started on preparing a report or just reading for fun.

10

Europe Becomes Christian

MONASTICISM

The Church Survives. The migrations of the barbarian tribes destroyed the peace and order of Europe for several centuries. The barbarians killed thousands of Christians and destroyed many churches. The very life of the Church was threatened by the barbarism of these wandering tribes. Yet, just as the Church had survived the Roman persecutions, so the Church survived these invasions.

The Church then had the opportunity to create a civilization founded on Christian ideas. It was a slow process that took centuries. In this great work, the *monks* (mŭngks) of the Church played an important part.

Monks of the East. During the early days of the Church, many Christians thought that the best way to save their souls was to withdraw from all worldly temptations. Many were like *St. Anthony* of Egypt, who lived between the years 250 and 350 A.D. He was a wealthy young noble, who decided to carry out the directions in the Gospel that Christ gave to the rich young man: "Sell all that thou hast, and give to the poor, and thou shalt have treasure in heaven; and come, follow Me."

St. Anthony retired to the desert where he spent many years in prayer and in trying to make himself perfect according to the teachings of Christ. For many years he did not see any other person. The fame of his holiness spread, and many others followed his example by adopting this solitary life. Each man lived alone in his own hut, but they all met together daily for

131

prayers, sermons, and readings from the Bible. These holy men were called *hermits* (hûr'mĭtz) or monks. Our word monk comes from a Greek word which means *living alone*. When a group of monks lived in one place, it was called a *monastery* (mŏn'ăs·tĕr'ĭ).

The Rule of the Eastern Monks. This type of holy life spread throughout the Church in the Eastern Roman Empire. A great scholar and bishop named *St. Basil* visited all the monasteries in Egypt, Pales- tine, and Syria. Then he wrote a set of rules for the monks in his own monastery. This *Rule of St. Basil* was adopted by all the monks in the East, and today it is still in use in that area.

* * * * *

Why do many young people enter the religious life today?

* * * * *

St. Benedict. A few years after the barbarians had driven the last emperor of the West from Rome, a

Pictured are Eastern monks at work in their fields. Notice that their monastery is built high on a mountain. Why, do you think, was the monastery made so hard to get to?

The famous Benedictine monastery at Monte Cassino was destroyed by bombs during World War II. The monastery, which has been completely rebuilt, is shown here during reconstruction.

son was born to a noble family in Italy. This boy whose name was *Benedict* attended school in Rome. He did not like the teachings of the pagans, and he did not like the wickedness and warfare in the world about him.

Benedict decided to become a hermit: so in the mountains not far from Rome he established himself in a cave. There he denied his body any comforts and pleasures. He ate only enough food to keep alive, he wore only the plainest and coarsest of clothing, and at night he slept on a bed of thistles. In this lonely cave he devoted himself to prayer and quiet thought.

The monks of a nearby monastery learned of Benedict's great

piety. They asked him to come and be their leader. Benedict agreed, and in the years that followed he founded a number of monasteries. The most important of the monasteries was at *Monte Cassino* (mŏn'tĕ kȧ·sē'nō), which is located halfway between Rome and Naples.

St. Benedict's Rule. St. Benedict saw that there was a need for rules to govern the monks. Like St. Basil, he thought that monks should live useful lives. He thought that they should eat enough food, wear enough clothing, and get enough sleep so that they could do useful work. He believed that idleness was a great source of wickedness. He thought monks should always be busy reading, working, or praying.

So he wrote his famous *Rule of St. Benedict*, which became the pattern of life in most monasteries in the western part of the Roman Empire.

St. Benedict expected his monks to follow the example of Christ, who by His own example—in the carpenter shop at Nazareth—showed the dignity of work. Benedict believed that the monks could raise all the food they needed on the monastery land, make their own clothes, and copy manuscripts for their studies. According to the Rule each monk had regular hours for work, for church services, and for prayer. St. Benedict summed up the idea of the Rule in his motto *To labor and to pray.*

*   *   *   *   *

St. Benedict emphasized the importance of prayer, study, and manual labor. Do you think that this is a good rule for everyone to follow?

*   *   *   *   *

The monks of each monastery elected a head called an *abbot* (ăb'ŭt). The word *abbot* is from an *Aramaic* (ăr'a·mā'ĭk) word meaning *father.* (Aramaic is the language which Jesus spoke while on earth.) The entire monastery was like a family. The abbot ruled the monastery as a father ruled a household.

Monastic Vows. The young men who wished to become monks took special vows. They promised to practice poverty, chastity, and obedience. The monastery could own land and property, but the individual monk had no personal possessions whatever. The monks all wore the same kind of plain robes, so that no one could be proud of his clothes.

Monastery Schools. Each monastery educated the boys who wished to become monks. In time, barbarian chiefs as well as Roman families sent their sons to the monasteries to be educated. In most places there were no schools except those in the monasteries. In this way the monasteries became the chief centers of civilization in the lands where the barbarians settled.

Education for Girls. St. Benedict's sister, *St. Scholastica* (skŏ·lăs'tĭ·ka), founded a convent for nuns not far from Monte Cassino. The nuns also adopted the Rule of St. Benedict. This convent became a great school for the education of girls. Other convent schools were founded throughout Europe.

St. Gregory the Great. One of the world's most remarkable monks was *St. Gregory the Great.* His family, which had been Christian for a long time, was one of the most impor-

Having saved Rome from the invasions of the Lombards, Pope Gregory turned his attentions to strengthening the Church. As a result of his efforts, the papacy became an important power.

tant in Rome. Gregory gave up a career as a lawyer and public officer to become a monk. He founded a monastery in his own mansion on one of the hills of Rome. He adopted the Rule of St. Benedict for this monastery and for the others that he founded.

In the year 590, the clergy and people of Rome elected Gregory as the pope. He was the first monk to become a pope. In his new position, he encouraged all the monasteries in the West to adopt the Benedictine Rule.

While Gregory was pope, the Lombards invaded Italy and threatened the city of Rome. There was no civil power left in Italy which was able to stop this new invasion. Pope Gregory, however, raised an army for the defense of Rome and central Italy. He made a treaty with the Lombard king, and Rome was saved from any further invasions by barbarian tribes.

* * * * *

Can you explain why it was good that Pope Gregory engaged in these non-religious activities?

* * * * *

THE FRANKS ARE CONVERTED

Barbarians Become Christians. The Franks, who had settled in ancient Gaul, were the first of the barbarian nations to accept Christianity. *Clovis* (klō′vĭs), the king of the Franks, had married *St. Clotilda* (klŏ·tĭl'dá), a Burgundian princess who was a devout Catholic. As a result of her good example and prayers, Clovis became interested in Christianity. On Christmas Day in 496, Clovis and three thousand of his warriors were baptized by *St. Remigius* (rĕ·mĭj'ĭ·ŭs), the archbishop of *Reims* (rēmz). In time, through the efforts of St. Clotilda and St. Remigius, the entire nation of the Franks was converted.

When the barbarians had gained control of most of the European continent, two places remained untouched. They were Ireland in the West and Constantinople in the East. Since its founding in 328 A.D., Constantinople had been the center of Christianity. A century later, the people of Ireland had been converted to the Faith. The first missionaries who were to win Europe for Christianity went out from these two areas, as well as from Rome.

Patrick. The man who had accomplished the conversion of Ireland was *St. Patrick*. Patrick was born in Britain about the year 389. His family were Roman nobles and devout Christians. The name *Patrick* means *noble* and comes from the same Latin word as *patrician*. As a boy, Patrick was captured by pirates and sold into slavery in Ireland. He lived there for six years. He learned to love the Irish people and to speak their Celtic language.

Patrick escaped from Ireland and returned to his own people, but he longed to return to Ireland and to convert the people to Christianity. For nearly twenty years, Patrick prepared himself for his missionary work.

* * * * *

How do the monks and nuns, who are the missionaries of today, prepare for their work in far-off lands?

* * * * *

Apostle to Ireland. St. Patrick secured the permission of the pope for his mission and was consecrated a bishop before he left for Ireland. In the year 432, he landed on the east coast of Ireland.

Knowing the Irish language and customs, he proceeded to the court of the *ardri* (ôrd·rē'), or high king of Ireland, at *Tara* (tăr'á).

While at Tara he converted and baptized *Conall* (kŏn'áll), brother of the ardri. Conall gave Patrick land for the building of a church which Patrick made his headquarters. St. Patrick then visited most of Ireland, preaching, converting, and baptizing.

Before his death St. Patrick had converted nearly all the Irish people. He established a native Irish clergy—made up of men who had been educated in the monasteries of Gaul (now modern France), before that Roman province had fallen to the barbarians.

Irish Monasteries. St. Patrick founded many monasteries in Ireland. Many of these were still small at Patrick's death in 461, but they continued to grow and prosper.

For two centuries the most important schools and colleges in all Europe were in the Irish monasteries. Scholars came from all parts of Europe to these monastic schools. Ireland became known as the *Isle of Saints and Scholars.*

As the barbarian nations began to settle down, Irish monks from these monastery schools went out as missionaries. They journeyed to all parts of Europe to carry on the important work of converting and civilizing the pagans.

Apostle of Scotland. One of the first of the missionaries to leave Ireland was *Columba* (kŏ·lŭm′bȧ). As a young man he had become a monk and had founded many churches and monasteries in Ireland.

When he was about forty-five years old, St. Columba decided to leave Ireland and go to Scotland to convert the people. He took with him twelve companions, after the example of Our Lord and His twelve apostles. St. Columba made his headquarters on the island of *Iona* (ī·ō′nȧ) off the west coast of Scotland. Iona became one of the most important monastic schools in Europe. Before his death in 597, St. Columba had won all Scotland for Christ.

Apostle to Central Europe. *Columban* (kŏ·lŭm′băn) was an Irish monk about twenty years younger than his namesake, St. Columba. St. Columban, like St. Columba, took twelve companions with him and journeyed to the kingdom of the Franks. There his preaching was so eloquent that he attracted a large number of followers. Then the king of Burgundy invited him to make his headquarters in that region.

St. Columba and his disciples arrive at Iona, where they established their monastery.

St. Columban and his disciples founded over one hundred monasteries. These were located in what is now modern Germany along the river Rhine, in Switzerland, and in northern Italy. The most famous of St. Columban's monastic schools was at *Bobbio* (bŏ′bĭ·ō), in Italy, the location of which place you can see if you look at the unit map on page 102.

Apostle of Switzerland. One of the Irish companions of St. Columban was *Gall* (gôl). He became fond of the people in what is now Switzerland. There, in the shadows of the mighty Alps, he established a monastery. The town which grew up around the monastery came to be known as *St. Gall.*

The monastery at St. Gall became one of the most famous in all Europe. The monastery also became a center of great learning. Its monks were so active in making copies of books that its library is still considered one of the best in Europe.

Apostle of England. When Pope Gregory decided to send missionaries to England, he selected a band of forty monks from his own monastery in Rome. He placed *St. Augustine* in charge of them.

If you look at the map on page 139, you can see the location of the seven small kingdoms of the Angles, Saxons, and Jutes who had invaded England and settled there. The Jutes had settled in *Kent* (kĕnt), in the southeastern part of the island. The Angles took over the northern section of England, where they had the three kingdoms of *Northumbria* (nôr·thŭm′brĭ·à), *Mercia* (mûr′shĭ·à), and *East Anglia* (ăng′glĭ·à). The Saxons set up three kingdoms which covered nearly all the southern part of the island. These were the kingdoms of *Wessex* (wĕs′ĕks), *Essex* (ĕs′ĕks), and *Sussex* (sŭs′ĕks).

Augustine and his companions arrived in one of these kingdoms, Kent, early in the year 597. *Ethelbert* (ĕth′ĕl·bẽrt), the king of Kent, had married a Frankish princess, *Bertha*, who was a devout Catholic. Ethelbert and the men of Kent refused to accept Christianity at first. Later, at Canterbury, the capital of Kent, Ethelbert gave St. Augustine permission to preach in his kingdom, and became one of the first converts. St. Augustine established his headquarters at Canterbury and became the first archbishop of Canterbury. He was known as the "Apostle of the English."

Apostle to Northern England. The Angles in the northern section of England had formed the kingdom of

Northumbria, which included the southern part of Scotland. One of the kings of Northumbria, *Oswald* (ŏz'wȧld), had spent several years in exile at Iona. After returning to his kingdom, he asked the Irish monks of Iona to send missionaries into Northumbria.

St. Aidan (ā'dăn) was selected for this task. After he was consecrated bishop, he went to England where he was welcomed by Oswald. The king gave St. Aidan the island of *Lindisfarne* (lĭn'dĭs·färn) in the North Sea. There St. Aidan built a famous monastery.

The successors of St. Augustine, working from Canterbury, and the successors of St. Aidan, working from Lindisfarne, soon converted the whole of England to the Faith. Just as in Ireland, the new converts in England became fired with a great enthusiasm to bring the Faith of Christ to pagan lands.

* * * * *

The Church's mission is still the conversion of souls. Can you give any evidence that the missionary zeal of the Church is just as fervent now as it was in the time about which you are studying?

* * * * *

SAXON ENGLAND
IN THE EIGHTH CENTURY

Lindisfarne

NORTHUMBRIA

CUMBRIA

Whitby

Irish Sea

York

IRELAND

North

Sea

WALES

MERCIA

EAST ANGLIA

ESSEX

London

R. Thames

KENT •Canterbury

Tintagel

WESSEX

SUSSEX

CORNWALL

English Channel

FRANKS

GERMANY IS CONVERTED

Apostle of Germany. A young Saxon noble named *Winfrid* (wĭn′frĭd) became one of the great missionaries of the Church. He entered the Benedictine school at *Exeter* (ĕk′sĕ·tẽr) in England as a young boy and later became a monk. His great ambition was to bring the faith to the pagan Saxons, who still lived in central Germany.

He left England and went to Rome to receive the blessing of Pope Gregory II (the Second). The pope changed Winfrid's name to *Boniface* (bŏn′ĭ·fās), which means *one who does good*. Boniface's work was so successful during his first

Under the suspicious eyes of the pagan Saxons, St. Boniface chops down the oak tree which they had considered as sacred.

three years in central Germany that the pope consecrated him a bishop.

In one area of Germany, the pagans held a gigantic oak tree in great veneration. It was dedicated to Thor, the god of thunder. St. Boniface with his own hands chopped down this oak, while throngs of pagans watched. They expected that Thor would strike down St. Boniface with a thunderbolt. When the monk remained unharmed, the pagans realized that their belief in these gods was false. Many pagans asked to be baptized immediately.

Boniface's Success. The missionary work of St. Boniface was so successful that he needed more priests. He sent to England, and a large group of monks responded to his call. In addition, a group of English nuns, some of them cousins of St. Boniface, came to Germany to found convent schools. The pope rewarded the missionary work of St. Boniface by making him an archbishop.

The most famous of the monasteries founded by St. Boniface was at *Fulda* (fŏŏl′dä) in central Germany. Fulda became the center of the Catholic Faith in Germany.

St. Boniface became very famous. Great leaders like Charles Martel sought his advice. It was St. Boniface, who at the request of the pope, crowned *Pepin* (pĕp'ĭn), about whom you will read, as king of the Franks.

Boniface's Martyrdom. When he was almost eighty years of age, Boniface resigned his archbishopric in order to become a humble missionary again. He had always wanted to convert the people of *Friesland* (frēz'lănd), a territory which forms that part of Germany and the Netherlands close to the North Sea. Despite his advanced age, Boniface's preaching brought many of the Frisians into the Faith.

One day as Boniface was preparing a group of converts for the sacrament of Confirmation, a band of pagans attacked them. The Apostle of Germany suffered the death of a martyr along with fifty-two others.

Apostle to Scandinavia. *St. Ansgar* (ăns'gär) preached the Faith to the people of Denmark and Sweden. He became archbishop of *Hamburg* (now in modern Germany), which he made the headquarters for his missionary trips to the countries of the North. He became famous for his works of mercy. The saint built hospitals, ransomed captives, and helped to reduce the slave trade.

Apostle to the Southern Slavs. An Irish monk who took the Latin version of his name and was known as *Virgil* (vûr'jĭl) became bishop of *Salzburg*, which is now in Austria. His diocese bordered the lands of the southern Slavic tribes. He devoted most of his energies to bringing the Faith to the people of the country which is now called *Yugoslavia*.

Apostle to the Northern Slavs. *St. Adalbert* (ăd''l·bĕrt) was a German monk who was made bishop of *Magdeburg* (măg'dĕ·bûrg) for the purpose of bringing the Faith to the Slavic people of the North. His missionary journeys took him into Prussia (now modern East Germany) and Poland.

A young Bohemian monk, who studied under St. Adalbert, took the same name as his great teacher. This second *St. Adalbert* became the bishop of *Prague*, now the capital of Czechoslovakia. He worked successfully among his own countrymen and in southern Poland. St. Adalbert was martyred in the year 1000.

St. Stephen of Hungary. *St. Stephen* was the son of the chief ruler of Hungary. Stephen's father and family were baptized Christians, but it was not until Stephen succeeded his father that the people of Hungary adopted the Catholic Faith.

The conversion of Hungary was due to the zeal of St. Stephen. He founded monasteries, established dioceses, and helped the priests spread the gospel of Christ. Stephen became the first real king of Hungary in 998 after subduing a number of rebellious nobles. In the year 1001, *Pope Sylvester II* sent him a consecrated crown, which each king of Hungary has since worn.

As Europe became more and more Christian, many pious people began to make journeys, or pilgrimages, to the Holy Land. With the conversion of Hungary to Christianity, a direct land route was open across Europe to the Eastern Roman Empire. St. Stephen gave the pilgrims protection throughout his kingdom. In addition, he established a *hospice* (hŏs′pĭs) at Rome, at Ravenna, and at Constantinople. A hospice was an inn where a pilgrim might find rest and refreshment. St. Stephen also established a monastery in Jerusalem to care for the pilgrims when they reached the birthplace of Christianity.

*   *   *   *   *

St. Stephen did many good works. Can you explain why these were an expression of his faith?

*   *   *   *   *

Eastern Missionaries. Missionaries came from the East to aid in the conversion of the Slavic peoples. The eastern emperors at Constantinople and the patriarchs of that city were interested in the spread of Christianity. Two of the chief missionaries from Constantinople were the brothers, Saints *Cyril* (sĭr′ĭl) and *Methodius* (mė̇·thō′dĭ·ŭs).

Cyril and Methodius worked as missionaries among the Bulgarians for several years. Then the duke of Moravia invited them to preach in his land, which today is a part of Czechoslovakia.

St. Cyril invented an alphabet which is still used in Slavic countries. The two brothers translated the Gospels and other books into the Slavic language. They were able to preach to the people in their own tongue, and the pope even permitted them to say Mass in Slavic.

Russia. *Vladimir* (vlăd′ĭ·mĭr) *the Great*, the ruler of Russia, had become interested in Christianity through his grandmother *St. Olga*. She had become a Catholic and had encouraged many of the people to accept the Faith of Christ.

Vladimir decided to become a Christian, so he asked the emperor at Constantinople to send a special mission to give him instruction. The people of Russia joined the Church in large numbers after the conversion of Vladimir in 998.

Vladimir gave up his earlier warlike career and gave his people a good government. He built churches as well as schools and did all he could to spread the work of conversion and civilization.

A Christian Continent. By the year 1000, nearly all of Europe was Christian. The missionaries had carried the Faith of Christ from Ireland to Russia and from Sweden to northern Italy. However, the work of the Church was not completed. There was a new Catholic Europe to build and many pagan lands to convert.

Summing Up. In the early centuries of the Church's history, men in both East and West desired to follow Christ's teachings by leaving the world. As these men came together and founded monasteries, they were inspired to carry God's word to all men. In so doing, much of barbarian Europe in the West was converted by the year 700 A.D. As each people received the faith of Christ, they were so fired with the Holy Spirit that they sent monks as missionaries to other lands. By about the year 1000 the whole of Europe, East and West, had been converted to the Catholic Faith.

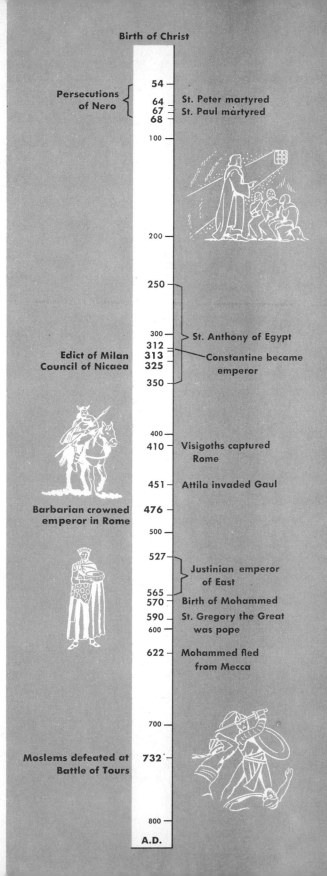

Birth of Christ

54	
Persecutions of Nero { 64	St. Peter martyred
67	St. Paul martyred
68	
100	
200	
250	
300	St. Anthony of Egypt
312	
Edict of Milan 313	Constantine became
Council of Nicaea 325	emperor
350	
400	
410	Visigoths captured Rome
451	Attila invaded Gaul
Barbarian crowned emperor in Rome 476	
500	
527	Justinian emperor of East
565	
570	Birth of Mohammed
590	St. Gregory the Great
600	was pope
622	Mohammed fled from Mecca
700	
Moslems defeated at Battle of Tours 732	
800	
A.D.	

FOR BETTER UNDERSTANDING

Checking Up

1. Explain the great task that the Catholic Church had in converting the barbarian nations.

2. What was the importance of the work of St. Benedict?

3. Tell what the Benedictine motto, *To labor and to pray*, means in the life of the monks?

4. Why was the work of St. Scholastica important?

5. Describe the career of St. Gregory the Great.

6. How were the Franks converted?

7. Why was Ireland known as the Isle of Saints and Scholars?

8. Describe the missionary work of St. Columba and St. Columban.

9. Tell how St. Augustine and St. Aidan converted the people of England.

10. Why is St. Boniface known as the Apostle of Germany?

11. Describe the work of Saints Cyril and Methodius.

12. Identify each of the following dates, and tell its importance: 496 A.D., 590 A.D., 998 A.D.

Yesterday and Today

1. The priests, brothers, or nuns, who are teachers in Catholic schools, live according to a Rule somewhat like that of St. Benedict. Find out the Rule followed by the Order at your school and compare it to that of St. Benedict.

2. Do you know the names of some of the missionary Orders or Societies and where their various missionary activities are? By writing to these Orders, you may secure magazines and pamphlets that will tell you about their present-day missionary work.

Persons, Places, and Terms

Identify: St. Anthony of Egypt, St. Basil, Conall, St. Gall, Ethelbert, Bertha, Oswald, St. Ansgar, St. Virgil, St. Adalbert (the older), St. Stephen, Pope Sylvester II, Vladimir, St. Olga, Clovis, St. Clotilda, St. Remigius.

Locate: Monte Cassino, Bobbio, Reims, Tara, Iona, Kent, Northumbria, Mercia, East Anglia, Wessex, Essex, Sussex, Lindisfarne, Fulda, Friesland, Hamburg, Salzburg, Magdeburg.

Define: hermit, monk, monastery, abbot, Rule of St. Benedict, ardri, hospice, pilgrimage.

Interesting Things to Do

1. Write a story about everyday life in a medieval monastery. Draw pictures and find photographs to accompany it. Put the story in your scrapbook.

2. Perhaps your teacher can secure for you the name and address of a boy or girl in a mission school in some foreign land. You could send pictures of your city, home, school, church, and a letter asking for information about the school, family, and parish church in their country.

UNDERSTANDING THE UNIT

For Discussion

1. Why is the birth of Christ the most important date in all history?

2. Was the fall of Rome due to internal weakness or due to invasions from without?

3. Why did Christianity become such a widespread religion so quickly?

4. Why were the Moslems willing to fight for their religion?

5. Explain why the work of the missionaries had great value in addition to value of religious conversion.

For You to Answer

1. How did the Emperor Augustus help to fulfill the prophecies concerning the birth of Christ?

2. Why were the early Christians persecuted at Rome?

3. What was the importance of the Council of Nicaea?

4. Describe the government of the Teutonic tribes.

5. How did the Moslems contribute to European civilization?

6. Tell about the conversion of Russia.

Linking Geography and History

1. How did the Romans use natural boundaries as a partial defense of their empire?

2. What two small islands played a great part in the conversion of England and Scotland?

3. Notice the great distances traversed by Roman legions, barbarian tribes, Christian missionaries, and Moslem armies. What natural obstacles would be met by these groups on their journeys?

Interesting Things to Do

1. Each of the words in the following list had its origin from some person, place, or thing in the events which you have studied about in this unit. Use a dictionary to find the origin and the present meaning of:

vandalism	Wednesday
gothic	arabesque
damask	mecca

2. The class might be interested in making a study of the Slavic and other non-Latin languages and rites used for saying Mass. Perhaps your priest might speak to the class about some of these rites.

Books to Read

Beaty, J. C., *Swords in the Dawn.*

Chubb, Thomas C., *The Byzantines.*

Cousins, Mary, *Tell Me about the Saints.*

Daniel-Rops, Henry, *A Catholic Child's Book About Saint Paul.*

De Wohl, Louis, *St. Helena and the True Cross.*

Fitch, Florence M., *One God, the Ways We Worship Him.*

Hunt, Marigold, *The First Catholics.*

Lansing, Marion, *Barbarian and Noble.*

Maryknoll Sisters, *Crusade, The Story of the Bible.*

UNIT 5
The Early Middle Ages

(400 A.D. — 1000 A.D.)

CHAPTER

11. A New Empire in the West
12. A New Political System
13. When Knighthood Was in Flower
14. The Church in the Middle Ages

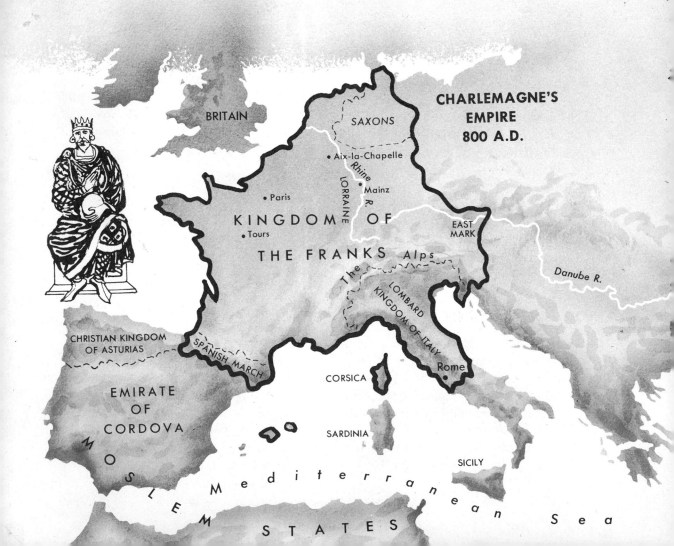

CHARLEMAGNE'S
EMPIRE
800 A.D.

BRITAIN

SAXONS

• Aix-la-Chapelle

Rhine R.

LORRAINE

• Mainz

• Paris

KINGDOM OF

• Tours

THE FRANKS   Alps

EAST
MARK

The Alps

LOMBARD KINGDOM OF ITALY

Danube R.

CHRISTIAN KINGDOM
OF ASTURIAS

SPANISH MARCH

Rome

EMIRATE
OF
CORDOVA

CORSICA

SARDINIA

SICILY

MOSLEM

Mediterranean Sea

STATES

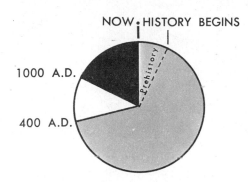

NOW HISTORY BEGINS

1000 A.D.

Prehistory

400 A.D.

INTRODUCTION

After the fall of the Western Roman Empire in 476 A.D. there was disorder throughout much of Europe. At length a strong king, Charles the Great—or Charlemagne, as he was called—established an orderly government in Western Europe. After his death there was no king who was strong enough to protect the people against invaders from the North and East, or against robber nobles who often seized the lands of their neighbors. A new system had to be found which would restore peace and order to Europe.

The people in Western Europe began to seek the aid of strong, fighting nobles who could protect them against such attacks. In return for protection, the people provided the nobles with various kinds of work and services. The weak nobles often turned over their lands to stronger nobles in return for protection. All parties had rights and duties in these arrangements and were bound to them by solemn prom-

ises. Thus, a system of protection and government developed which provided advantages for all. The new system was called *feudalism*.

As you read this unit, you will learn about this system, and how the Church influenced it. You will see that the Church introduced customs which helped to reduce the warfare and fighting so common at the time. It introduced the ideals of chivalry and knighthood. It provided religious instruction for all of the people, and education for many. It preserved and added to the learning which was handed down from the ancient world. In addition the Church provided a spiritual and cultural bond which helped to draw the various peoples of Europe together.

11

A New Empire in the West

THE FRANKS AND THEIR KINGDOM

A Young King. Among the invading Teutonic tribes that overran the Roman Empire were the Franks. They established the strongest of the new nations.

The Franks did not desert their homeland when they invaded the Roman Empire. Instead they kept what territory they had and slowly extended it until they controlled the Roman province of Gaul. In this way, the Franks gained a firmer hold on the territory that they captured than did the tribes who wandered far from their homeland.

In 481, five years after the barbarians had driven the last Roman Emperor of the West from his throne, a fifteen-year-old boy named *Clovis* became king of the Franks. Despite his youth, he was a good leader and a strong ruler. He defeated the Roman governor of Gaul. He also defeated all the other Teutonic tribes in that region.

Clovis was the first Teutonic king to become a Catholic. After his conversion, the Franks gave strong support to the Church.

Clovis was able to unite the various Frankish tribes into one strong nation. He provided law and order for a large section of Western Europe. The Eastern Emperor at Constantinople gave Clovis the titles of *Patrician* and *Consul*. Clovis gladly accepted these honors and appointed many western Romans to important positions in his kingdom. In this way, he helped to unite his Frankish people with the Romans of Gaul. The language of the Franks became more and more like Latin. The people of the Frankish kingdom adopted many Roman customs and manners.

149

Mayors of the Palace. When Clovis died in 511, his kingdom was divided among his four sons. These sons, and the rulers who followed them, quarreled among themselves. The hundred years after the death of Clovis were years of rivalry and bloodshed. Much of the civilizing work of Clovis was lost.

A series of weak kings gradually permitted the men who were the mayors of the palace to take over most of the important tasks in the kingdom. In time, the mayor of the palace became more powerful than the king himself.

When the Mohammedans crossed the Pyrenees Mountains and threatened to conquer all Europe, it was the Frankish mayor of the palace, Charles Martel, who defeated them. He did this at the Battle of Tours in 732. After this great victory the people looked upon Charles Martel as the real ruler of the Franks.

A New King. Charles Martel did not take the title of king, even though he was the actual ruler. After his death, one of his sons, Pepin, became ruler of all the Franks.

After he had ruled as mayor of the palace for ten years, Pepin sent a bishop and an abbot to Rome. They went to see *Pope Zacharias* (zăk′*a*·rī′ăs) and asked him who should be king—a weakling who had only the title of king or the man who actually ruled the kingdom. The pope's reply was that the man who actually ruled the kingdom should be called king.

Pepin set aside the last of the weak kings that were the descendants of Clovis. With the consent of the bishops and nobles, Pepin then became king. St. Boniface, the Archbishop of *Mainz* (mīntz), anointed the new king in the same manner in which the Old Testament tells us that the prophet Samuel anointed King Saul.

*   *   *   *   *

What type of impression would that ceremony have on the Frankish people?

*   *   *   *   *

The Papal States. For many years each succeeding Eastern Emperor at Constantinople had claimed to be the ruler of Italy. However, when the Lombards invaded Italy, the Eastern Emperor did very little to stop them. In order to defend Rome and central Italy, the pope was obliged to raise an army and try to check these warlike people. The pope also appealed to Pepin for help against the Lombards' continuing attacks. Responding to the pope's plea, Pepin led his army against the Lombards and defeated them. Then he gave the land of central Italy to the pope. This made the pope a civil ruler as well as the spiritual head of the Church. This civil power of the pope prevented any other ruler from interfering with the spiritual work of the head of the Church. Today, the pope is still a civil ruler. He is the head of a small section of the city of Rome, which is an independent state, or country, called *Vatican City*.

THE FRANKISH KINGDOM EXPANDS

Charles the Great. After Pepin's death his son Charles became king. So great a king was Charles that he is even today known as *Charlemagne* (shär′lē·mān), which means *Charles the Great*. He ruled for forty-six years, from 768 to 814.

Charlemagne had a secretary who wrote down many things about him. This secretary tells us that Charlemagne was a big man, more than six feet tall. He had fair hair, blue eyes, and a prominent nose. He was also a man of dignified bearing.

Charlemagne was very energetic. He enjoyed riding and hunting and was an expert swimmer. He never ate or drank too much. His frequent exercise and his good habits in eating and drinking made his body strong and his mind bright.

Charlemagne and the Barbarians. Charlemagne wanted to bring all the Teutonic peoples together into one great Christian nation, and he did much toward accomplishing this.

The Saxons, who lived in what is now northern Germany, were one of the fiercest of all the Teutonic tribes. The unit map on page 146 shows the location of their home. It took Charlemagne thirty years to bring them under his rule. After conquering these peoples, he aided and encouraged missionaries in the work of converting and civilizing them. By one hundred years later the Saxons had developed the most important Germanic kingdom.

This conquest of the Saxons brought Charlemagne into contact with the Slavic tribes to the east. In a single campaign, Charlemagne forced the Slavic tribes to accept him as their overlord. Then he established several *marches* along the eastern boundary of his dominions. A *march* was a military district set up to protect the rest of the country from invasion. The Eastern March became one of the most important districts. It later developed into the country of Austria.

Charlemagne in Spain. When Charles Martel defeated the Moslems at Tours in 732, he had pushed them back across the Pyrenees Mountains. From time to time, however, the Moslems continued to invade southern France. For twenty years Charlemagne waged war against the Moslems in Spain. He succeeded in keeping southern France free and in conquering a part of northern Spain.

One of the men who accompanied Charlemagne in his battles against the Moslems was a very brave knight named *Roland* (rô′län′). Many famous stories are told about him in the medieval tale, *The Song of Roland.*

Charlemagne in Italy. Like his father, Charlemagne wanted to protect the pope against the Lombards in Italy. He made several expeditions against them and finally deposed the Lombard king. Then Charlemagne took the Iron Crown of Lombardy and placed it upon his own head. Thus, he became king of the Lombards as well as king of the Franks.

* * * * *

The Iron Crown of Lombardy was a symbol of power that Charlemagne used to show his new authority. What symbols of authority do we have and use in our country today?

* * * * *

THE FRANKISH KINGDOM BECOMES AN EMPIRE

Charlemagne as Emperor. By his vast conquests, Charlemagne made himself ruler, either in whole or in part, over the section of Europe that today includes Spain, France, Belgium, Holland, Germany, Austria, Hungary, Italy, and Switzerland. Western Europe had once again been united. This time a German and not a Roman had estab-

One of Charlemagne's great interests was the welfare of the Church. He is remembered as a champion of Christianity. He especially worked to spread Christianity to all classes of people.

Charlemagne is shown placing the Iron Crown of Lombardy upon his head. With the defeat of the Lombards, the Church became safe from further barbarian attacks.

lished law and order in the western half of Europe. A German empire had taken the place of the Western Roman Empire. The Anglo-Saxons in England and the Scandinavians were the only Teutonic groups not included in this empire.

Even though Charlemagne had formed a vast empire, he was still only a Teutonic king. Then, on Christmas Day in 800, *Pope Leo III* crowned him *Emperor of the Romans* at Mass in St. Peter's Church in Rome.

The coronation of Charlemagne made a great impression on all the people of Europe. It gave him no additional power and no new territory. Yet, Charlemagne was considered to be the successor of the Western Roman Emperors both in power and possessions. His empire, however, was very different from that of the Roman Emperors. The ruling people were not Romans but Teutons. Charlemagne's capital city was not Rome, but the German town of *Aachen* (ä′ĸĕn), which is generally known by its French name of *Aix-la-Chapelle* (āks′lä·shă-pĕl′).

Charlemagne Governs. Governing the empire was a great task. Charlemagne did not revive the old Roman methods, but worked out new methods of his own.

There was, in Charlemagne's empire, no system of general taxation for the support of the government. Instead, Charlemagne had to depend on the income from his royal estates. Therefore, he took great care to see that his estates were well cultivated and that the accounts of their produce were accurately kept.

Charlemagne divided his empire into divisions called *counties*. In order to manage local affairs, he appointed a noble, with the title of *count*, to rule over each of these divisions. It was the duty of the counts to act as judges when disputes arose among the landowners. It was also the counts' duty to keep order and to raise troops for Charlemagne. Sometimes several counties were combined into a *duchy* and the ruler was given the title of *duke*.

Charlemagne invented a system of keeping a check on the counts. Each year two inspectors were sent out to every county. One was a bishop, and the other a noble from the royal court. They were instructed "to do justice to churches, widows, orphans, the poor, and all the people." These inspectors called the people together to find out whether there were any complaints. The inspectors gave Charlemagne a complete report on the affairs in each county. In this way, he knew what was happening in each section of his large empire.

Each spring, at Aix-la-Chapelle or at some other center in his empire, Charlemagne held a great outdoor meeting called a *May-field*. At this meeting, Charlemagne discussed the laws with his people and explained to them the purposes of new laws. Sometimes he even let the people vote on some question. Having these meetings was wise. Such meetings made the laws known to the people, and, thus, made it difficult for unfair judges to change the laws to please themselves.

* * * * *

Can you name some other advantages of the annual May-field?

* * * * *

Education under Charlemagne. Charlemagne wished to educate his people and to develop great schools. He himself was a grown man before he learned to read and to write. Yet, he learned to speak Latin as fluently as his native German, and he also learned to understand Greek. He was then able to listen to the great scholars when they lectured.

At Aix-la-Chapelle, he founded a great Palace School. His children and the children of the nobles were educated there. He wanted to train these children for the duties they would have later in helping to govern the empire. To his Palace School, he brought the best scholars in Europe. Charlemagne himself often visited the school. In spite of his duties as emperor, he found time to study religion, grammar, astronomy, and history.

154

The greatest of the scholars at the Palace School was a Saxon from England. This was *Alcuin* (ăl′kwĭn), who had been educated at the Cathedral School of York in England. Charlemagne made him director of the Palace School. Alcuin also helped Charlemagne plan the other schools of the kingdom.

Charlemagne ordered that every monastery and cathedral should open a school. These schools were open to all boys no matter how poor their parents might be. If a boy wanted a good education and was willing to study hard, he might attend one of these schools without charge. In every village, Charlemagne tried to have an elementary school, which was under the direction of the parish priest.

Although Charlemagne ruled for over forty years, his plan for schools was never completely carried out. It would have taken many more years to put all his educational plans into effect. Unfortunately, his successors showed little interest in promoting learning. Charlemagne's efforts were not, on the other hand, all in vain. Never again was the lack of learning so widespread in Western Europe as it had been before his time. For instance, documents, letters, and writings of the period after Charlemagne's rule show a great improvement in spelling, handwriting, and grammatical accuracy. At some monasteries and cathedrals, the schools which Charlemagne encouraged and supported continued to exist, and some grew into great universities.

Charlemagne and the Church. Charlemagne was devoted to the Christian religion. He was especially eager that all church ceremonies and services be conducted in the proper manner, so he established schools for church music and ceremonial.

He attended Mass and other services regularly at the cathedral of Aix-la-Chapelle. To this church Charlemagne gave many gifts—fine vestments, candlesticks of silver and gold—as well as other ornaments for the church and altar. The church at Aix-la-Chapelle was not the only one which knew his generosity. He gave rich gifts to other churches in his empire, especially to St. Peter's at Rome.

He was very generous in giving to the poor and even sent gifts to needy Christians at Jerusalem, Alexandria, and in North Africa.

In his zeal to extend Christianity, Charlemagne required the people whom he conquered, especially the Saxons, to be baptized. He believed that they could be more easily

Charlemagne gave many beautiful and valuable gifts to churches. He was especially generous in his gifts to the cathedral at Aix-la-Chapelle and to St. Peter's Church in Rome.

civilized if they were converted to Christianity. Alcuin and some of the bishops warned Charlemagne that if these people were forced to accept Christianity they would, as a rule, be Christians in name only. Gradually, however, the monks and missionaries helped the Saxons become true and faithful Christians. In a very few generations, the very people upon whom Charlemagne had forced Christianity spoke of him as their friend and as a great teacher of the Faith.

Charlemagne's Empire is Divided. Charlemagne died in 814 at the age of seventy-two. He was buried in the cathedral of Aix-la-Chapelle.

Charlemagne was succeeded by his son, *Louis the Pious*. Louis was not so strong a ruler as his father. Louis decided, and in part was forced, to divide his empire among his sons. One son, *Charles the Bald*, took as his kingdom the western part of the empire that later became known as France. Another son, *Louis the German*, took the eastern part of the empire. This section became Germany.

Lothair (lŏ·thâr'), the oldest son, received as his kingdom northern Italy and the land between the kingdoms of his brothers. Because of his ambition to extend his territories, Lothair was often at war. Even before his death the in-between territory, which is now known as the *Lorraine* (lŏ·rān'), became a battleground over which

Lothair's brothers, Charles and Louis, fought. In more recent times it has remained a cause of conflict and a battleground between France and Germany.

The unity which Charlemagne had given to Western Europe was broken again, but the idea of unity remained in the thoughts of the people of Europe.

* * * * *

Has the present political situation in Europe revived the idea of closer union among the European countries? If so, why?

* * * * *

Summing Up. As the barbarians began to settle down after their invasions of the Roman Empire, the Franks came to dominate all Europe. Under Clovis, the Franks adopted many Roman ways and were converted to Christianity.

The Frankish kings became so weak that, in time, their mayors of the palace began to usurp their powers. In the person of Charles Martel, conqueror of the Moslems at Tours, the mayor of the palace became ruler in all but name. Charles's son, Pepin, deposed the last Frankish king and assumed the crown with the approval of the pope and nobles.

Pepin's son, Charlemagne became the greatest ruler of the age. Charlemagne was great because of his conquests of lands and peoples, his encouragement of the Church, his re–establishment of learning, and his refounding of the empire of the West. The progress made under Charlemagne was great but short lived, for his son and heirs fell to quarreling after his death. Then Europe once more fell into a semi-barbarism that took many centuries to overcome.

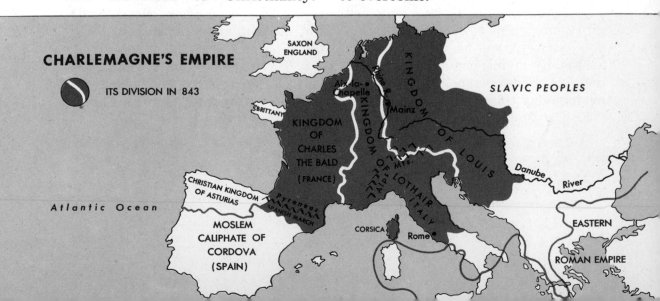

CHARLEMAGNE'S EMPIRE

ITS DIVISION IN 843

FOR BETTER UNDERSTANDING

Checking Up

1. Explain why the Frankish kingdom became so important.

2. What position did Charles Martel hold in the Frankish kingdom?

3. What is the importance of Charles Martel in European history?

4. What were the Papal States set up by Pepin?

5. Tell what methods Charlemagne used to govern his empire.

6. Tell how Charlemagne encouraged education.

7. How did Charlemagne aid the Church?

8. How was Charlemagne's empire divided after his death?

9. Identify and tell the importance of each of the following dates: 481, 732, 768, 800, 814.

Yesterday and Today

1. What measures have been taken or planned to bring about closer unity among the many European nations of today?

2. Is it difficult for a nation to engage in war and at the same time improve conditions for its people? Can you either prove or disprove your answer by giving examples from the reign of Charlemagne? What about modern-day countries?

3. The stories about Roland and Charlemagne are often called hero stories. About what men living today could hero stories be written?

Persons, Places, and Terms

Identify: Clovis, Charles Martel, Pepin, Pope Zacharias, Roland, Alcuin, Charles the Bald, Louis the German, Lothair.

Locate: Rome, York, Austria, Lombardy, Lorraine, Aix-la-Chapelle.

Define: count, march, duchy, Mayfield, Palace School.

Interesting Things to Do

1. Pretend that you are a radio or television news announcer. Present a broadcast to the class about the crowning of Charlemagne as Holy Roman Emperor in St. Peter's Church on Christmas Day, 800 A.D.

2. Make a color map of the battlefield at Tours in France where Charles Martel defeated the Moslems. Write the story of this battle after you have read about it in your encyclopedia. Put the map and story in your scrapbook.

3. Have a story hour. Various members of the class can read songs and stories that the troubadors sang about Charlemagne and Roland.

12

A New Political System

AFTER CHARLEMAGNE

The People and the Land. Since the time of the Roman Emperor, Justinian, the great majority of the peoples of Western Europe had gained their living from the land. Even after the Roman Empire had been overrun by the barbarians, the people still resided on the great landed estates. The barbarian tribes as they settled down and formed semi-civilized nations also lived from the land. You may remember reading that many of these tribes had originally lived and farmed in and around small villages. The system of the people working for and living on the land of a powerful noble or chief is called *manorialism* (má·nō′rĭ·ăl·ĭz'm), after the *manor*, or estate, of the lord. Even Charlemagne received the main part of his income from his vast estates, or manors, which were the homes and

livelihood of many thousands of people.

* * * * *

How do today's methods of earning a living compare with those of Charlemagne's time?

* * * * *

A New Security. After Charlemagne's death, his empire broke up into smaller divisions as quarrels and wars broke out between his sons, grandsons, and their descendants.

In addition, Northmen—barbarians from the Scandinavian countries—invaded the lands once controlled by Charlemagne. These invaders not only raided the coasts, but made their way inland and robbed and destroyed many towns. The Moslems in Spain continued to attack the Frankish people. Barbarian tribes in Eastern Europe and Western Asia again threatened the people of the West.

In all of Western Europe there was neither king nor army strong enough to protect the people from these continuing dangers. Usually, then, a noble whose land was vast enough to support a small private army would protect the people in his area.

Some of the Frankish kings had given vast stretches of land to nobles who had performed some military service. After the death of Charlemagne many nobles, or counts, seized the lands, or counties, over which they had ruled. Often the weaker nobles, who had only a little land, gave their land to some powerful noble in return for his promise to protect them and the people who lived and worked on their estates. Then these nobles and their *serfs* (sûrfz), the common people who tilled the soil, would be allowed to continue living on the land. These lesser nobles were said to be the *vassals* (văs'ălz) of the powerful lord. This plan for protection is known as the *feudal* (fū'dăl) *system*, or *feudalism* (fū'dăl·ĭz'm). In time, feudalism came to take the place of manorialism. The common people who lived on the estates accepted this arrangement since it offered the greatest protection.

The feudal system was like a bargain or a contract. The great noble

Because they lived in an age of constant warfare, the chief duties of the vassal to his overlord included military service and loyalty. Under the feudal system the vassals provided soldiers to serve under the lord who protected both the vassals and their serfs.

promised to give protection to those vassals who lived on his land. In return, the vassals made several promises to help the lord. This system extended protection from the king to the lowliest person in the kingdom.

Lords and Vassals. The kings of Western Europe believed that God permitted them to have great possessions and wealth in order that they might perform a service to God by ruling His land justly and wisely. Some of the kings presented their entire kingdoms to the pope, as the representative of God upon earth. The pope returned the kingdoms to the kings who were to rule as the vassals of God according to the commandments of God. This was a beautiful and wonderful idea. However, many kings were selfish and unworthy, and did not live up to this noble idea.

Very few kings after the time of Charlemagne really ruled their kingdoms because the nobles were as powerful as the kings were. However, a king usually kept his title and his claim to all the land in his kingdom. A king granted the use of great areas of land called *fiefs* (fēfz) to the great nobles. These nobles then became vassals of the king.

A vassal was not to have the use of the land for just a period of years but for his whole lifetime. Upon his death a vassal's oldest son was to inherit the fief with the same privileges and obligations.

When a noble received a fief from the king, he promised to supply the king with a certain number of soldiers. He also had to promise to supply money to the king on certain special occasions.

You will remember reading that the powerful nobles had vassals, too, for every great estate was made up of fiefs of the lesser nobles. These lesser nobles were the vassals of a great noble, who was known as their lord. The great noble promised to let them live on his land, which in the beginning had often been promised or given to him in return for protection. These lesser nobles, in turn, promised to furnish soldiers to the lord and to give him money on special occasions. The king and the great nobles always kept serfs and lands for their personal income and food supply.

Thus, the great nobles were at the same time vassals and lords. They were vassals pledged to the king and overlords of the lesser nobles. Lesser nobles granted their land into fiefs and gave these small fiefs to men who promised loyalty and became their vassals.

The Homage Ceremony. When a lord presented a fief to a vassal in later times, the event was marked with a solemn ceremony. The vassal approached the lord with his head uncovered and without weapons or armor. He knelt before the lord and placed his hands in those of the lord. The vassal promised undying loyalty to his lord. The lord then gave the vassal the *kiss of peace* and promised to protect him in return for his faithful service. Finally, the lord invested the vassal with the fief by giving him some token such as a flag, a staff, or a clod of earth.

This ceremony of homage provided a strong bond between lords and vassals. In this manner every nobleman in the kingdom took a pledge of loyalty to the lord immediately above him. In the feudal period, a personal pledge of loyalty was made by one man to another; in our country, we pledge our loyalty to the government of the United States of America.

*   *   *   *   *

Why would the men of the Middle Ages not have understood our use of the word patriotic?

*   *   *   *   *

When there was a dispute between vassals, the case was tried in the lord's court. In addition, the lord was commander of the soldiers that the vassals were required to provide for him. The feudal lord was sort of a king over all his own lands. Yet, the vassals expected the lord to carry out his promises.

Everyone realized that even the lowliest man in the kingdom had certain rights. The contract between the lords and their vassals (land for service) and the contract between the nobles and their serfs (protection for work) guaranteed everyone his rights. The serfs, however, could not be fired, or put out of work, since they were bound to the land. You will be reading more about the serfs and their life in the next chapter.

*   *   *   *   *

How are the rights of the individual citizen protected in our country today?

*   *   *   *   *

A New Era. As the political system of feudalism developed in the centuries that followed Charlemagne's death, mankind entered the period of history that we call the *Middle Ages*, or the *medieval* period. This is the name we give to the thousand years following the ancient civilizations—the period from 500-1500 A.D.

LIFE IN A FEUDAL CASTLE

A Walled Fortress. During the Middle Ages, each noble had to provide protection for his vassals and serfs, so the nobles began the practice of building great castles. These castles were not only places of protection for the people who lived in each castle's neighborhood, but at the same time were the homes of the various nobles.

Castles were usually built upon high hills in order that they might be more readily defended. Each castle was not just one building. It was a group of buildings surrounded by stone walls that were perhaps twenty feet in height. These outside walls were too high for an enemy to scale and too thick for him to batter down.

Along the top of the massive walls were openings through which the defending soldiers could hurl rocks or hot tar. There were also narrow slits in the walls through which the defenders could shoot their arrows.

At intervals along the outer walls were great towers. At first these were square, but later they were rounded in order to prevent invading soldiers from hiding in the outer corners. Inside these towers were the staircases that led from the courtyards to the tops of the walls, or battlements.

Outside the castle walls was a deep ditch filled with water. This ditch was called a *moat* (mōt). At the outer edge of the moat was a strong fence made of heavy posts driven into the ground. This fence was called a *palisade* (păl'ĭ·sād').

The only way to cross the moat was by means of a drawbridge. A gatekeeper guarded the castle's only entrance and the drawbridge. From his tower he operated the ropes, or chains, which raised or lowered the bridge. He would not let the drawbridge down until he was sure that those who wished to cross were welcome to enter. Even if an enemy succeeded in crossing the moat before the drawbridge could be raised, there was a heavy gate, or door, which could be closed to block the way.

Inside the Castle Wall. Inside the castle gate was a courtyard known as the *outer ward*. This was often large enough to hold all the people in the neighborhood and their cattle in time of danger. The outer wards of some castles were paved with rough cobblestones; in other castle courtyards, grass grew. In the outer ward were the stables and the shops of the blacksmiths, the carpenters, the bakers, the tailor, and the other skilled workmen of the castle.

*   *   *   *   *

If a castle were preparing for a siege by an approaching enemy, what are some of the things that the serfs would bring inside the castle walls?

*   *   *   *   *

Another heavy wall separated the outer ward from the second, or inner court. This gave added protection to the main buildings, which were situated in the inner court. The most important building in the inner court was the *keep*, or *donjon* (dŭn'jŭn). This was where the lord and his family lived. Close by was the chapel where the people of the castle attended Mass.

The donjon, or keep, was a tower-like, thick-walled building having very few windows. There were few windows because every window was an opening through which an attacking enemy might hurl his spears or shoot his arrows. The windows that were in the keep were extremely narrow and admitted very little light or sunshine. Prisoners were usually jailed under the donjon. Our word *dungeon* (dŭn'jŭn) comes from this medieval word.

The noble's family lived in the upper rooms of the keep. The thick walls failed to keep out the bitter winter cold. Floors were covered with dried rushes or reeds. The rooms were small and dark and had very little furniture.

The Great Hall. The main room of the keep was the great hall. Sometimes the great hall was a separate building attached to the keep. This hall was a combined living room and dining room. In some castles it was as much as forty feet wide and sixty feet long. Sometimes rugs made from the skins of animals were scattered about on the floor. As a rule, the ceiling of the great hall was very high, and often it was made of heavy beams of oak.

On the walls of the great hall hung weapons and armor always ready for use. The lord's battle flags and banners, as well as tapestries depicting religious and military scenes, also adorned the walls.

The great hall had at least one large fireplace. In the winter, logs were heaped high in the fireplace, and a roaring fire helped to give the hall some warmth and cheer.

The Castle Meals. During early feudal days, a few rough chairs and benches and perhaps a chest or wardrobe closet were the only furniture in the great hall. At meal time wooden trestles were brought in,

FARMLAND

SERFS' VILLAGE

MILL

FARMLAND

WOODLAND

PASTURELAND

Chateau de Charleson 1300

POSTERN

KEEP

CHAPEL

GREAT HALL

GARDEN

BATTLEMENTS

STABLES

COURTYARD

STOREHOUSE

MAIN GATE

BARBICAN GATE

DRAWBRIDGE

PASTURELAND

MOAT

PALISADES

and long boards were placed upon them to make a table. Permanent tables and benches were added later. All the members of the lord's household ate at this great table, except some servants who ate in the kitchens.

Meat and bread were the chief foods served at the lord's table. As many as three or four kinds of meat were often served at a single meal. In later feudal times, all the meats were highly seasoned with pepper and other spices. Salt was used sparingly, for it was hard to get. Other foods were boiled vegetables, especially beets, cabbage, and turnips. Since the people of that time did not have sugar, they used honey for sweetening their food.

In the kitchens the food was cooked over the open fire in large fireplaces. Copper or iron kettles, hung from hooks above the fire, were used for boiling meat, vegetables, and puddings. Big roasts were cooked over the fire on a slowly turning rod, or spit. The roast was ready for the table when it was "done to a turn."

* * * * *

Why would you think that the types of food we eat and our modern ways of preparing food are superior to those used in the Middle Ages?

* * * * *

Entertainment. After the evening meal was over, the lord and his household were sometimes entertained by the songs of a wandering *minstrel* (mĭn′strĕl), who sang of heroes and battles. In southern France and northern Italy, these minstrels were called *troubadours* (trōō′bȧ·dōōrz). Sometimes a minstrel's song was a story about beautiful ladies and how they were rescued from danger by a very brave hero.

If there was no minstrel to sing, perhaps a stranger, who had sought a night's lodging within the castle walls, entertained the lord and his household by telling stories of his

Because so many people were sheltered within castle walls, the kitchen help had to work continually to prepare the meals of the day.

travels and adventures. Sometimes the evening was made gay with games of cards or chess.

Usually the lord had a *court jester*, or fool, who was dressed in brightly colored clothes. It was the jester's business to keep his master entertained by playing jokes and by doing and saying funny things.

Outside a castle's walls were the forests in which a lord and his friends hunted deer, pheasants, and sometimes bears. When the nobles went hunting, they took their falcons with them. These falcons were birds of prey that had been trained to hunt pheasants, rabbits, and other small animals.

The Ladies of the Castle. In the inner ward, or court, of most castles, there was a private garden surrounded by high walls. Here, during the day, the local lord's wife and her ladies often walked among the flowers or sat together sewing and embroidering.

Adjoining the garden was a room in which the ladies spent much time spinning, weaving, or sewing. The tapestries that adorned the great hall of a castle were made by the lord's wife and her ladies; so were the clothes of all the household.

The wife of the lord had many duties. She managed the household, supervised the servants, planned the meals, and saw that her husband's guests were comfortable. The young girls were trained to spin, weave, and embroider. They were also taught first aid so that they might help the knights when these men were wounded in battle. Since herbs were an important part of medieval medicine, the lord's wife took great care of the herb garden.

Summing Up. As new nations arose in the West, the chief way of life for all the people was agriculture (manorialism). However, after the breakup of Charlemagne's empire, a new system of government had to be found to protect the land and people. So feudalism, a noble ideal involving every person in the land, came into being. Weaker nobles promised their lands to stronger nobles in return for protection, and these greater nobles, in turn, promised loyalty to the kings in return for protection.

This noble and practical ideal of feudalism did not always work because of the weakness of men, but it provided the best protection for the most people in those troubled times.

Life in feudal times may seem exciting and romantic to us, but even life in the castles was not really very pleasant.

FOR BETTER UNDERSTANDING

Checking Up

1. What is meant by the term manorialism?

2. What is meant by a fief?

3. What were the obligations of a vassal to his lord; of a lord to his vassal?

4. What authority did a lord have over his vassals?

5. Describe the outer ward and the donjon of a typical castle.

6. Give a description of the great hall of a castle.

7. How did the ladies of a medieval castle pass their day?

Yesterday and Today

1. Compare the types of taxes paid in our country today with those paid by the men of the Middle Ages. How do you account for the differences?

2. List some of the conveniences, which many people in America have, that make our lives so much easier than the lives of the medieval knights and ladies.

3. Make a list of games that boys and girls of today play, which were also played during the Middle Ages.

Terms

Define: manor, count, serf, vassal, feudal system, fief, Middle Ages, moat, outer ward, donjon, keep, troubadour, minstrel.

Interesting Things to Do

1. Find pictures and sketches of various castles and of the many activities that were part of medieval castle life. Make a display for the class bulletin board or your scrapbook.

2. Construct a model of a feudal castle using cardboard or clay. The work for this project could be divided among several groups in the class. Some might like to make small costumed figures for the castle courtyard, while others build the castle itself.

13

When Knighthood Was in Flower

FEUDAL TIMES

Military Training. During feudal days, if one noble wanted land held by another, he set out to take it by force. War was then the chief business of the nobles. Almost every noble was constantly engaged in warfare either to keep his lands from being seized or to add to his possessions by seizing some other noble's land.

For these reasons each castle was a training school for knights. Every great noble had his own military academy. The boys of the noble families had a special type of education and training which prepared them for knighthood.

The Page. In the first stage of this training the boy was called a *page*. At the age of seven, he was often sent to some great nobleman. There, until he was fourteen years of age, he served as a page.

During this training period, a page was taught that his main duty in life was to be of service to God and his fellow men. The page attended his lord and lady constantly. He waited on them at table. He ran errands for them. He held their horses while they mounted. He accompanied them when they went hunting.

He learned to read and write, but he did not have much education of this type. The lady of the castle taught him to be gentle and courteous and gracious. The page also learned to sing and to play the lute or harp. The lord taught the boy how to ride and to hunt. In addition, the boy learned to swim, to box, and to use the bow.

The page was given a good religious training. He was taught the truths of the Catholic religion. He was taught morning and night prayers and how to pray at Mass as well as at other religious ceremonies. The lady of the castle told him stories about the saints and about brave and good knights.

The Squire. When the page was about fourteen years old, he became a *squire*. As a squire he was the attendant of a knight. As a squire he also became skilled with the lance, the sword, and the spear, the weapons used by the knights. Among his duties was that of keeping his knight's armor polished.

A knight weighted down with his heavy armor could do little to help himself when he was hurt. The squire, therefore, went with his knight to battle. When a knight was wounded or killed, his squire helped carry him from the field of battle.

The Knight. If a boy served well as a page and squire, he would be made a knight when he reached the age of twenty-one. The ceremony of becoming a knight was long and solemn. Some great feast day of the Church was selected for the event.

On the evening before the squire became a knight, the ceremonies began with the bath of purification. After the bath the squire put on a red garment, which meant that he was willing to shed his blood for the Church or for some other worthy cause. Then he put on a white garment, which was a symbol of his purity in mind and deed. Lastly he put on a black garment, which was a reminder that all men must die.

Then the squire went to the castle chapel and laid his suit of armor on the altar steps as a sign that it would be used only for a good and just cause. Through the entire night, the young man kept a vigil before the Blessed Sacrament. He prayed that he might become a true and worthy knight.

In the morning the squire went to confession, attended Mass, and

The education of a knight began at an early age. As a page, he learned the code of courtesy expected of a knight. He also learned to ride and to handle weapons. The squire acted as a valet and attended his master in many ways. The outcome of this training was knighthood.

received Holy Communion. After Mass, the young man took the oath of knighthood. It was a solemn promise to be brave, loyal, and honorable; to defend the Church; to protect the poor and oppressed; and to lead a life of purest chastity.

*　*　*　*　*

Are the aims of the education for the knighthood similar to the aims of the education you are receiving?

*　*　*　*　*

After taking the solemn oath, the squire went out into the castle courtyard where he put on his new suit of armor and his sword. Usually, a large throng of knights and ladies gathered for the final part of the ceremony. The lord of the castle or some older knight touched the squire on the shoulder with a sword and said: "In the name of God, of St. Michael, and of St. George, I dub thee knight; be brave, bold, and loyal." Then the young man proudly took his place among the knights of his lord.

Weapons and Armor. Each knight had a suit of armor which was made by the blacksmith of the castle. The smith also made the swords, lances, and spears for the knights. When any of these weapons were broken, they were sent to the blacksmith shop for repair.

Knighthood was a religious and military occasion of elaborate ceremony and solemn vows.

In the early feudal days, the knights had protected themselves in battle by wearing clothing of leather. Then they added quantities of metal rings fastened together. In time, they wore an entire coat of this chain mail. Ultimately, the suit came to be made entirely of metal plates, or armor. This was done to give greater protection. The knights also developed metal helmets in order to protect their heads.

When a large group of knights in full armor were gathered together, it was difficult to tell one from the other with their heads and faces covered by their helmets. As a result, each knight wore on his armor or shield some special mark to proclaim who he was. Perhaps this mark was the picture of a lion or some animal noted for its strength. Perhaps it was some bird known for its speed. Perhaps it was some flower, which suggested goodness or another quality. Perhaps this symbol was a design that represented some deed for which its wearer was famous. Every man chose his own special mark. Out of this grew the practice of having a family coat of arms.

Tournaments. If you have ever engaged in a sports tournament at your school or neighborhood playground, you were following a custom similar to that followed by the knights of the Middle Ages. Our tournaments are quite different and, of course, far less dangerous.

When the knights were not engaged in real warfare, they often took part in sham battles, or tournaments. Tournaments were very popular. People traveled many miles to attend them.

The field in which a tournament took place was called the *lists*. From the sides of the lists throngs of onlookers watched the tournament. Some of the ladies wore the colors of their champions, knights who fought for them. Banners carrying the coats of arms of the contestants were placed around the field.

The knights lined up dressed in full armor and seated on horseback. Sometimes there were as many as fifty knights on each side in a contest. When the signal was given, the knights advanced and engaged in the sham battle. Each knight charged across the field with his lance aimed at his opponent's helmet or shield. The object was to strike an opponent so hard that he would fall from his horse. The side that had the most men on horseback after three charges won. Sometimes the defeated knights had to give their horses and armor to the winners.

Below are the coats of arms of five Norman-English knights from the year 1280. Each knight had his own personal design on his shield so that he could be distinguished in battle. When a knight was in full armor, his coat of arms was usually the only means of identifying him.

Jousting was a popular event at medieval tournaments. Each knight carried a blunted lance and tried to unseat his opponent. Jousting was done in such earnest that the sport was extremely dangerous. Many knights were wounded and some were killed during the encounter.

At a tournament, a great knight usually challenged the other knights to meet him in single combat. Any knight brave enough to fight against the challenger came forth and fought with him. A single contest of this sort was called a *joust* (jŭst).

Often the knight who won the greatest distinction in the combats was allowed to choose the queen of the tournament. After the tournament was over, the queen was crowned, a great feast was held, and there was much merry-making.

THE ORDINARY PEOPLE IN THE MIDDLE AGES

The People's Life. Not far from each castle were the homes of the people who tilled the lord's land. For protection the people lived close together in villages. These people were called *serfs* or *villeins* (vĭl′ĭnz). (Our word *villain* originally meant a common man.)

The serfs had very little freedom. A serf could not move from the estate on which he was born. He could not leave it even for a short time without the permission of the lord; however, he could not be evicted from his land either.

You may wonder how men became serfs. It all began at the same time when the nobles were seeking protection from invading barbarian tribes. Men who had no land came to the estates, or manors, of the lords seeking protection. The lords, or nobles, made these humble villeins, or serfs promise to serve them as long as the serfs lived. In return, the lord promised to protect

173

the serfs, and see that they were housed, fed, and clothed. In addition, the lord, or noble, gave each serf a strip of land to farm. This land was to be passed down from father to son like the lord's own fief.

The serfs were not slaves. The Middle Ages was the time when the first great civilization that was not founded on slavery came into being. The serf, however, was bound to the soil, or land, and not to any master. The lord who lived in the castle might be conquered by a more powerful noble and lose his castle, but the serfs remained on the same land. Their rights to the land were secure. A typical family of serfs stayed on the same estate for hundreds of years.

*   *   *   *   *

In how many ways did the position of the serf differ from that of a slave?

*   *   *   *   *

In early feudal times, there were few ways by which a serf could escape from the estate on which he was born. To leave serfdom some became priests or monks. For example, if the parish priest found a brilliant boy in the village school, he could request the lord to permit the boy to enter the religious life. Some of these children of serfs rose to high positions. For instance, a son of serf parents, *Suger* (sü′zhâr′), became abbot of the Monastery of St. Denis near Paris. He was the chief adviser to several kings of France. At one time, when King Louis VII went on a Crusade to the Holy Land, Suger was left in charge of the kingdom. *Gerbert* (zhĕr′bâr′), who was famous as one of the greatest scholars in Europe, was another prominent man born of serf parents. He became archbishop of Ravenna, Italy, and in the year 999 he was crowned as *Pope Sylvester II.*

The only other way to escape was to run away. If a serf could hide himself for a year and a day and avoid being sent back to his lord, he was free according to the law. During the early part of the Middle Ages it was almost impossible for a serf to gain his freedom in this way. If he ran away, he had no place to go. There were very few towns, and other feudal estates did not usually want a runaway serf for fear of trouble with the lord of the serf.

Obligations. Not only was the serf bound to the soil, but his freedom was limited in other ways. Serfs were required to have their grain ground at the lord's mill and to pay the miller for grinding it. Payment was not made in money, but in a certain portion of the grain.

In the Middle Ages, justice varied greatly from one manor to the next. If a serf was accused of a crime, he was usually tried at the lord's court in the castle. However, it was not uncommon for a serf to be punished or even killed for an offense without ever appearing in court.

Not only was the serf forbidden to kill the deer and the other animals in the lord's forests, but he did not even dare to enter these forests. The forests were guarded by the lord's gamekeepers. If a serf was caught trespassing, he was severely punished.

Protection. All the serfs of a village had rights in certain common lands. Their cattle and sheep could graze on the common pasture land. The serf could gather fuel in the common woodland. He was entitled to a certain amount of the hay from the common meadow. This same idea was brought to America by some of the early settlers. For instance, every colonial town and village in New England had its common, which today is used as a park.

If a serf was accused of wrongdoing or if he got into trouble with his neighbors, he was tried in the lord's court. The court was usually held in the castle with the lord as judge. In England, the serfs sat on juries in most cases, and in this way they were able to preserve their rights.

The serf was obliged to work two days a week for the lord. During the planting and harvesting seasons, the lord might require him to work additional time on the estate's fields. However, the serf usually had enough time to work on his own fields as well.

As towns grew up in Europe during the latter part of the Middle Ages, the serfs were able to sell some of their products to the townspeople for money. As a result, many of the serfs were gradually able to save enough money in order to buy their freedom.

The Serfs' Village. The little village in which the serfs lived was not very attractive. Its streets were usually narrow, crooked, and filled with rubbish.

The houses of the village were small. They were built of rough materials, and their roofs were thatched; that is, made of straw or grass. There were only a few windows in each house.

As in the early days of our own country, the window openings were covered with heavy paper or cloth that had been soaked in oil to make it weatherproof. Of course, such windows let in very little light.

The cracks in the walls were filled with mud or straw. The floor in the house was but bare earth, usually covered with rushes or straw. Rugs were rarely used in these houses.

The serf did not have a very comfortable home. Yet, these dwellings were not very different from the huts that the American pioneers built on the frontier of our own country. Abraham Lincoln was born in a log cabin that was similar to the home of a feudal serf.

* * * * *

Can you list other ways in which a serf's daily life was similar to the everyday life of a pioneer settler in our own country?

* * * * *

Life's Necessities. In general, the serf's clothing was made of a coarse, homespun cloth that was woven on the lord's loom. The serf had to buy this cloth from the lord's weaver. As a result, the serf did not have many clothes. His chief garment was a loose tunic that hung from the neck to the knees, leaving the arms and legs bare. To keep his legs warm in winter, the serf wrapped pieces of cloth around them. For shoes, he wrapped his feet in wool cloth and strapped wooden soles to them.

The serf's food was very simple.

Living in poverty and filth, serfs often shared their already overcrowded houses with cattle. Famine and plague became frequent visitors to the manorial village.

It consisted mainly of bread and vegetables. The bread was very coarse and dark in color. It has often been called *black bread*.

Fun. There was a cheerful side to the life of the serfs. On Sundays and on the many holydays, there was no work. After Mass, the serfs gathered together in an open space in their village. At these gatherings they danced and played games. Some of the folk dances of today had their origin in feudal times. Perhaps you have seen some of these folk dances done in your own community.

FARMING

A Hard Life. The people of the Middle Ages knew very little about the soil. They did learn, however, that land used year after year produced poor crops. In an effort to keep their soil from wearing out, many feudal lords divided their farming land into three great fields, or areas. This is sometimes called the *three-field system*.

One year, during the autumn season, the first field would be sown with wheat. In the spring, the second field would be planted with grain, like rye or barley. Both of these crops would be harvested in the late summer. At the same time, the third field would be left idle in order to allow the richness to return to the soil. The next year, the third field would be the wheat field, the second field would be idle, and the first field would have the rye or barley.

The serf did not have all his land in one place as do most farmers of today. The three big fields on the feudal estate were generally divided into many small strips, each containing only a few acres. Several of these small fields were permanently assigned to each serf and his family. One serf might have to cultivate as many as five to ten such strips of land, which were probably scattered about in various parts of the estate. In this way, no one serf had all good land or all poor land.

This method of dividing the fields is sometimes called the *open-field system*. There were no fences to separate the strips of land. They were divided instead by balks, or strips, of unplowed turf. This was wasteful, since crops were not raised on the balks.

How the Serf Farmed. The methods of cultivation that the serf used were simple and crude. Sometimes, the serf had oxen to pull his wooden plow: sometimes, he and his wife pulled the plow themselves. He sowed grain by hand in the same manner as had the farmers in the time of Our Lord. When the grain was ready to be harvested, the serf cut it by hand with a sickle. He threshed the grain with a hand *flail* (flāl).

* * * * *

Why were there so few improvements made in the methods of farming up to the time of the Middle Ages?

* * * * *

A part of everything the serf raised had to be given to the lord of the estate. When the hay was cut, great loads of it were taken to the castle where it was used for the lord's war horses. When the grain was harvested, a man came from the castle to set aside the lord's share.

In the fall, the lord sent a man to collect his share of the season's pigs. In the spring, a man from the castle took the lord's share of the sheep and the lambs. The lord might collect cattle and poultry at any time.

The Community. As you have read, the life of the nobles in the castle was very different from the life of the serfs in the village. Yet, both were necessary parts of the same feudal community in the early days. The noble protected the serfs from invading tribes and, in the later Middle Ages, from plundering

Caring for his master's fields consumed about half of a serf's time. Storing the harvest, grinding the grain, cutting firewood, hauling water, weaving cloth, and repairing buildings were some of the other duties expected of a serf in return for a noble's protection.

A lord collects "rent" from his serfs—sacks of grain in exchange for allowing them to work on the land. Usually, the largest portion of a serf's harvest had to be turned over to the lord.

barons. In return for this, the serfs supported the noble and his family by supplying them with food and labor.

Each estate, or manor, produced nearly everything that was needed for the entire community—food, clothing, weapons, tools, and fuel. Salt, millstones, and iron were the only products that an estate had to secure from outside.

One of the chief features of life on a feudal estate was the community spirit. In any kind of work that was especially hard or difficult, the serfs helped each other. Much of the community life centered around the parish church and the feasts of the Catholic Faith. Such was life in the Middle Ages.

Summing Up. The noble boys of feudal times were educated in the castles, which were military training schools as well as places of protection. First as a page, then as a squire, and finally as a knight, a noble was instructed in the truths of the Catholic Faith, the ideals of chivalry, and the arts of war.

The life of the nobles was filled with hunting, jousting, and fighting. The life of the serfs, on the other hand, was very hard. Ordinarily, the serf tilled his own land and that of his master from dawn to dusk. The serf had few tools to work with, and he lived and dressed in a very primitive way. Yet, the serf was not a slave and could not be evicted from his land. While life was hard, there were certain privileges and advantages—such as the protection offered by the feudal system and the guidance of the Church.

FOR BETTER UNDERSTANDING

Checking Up

1. Was the training of a page well suited to the type of life he was to lead in later years?

2. What were the duties of a squire?

3. Describe the ceremonies that a squire performed just preceding his being knighted.

4. Tell what happened at a feudal tournament.

5. Why were the serfs not slaves?

6. What were the rights and duties of the serfs?

7. Describe the home life of the serfs.

8. What type of amusements did the serfs enjoy?

9. Describe what is meant by the three-field system.

Yesterday and Today

1. Compare the life of a feudal serf who was a farmer with the life of an American farmer of today.

2. List some rights that we have that the serfs of feudal times did not have.

3. Would the education that a noble boy received in the Middle Ages be suitable preparation for a career today? Explain your answer.

Persons and Terms

Identify: Suger, Gerbert.

Define: squire, knight, vigil, armor, coat of arms, tournament, lists, joust, serf, villein, open-field system, sickle, flail.

Interesting Things to Do

1. Write a report for your scrapbook on one of the following topics: *A Day in the Life of a Page, The Exciting Adventures of a Squire, Why I Should Like to Have Been a Knight, The Life of a Medieval Lady.*

2. Various members of the class could prepare a map of a feudal manor. Be sure you show the three-field system, the commons, the homes of the serfs, as well as the parish church and castle.

3. You might be interested in studying the main features of various coats of arms by looking in your classroom or library encyclopedias. Then you could ask your teacher to help you read and understand the coat of arms of the bishop of your diocese.

14

The Church in the Middle Ages

SPIRITUAL AND WORLDLY POWER

The Church's Role. The Catholic Church was founded, as you have read, during the days of the Roman Empire. It took some of its organization from the plan of the Roman Empire. When the empire in the West collapsed, the Church not only survived but also succeeded in saving much of the best of the ancient civilizations, Greece and Rome.

As feudalism developed among the Teutonic nations, the Church adapted much of its organization to the new system. The Church thus encouraged a system of government that protected the weak and recognized the rights of the common man.

The Church did more than this. It helped feudalism to grow and develop in the proper way. The Church did much to curb the war-like spirit of the feudal nobles, it became the teacher and adviser of all Europe, and it led the peoples of Europe—Roman and Celt, Teuton and Slav—into the great Catholic civilization of the Middle Ages.

The Bishops. Faithful Catholics have always been in the habit of making gifts to the Church in order to help with works of charity. During the Middle Ages, kings and nobles made their gifts in the form of land that was the chief type of wealth at the time. These gifts of land were usually made to the local bishop, and, in time, many of the bishops became great landowners.

In the early part of the Middle Ages, the clergy were the best-educated people in Europe. Kings frequently asked their advice concerning the government of kingdoms. For centuries priests and

Administered confirmation

Directed his diocese

Advised king

Provided soldiers
for king

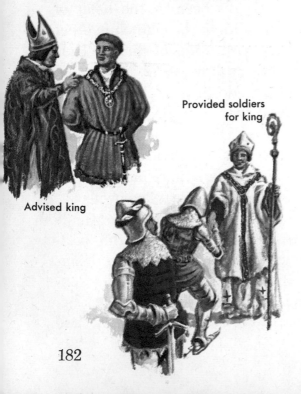

bishops were the chief advisers of kings and emperors. A king would sometimes turn over the administration, or government, of an entire county to a bishop because he knew that the bishop would be good, wise, able, and just. In this way, many bishops became political as well as spiritual leaders of the people. This practice had many good results, but there was danger in it.

When a bishop was placed in charge of a county, or other large area of land, he received it as a fief and became a direct vassal of the king. He had to provide the king with the regular feudal services. This included military service, and sometimes a bishop would have to lead a group of his vassals in battle. You can see that, in some cases, the bishops would become so busy with governing that they would not be able to devote enough attention to the spiritual guidance of the people.

When a bishop died, it was the law of the Church that his successor should be elected by the priests and the faithful people of his diocese. However, the kings began to interfere in the elections of the bishops because they wanted to make certain that each new bishop would be a loyal vassal. At length, a great struggle broke out between the popes, who wanted the bishops to be pious and learned, and the kings, who wanted the bishops to be strong rulers.

* * * * *

Why does this problem of governmental interference in the Church's affairs not exist in the United States today? Did it ever exist in our country?

* * * * *

The same problem grew up in regard to the abbots of the monasteries. Sometimes in order to secure protection for the monastery, an abbot would become the vassal of a noble. If the noble was not pleased with the abbot elected by the monks, the nobleman might try to interfere in the election of the next abbot. Sometimes the kings and lords used force to secure their way.

It is easy to see that the practice by which bishops and abbots became great feudal lords had some features harmful to the Church. It was most important for the Church that the bishops and abbots should be great spiritual leaders rather than great feudal lords. It has always been necessary for bishops to teach the gospel of Christ without fear of any ruler: the bishops have always needed to be able to correct any wrongdoer, whether he is a king or a common man.

Feudal nobles often interfered in the election of bishops and abbots of monasteries.

Medieval bishops provided service to kings and advised them on many matters.

THE CHURCH BRINGS PEACE

A New Ideal. Even though many bishoprics and monasteries became a part of the feudal system, the Church itself remained independent of feudalism. The main purpose of the Catholic Church was and is to lead men to know God, to love God, and to do God's will. The Church found that there were many features in feudalism that were not helpful in carrying out this mission.

One of the worst features of the the early feudal period was the constant warfare between nobles. Early in the Middle Ages the popes tried to stop this constant, petty warfare just as in modern times the popes have tried to prevent wars between nations.

By introducing the ideas of *chivalry* (shĭv′ăl·rĭ), the Church was able to make the methods of warfare less cruel. Chivalry means the rules, customs, and manners followed by the knights.

Originally, the knights were interested only in making war. It was the Church that taught the knights the ideals of truth, honor, purity, and loyalty. The beautiful oath of the knights was a part of the ceremony established by the Church.

The Church tried to turn the knights away from warfare conducted for selfish reasons. If a knight wanted to do battle, he was provided with many worthy causes that he might champion or defend. Under the code of chivalry, a knight could not refuse to champion the cause of widows, orphans, or those who were helpless.

The Peace of God. The Church tried to restrict the places where warfare could be carried on. Under the *Peace of God*, the Church, particularly in the area we today call France, forbade the knights from carrying on warfare in the vicinity of churches, monasteries, or other sacred places. It also tried to prevent the warring knights from attacking unarmed people such as priests, serfs, pilgrims, and merchants.

The Church instituted the *right of sanctuary* (săngk′tū̆·ĕr′ĭ). For example, if a person was accused of a crime by some lord, he might seek safety, or sanctuary, in a church. Then a priest or bishop would examine the case and if the accused were innocent, he would be freed. If he were guilty, he would be handed over to the proper legal authorities. By this method, the Church prevented many innocent persons from being put to death.

The Truce of God. The Church reduced the number of days in the year on which fighting might take place. The *Truce of God* at first prevented the knights from fighting on Sunday, which was interpreted as being from Saturday evening until Monday morning. Later, the truce was extended from Wednesday evening to Monday morning.

The truce also forbade fighting during the seasons of Lent and Advent. The Lenten truce was later extended from the end of Lent to Pentecost Sunday, fifty days after Easter Sunday. Later, the Lenten truce was extended from Pentecost Sunday to St. John's day, which is celebrated on June 24. This was done to protect the serfs during the season of plowing and planting.

In the same way, the Advent truce was extended as far as *Epiphany* (ĕ·pĭf′à·nĭ), which is twelve days after Christmas. Another period of truce was added. This went from the Feast of the Assumption of the Blessed Virgin on August 15 to the Feast of St. Martin on November 11. This gave protection to the serfs by forbidding war during the harvest season. If a noble wanted to make war, he had to do so during the very hot or the very cold months.

The Church had no army to enforce these rules. Yet, the popes and councils of the Church gave strong support to the Peace of God and the Truce of God. The Church had one weapon that it could use against those who violated either the Peace or the Truce of God. It was the weapon of *excommunication*. If the Church excommunicated a person, it meant that he was not allowed in a church; he could not receive the sacraments; and he could not be buried in consecrated ground. In addition, no other person would speak to him or do business with him. This was a very severe punishment, but the Church was trying to wipe out the cruelty and harshness of feudal warfare.

*   *   *   *   *

Why was it necessary for the Church to attempt to control outbreaks of feudal warfare?

*   *   *   *   *

We see that the Church was able to restrict fighting to certain places, times, and conditions. On the other hand, the Church was able to use the fighting spirit of the knights in a very great cause. This worthy cause was the Crusades, which were started to free the Holy Land from the Moslem Turks. You will read more about the Crusades in Chapter 21.

THE CHURCH LIGHTS THE WAY

Centers of Civilization. As you have read, the Church established monasteries throughout Europe even before the days of the first barbarian invasions. As the monasteries grew, and their work broadened, they came to have a strong influence on the lives of the people.

In a Monastery. Each monastery consisted of many buildings grouped together, somewhat like a castle. Some monasteries were surrounded by walls and moats, for in those troublesome times even the monasteries were attacked by invaders. Most monasteries, however, were not fortified because they were protected by the rules of the Peace of God.

The gates of the medieval monastery opened onto a large cobblestone courtyard. Some of the main buildings of the monastery were built around this courtyard.

Monasteries performed a great service in a day when there were no hospitals, schools, or inns. The monks cared for the sick, conducted schools, and took in travelers. They also recorded events of the day—chronicles which contribute greatly to our knowledge of the Middle Ages.

HOSPITAL
DORMITORY
CLOISTER
CEMETERY
Chapter house
REFECTORY   KITCHEN
CHURCH
Abbot's house
STOREHOUSES
GUEST HOUSE
COURTYARD
GATE

The Chapel. On one side of the courtyard was the church where the monks attended services. In the early monasteries, the church was a plain, rough, wooden building with hard, wooden benches. As time went on, the church was usually rebuilt of stone. Beautiful colored-glass windows were added, and gold and silver ornaments were often provided for the altar. Wealthy people sometimes gave gold and jewels or property to the monastery when they came to pray for some special intention, or to give thanks for some favor received. Many people bequeathed the monasteries such wealth so that they might have prayers and Masses said for their souls.

The Monks' Quarters. Another important building was the dormitory where the monks slept. In the first monasteries the dormitory was usually one big room. In later monasteries the dormitory was divided so that each monk might have his own room. Below the dormitory was a garden and a covered walk called a cloister (klois'tẽr), where monks could walk and meditate.

A monk's room was called a cell. It was a tiny room, with a bed of rough boards and a thick board for a pillow. The later dormitories had rows of such tiny rooms. Usually,

A monk meditates in his small cell surrounded only by the barest necessities.

each room had an open archway instead of a door. Beside the bed was a rough bench where a candle could be placed. On the wall there was usually a crucifix or a statue of Our Lord.

Another important part of the monastery was the *refectory* (rẽ·fĕk'tô·rǐ), or dining room. There the monks sat at long wooden tables and ate their simple meals. While they ate, one of their members read aloud from the Bible or from some other religious book.

Other parts of the monastery were the writing rooms, the kitchen, the hospitals, the abbot's house, the chapter house where the monks met together, and the guest house where

SOME DUTIES OF MEDIEVAL MONKS

Prayed many times

Performed special work

Cared for the sick

Raised their own food

travelers could find lodging. There were also sheds, or barns, where the cows and other animals of the monastery were kept.

Monastery Life. The monks arose very early for Mass, after which they breakfasted on wine and bread and then were at work by sunup. Some monks worked in the gardens and fields, some cultivated the vineyards and made the wine. Others preached missions, taught, copied manuscripts, or tended the sick. Every monk did the work given him by the abbot since obedience was one of the things each man had promised when he became a monk.

When a new monastery was established, the monks did most of the construction work since the monks thought manual labor was honorable for a man. One of the great things that the monks taught the peoples of Europe was the dignity of labor. In all previous civilizations, the hard work had been done by slaves or women. Following the example of the monks, the freemen of the Middle Ages began to have a great pride in their work.

The monks had their dinner, the only really full meal of the day, at noon. In some monasteries, only the sick monks were allowed meat. The others had vegetables, bread, wine, and cheese. We must remember that all Europeans drank wine or ale because in many places there was no pure drinking water. They had not learned how to keep wells pure and clean. Such knowledge is really very modern.

After dinner, the monks were allowed to rest or to read for an hour or two before returning to their work. In the late afternoon, there was a service in the church called *Vespers* (vĕs'pẽrz). This was followed by supper of bread and wine; then came evening prayers. By 8:30, the monks were ready for bed. In most monasteries, they were awakened at midnight for another church service called *Matins* (măt'ĭnz), which was like morning prayers. Then they returned to their beds until time for Mass.

*　*　*　*　*

What was the purpose of the readings during mealtimes?

*　*　*　*　*

Work and prayer were the chief elements in the life of a monk. Even their simple meals were eaten in silence while the monks listened to passages being read from some religious book.

MONASTIC LEARNING

Manuscripts. Any man who wished might become a monk if he were found worthy. So the monasteries had all classes of men from serfs to the sons of kings. All were supposed to be treated alike. Naturally, however, some men were better fitted for certain tasks than others. Those who read and wrote well were usually assigned to copy manuscripts. This was a very important work. Most of the Greek, Roman, and early Christian writings had been written on papyrus. In time, this papyrus began to crumble. These manuscripts would have been lost forever if the monks had not copied them. In this way, the monks preserved much of the knowledge of the ancient world for us.

The monks made their copies of manuscripts on long rolls of parchment. Parchment was made from sheepskin or calfskin that had been washed, scraped, and dried several times. Then it was dusted with powdered chalk, rubbed smooth, and stretched on frames to dry. These parchment sheets were very strong and lasting.

In the later Middle Ages, the sheepskin was cut into sheets, or pages, and bound together. Thus, books, similar to those we know today, were made. As you can see, such books were easier to handle than were the long rolls.

From the herbs grown in the monastery garden or gathered in the woods, the monks made their own ink. *Quill* (kwĭl) pens were made from feathers.

Copying a manuscript was a very slow task. Even working all day nearly every day, it sometimes took

In order to make each page as fine as possible, the monks "illuminated" their work by painting small pictures and elaborate decorations around the most important capital letters.

Women, too, were eager to serve in the religious life. As nuns, their duties were similar to those of the monks. In addition to frequent prayer, the nuns cleaned the convent, wove their own clothing, cared for the sick, and worked in the fields to raise their own food.

a year or more for a monk to copy one book.

* * * * *

Why did the monks feel that there was value in this slow, difficult copying of books?

* * * * *

You can easily understand why books were not as numerous in the Middle Ages as they are now. Because the task of copying a book was so great, each book became a precious treasure which was carefully guarded.

Many of the books which were copied by the monks of the Middle Ages are still in existence. Some of them are done in very beautiful writing and are decorated with colorful and carefully drawn capital letters and pictures.

The monks also wrote new books. They wrote accounts of the lives of the saints. They wrote histories of what was going on at the time. These writings give us some of the best information that we have concerning the people of the Middle Ages. The world owes a great debt to the monks for preserving the best that had been produced by the ancient civilizations, as well as leaving us such good accounts of the Middle Ages.

Convents. You have studied about the founding of convents for nuns. These convents had rules similar to those of the monasteries. The nuns elected a superior, who was called an *abbess* (ăb′ĕs).

In the convents, the belief that work was good was also very strong. Every nun was assigned a long day of hard work by the abbess. Some of the nuns looked after the garden. Some nuns did the cooking and housework.

Each convent tried to develop some special work. Some had hospitals that were so good that many valuable gifts were given to them.

Medieval nuns were one of the first groups to realize the importance of an education for girls as well as for boys. The nuns encouraged girls to adopt the Blessed Virgin as their model in life. They taught the girls useful arts such as fine sewing, embroidering, and lace-making as well as many other practical things.

Monastic Arts. The work of the Church in educating the people of Europe was not confined to convents and monastery schools. It was not necessary for everyone to become skilled at book learning. It was necessary for them to know how to make a living and to improve their situation. The monks were the leaders and teachers in this work also.

The monasteries usually had the best farms in the Middle Ages. The monks taught the serfs in the neighborhood to raise better crops. They showed the serfs how to improve the quality of their cattle, pigs, and sheep. The monks encouraged the serfs to clear forest land that was idle. They also encouraged them to drain swampland and to place it under cultivation.

Some of the best paintings and statues of the Middle Ages were made by monks. In some monasteries, there were also skilled craftsmen such as goldsmiths and shoemakers. When a man became a monk, he was encouraged to set up his workshop and to carry on his trade. Each monk was given a good deal of freedom in using his trade to supply his monastery's needs, provided that he did his work humbly and did not become vain.

Doing the Lord's Work. Early in the Middle Ages, there were no hospitals as we know them. Doctors at that time knew very little about medicine and surgery. Often a doctor was simply a barber. His only equipment consisted of his barber knives, a few roots and herbs for making teas, and a certain kind of worms called *leeches* (lēch'ĕs). Doctors of the Middle Ages often used leeches to suck blood from sick people.

The monks were kind and patient, and people who were sick or injured turned to the monks for help. Many times during the Middle Ages the monks carried the wounded from battlefields and nursed them through long periods of recovery. Rich and poor alike sought comfort at the monasteries. In time, monastery hospitals developed. As you have read, the sisters in many convents also developed hospitals. In the monastery and convent gardens, many herbs were raised that were used for medicines.

The monasteries helped the poor by giving them food or other gifts. It was not an uncommon sight to see a monk giving bread to a beggar.

There were no inns for travelers in those days. Pilgrims on a journey to the Holy Land or some famous shrine could always find a welcome and a night's lodging at a monastery. The monks were famous for their hospitality to pilgrims and travelers.

You can see how the Church helped in many ways to make up for the weaknesses in the feudal system and also established Godly customs that have continued throughout the centuries to the present time.

Summing Up. During the Middle Ages, the Church strove mightily to correct the many weaknesses of the feudal system. The Church turned the warlike behavior of feudal knights into good channels by introducing the ideals of chivalry. The Church, through excommunication, enforced both the Peace of God and the Truce of God. This peace and the truce helped to curtail fighting, protect the serfs and their crops, and ensure the safety of churches and of helpless persons.

In the monasteries and convents of the Middle Ages, learning was preserved, hospitals were established, and the ideals of work and prayer were lived. Thus, the great heritage of the ancient world and the great ideals of Catholic civilization were passed down to us.

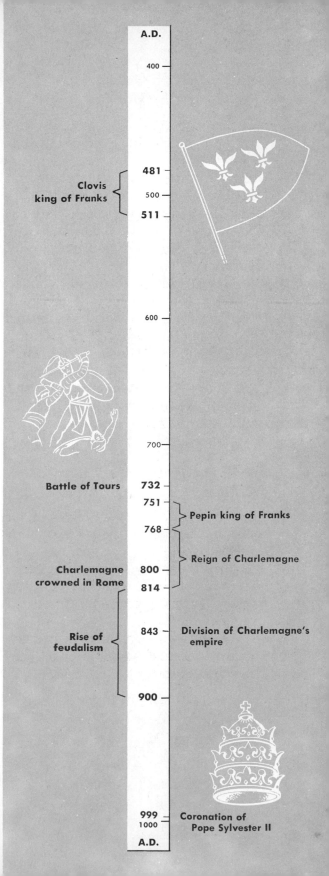

A.D.

400

481
Clovis
king of Franks
500
511

600

700

Battle of Tours   732
751
> Pepin king of Franks
768
> Reign of Charlemagne
Charlemagne   800
crowned in Rome
814

Rise of   843   Division of Charlemagne's
feudalism   empire

900

999   Coronation of
1000   Pope Sylvester II
A.D.

FOR BETTER UNDERSTANDING

 ### Checking Up

1. Explain how the Church was part of, yet different from, the feudal system.

2. Why did many bishops become important feudal lords?

3. What methods did the Catholic Church use to reduce feudal warfare?

4. What were the main parts of a monastery?

5. How did an ordinary monk spend his day?

6. Why was the work of a monk who copied manuscripts important?

7. During the Middle Ages, what type of education did girls receive?

8. What improvements did the monks make in farming?

9. Describe the charitable work of the monasteries and convents.

 ### Yesterday and Today

1. Show how the Church plays as important a part in our daily lives as it did in the lives of the people of the Middle Ages.

2. Are there any present-day agencies with enough influence to curb warfare as the Church was able to do in feudal times?

3. Tell how the Church continues to carry on great works of charity in the world of today.

 ### Terms

Define: chivalry, Peace of God, right of sanctuary, Truce of God, excommunication, cloister, dormitory, cell, refectory, Vespers, Matins, abbot, abbess.

Interesting Things to Do

1. Imagine that you are a monk or a nun of the Middle Ages. Write a diary entry for your scrapbook, in which you tell how you spent an ordinary day.

2. As a class project, construct a model of a monastery from clay or cardboard. Several groups can be formed to help do this. One group can make the buildings, another the monks at work.

3. Have a display on the class bulletin board. Collect pictures and photographs of ancient manuscripts and of manuscript writing done by the monks of the Middle Ages.

4. Many religious orders today have pamphlets that describe their purposes, daily routine, and special mission. Ask your teacher to help you secure some of these pamphlets and then compare what they tell you about modern religious life with the religious life of the Middle Ages.

UNDERSTANDING THE UNIT

For Discussion

1. What is the meaning of the name *Charlemagne?*

2. How did the feudal system provide law and order for the Middle Ages?

3. Tell in what ways a medieval manor was self-sufficient.

4. What problems were created when bishops and abbots were made vassals of kings and nobles?

For You to Answer

1. List similarities and differences between Charlemagne's empire and the old Roman Empire.

2. Tell how every feature of a medieval castle was designed to make it very difficult for an attacking army to conquer it.

3. What were the terms of the feudal contract and the obligations that each party had to the other?

4. How did the Church try to lessen fighting and warfare during the feudal period?

5. Tell how men originally became serfs and what the duties and rights of the serfs were.

Linking Geography and History

1. Draw a map of Europe that will show:

   a. in red color, the sections of his empire that Charlemagne inherited;

   b. in blue color, the sections he conquered;

   c. in yellow color, the parts of the old Roman Empire of the West that were not included in Charlemagne's empire.

Interesting Things to Do

1. The following group of words had their origin in the events and practices of the Middle Ages. Each word has had interesting changes in its meaning. Use your dictionary to find the original meaning and the present-day usage of:

castle	homage
chivalry	list
domain	manor
feud	villain

2. Use your classroom or library encyclopedia to find out the average life span of people during the Middle Ages. Then check on the diseases, diet, and other circumstances that caused many of the medieval people to die at an early age. Report to the class on how we today fight and control these factors in order to lead longer lives.

Books to Read

Boardman, Fon W., *Castles.*
Brady, Charles A., *The King's Thane.*
Davis, William, *Life on a Medieval Barony.*
De Angeli, Marguerite, *Door in the Wall.*
Gladd, Anthony, *The Saracen Steed.*
Hartman, Gertrude, *Medieval Days and Ways.*
Sutcliff, Rosemary, *Knight's Fee.*
Tappan, Eva, *When Knights were Bold.*
Willard, Barbara, *Son of Charlemagne.*

UNIT 6
Early England

(600 A.D. — 1300 A.D.)

CHAPTER

15. England's Early History
16. The Normans in England
17. England in the Late Middle Ages

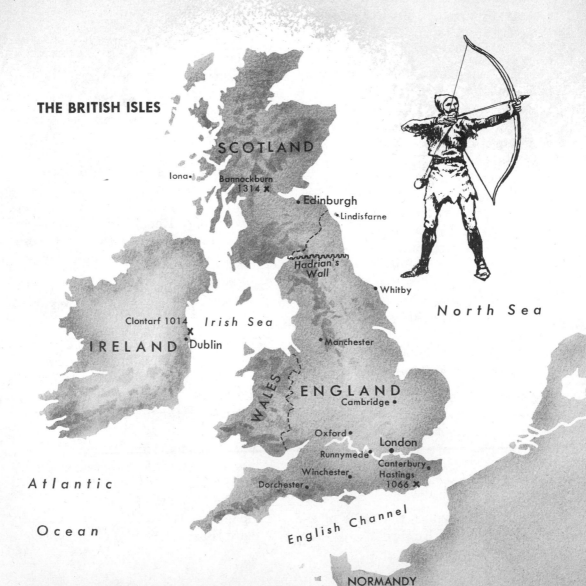

THE BRITISH ISLES

SCOTLAND

Iona•
Bannockburn
1314 ✗

•Edinburgh
•Lindisfarne

Hadrian's
Wall

•Whitby

North Sea

Clontarf 1014 Irish Sea
✗
IRELAND •Dublin

•Manchester

WALES ENGLAND
Cambridge •

Oxford•
London•
Runnymede•
Winchester• Canterbury•
Dorchester• Hastings
1066 ✗

Atlantic

Ocean

English Channel

NORMANDY

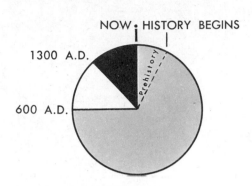

NOW · HISTORY BEGINS

1300 A.D.

600 A.D.

Prehistory

INTRODUCTION

When the Roman Empire was at the peak of its power, one of its provinces was Britannia, in the country which we now call England. When their empire began to decline, the Romans withdrew from Britannia, and Teutonic tribes invaded the land. These tribes, the Angles, Saxons, and Jutes, established a number of small kingdoms throughout England. They were pagan barbarians who brought their own language and customs to the lands they conquered.

For several hundred years there was no central government. Then, about 875 A.D. a strong Saxon king, Alfred the Great, brought much of England under his rule. He tried to raise the cultural level of his people and to promote education. Almost 200 years later, in 1066, Duke William of Normandy led an army of Normans across the English Channel from France into England and seized the English throne. William and the Norman kings who followed him took steps to reduce the power of the nobles and to increase the power of the king. Later, the English set out to extend their influence and government throughout the British Isles.

In time a system of uniform laws and courts developed in England which helped to protect the rights of the people against the power of the king. Also, the people gained the right to have their representatives take part in making the laws.

As you read this unit, keep in mind the fact that in later centuries many people left the British Isles and came to North America. These people brought with them ideas about freedom, justice under law, representative government, and respect for individual rights which had developed in England.

197

15

England's Early History

THE CELTIC PEOPLES

The British Isles. If you look at the map on page 196 you will see the location of a group of islands known as the *British Isles*. There are hundreds of islands in the group. The two largest are Great Britain and Ireland. Modern Great Britain is made up of three countries— England, Scotland, and Wales— called *The United Kingdom.*

Surrounded by the sea, it was natural that the people of these islands should turn to the sea to make a living. In the early part of the Middle Ages, Ireland produced many great mariners. *St. Brendan* (brĕn'dăn), the founder of the monastery at *Clonfert* (klŏn'fẽrt) in Ireland, was a famous navigator. His own story of the voyages that he made into the western ocean influenced Columbus in making his voyages of discovery.

Celtic Tribes. When we first hear of the British Isles in history, they were inhabited by Celtic tribes. The Teutonic tribes had pushed these Celtic peoples to the western rim of Europe. The Celts spoke a language which was different from that of the Teutons. The Celtic language survives as Irish and Scottish *Gaelic* (gāl'ĭk). Irish Gaelic is the official language of Ireland today.

In his writings, Julius Caesar has left us a vivid description of the Celts. They were tall, strong, and blue-eyed. Their hair was light in color, and it was worn very long, hanging down over their shoulders. In order to make themselves more frightening in battle, they painted their bodies blue. This was done by using a dye made from a weed which grew on the islands. The island of Great Britain was called

Britannia (brĭ·tăn′ĭ·à) by the Romans.

Tribal Wars. Early Britons, or Celts, were not united under one ruler. There were many tribes, each with its own king. These tribes were frequently at war with one another. In warfare, the Britons used swords and spears made of iron or bronze, short knives, and bows and arrows. Their shields were usually made of wood covered with animal hide.

Their most remarkable piece of war equipment was the war chariot. These chariots were low, two-wheeled carts drawn by well-trained horses. Sticking out from the hub of each wheel was a sharp scythe-like blade. In each chariot rode a driver and one or two warriors.

*   *   *   *   *

What ancient peoples also used chariots in their warfare?

*   *   *   *   *

Celtic Religion. The early people of Britain, like other pagan peoples, worshiped the forces of nature. Every tree, stone, or spring was looked upon as the dwelling place of some deity. Thunder, lightning, wind, rain, and fire were the forces these people also worshiped.

Among the Britons, men called *Druids* (drōō′ĭdz) had charge of all religious rites and ceremonies. If a boy wished to become a Druid, he had to spend many years in committing to memory the Druid teachings. None of these teachings was ever put in writing, but they were handed down by word of mouth from the older Druids to the younger.

The Druids spent much time in studying the heavens, and claimed they could foretell the future by observing the stars. They looked upon the oak tree and the mistletoe as particularly sacred. The Druids conducted sacrifices to their gods; they practiced magic; they judged disputes and fixed penalties.

The Celts, who used iron weapons and tools, gradually subdued the earlier peoples in Britannia. Archaeologists have discovered elaborately decorated weapons left behind by Celtic tribesmen.

Parts of Hadrian's wall still stand five to six feet high and are broad enough to walk on.

THE ROMANS IN BRITAIN

Caesar in Britain. When Julius Caesar was trying to conquer the people of Gaul, he realized that they were receiving aid from their Celtic kinsmen in Britain. So Caesar determined to conquer the Britons, too. Twice he led his army into Britain, but he was unable to subdue the country.

Nearly one hundred years after Caesar, a Roman emperor sent an army to Britain in order to subdue the natives and to make the territory a Roman province. The Celts, however, did not peacefully accept Roman rule. It took the Romans forty years to conquer the section of Great Britain that became the Roman province of Britannia. The Romans failed to conquer the Celtic tribes in Wales and in northern Scotland.

In order to protect the province of Britannia from the *Picts* (pĭkts), as the tribes in Scotland were called, the Roman emperor, Hadrian, had a wall built across northern England. This wall of Hadrian was about seventy-five miles long and extended from the Irish Sea on the west to the North Sea on the east. It was about eighteen feet high and nine feet thick. At various places along the wall, great forts were built so that soldiers could be quickly rushed to any place where there was an attack. The wall, built between 122 and 127 A.D., still stands.

The Romans built up the province of Britain just as they tried to improve all their provinces. They constructed great roads, aqueducts, and baths. The remains of many of these can be seen today. The Romans built over fifty walled towns. Some of these were originally military camps and were called by their Latin name *castra* (kăs'trȧ). In time the English changed this *castra* to

201

chester. When you see *chester* in the name of a city like—*Rochester, Dorchester, Winchester,* or *Manchester*—you know that the name originally referred to a Roman camp in England.

The Roman Withdrawal. When the barbarian nations began to threaten Rome itself, the troops were brought back from the provinces to protect the capital. Among those called back were the Roman troops in Britain. After that, the Romans never regained control of Britain.

Although the Romans were in Britain for nearly four hundred years, England never became a Latin nation like the other sections of Europe that had been part of the Roman Empire. In England, we can see today the remains of Roman towns, roads, forts, and baths; but there is not much more to remind us of Roman rule. The English language today is not a Latin language like French or Italian. The old Roman law is the basis of the laws in most countries on the continent of Europe. England, however, developed its own system of laws. Even most of the Christian churches founded during the time of the Romans were destroyed.

* * * * *

Why did England not become a Latin country in language, law, or customs?

* * * * *

The Roman army provided the military power that made the Roman Empire great. Army camps, such as this, served as centers of Roman influence and culture in far-off countries.

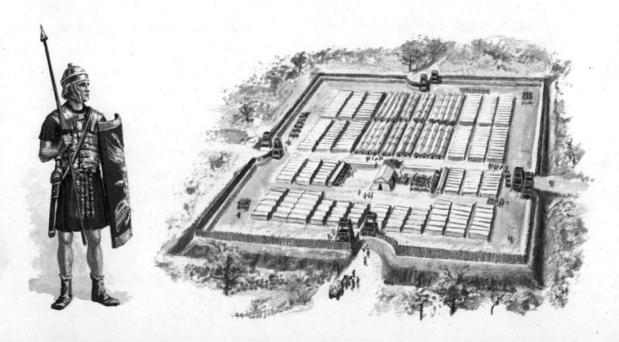

King Arthur, a heroic Celtic warrior, fought bravely against the Anglo-Saxon invaders. These battles are described in the legends of King Arthur and his Knights of the Round Table.

ANGLO-SAXON TRIBES

The Teutonic Invasions. Bands of Saxons raided the coasts of Britain even while the Romans were still in control of the island. Yet, the Saxons were not able to make any settlements as long as the Roman legions remained.

When the Romans withdrew, the Saxons and other Teutonic tribes made new efforts to invade Britain. Since the Britons were not able to defend themselves against these invasions from the north and west by the Picts and the Scots, the Britons invited some Teutons to aid them.

First to arrive were the Jutes, who came from *Jutland* (jŭt'lănd) in western Denmark. The Jutes had settled in Kent in the southeast section of Britain. They were followed by larger numbers of Angles and Saxons, who came from the area that borders on the North Sea and today is part of modern Germany.

These Teutonic tribes helped the Britons to drive out the Picts and the Scots. Then they began to take the Britons' land for themselves.

The Britons were then forced to fight a new enemy. In battle after battle the Britons tried to expel the Teutonic tribesmen.

The Angles, Saxons, and Jutes were victorious. They drove the Celtic tribes into the hill country of the west and the north. Some of the Britons crossed over into France

203

The city of Canterbury in southern England was the ancient religious center of Britain.

to the area which became known as *Brittany* (brĭt″n·ĭ).

With the Teutonic tribes in possession of Britain, the country was named after the Angles and became *Angleland* (ăng′g′l·lănd), or *England*. Since the Angles and the Saxons were more numerous than the Jutes, the term *Anglo-Saxon* is usually used to refer to all the Teutons in Britain.

West-Saxon Supremacy. As described in Chapter 10, the Teutonic tribes formed seven small kingdoms in England. There was constant rivalry and warfare among these seven kingdoms. For a time Kent was the leading kingdom. Its capital was Canterbury. After Kent lost the supremacy, it passed first to one and then to another Anglian kingdom. At length, one of the Saxon kingdoms became stronger than any of the other kingdoms. This was the kingdom of Wessex.

The man who brought Wessex to the leadership of England was a prince named *Egbert* (ĕg′bẽrt), who lived from about the year 775 to 839 A.D. Before he became king of Wessex, he had been in political exile at the court of Charlemagne. He had seen how Charlemagne had united the Franks and had established a great kingdom on the continent. Egbert had noticed that the policies of Charlemagne brought greater opportunities for the spread of religion, education, and civilization because there were fewer wars.

No sooner had Egbert become king of the West Saxons than he began the work of increasing his power. One after another, the other kingdoms of England and even the Celtic kingdoms of Wales recognized Egbert as overlord.

The Church in England. In Chapter 10, you have read how Pope Gregory sent St. Augustine and forty monks to convert the Teutonic people of England, and how

Canterbury became the center of religious life in southern England.

In the northern part of Great Britain, there were two great monasteries, Iona and Lindisfarne. The Irish and Scottish monks from these monasteries had converted the people of that area.

The Irish monks and those who came from Rome with St. Augustine all taught the same Catholic truths. However, in a few items they each had a different way of doing things. For instance, the Celtic monks and St. Augustine's monks disagreed on how to find the date of Easter and about what forms of baptism to use.

In order to reach agreement on these details, a Church council was held at *Whitby* (hwĭt′bĭ) in the year 664 A.D. After much discussion the council decided to follow the practice and customs of the monks who had come from Rome. This agreement made it possible to organize the Church in England as one united body.

At Church councils men from all the various kingdoms came together. In this way, prejudices were broken down. Naturally, when the people throughout England came to have the same religious practices and to have the same Church rules, it was thus easier to unite them under one government.

The council at Whitby was held at St. Hilda's abbey. The result of the council was that differences in religious practices and observances were ended and the Church was unified.

INVASIONS FROM THE NORTH

Northmen. As Anglo-Saxon England grew, Teutons settled in Norway, Sweden, and Denmark—the area we call *Scandinavia* (skăn′dĭ·nā′vĭ·a). These countries are situated on peninsulas, and the inhabitants were as much at home on the sea as they were on land. Sometimes these peoples were called *Northmen*, sometimes they were called *Danes* (dānz). Sometimes the name *Vikings* (vī′kĭngz) was given to these hardy sea rovers.

Some of the Northmen had invaded the land of the Franks after the death of Charlemagne. Others plundered the coasts of England and Ireland. Some invaded Russia and became the rulers of parts of that vast land. Others found their way to southern Italy, where they established a kingdom. After the Northmen of Scandinavia were converted to Christianity and had become civilized, they continued their explorations. Around the year 1000, a group of Vikings under the leadership of *Leif Ericson* (lāv ĕr′ĭk·s′n) came to North America. There they explored a section that they called *Vinland* (vĭn′lănd).

The Danes who made raids on the coasts of England and Ireland were not civilized. They were pagans and worshiped Woden, Thor, and the other Teutonic gods. Coming in

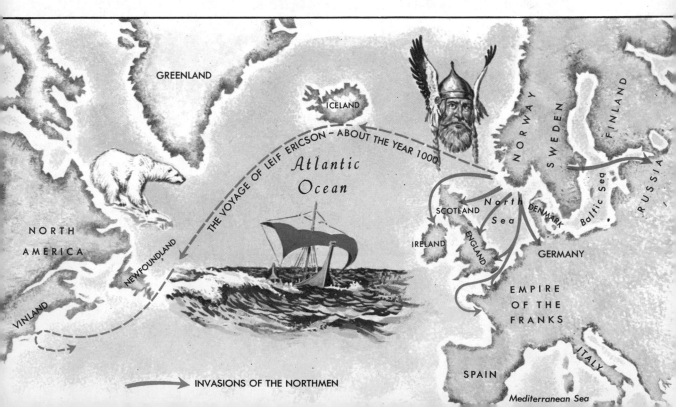

INVASIONS OF THE NORTHMEN

Alfred the Great made several trips to Rome to visit the pope. His travels to the more civilized parts of Europe impressed young Alfred with the backwardness of his country—England.

their swift, long boats, these men from northern Europe attacked the coast towns, plundered monasteries and churches, burned whole villages, and were gone before the unfortunate settlements could defend themselves or summon aid.

Shortly after Egbert succeeded in making all England recognize his supremacy, the Danish raids became more frequent and more destructive. As a result, Egbert had no time for organizing his new kingdom and making himself the real ruler of all England. He had to give his attention to defending his home kingdom, Wessex, from the invaders.

A Great King. It was not until Ælfred or Alfred (ăl'frĕd), a grandson of Egbert, came to the throne of Wessex in the year 871 A.D. that the Danes were stopped. This young man, who was only twenty-two years old when he became king, is known as one of the great kings of the Middle Ages. For many reasons he deserves the title, *Alfred the Great*. While he was still a young prince, he had made a trip to Rome, with *King Ethelwulf* (ĕth'ĕl·wōolf) his father, to meet the pope.

* * * * *

Do you believe such a trip to Rome would benefit a young prince like Alfred? If so, explain why.

* * * * *

When Alfred became king of the West Saxons, the Danes were in

207

Provided an alert force ready for battle

Manned watch towers along the Danelaw border

Farmed to maintain the food supply

possession of northern and eastern England and were still making frequent attacks upon the West Saxons. For a time it seemed they would succeed in taking Wessex. Alfred rallied his people to resist them.

At length, after many encounters with the Danes, Alfred made them agree to a line separating Saxon and Danish lands. By this agreement almost all England was divided into two parts, with Alfred as king of them both. The southern and western part was to be governed by Saxon laws. The northern and eastern section became known as the *Danelaw* (dān′lô′), for in that region all matters were settled according to Danish law. By this agreement, Alfred in effect gave up half of his kingdom to the Danes for a time in order to save the rest from their attacks.

Military Reforms. King Alfred realized that his country needed an army that was prepared to fight any invaders. So Alfred divided the men of his own kingdom into three groups. One group was always to be armed and ready for battle. Another group was to be stationed in forts that Alfred built along the Danelaw border. The third group was to till the fields to maintain the supply of food.

Alfred succeeded in checking the advance of the Danes and in forcing them to acknowledge his overlordship. He allowed them to manage their local affairs according to Danish laws, but he made them recognize him as king. Thus, Alfred became king of all England.

* * * * *

Why was it wise of Alfred to allow the Danes to manage their local affairs?

* * * * *

Learning, Religion, and Government. Alfred did everything he could to encourage literature and learning. He became a student of Latin and translated several important books from Latin into the language of his Saxon people. He also ordered the writing of the *Anglo-Saxon Chronicle*, which was the first history of England written in that early English language. It was Alfred's wish that his people should be able to read and write their native tongue.

When he became king, he founded a Palace School at Winchester. He encouraged the founding of schools in all the monasteries.

Alfred was a devoted Catholic. He did much for the churches and

Windsor Castle is the main home of Britain's royal family. The site of the castle was chosen by William the Conqueror. The round tower, or keep, is eighty feet high and can be seen from a long distance. The castle and the grounds cover about twenty-four acres.

monasteries in England, and he contributed regularly to the support of the Holy Father in Rome. Alfred devoted much attention to the conversion of the Danes.

Alfred's kingdom was divided into a number of districts, called *shires* (shīrz). These were like our counties. The shires were governed by officers directly responsible to the king. The *shire reeve* (shīr′rēv′), or *sheriff*, collected taxes and enforced the law. The *ealdorman* (ôl′dŏr·măn), or *alderman*, was the chief agent of the king in a shire. Bishops also had a very prominent part in the government of the shires.

Alfred's Descendants. Alfred died in the year 899. His son and grandsons devoted themselves to making England one united nation. Little by little, they brought the Danelaw under the rule of Anglo-Saxon laws. Gradually, the Danes became absorbed by the Anglo-Saxons, and the differences between the two peoples began to disappear. When *Edgar* (ĕd′gẽr), Alfred's great-grandson, became king in 959, all England was one united kingdom. Common language, common law, common customs, and one religion had helped unite the inhabitants of England.

Edgar was crowned by the archbishop of Canterbury at a very solemn ceremony. This became the pattern for all later coronations of English kings. Edgar's solemn oath to rule with justice and mercy has been taken by all later kings.

Disorder in England. For more than a hundred years after Edgar's time there was much disorder and confusion in England. Quarrels among the noble landowners caused many civil wars. To add to the troubles, England was threatened by attacks from without. From Denmark and Norway came a new horde of invaders. This Danish invasion differed from that of Alfred's time. The invaders of Alfred's time had been separate tribes without one central leader and without a unity of purpose. The new invasions were led by Danish kings supported by large armies.

A New King. So successful were these Danish invaders that for a time England was ruled by Danish kings. Canute, who ruled in England from 1016 to 1035, was the greatest of these Danish kings.

You perhaps know the story about King Canute who, after listening to the flattery of his courtiers, tried to command the tide to stop rising. As the waves continued to rush onward, Canute realized that only God can control the wind and the waves.

Canute gave up his pagan religion and became a fervent Catholic. He founded monasteries and made many gifts to the cathedrals of England. He even made a pilgrimage to Rome.

Canute was a very important man in Europe because he ruled Denmark, Norway, and Sweden as well as England. Although he was an invader, the English people admired him because he was wise and just. He was crowned by the archbishop of Canterbury and took the same oath as the earlier English kings. He kept the best of the English laws of Alfred and Edgar. Canute appointed Englishmen to most of the important positions in the kingdom. He kept the taxes low and tried always to rule for the benefit of the people.

*   *   *   *   *

Why, do you think, would Canute's policies win him the loyalty of the English people whom he had subdued?

*   *   *   *   *

Summing Up. The British Isles were the home of the Celts, who were conquered by the Romans. After the Romans left Britain, the Celts were driven out by the Teutonic tribes of Saxons, Angles, and Jutes.

The next group to invade Great Britain was the Danes, who conquered a large part of England and set up the Danelaw. In time, through the influence of great Anglo-Saxon leaders like Alfred the Great and Edgar, as well as Danish kings like Canute, each who ruled England as one country, a united nation began to take shape. The influence of the Church also helped to pacify and unite the Danes and Anglo-Saxons into one people.

When the tide refused to stop rising at his command, King Canute said: "Let all men know how empty and worthless is the power of kings; for there is none worthy of the name but Him whom heaven, earth, and sea obey."

FOR BETTER UNDERSTANDING

 ### Checking Up

1. Describe the Celtic inhabitants of the British Isles.

2. Who were the Druids?

3. Why was Julius Caesar interested in Britain?

4. Why did the Romans withdraw from Britain?

5. What reminders of Roman rule may be seen in England?

6. What Teutonic tribes settled in England?

7. How did Egbert increase the power of the West Saxon kingdom of Wessex?

8. How did the Church help to unify England?

9. How did King Alfred encourage religion and learning?

10. Describe the results of the later Danish invasions.

11. Tell the significance of each of the following dates: 664, 959, 1000, 1016.

 ### Yesterday and Today

1. The Celts who lived in the British Isles had many superstitions. For example, they believed in fairies and elves. What superstitions do some people believe in today?

2. How do the duties of the sheriff in your county differ from those of a sheriff in the England of King Alfred's time?

3. Tell why a defense system like the wall of Hadrian would not be very effective for protection today.

Persons, Places, and Terms

Identify: St. Brendan, Ethelwulf, King Arthur, Egbert, St. Augustine, Alfred, Edgar, Canute.

Locate: Scotland, Wales, Ireland, Denmark, Canterbury, Dorchester, Winchester, Manchester, Whitby, Hadrian's Wall.

Define: Gaelic, Britannia, Druids, Picts, Council of Whitby, Vikings, Danelaw, *Anglo-Saxon Chronicle*, shire, shire reeve, ealdorman, courtier.

Interesting Things to Do

1. Draw a color map of Great Britain showing the seven Anglo-Saxon kingdoms. Also show the sections of that island that remained under Celtic control.

2. Make a list of the cities, towns, and counties in your state that are named after places in England.

3. For your scrapbook, make a chart of the various peoples that invaded Britain before the year 1000. Show the name of the group, where they came from, and where they settled. Be sure to include dates, names of leaders, and their accomplishments.

_16_

The Normans in England

INVADERS FROM THE NORTH OF FRANCE

King Edward. Canute's sons were harsh and cruel. Fortunately for the people of England, they ruled only a few years. Then the English nobles elected _Edward_, the grandson of King Edgar and a descendant of Alfred the Great, as their king. Edward was such a religious man that he is known as _St. Edward the Confessor_.

* * * * *

Do you know why saints such as King Edward are known as Confessors?

* * * * *

Edward had spent most of his early life in northern France, just across the channel from England. There he grew up in the care of his uncle, the _duke of Normandy_ (nôr′măn·dĭ).

In France. Normandy was a region that had been overrun by Northmen after the time of Charlemagne. These invaders made permanent conquest and settlements in this land of the Franks at about the same time that other Northmen were taking possession of northern England and setting up the Danelaw.

You have read how the Danes in England came to adopt the language and customs of the Anglo-Saxons. The Northmen who settled in northern France were likewise influenced by the Franks whose land they invaded. This area of the Franks' homeland came to be called _Normandy_, or the land of the Northmen, and the people became known as _Normans_. In language and customs the Normans were _Frankish_ or, as we say, _French_.

Brought up among the Normans,

EDWARD THE CONFESSOR

HAROLD

WILLIAM THE CONQUEROR

Edward the Confessor was Norman in speech and manner. When he became king of England, he brought many Norman nobles with him and gave them high positions in his kingdom.

A Power Struggle. Edward was not the real ruler of England. His Norman nobles were not very powerful either. The real rulers of England were a man named *Godwin* (gŏd'wĭn) and his son, *Harold*. These powerful West Saxon nobles, as advisers to the king, exercised kingly authority for the pious but weak Edward.

In January of the year 1066, Edward the Confessor died leaving no son to succeed him. According to custom it was the duty of the nobles to choose a new king. Harold was chosen as king.

No sooner was Harold declared king than a powerful rival set out to take the kingdom from him. This rival was *William*, duke of Normandy.

William was Edward's cousin, and William's wife was a descendant of the line of Alfred the Great. William claimed that Edward had promised him the English throne. Harold himself had once even made a promise to support William as Edward's successor. William was a very powerful noble, who by the time he was twenty-four had made himself the strongest lord in all of France.

The Battle for England. William made a public announcement of his intended conquest of England in order to secure the throne. To his banner came many adventurers from nearby regions. He gained the support of many Norman noblemen by promising them lands in England. In a short time, he gathered about him a large band of followers. In the fall of 1066, William crossed the English Channel. At *Hastings*, about fifty miles south of London, the forces of Duke William and King Harold met in battle.

Harold and his English soldiers took their stand on a small hill and waited for the Normans to attack. The English were armed with lances and battle-axes. These weapons were only useful when the enemy was at close range.

The Normans had many skilled archers. From a safe distance they were able to send great showers of arrows against the English foot soldiers. Many of the Norman knights were on horseback and this permitted them to make sudden charges against Harold's soldiers.

The English fought bravely and valiantly, but by the close of the day Harold had been killed, and the English had been defeated.

William's Victory. After his victory at Hastings, William marched toward London. Seeing William's powerful forces, a group of influential nobles and churchmen decided that it was useless to oppose him, so they agreed to accept him as king. When William reached London, the city opened its gates to him. In Westminster Abbey, on Christmas Day, 1066, William was crowned king of England.

The Norman forces of William the Conqueror crossed the stormy English Channel in boats similar to those used by their ancestors when they traveled from Scandinavia to France.

The Tower of London is a group of stone buildings that includes a fortress, a castle, and a prison. The Tower has played an important role in the history of England.

WILLIAM'S REIGN

England Changes. The Norman duke, William, by virtue of his conquest of England, became known as *William the Conqueror*. Under William a great many changes began to take place.

The Conqueror declared that he would keep the laws, customs, and government as they had been organized during the reign of Edward the Confessor. The people, therefore, continued to settle their disputes in the local courts according to Anglo-Saxon laws. The local officials who governed the people kept their Anglo-Saxon titles and duties. William even kept the *Witan* (wĭt'ăn), which was a council of bishops, abbots, and nobles. This council gave advice to the king and assisted him in governing the kingdom. In many ways it seemed as if no changes had been made by the Conqueror.

William, however, began to appoint Normans to all the high positions in England. He distributed great areas of land to his Norman followers. Great Norman castles of stone began to be built all over England. William ordered that a great castle fortress be built for himself in London. This castle, known as the *Tower of London*, still stands and is in use after nearly nine hundred years.

* * * * *

Do you know what use is made of the Tower of London today?

* * * * *

216

When William gave land to a Norman noble, he was careful that the noble would not have too large an estate in any one area. Instead he gave a noble several small estates scattered in various parts of England. This prevented a noble from becoming too powerful. A noble could not collect a large army in any one place. No noble would then be strong enough to revolt against the king.

William required every land-owner, from the lords of the great estates to the men who held only a few acres, to take an oath of loyalty and service to him. By taking this oath, all English landholders became vassals to the king. This was a change in the customs of feudal-ism, according to which a man owed allegiance to the lord above him. From then on in England, a man's first allegiance was to the king.

William's Census. William wanted to know all about the land and the people that he had conquered. He ordered a census to be taken. Today in the United States, a census is taken every ten years, but in William's day a census was rarely taken.

William's remarkable census was recorded in a book of two volumes. Partial copies of this book still exist. This record was looked upon as a final authority for levying and collecting taxes.

To get the information for the *Domesday* (dōomz′dā′) *Book*, as

The census takers in each district were people who came from the district and knew the area well. In this way William was reasonably certain of an accurate accounting.

the volumes of census records were called, William sent commissioners into every shire (county) and town. The census takers called the people in each area together and asked them questions about their families and their property. In this way, it was found out how much farm land there was in England and who were the owners. Every single piece of property, including the livestock and the crops, was recorded.

*   *   *   *   *

Every ten years, a census is taken in the United States. What kinds of questions are asked by the census takers?

*   *   *   *   *

Perhaps the greatest influence of the Normans in England was their influence upon the language which we speak, read, and write. As you have read, the Normans had adopted the language of the Franks, a language so mixed with that of the Romans that it was more Latin than Teutonic. Naturally, the Normans carried this language with them to England.

For some time after the Norman conquest, three languages were used in England. The rulers, who were small in numbers, spoke Norman-French. The mass of the people continued to speak Anglo-Saxon. At the same time the language of the Church and the official documents of the government was Latin.

The Norman conquerors and the conquered Anglo-Saxons spoke different languages. Yet, it was necessary for each group to understand the other, so both began to learn and to use words of each other's language. At length the languages

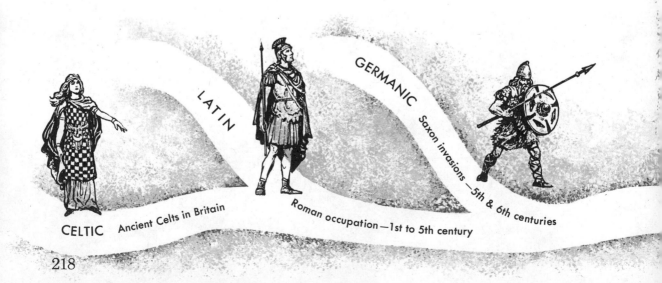

CELTIC   Ancient Celts in Britain

LATIN   Roman occupation—1st to 5th century

GERMANIC   Saxon invasions—5th & 6th centuries

were mixed together to form one language, English. Usually, the Anglo-Saxon words for common everyday things remained in use, but in many cases the Norman-French words took the place of the Anglo-Saxon words. Thus, a large part of our present-day English language is of French-Latin origin. Some words like *Mass* and *Benediction*, however, entered the English language directly from the Latin.

Our modern English language was greatly enriched by the addition of Norman-French. Today we often provide two words for the same thing. For example, *hue* is the Anglo-Saxon word, while *color* is the Norman word. The Anglo-Saxon word is *storm*, while the Norman word is *tempest*.

Summing Up. After Canute's death, St. Edward the Confessor, a descendant of Alfred the Great, was elected king of England by the nobles.

Upon Edward's death, Harold, a powerful West Saxon noble, was elected King. His claim to the throne was immediately challenged by Duke William of Normandy, a cousin of Edward.

At the Battle of Hastings in the year 1066, the Norman-French forces of William defeated the Anglo-Saxon forces under Harold. Then William the Conqueror became the king of all England.

Under the Conqueror many changes took place. Normans were appointed to all high posts in the kingdom and every landowner took the feudal loyalty oath only to the king, not to other powerful nobles. Gradually, the Anglo-Saxon and Norman-French languages began to change into our own English language.

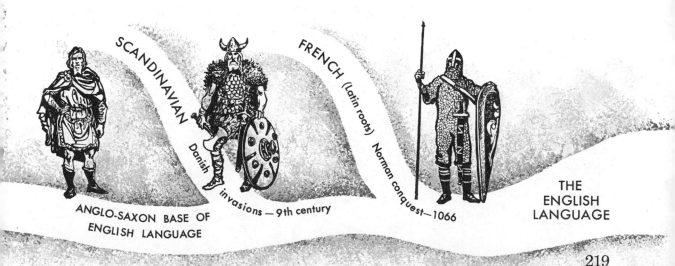

SCANDINAVIAN

FRENCH (Latin roots) Norman conquest—1066

Danish invasions — 9th century

ANGLO-SAXON BASE OF ENGLISH LANGUAGE

THE ENGLISH LANGUAGE

FOR BETTER UNDERSTANDING

 ## Checking Up

1. Who were the Normans?

2. Why did Harold claim to be king of England?

3. Why did William of Normandy claim the throne of England?

4. Tell why the Normans won the Battle of Hastings.

5. What were some of the changes that William made in England?

6. What was the importance of the *Domesday Book?*

7. What changes took place in the English language as a result of the Norman conquest?

8. Why is the date, 1066, important in the history of England?

 ## Yesterday and Today

1. Does your local community have any system of records similar to the *Domesday Book?* What is the purpose of these records? Where are such records kept?

2. Even though he was a very holy man, St. Edward the Confessor was a weak ruler, who was controlled by Godwin and his son Harold. Can you think of any modern-day situations where good men have been the rulers but others have actually held the power? Is this a good thing for a country?

 ## Persons, Places, and Terms

Identify: Edward the Confessor, Godwin, Harold, William of Normandy.

Locate: Normandy, Hastings, London.

Define: archer, Witan, *Domesday Book.*

 ## Interesting Things to Do

1. Plan and present a special news program on the Battle of Hastings. Imagine that several members of the class are correspondents who have covered the battle. Have them interview important participants as well as give an interpretation of the aftereffects of the fight. Be sure you have one of the correspondents give the background of the battle.

2. The boys in the class might make a survey of the kinds of armor and weapons that men used during the Middle Ages. The boys can check your local library, or a local museum, for information to help them in the project. Then they can make drawings and models of the various types used. Models can easily be made from cardboard and aluminum foil. Be sure that each item and picture is clearly labeled.

17

England in the Late Middle Ages

Henry II. William brought peace and order to England. For example, it was said that a man could travel all through England with a great bag of gold and never be robbed. As a result, trade and commerce prospered. The sons of William the Conqueror, however, did not have their father's ability to rule well. Under William's successors new wars between nobles broke out, and there was great disorder throughout the kingdom.

About one hundred years after William the Conqueror, a man named *Henry* inherited the throne. He was known as *Henry II*. His mother, *Matilda*, was the granddaughter of William the Conqueror. Henry's father, *Geoffrey*, was a French noble who from boyhood had worn on his cap a little sprig of yellow broom plant called *planta genesta*. For this reason, Geoffrey's family became known as the *Plantagenets* (plăn·tăj′ĕ·nĕts). Henry II and his descendants who ruled England are called the *Plantagenet kings*.

Henry II was one of the most powerful rulers of his day. Not only was he king of England; he was also feudal lord of half of France. He had six times as much land as the king of France.

Henry and the Nobles. Even though Henry divided his time between England and his possessions in France, he was one of England's strongest kings. No sooner had he become king than he began to strengthen the government of England.

Henry encouraged the nobles to pay money into the king's treasury instead of providing knights for the king's army. As the nobles gave up the practice of keeping armies for the king's service, it was less easy for a noble to gather an army for war against another noble or against the king.

Henry destroyed the castles of any rebellious nobles and allowed no new castles to be built without his permission. When a noble rebelled, his title was taken away, and any noble who had gained his title as a reward for fighting during England's civil wars was deprived of his rank. This meant that it was difficult for nobles to use either their power or prestige to undermine the king.

Henry's Court Reforms. King Henry thought of a plan that would improve the courts, increase his own authority, and weaken the power of the nobles all at one time. According to his plan, Henry appointed well-educated men as judges and sent them throughout the kingdom. These judges were to see that the king's courts, which settled disputes between the great lords, and the local courts in each shire, or county, were conducted properly.

Henry's judges were to visit each shire at least once a year and hold a meeting called an *inquest*. At the inquest the judges called together twelve of the most trustworthy men in the area. The twelve men whom the judges called together each took this oath, "I swear to tell the truth, the whole truth, and nothing but the truth." The Latin word for *I swear* is *juro*. So the twelve men became known as *jurors*.

The jurors were asked to tell

about anyone in their neighborhood who had committed or had been suspected of any crime during the past year. Everyone whom these jurors accused of crime was then summoned to trial. Thus, Henry II began a practice out of which the *grand jury* system of today has grown. The word *grand* comes from a Norman-French word which means *large*. There was also a small, *petit* or *petty jury*.

The petty jury was developed by the judges of Henry II, too. When a case came before the king's justices, they selected twelve men from the neighborhood who knew nothing about the crime. These twelve served as the petty jury. The jurors listened to witnesses who could tell of the crime. Then the jurors decided the case from the evidence presented by the witnesses. Although Henry's judges did not begin trial by jury, they made it more nearly like the form we use today.

Whenever the king's judges made a decision, it was written down. It then became a model for similar decisions made later by other judges. In this way there developed in England a *common law* for all the people. It was a law that did not simply depend on local feudal customs. This common law was brought across the sea to America by the English settlers, and it is the basis for the law in our country today.

* * * * *

What advantages are there in having standard laws throughout a nation?

* * * * . *

Today's grand jury system is based upon that begun by Henry II. Persons charged by the grand jury are then brought to trial.

St. Thomas à Becket's feast day is celebrated on December 29, the day he was murdered while at vespers in the cathedral. He was declared a saint by Pope Alexander in 1172.

Henry and the Church. In 1162, Henry had helped to make his friend, *Thomas à Becket*, the archbishop of Canterbury. Thomas was a cleric who had been the chancellor of England, that is, chief official of the king. After becoming archbishop, Thomas began to defend the rights of the Church against royal interference, for Henry was trying to take away some of the rights and freedom of the Church. As you know, the Church always insists on maintaining its freedom, which is necessary for carrying on the work of God.

This struggle between the king and the archbishop lasted for years. One day in a burst of anger, Henry said that he wished he were rid of Thomas. Four of the king's knights then went to Canterbury and killed the archbishop in his cathedral, four days after Christmas in the year 1170.

The whole of Western Christendom was shocked at the murder. Thomas à Becket was canonized as a saint within three years. Every year great pilgrimages from all over England went to his tomb at Canterbury.

One of the oldest and greatest pieces of literature in the English language is the work of *Geoffrey Chaucer* (chô'sẽr) and it is called *The Canterbury Tales*. This collection of stories, many of which are in verse, tells about a group of pilgrims journeying to the shrine of St. Thomas à Becket about two hundred years after his death.

ENGLAND AFTER HENRY II

The Lionhearted King. Henry II was followed on the throne by his son, *Richard*, who is one of the best-known kings of the Middle Ages. Richard was a daring and reckless warrior, noted for his exciting adventures. Because of this, he is known as *Richard the Lionhearted*. He was one of the leaders of the Third Crusade to rescue the Holy Land from the Turks. In Chapter 21, you will read more about Richard and the Crusades.

Richard, who became king in 1189, did not earn any great reputation in England. The English raised large sums of money to finance his expedition to Jerusalem. When he was returning from the Holy Land, Richard was captured and held for a time as a prisoner in Austria. The English people were obliged to supply a huge amount of money for the king's ransom. You can see why Richard wasn't too popular.

Henry's Son, John. Richard was succeeded as king by his younger brother, *John*. While Richard was in the Holy Land, John had tried by treachery to seize the throne for himself. This failing, he had to wait until Richard's death in 1199.

John became very unpopular after the king of France captured Normandy and practically all of the other English feudal holdings on the continent of Europe. In the long run, however, the loss of the French lands was good for England. From that time on the English kings could devote all their time to affairs at home instead of journeying between England and France.

While John was king of England, there was much lawlessness in the land. Travelers were constantly in danger of being robbed. The nobles were continually at war with each other. The poor people were oppressed by greedy nobles.

Richard the Lionhearted was a poet as well as a bold fighter, but he was too careless of his duties to be called a great king.

Robin Hood, the bold outlaw, was a legendary hero of the common English people, just as King Arthur was a hero of the English upper classes. He became known as a protector of the poor.

Conditions were so bad that people dreamed of a brave hero who would protect them. Perhaps, there really were some men who became outlaws in order that they could rob the rich and unjust and give to the poor. A story or legend grew up about such a protector of the poor. He was called *Robin Wood*, or more popularly, *Robin Hood*.

*   *   *   *   *

Can you guess where the name Robin Hood, or Wood, came from? You can get an idea by making three words of the name Robin Wood.

*   *   *   *   *

King John and the Pope. Pope Innocent III had appointed as archbishop of Canterbury a very learned and capable man. This was *Stephen Langton* (lăng′tŭn), who had spent many years in Rome and was already a cardinal. King John was displeased at the appointment because he wished to have a man who would be dependent upon him. John refused to admit Stephen Langton into England and seized the estates that belonged to the diocese of Canterbury.

For this mistreatment of the Church, Innocent III placed England under an *interdict* (ĭn′tẽr·dĭkt), that is, all churches in England were closed. Mass could not be celebrated and marriages and funerals could not be solemnized. The people in England were pious Catholics and they grumbled against the king who had brought such punishment on the kingdom.

After five long years, John made peace with the pope. In order to restore peace to the country and keep his crown, John presented the kingdom of England to Pope Innocent III and paid homage to him as his overlord. The pope immediately returned the kingdom to John as a fief. Stephen Langton was then permitted to take up his duties.

THE GREAT CHARTER

English Liberty. Heavy taxes had been placed on the people by King Richard. King John increased the taxes and yet accomplished nothing. He was a tyrant who ruled without regard for the rights of his people. The people began to resist. A group of English churchmen and nobles determined to put an end to the tyranny of the king. Led by the cardinal-archbishop of Canterbury, Stephen Langton, the bishops and barons wrote out a list of the rights of the Church and the rights of the few English freemen.

This list, or charter, did not contain anything new. The rights mentioned in it were not thought up by

The barons force King John to put his signature to the Magna Carta, one of the most important documents of English history.

The lines from the Magna Carta reproduced here include the article that guarantees all freemen in the kingdom the right to a trial. Notice the elaborate style of the writing of the period.

the nobles. Instead, they were rights which had been assured to the nobles since the early days of England. They were the rights John had ignored.

On June 15, 1215, in a meadow called *Runnymede* (rŭn'ĭ·mēd), on the south bank of the *Thames* (tĕmz) *River*, the bishops and barons met King John and they demanded that he sign the charter. Because of the nobles' power, John was afraid that he might lose his crown, so he signed the charter.

This charter is known as the *Great Charter* or *Magna Carta* (măg'nà kär'tà). Even today it is considered one of the most important steps on the road to democratic government. You will find many of its principles contained in the Constitution of the United States.

One of the most important statements in the Great Charter was that no noble or freeman should be arrested, held in prison, deprived of his land, or banished except under the law. Further, no noble could in

any way be punished except by the judgment of men of his own rank and according to the law of the land. Another statement of great importance declared that justice should not be sold, refused, delayed, or denied to any freeman.

The Great Charter declared that the king could not ask for extra taxes without the consent of the Great Council, or Witan. Five and a half centuries later the American colonists reminded the English king of this principle. These colonists said there should be no taxation without representation.

In the Great Charter the king also promised that the Church should be free. This meant, in one respect, the Church would be free to select its bishops without interference from the king.

King John had no intention of living up to the Great Charter. In fact, he gathered together an army and prepared to make war on the bishops and nobles. John, however, did not succeed. He died in 1216.

PARLIAMENT DEVELOPS

The King's Council. From the earliest times, the people of England had some kind of an assembly. Among the early Celts the tribal chieftain had as his advisers the leading warriors of his tribe. Later, the Anglo-Saxon kings were advised by a group of the leading men of the kingdom. This group, you may remember, was called the *Witan*, or the *meeting of the wise men*.

The Witan was not elected by the people. It was composed of relatives and friends of the king, of men who held important Church positions, and of nobles who held great tracts of land.

The Parliament of 1265. *King Henry III*, the eldest son of King John, also proved to be a tyrant.

As a result, the nobles revolted against him. The nobles were led by a brave man named *Simon de Montfort* (mŏnt'fĕrt). Under his leadership they gained control of the government in 1264. Just fifty years after the signing of the Great Charter, Simon called together an assembly to discuss matters of common interest. The assembly was given a new name by these Norman rulers. It was called a *parliament*, after the French word *parler*, which means *to speak* or *to discuss*.

The assembly which Simon called in 1265 was different from the earlier assemblies in England. The bishops and the nobles were called to this parliament as they always had been. Simon, however, wanted

The royal procession to the opening of Parliament is a colorful tradition, filled with pomp and splendor. The British enjoy the pageantry that accompanies their ancient traditions.

When the Model Parliament met at Westminster in 1295, Edward summoned not only churchmen and nobles, but knights and townsmen as well. The House of Commons was made up of the knights and townsmen.

the support of other groups, too. So he invited each shire, or county, to send two knights, lesser noblemen, and each town to send two leading citizens.

Simon de Montfort was overthrown in 1265 by *Edward I*, the son of Henry III. Edward knew that both his father and his grandfather had been hated for their tyranny. When he became king, Edward promised to recognize the rights of the people.

Edward's Model Parliament. Edward I needed money to pay the expenses of his army, so he called a meeting, or parliament, to get new taxes approved. This parliament that he assembled in the year 1295 consisted of representatives

from the towns and counties, as well as of nobles and churchmen. This parliament differed in two respects from the parliament that had met thirty years earlier. First, Edward's parliament was called together by a king and not by a rebel leader who was fighting against the king. Second, it represented all the English nobles and freemen, not just those under the control of a rebel leader. Historians refer to Edward's parliament as the *Model Parliament* because it became the model for later parliaments in England.

At first, the parliament met chiefly to grant the king's requests for money. In time, the parliament began to present petitions to the king in order to correct or improve

230

conditions in the kingdom. Later, the king found that if he did not grant the requests of the parliament, no money was voted for him. As time passed, the other acts passed by the parliament began to receive the consent of the king, and thus became the laws of England. About thirty years after the Model Parliament met, parliament was so strong that it forced the son of Edward I, *Edward II*, to give up his throne and in his place elected Edward I's grandson, *Edward III*.

In the beginning, those who came to represent the shires and the towns met in the same body with the nobles and clergy. After a time, the parliament began to meet as two groups, or houses. The upper house, the group made up of the nobles and the bishops, became what is now called the *House of Lords*. The lower house, or *House of Commons*, was made up to represent the towns and shires. Today the House of Commons is the main governmental body in Britain.

ENGLAND GAINS TERRITORY

The West of England. As you have read, the entire island of Great Britain was at one time inhabited by the Celtic tribes. When England was invaded by Romans, Anglo-Saxons, Danes, and Normans, in turn, the Celtic people were driven to the far western and the far northern sections of the island. The people of *Wales*, as the western section of Great Britain came to be called, continued to carry on a border warfare with the rulers of England.

Edward I determined to unite the whole of the island of Great Britain under his control. He led an army

Harlech Castle in Wales is typical of the castles built by the Norman kings. Why, do you think, did the kings have castles built throughout the island?

into Wales and subdued the native leaders in 1256. Then he divided their land into shires and introduced English laws. In order to make the conquest more pleasing to the people of Wales, he gave to his eldest son, Edward II, the title *Prince of Wales*. Since that time the eldest son of every English monarch, with one exception, has held this title.

Scotland. The conquest of Scotland was more difficult. The Celtic tribes that had been driven to the northern, or highland, section continued to speak Celtic. Anglo-Saxons had settled in the southern, or lowland, section of Scotland. These two groups were ultimately united under a king, who had his capital at *Edinburgh* (ĕd″n·bûr′ŏ).

Edward I insisted that the king of Scotland should recognize the king of England as overlord. When Edward tried to enforce this demand, the Scots, led by *William Wallace*, rose to defend their country.

This war was unsuccessful and Wallace was beheaded in 1305, but a few years later another armed conflict led by *Robert Bruce* was more successful. Bruce and his followers defeated the English under Edward II at *Bannockburn* (băn′ ŭk·bûrn′) in 1314. As a result of this battle, the Scots were able to keep their independence for three hundred years.

English Expansion in Ireland. You have read how the Danes, after repeated attacks on England, were finally able to set up a kingdom there during the time of King Canute. During this time the Danes made repeated raids on Ireland and destroyed many of the famous schools and monasteries.

About the year 1000, the Danes invaded Ireland in large numbers. An Irish leader, *Brian Boru* (bŏ·rō′), united the Irish tribes against the Danes. The Irish and the Danes met in a great battle at *Clontarf* (klŏn·tärf′), on Good Friday in the year 1014. Although Brian Boru was killed in this battle, the Danes were defeated and Ireland remained free.

The Norman kings of England were anxious to bring Ireland, as well as Wales and Scotland, into their domains. Henry II entered Ireland with a strong force. The Irish were helpless in fighting against the well-armed Anglo-Normans. Thus, many of the Irish chieftains accepted Henry as their overlord.

The English conquest of Ireland was not complete, because the invaders were confined to a fairly small area around Dublin called *The Pale*, which means a *fenced-in area*.

* * * * *

Why was the resistance of the Scots and Irish against the English like the efforts of today's native peoples throughout the world to gain their independence?

* * * * *

Summing Up. Between the years 1150 and 1400 the English people gained many rights from their kings. Henry II made wise changes in the courts and laws. Out of these changes came the common law, which is the basis of our laws today. Juries were set up to try people accused of doing wrong. King John signed the Magna Carta, which listed the rights of the nobles and freemen that the king had to respect.

The council which advised the king became an assembly called parliament. All classes of freemen, as well as the nobles and Churchmen, sent representatives to that body. That body was the beginning of representative government such as we today enjoy.

During the centuries from 1150 to 1400 the English kings also extended their influence over almost all of the British Isles.

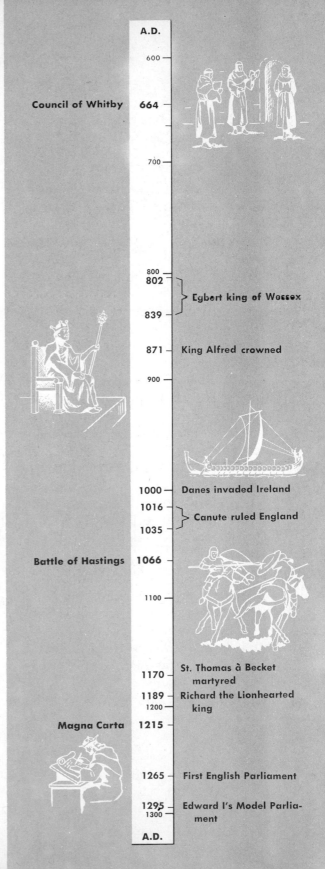

A.D.

600

Council of Whitby — 664

700

800
802
Egbert king of Wessex
839

871 — King Alfred crowned

900

1000 — Danes invaded Ireland
1016
Canute ruled England
1035

Battle of Hastings — 1066

1100

1170 — St. Thomas à Becket martyred
1189 — Richard the Lionhearted king
1200

Magna Carta — 1215

1265 — First English Parliament

1295 — Edward I's Model Parliament
1300

A.D.

FOR BETTER UNDERSTANDING

 Checking Up

1. How did Henry II weaken the power of the nobles?

2. In what ways did Henry II improve the courts?

3. What was the cause of the quarrel between King Henry II and St. Thomas à Becket?

4. Who was Richard the Lionhearted?

5. Why did King John quarrel with the pope?

6. Under what circumstances did King John sign the Magna Carta?

7. What are some of the chief points of the Great Charter?

8. Show how and why Simon de Montfort created a new type of parliament.

9. Why was the Model Parliament so called?

10. How did parliament increase its power?

11. Identify the following dates and tell their importance: 1189, 1215, 1265, 1295.

 Yesterday and Today

1. Find out who represents your district and state in our nation's Congress. Tell how these persons are selected and compare their selection with that of the members of early English parliaments.

2. Show how the power to raise taxes was important in the development of the English parliament. Which part of our government holds this power?

 Persons, Places, and Terms

Identify: Henry II, Thomas à Becket, Chaucer, Richard the Lionhearted, King John, Robin Hood, Stephen Langton, Simon de Montfort, Edward I, Edward II, Edward III, William Wallace, Robert Bruce, Brian Boru.

Locate: Runnymede, Bannockburn, Clontarf, Wales.

Define: Plantagenets, inquest, juror, grand jury, petty jury, common law, Canterbury Tales, interdict, Magna Carta, parliament, House of Lords, House of Commons, Prince of Wales.

 Interesting Things to Do

1. For your scrapbook, prepare a report on how a jury of today works. You might ask your parents or a teacher who has served on a jury to help you.

2. Look up our American Bill of Rights (first ten Amendments to the National Constitution) and compare them with the rights listed in the Magna Carta.

3. Secure pictures of England from old magazines, then arrange an interesting display of these pictures on the class bulletin board.

UNDERSTANDING THE UNIT

For Discussion

1. Why was the Roman conquest of Britain not permanent?

2. How did Charlemagne influence King Egbert?

3. Why was the Norman conquest one of the most important events in the history of England?

4. Why was the development of Common Law important to England?

5. Why was Henry II one of the most powerful rulers of his day?

6. Briefly tell the story of the growth and development of the English parliament.

For You to Answer

1. Compare the policies of Charlemagne and Alfred the Great.

2. How did the Norman Kings of England weaken the old feudal system?

3. Why was King John so unpopular?

4. Explain the rights of the English nobles and freemen that were assured by the Magna Carta.

5. Briefly tell of the English attempts to conquer Scotland and Ireland.

Linking Geography and History

1. Tell how England's being an island kingdom affected the lives of its people.

2. Tell what natural features helped to keep the English attempts to conquer Scotland and Ireland from being successful.

3. What are some of the difficulties of a ruler whose territories are separated from each other? Use examples from the history of England.

Interesting Things to Do

1. For your scrapbook, make a chart which lists all the English kings told about in this Unit. Be sure you include dates and the important happenings in the reign of each king.

2. Have your teacher help you invite someone to talk to your class about England. Perhaps a friend or relative has visited or lived there and can show pictures or slides to the class, as well as tell you many interesting things about the country.

3. Write a life of St. Edward the Confessor for your scrapbook. Draw colorful pictures to illustrate your report.

Books to Read

Bryner, Winifred, *Fourteenth of October*.

Daughtery, James H., *Magna Carta*.

Foster, Harold, *Prince Valiant*.

Hutton, Clark, *Picture History of Britain*.

Leighton, Margaret, *Journey for a Princess*.

Malory, Sir Thomas, *Boy's King Arthur*.

McSpadden, Joseph W., *Robin Hood and his Merry Outlaws*.

Robinson, Mabel L., *King Arthur and his Knights*.

Sellman, R. R., *The Vikings*.

UNIT 7
European Nations Develop

(900 A.D. — 1500 A.D.)

CHAPTER

18. France Becomes a Nation
19. Two Nations: Spain and Portugal
20. Other Lands Become Nations
21. Wars to Rescue the Holy Land

WESTERN EUROPE AT
THE TIME OF THE CRUSADES

→ MAIN CRUSADE ROUTES

ENGLAND
London

Atlantic
Ocean

HOLY
ROMAN
EMPIRE

POLAND

Paris
FRANCE

Ratisbon

Lyons
Clermont

HUNGARY

Venice

PORTUGAL
SPANISH
CHRISTIAN
KINGDOMS

Genoa

Danube R.
ROMAN

Black Sea

MOSLEM STATES
IN SPAIN

Rome

EASTERN
EMP.

Constantinople

DOMINIONS OF THE TURKS

ASIA MINOR

M e d i t e r r a n e a n   S e a

K. OF
SICILY

MOSLEM STATES IN AFRICA

HOLY
LAND
Acre
Jerusalem

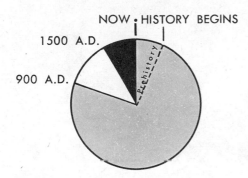

NOW • HISTORY BEGINS

1500 A.D.

900 A.D.

Prehistory

INTRODUCTION

During the time that England was becoming a strong and united nation, other nations were developing on the continent of Europe. France, Spain, and Portugal all became strong, independent nations, and several other nations such as Switzerland, Poland, Sweden, and Denmark had been established by the year 1500.

Central Europe attempted to work out a different plan of unity. Efforts were made to re-establish an empire which would include both the German and Italian states. As a result neither Germany nor Italy became independent nations during this period.

As the nations of Western Europe began to emerge, Pope Urban II called on the people of these countries to drive the Turks from the Holy Land. Answering the pope's call, men of all classes—from kings to serfs—enlisted in the Christian armies. For the nobles, this meant a sacrifice of land and wealth because they were supporting the venture. For all men who took part in the effort, going to rescue the Holy Land meant suffering the dangers and hardships of war.

The effort to rescue the Holy Land continued for many years and had a lasting effect upon European culture and trade. New ideas and goods were brought from lands in the East. New trade routes were developed, which, in turn, stimulated trade and commerce. The towns prospered and gained new rights for their citizens. The powers of the nobles declined and those of the kings increased. Serfs found ways to leave the feudal estates and live in the towns as free men. These changes all had a part in the development of modern nations in Europe.

18

France Becomes a Nation

THE KINGDOM OF CHARLEMAGNE CHANGES

Land of France. If you look at the map on page 245, you will see that France has natural boundaries on all sides except the northeast and the east. The English Channel, the Bay of Biscay, and the Mediterranean Sea provide protection on the northwest, on the west, and on the south. The Pyrenees Mountains form a natural barrier between France and Spain to the southwest, while the mighty Alps separate France from Italy on the southeast.

Charles the Bald. When the empire of Charlemagne was divided among his grandsons, *Charles the Bald* became ruler of that part we today call France. Charles tried to rule France according to the example set by his famous grandfather, but this territory was not easy to rule, and Charles was beset with difficulties. The Vikings from the north were constantly invading France. They destroyed crops, burned towns, and carried away prisoners and valuables. Southern France was often attacked by Moslem invaders from Spain and North Africa. Frequently, Charles the Bald was also at war with his brothers who held the lands to the east of his kingdom.

* * * * *

By looking at the map of France on page 245, can you tell why the country was so vulnerable to enemy attacks? From which directions might invasions come?

* * * * *

The Nobles. The great landowning nobles in France were very powerful, and the common people

239

turned to them for protection against the various invaders. Thus, Charles the Bald and his successors had little power because the nobles were often more powerful than the king.

In France, each feudal lord or noble governed his land according to his own laws. Each district had its own kind of money. You can easily see that while the descendants of Charlemagne called themselves kings, they had a difficult time trying to make the nobles obey them.

During these troublesome times, a man named *Odo*, by warding off the Viking attacks, gained great favor among the French nobles. At the time Odo became famous, the king of France was *Charles the Fat*. As his name suggests, Charles was a weak and lazy ruler. The nobles of France had no intention of obeying any king. The nobles, however, admired Odo, so they took the throne away from Charles the Fat and chose Odo, who was the count of Paris, as their king in 888. This happened during the time that Alfred the Great ruled in England.

A New Line of Kings. For the next one hundred years after Odo had ruled, many nobles in France supported the descendants of Charlemagne as king. Other nobles sup-

ported the descendants of Odo. Naturally, there was much warfare. At last in 987, the French nobles chose as king a man named *Hugh* (hū) who was the count of Paris and the duke of France. The new king was a grandnephew of Odo. Because Hugh always wore a cape, he became known as *Hugh Capet* (kā′pĕt). Thus, the descendants of Hugh who ruled France came to be called the *Capetian* (kȧ·pē′shăn) kings.

The Capetian kings were interested in uniting all of France into one strong nation. In order to do this, they realized they had to lessen the power of the nobles and increase the power of the king.

First Strong Capetian King. In the year 1180, *Philip Augustus* came to the throne of France as a boy of fifteen. At that time, Henry II was king of England. Many of the policies of Philip were similar to those of Henry. Henry II was also duke of Normandy and his wife was heiress to other great areas in France. This made Henry a vassal of Philip, king of France, as well as being king of England.

In France, as in the other countries of Europe during the Middle Ages, there were three classes of people other than serfs. The clergy made up the first class, or *First Es-*

tate as they were called in France. The nobles belonged to the second class, or the *Second Estate*. The common people who lived in the cities and the towns made up the third class, or *Third Estate*.

Philip Augustus set out to weaken the power of the nobles, or Second Estate. To do this, he gave many favors to the other two estates, or classes. Philip appointed outstanding churchmen to important positions. The Church, in turn, was interested in uniting all France under the king, in order to stop the constant wars between the feudal nobles.

Philip Augustus and his successors encouraged the serfs to buy their freedom and to live in towns where they could engage in trade and industry. This process deprived the lords of their field workers and potential soldiers.

To many of the towns, Philip Augustus granted charters which gave them certain rights and liberties. He protected the seaports against pirates. As a result of these measures, trade flourished, and the cities became prosperous. In return for his protection and fair treatment, the towns paid taxes to Philip and recognized him as king. In gaining the support of the towns, Philip Augustus lessened the power of the feudal nobles on whose lands the towns had grown up. With the taxes which he collected from the towns, he hired troops. He used these troops to subdue the feudal nobles who refused to obey him, and he was, thereby, able to make the nobles pay taxes.

* * * * *

Was there a similarity in the way that the power of the kings in England and France developed at this time? Why or why not?

* * * * *

The three French estates formed a council called the Estates-General. In the late Middle Ages, kings began to invite leaders from each estate to discuss legislative and financial matters.

FIRST ESTATE

SECOND ESTATE

THIRD ESTATE

France Is Enlarged. There was always a great rivalry between Philip Augustus and his chief vassal, Henry II of England. Henry II was, however, too strong for Philip to challenge. After the death of Henry, Philip Augustus was busy with a Crusade to the Holy Land. This Crusade was led by Philip Augustus and the new king of England, Richard the Lionhearted.

When Richard died, and his brother John became king of England, Philip succeeded in capturing Normandy and other English holdings in France from John.

Through his own marriage and by the marriage of his son, who later became *Louis VIII*, Philip gained new territory for France. Thus, Philip brought two thirds of France under his personal rule. Then the king was more powerful than any noble in France.

A Popular King. Perhaps the most popular of all French kings was *Louis IX*, son of Louis VIII and the grandson of Philip Augustus. Louis IX was a remarkably wise, just, and capable ruler. He was very religious, and attended Mass frequently. He spent a great deal of time in prayer, fasting, and penance. His concern for the poor was remarkable. He often fed the poor from his own table, and then he, the king, ate what remained. He washed the feet of the poor, in imitation of Our Lord. He founded many hospitals which gave special care and attention to the blind and the lepers.

Louis was a brave soldier. Twice

King Louis IX was one of the most virtuous kings of France. He was a pious, generous, and just ruler who was popular with the French people. He often shared his table with the poor.

he led Crusades to free the Holy Land from the Turks. During the Seventh Crusade, Louis gave up his life. Very shortly thereafter the Church declared him a saint. To this day he is referred to as *St. Louis*.

St. Louis was a lover of justice. Like Henry II of England, he believed that the feudal courts conducted by the nobles were often unfair. In the feudal courts, a man often had to fight a duel in order to prove his innocence. Like his grandfather, Philip Augustus, St. Louis wanted to abolish all unnecessary fighting. St. Louis offered the people the opportunity of settling their disputes in the king's courts, where the old Roman method of trial was used. There all cases were decided by the law and not by combat. Louis also established a regular system for appealing the judgments in all cases in the feudal courts to the royal, or king's, courts.

A Handsome King. When the grandson of St. Louis, *Philip IV*, became king of France, he found a well-organized kingdom. Philip IV was so handsome that he was called *Philip the Fair*. He proved to be an able king as well as a handsome one.

He created a national army. He encouraged all classes of the people to enlist in the king's army, and

In medieval trials by combat (above), the strongest man always won. The modern justice of our court system (below) owes much to reforms made by Henry II and Louis IX.

The Estates-General, although somewhat similar to English Parliament, never really gained power. By the time of Louis XI, the king was asked to govern without the Estates-General.

paid his soldiers from the royal treasury. This was a great blow to the feudal lords.

The royal courts and the national army were an added expense for the king's treasury. So Philip introduced a new system of taxation by which every person in the kingdom was obliged to pay taxes to the royal treasury.

The Estates-General. The reign of Philip was important for the first meeting of the *Estates-General*. The first Estates-General was an assembly similar to the first English Parliament. As the name, Estates-General, suggests, this assembly was made up of representatives of all three classes, or estates. Edward I of England had called his Model Parliament together in 1295 so that English freemen might agree to his plans for taxation. It was in 1302, seven years later, that Philip the Fair called a meeting of the first Estates-General in France for the same purpose.

When the Estates-General first met, it was very similar to the English Parliament. However, important differences developed. The English Parliament separated into two houses. The Estates–General divided into three groups, each estate voting by itself. The English Parliament became very powerful. The Estates-General never became as important. The members of the Estates–General only met when summoned by the French king. They were not able to make laws. Most of the later kings of France ruled without ever calling a meeting of the Estates-General.

A CENTURY LONG WAR

France and England. Even though the English had lost most of their French territory during the reign of King John, the English kings continued to be feudal lords of the duchy of *Guienne* (gü·ē′yĕn′) in southern France. In this way, the English king continued to be a vassal of the French king.

In the year 1328, *Charles IV*, the last of Philip the Fair's sons, died leaving no son to inherit the throne. A nephew of Philip the Fair, *Philip VI*, was chosen as king of France. At that time, the king of England was *Edward III*, a grandson of Philip the Fair. Edward III declared that for this reason he had a better claim to the French throne than did Philip VI.

Philip VI showed little respect for the rights of the English king, Edward III, in Guienne. Philip also sent French troops to England to aid the Scots in a rebellion against the English. So Edward invaded France in order to make himself king of that country.

This conflict between the English and the French was the beginning of a period of warfare which continued for more than a hundred years. Those long years of war and bloodshed are known as the *Hundred Years' War*. The Hundred Years' War was really not one war. It was a series of wars and periods of peace lasting through the reigns of five French and five English kings.

FRANCE
AT THE TIME OF JOAN OF ARC

FRENCH TERRITORY UNDER
ENGLISH AUTHORITY

The Longbow. Large numbers of English foot-soldiers were armed with a new weapon, the longbow, at the beginning of the Hundred Years' War. The longbow was six feet in length—taller than the man who carried it. It had such force that an arrow shot from it could pierce a suit of armor 200 yards away. A skilled archer could shoot as many as twelve arrows a minute.

The English began their battles by sending an immense shower of arrows against the heavily armored enemy knights, who were on horseback. This usually caused confusion in the ranks of the knights, and they would flee in disorder. As you can see, the use of the longbow in battle was a direct cause of the decline in importance of the heavily armored knights.

During the Hundred Years' War the French invented a cannon which could be used to make a breach in the wall of a town or a castle. With these cannons, the feudal castle was no longer a strong fortress that could resist all attack. This caused a great change not only in warfare, but in the life of the times as well.

* * * * *

What, do you believe, were some of the important effects of these changes in the methods of warfare?

* * * * *

French knights, wearing heavy and awkward armor, were no match for the English longbowmen during the Hundred Years' War.

St. Joan of Arc. As the war progressed, the English made great gains, defeating the French in battle after battle. This, however, was destined to be changed through the influence of a simple French peasant, or serf, a girl named *Joan*.

Joan was born in the village of *Domremy-la-Pucelle* (dônr′mē′ là pü′sĕl′) in eastern France, in the year 1412. It was there that she spent her childhood. Joan was very religious, and spent much time in prayer. As she grew older, she began to be concerned about the troubles of her country. One day when she was thirteen, she was startled by the sound of voices calling to her. *St. Michael the Archangel*, *St. Catherine*, and *St. Margaret* appeared to her from time to time. They told her that she must save her country from the English, and that she must see that the *Dauphin* (dô′fĭn) was crowned king of France.

The Dauphin was the heir to the throne of France. The name Dauphin was originally the title of the lord of *Dauphine*, a province in France. It had become customary to confer the title of Dauphin on the eldest son of the king of France, just as it was customary in England to name the eldest son of the king as the Prince of Wales. *Charles*, who was the Dauphin of France, was doing nothing to arouse his people to resist the English.

Joan could hardly believe that she had been chosen to save France: the voices kept insisting, "It is God who commands it." When Joan was sixteen, she became convinced that she must carry out the commands of the saints who appeared to her. She determined to go to the Dauphin and to raise an army to fight the English. She believed that she must see that Charles, the Dauphin, received the crown as king of France. Joan's parents and friends tried to persuade her to give up her ideals, but she refused. She felt she must carry out the will of God. When she asked various nobles and officials to take her to the Dauphin, they laughed at her.

Joan's Victory. At length the English were in possession of almost all northern France and were besieging the city of *Orléans* (ôr′lā·äN′). Only then did the officials agree to let Joan see the Dauphin.

The Dauphin, however, continued to delay in taking action to save France. Finally, the situation at Orléans, where the Dauphin was besieged by the English, became desperate. The common people who had come to have great faith in Joan, begged the Dauphin to give

Guided by her strong faith in the voices and visions that advised her, Joan of Arc mounted a horse and set out, at the age of sixteen, to save France from the English.

her a chance to save France. So it was that Joan led the French against the English at Orléans. She was dressed in armor and carried the banner of France—a white banner decorated with yellow lilies. Joan's great faith and her brave spirit gave the French soldiers new courage. Under her leadership, the French defeated the English. Joan was afterwards referred to as the *Maid of Orléans*.

After her victory at Orléans, Joan led Charles to Reims. There in the great cathedral, she saw him crowned as *Charles VII*, king of France, in the year 1429. The vic-

tory won by Joan awakened in the French people a great feeling of patriotism for their country and for their king. The French began to defeat the English.

Some of the officers of the French army became jealous of Joan's success as she led the armies to victory after victory. During a battle some of these men allowed her to fall into the hands of the hostile, pro-English duke of Burgundy. The duke of Burgundy sold his famous captive to the English. King Charles made no attempt to rescue Joan, the young girl who had brought him victory and the French crown.

Martyrdom of Joan of Arc. Young Joan was not treated as an ordinary prisoner of war. Instead she was accused of witchcraft. Her captors declared that she had gained her strength at Orléans not from God but from Satan. She was tried and sentenced to death. In the market place of *Rouen* (rōō·än′), the courageous girl was tied to a stake and burned to death. She asked for a cross which she held before her eyes, and continued to pray the name of Jesus to give her strength during her ordeal. So bravely and nobly did she face death that even her executioners were moved. One English soldier who witnessed her death cried out, "We are lost for we have burned a saint."

Exit the English. Indeed, the English cause was lost. Aroused by the cruel death of the Maid of Orléans, the French soldiers went on to win many battles. In 1453, the English lost the last of their great holdings in France. Of all their vast lands there, they retained only the town of *Calais* (kȧ′lĕ′) on the English Channel. The Hundred Years' War finally came to an end, and with it came the end of England's attempt to rule France.

Today, the heroic Joan of Arc is everywhere spoken of with reverence. The Catholic Church raised Joan of Arc to sainthood in 1920. Her faith, her courage, her service to France, and her tragic death have inspired not only the people of France, but many great writers, painters, and sculptors.

England and France were both

At a time when Joan needed their help most, Charles and the French people appeared conveniently to have forgotten her. She was burned at the stake in the market place of Rouen in 1431.

exhausted at the end of this long struggle. As most of the fighting had been on French soil, the people of France had suffered the greatest loss.

* * * * *

Do you think that England's loss of territory in France was a good thing for both countries? If so, why?

* * * * *

The Black Death. A great plague, called the *Black Death,* swept across Europe during the middle 1300's. English soldiers returning from France brought it to England with them. Many millions of people died; almost one half of the entire population of Europe was destroyed. When priests went to help the afflicted, they were often stricken with the disease. In some sections of Europe, there was not a single priest alive when the plague was over. Entire monasteries and convents were wiped out.

The Black Death and the Hundred Years' War each provided a great blow to the feudal system. You have read how the new methods of warfare reduced the importance of armored knights and feudal castles. The king of France had developed a new national army and did not need the support of the feudal nobles. Labor was so scarce after the Black Death, that workers were able to secure much higher wages and better working conditions. Many serfs were able to buy their freedom and many moved into the towns. There was hardly a serf left in France at the end of the Hundred Years' War. Most of the people were townspeople or free peasants.

THE KING BECOMES ALL-POWERFUL

Supreme Rulers. After the Hundred Years' War, the kings of France were absolute monarchs. This growth of power was a gradual process. Philip Augustus, St. Louis, and Philip the Fair each had in various ways increased the power and influence of the king. There was also no real threat to the king's power since the nobles were without armies and strongholds. The Estates-General was weak, and the king was supported by direct taxes and a standing army.

Louis XI. After the death of Charles VII, his son *Louis XI* became king of France. Louis was far from kingly in appearance. He was a bony, awkward man with a disposition as ugly as his looks. He had a long, thin nose, deep-set eyes, and hollow cheeks. He wore rough, plain clothing. His one ambition was to improve his position as absolute ruler of France.

In order to accomplish his purpose, he was continually weaving plots against his own nobles as well as the other monarchs of Europe. His plots appeared to go in all directions like the web of a spider. For this reason he was called the *Spider King*.

By his plottings, Louis was able to add several other regions of France to the royal domain. Only the great independent duchy of Brittany remained outside of his control. However, *Charles VIII*, the son of the Spider King, married the heiress of the duchy of Brittany. When Charles VIII died in 1498, France was a united kingdom. *Louis XII*, who followed Charles VIII to the throne, was the first king to be the absolute ruler of all France.

* * * * *

Are there any countries in the world today that have absolute rulers?

* * * * *

Summing Up. When Charlemagne died, his empire was distributed among his three grandsons. Charles the Bald took the part that is now called France. With enemies on all

A sly and unscrupulous king, Louis XI would break promises as easily as he made them if it suited his needs of the moment.

sides he failed to keep order. People asked powerful nobles to protect them. In this way, feudalism developed in France.

In later years Philip Augustus, a descendant of Hugh Capet, united much of France into one nation. Philip gave favors to Churchmen and townspeople. These groups helped the king get a good army and force the nobles to obey him. The Estates–General, although it never became powerful, helped unify France, too.

The Hundred Years' War with England seemed lost until Saint Joan of Arc helped the French win. After the war the king forbade private armies and taxed all the land. The noble's power was thus broken and by 1498, when Louis XII came to the throne, all France was united as one nation under a supreme king.

FOR BETTER UNDERSTANDING

Checking Up

1. Describe the natural boundaries of France.

2. What was the origin of the Capetian line of kings?

3. What was the feudal relationship of King Henry II of England to Philip Augustus?

4. How did Philip Augustus weaken the power of the nobles?

5. Describe the character of St. Louis IX.

6. Describe the organization of the Estates-General.

7. What were the causes of the Hundred Years' War?

8. How did St. Joan of Arc save France?

9. Explain what is meant when it is said that the kings of France were absolute rulers.

10. Identify each of the following dates and tell its importance: 987, 1180, 1302, 1453, 1498.

Yesterday and Today

1. Recall some of the nicknames or colorful descriptive titles given to the French kings. Do we call our Presidents and other leaders by such terms?

2. A number of the French provinces, or states, were mentioned in this chapter. Make a list of them, and see if you can recall any modern happenings that occurred in each.

Persons, Places, and Terms

Identify: Charles the Bald, Odo, Charles the Fat, Hugh Capet, Philip Augustus, Louis VIII, St. Louis IX, Philip the Fair, Charles IV, Philip VI, St. Joan of Arc, Louis XI, Charles VIII.

Locate: Paris, Guienne, Domremy-la-Pucelle, Orléans, Reims, Rouen.

Define: Estates–General, Hundred Years' War, longbow, Dauphin, Black Death.

Interesting Things to Do

1. Our famous Statue of Liberty is a gift from the French people to the American people. Try to find out how the statue was planned, paid for, and set up on Liberty Island in New York Harbor.

2. Your group can make a report to put in your scrapbook. Have your report show how the French people live today. Here are several things you may want to learn about them:

    a. the names of important French leaders,

    b. the way the people dress,

    c. the kind of music they enjoy,

    d. the kinds of food the people eat,

    e. their favorite games and sports.

3. Make a list of towns and cities in the United States named after important people or places of France.

19

Two Nations: Spain and Portugal

SPAIN BECOMES A NATION

Southwest of France. To the southwest of France lies the *Iberian* (ĭ·bḗr´ĭ·ăn) *Peninsula* on which there are two countries, Spain and Portugal.

The Iberian Peninsula is surrounded on three sides by bodies of water. The Bay of Biscay lies northeast of the peninsula; the Atlantic Ocean is west of the peninsula; and the Mediterranean Sea forms the eastern and most of the southern boundary of the peninsula. The lofty Pyrenees Mountains on the northeast divide the Iberian Peninsula from the rest of Europe. Because of these mountains, trade and travel between the peninsula and France have always been difficult. The many natural boundaries of the Iberian Peninsula can be seen by looking at the map shown on page 254.

On the south, Spain is very close to Africa. In fact, at the narrowest point Spain is separated from Africa only by the narrow Strait of Gibraltar. This has made it easy for invaders to enter Spain from Africa.

Ancient Days. The people of ancient Phoenicia traded with the Celtic tribes who lived in Spain. When the Phoenician colony at Carthage became powerful in the Mediterranean area, it founded many important trading centers in southern Spain. In time, most of southern Spain became a Carthaginian province.

The Punic Wars. Spain was a battleground between Rome and Carthage during the Punic Wars. It was in Spain that Hannibal prepared for his famous expedition into Italy. Rome defeated Carthage, and Spain became a Roman province.

THE IBERIAN PENINSULA
IN 1490

Bay of Biscay

FRANCE

Atlantic Ocean

León

KINGDOM

OF

CASTILE

AND

LEÓN

KINGDOM OF PORTUGAL

Salamanca

Madrid

Toledo

Lisbon

Cordova

Seville

ANDALUSIA

MOORISH
Granada
KINGDOM OF GRANADA

Gibraltar

K. OF NAVARRE

Pyrenees Mts.

KINGDOM

OF Barcelona

ARAGON

Valencia

Mediterranean Sea

MOSLEM STATES IN AFRICA

In time, the people of Spain dropped much of their own language and adopted Latin. Two modern languages, *Spanish* and *Portuguese*, have developed from this blending of the older Iberian tongues with ancient Latin.

While Spain was a Roman province, its people were converted to the Catholic religion. Later, because of their desire to spread the Catholic Faith, Spanish and Portuguese explorers came to America. They were among the earliest voyagers to our continent.

The Barbarians and Spain. As the barbarian tribes began to overrun Western Europe, some of them made their way into Spain. These tribes wandered through the peninsula, pillaging and destroying. The Vandals were in control of Spain for a time. They later crossed into Africa, leaving the name *Andalusia* (ăn′dȧ·lōō′zhȧ), or *Vandal land*, to a region of southern Spain.

The Visigoths, or West Goths, invaded and finally became masters of Spain. They set up a kingdom and brought the whole peninsula under their rule. These Goths mingled with the Romanized inhabitants of Spain and adopted their language.

The Visigoth king had very little power. He was unable to control his nobles. This condition, as you have read, existed in other countries in the early Middle Ages. The Visigoth kings might have been able to unite their country, as did France and England, had not the Mohammedans from North Africa invaded Spain. These Mohammedans overthrew the kingdom of the Visigoths in the year 711.

Other Conquests. You may remember reading that the Mohammedans had conquered all of northern Africa; that they had crossed into Spain and soon conquered the entire peninsula; and that they had even crossed the Pyrenees and threatened to subdue all of Europe. They were finally stopped in 732 by Charles Martel and the Franks at the Battle of Tours. Charlemagne, the grandson of Charles Martel, drove the Mohammedans back across the Pyrenees and freed the northern part of Spain from their control. It took another seven hundred years, however, for the Spaniards to drive the Moslems from the peninsula.

The *Moors* (mŏŏrz), which is the name the Spaniards gave to the Moslems who came from northern Africa, have left many reminders of their long stay in Spain. The city of *Cordova* (kôr′dŏ·vȧ) became their capital, and they made it one of the most beautiful and thriving cities in the world.

You may remember reading in Chapter 9 how the Mohammedans established great civilizations. The Moors brought new goods and ideas to the people of Spain and Europe. They founded the first universities in Spain, for example, and constructed beautiful buildings, many of which can still be seen today.

Highly ornate geometric designs of Moorish architecture developed when Islamic law prevented artists from making life-like images of objects. The walls and ceiling of the Alhambra at Granada, Spain, are painted with foliage colored in red, blue, and gold.

Northern Spanish Kingdoms. In the northern section of Spain, which had been freed from the Moors by Charlemagne, several small Christian kingdoms developed. Among these were the kingdoms of *León* (lā·ôn'), *Castile* (kăs·tēl'), *Navarre* (na·vär'), and *Aragon* (är'a·gŏn).

The kings of León fought their way down the west coast of the Iberian Peninsula and freed the area that later became the kingdom of Portugal. The kings of Aragon were successful in conquering much of the peninsula's eastern coast. The Aragonese began a prosperous trade with other sections of the Mediterranean region and built a strong navy to protect their merchant ships. The kingdom of Castile was extended through the area in the center of the peninsula. As the Castilian armies advanced against the Moors, the Christian nobles erected a line of strong castles in order to secure their gains and hold the Moors in check. The kingdom was called Castile, because it was a kingdom of so many castles. Over the years, the Moors were gradually driven back. In the year 1212, after being defeated, the Moors were confined to the small area of *Granada* (gra·nä'da) in the south of Spain.

SPAIN IS UNITED

Ferdinand and Isabella. The marriage of *Princess Isabella* to *Prince Ferdinand* in 1469 was a very important event for Spain. The beautiful and talented Isabella was the sister of the king of Castile. Ferdinand was the son of the king of Aragon. Through their marriage Castile and Aragon were joined.

*   *   *   *   *

Can you think of any marriages of nobility that have helped to unite other countries about which you have studied?

*   *   *   *   *

Queen Isabella was a woman of remarkable courage and determination. She was a very devoted Catholic. Many of the great actions of her life were influenced by her desire to spread the Faith of Christ.

Ferdinand and Isabella together were wise and able rulers. Their first great project was to completely drive the Moors from Spain. Spaniards from every corner of their realm joined the armies of Ferdinand and Isabella. Christian knights from other countries also gave their aid. For ten long years, the Spaniards fought the Moors. On

St. Dominic's constitution for his Order is considered an exceptional legislative work.

January 2, 1492, the Moors surrendered their last stronghold—the city of Granada. The entire Iberian Peninsula was then under the control of the Spanish monarchs.

Land of Saints. The people of Spain then set out to develop their newly united country into a great Catholic nation. Spain had already given to the Church many great saints. One of these was *St. Dominic*, who founded the Dominican Order and who gave to us the rosary. Many other saints came from Spain in the century after the expulsion of the Moors. These included *St. Teresa of Ávila—St. Ignatius Loyola*, founder of the Society of Jesus—and *St. Francis Xavier*, the Apostle to the Far East.

The defeat of the Moors at Granada, early in 1492, was an event which was important for Americans of today. When the victorious Spanish soldiers entered the city of Granada, *Christopher Columbus* was with them. A few months later, Isabella was able to provide Columbus with the funds necessary for his famous voyage.

Absolute Kings. Ferdinand and Isabella succeeded in uniting the entire peninsula, with the exception of the independent kingdom of Portugal. They then wanted to unify the people into one nation. In order to bring this about, they planned to weaken the power of the feudal nobles. So Ferdinand and Isabella controlled the number of castles built, they punished warring nobles, and they established their own military force to maintain law and order.

The king and queen also formed a sort of an alliance with the towns

St. Teresa of Avila, zealous Carmelite reformer, wrote autobiographical books as well as spiritual and mystical books.

against the nobles. This alliance worked effectively in the Spanish parliament.

The *Cortes* (kôr'tĕz), or Spanish parliament, like the French Estates-General, never became important. It was, however, in 1188 that men from the towns were added to the Cortes of the kingdom of León. Ferdinand and Isabella continued to favor the townsmen in the Cortes of united Spain.

* * * * *

Can you check to see in which kingdom the townspeople were first represented in a king's council, León or England?

* * * * *

In many important questions, the townspeople supported the king and queen against the nobles. Thus, in time, the Spanish kings became absolute monarchs like their kingly neighbors in France.

PORTUGAL BECOMES A NATION

Early Times. Spain and Portugal not only share the same peninsula—for a long time they shared the same history. Both had belonged to Carthage, both were under Roman rule, and both had been overrun by the barbarians and Moors.

All these invasions and changes in rulers had less effect upon Portugal than they did upon Spain. If you look at the map of the Iberian Peninsula on page 254, you can see why this was true. Portugal lies in the extreme western part of the peninsula. None of the invaders approached from that direction. The Carthaginians invaded the peninsula from the south. The Romans came from the east. The barbarians came from the north and

east. The Moors came from the south. So while Spain was the center of each of the invasions, Portugal was merely on the western edge.

When the Christian kingdoms in the north—León, Castile, Aragon, and others—began to push back the Moors, Portugal was a border fief of the kingdom of León. You will remember that Christian knights from many countries came to aid the Spaniards in expelling the Moors.

Among these knights was *Henry*, count of Burgundy. Henry did not return again to his native land. Instead he stayed in Spain and in the year 1094 married *Theresa*, a daughter of the king of León.

As a dowry Theresa's father gave

her Portugal. So it was that Henry of Burgundy became the count of Portugal. Henry was then the vassal of the king of León. Henry and his descendants not only made Portugal independent of León, but made it a separate kingdom. Henry's son, *Alfonso* (ăl·fŏn′sō) *I*, became the first king of Portugal in 1139.

By the year 1262, Portugal had succeeded in driving out the Moors. This was more than two hundred years before they were finally driven from Spain.

Nation by the Sea. While Spain was busy trying to expel the Moors, the rulers of Portugal were able to set up a strong kingdom along the western edge of the Iberian Peninsula. With such a long sea coast the people of Portugal naturally turned to the sea to make a living both as fishermen and traders. At a very early date, merchants from Portugal traded with England. Venetian merchants on their way to the cities of northern Europe stopped and traded with the Portuguese.

*   *   *   *   *

In what ways do you suppose Portugal's trading helped make her a free land?

*   *   *   *   *

Besides building up their commerce, the people of Portugal built a language of their own. They took words from the languages of the various people who came to live in Portugal.

The Portuguese also became bold and courageous sailors, and they developed their own trade and commerce. In another chapter you will read how the Portuguese made many contributions to the science of navigation. They also became among the most important explorers of the New World.

Summing Up. The countries of Spain and Portugal are on the Iberian Peninsula. Over the years Phoenicians, Greeks, Romans, barbarian tribes, and Moors came to the peninsula. Each of these groups settled on the land and had its part in developing these countries.

In 1492, the Moors were driven out by the united Spanish kingdoms under Ferdinand and Isabella. This was done nearly two-hundred and fifty years after the Moors were expelled from Portugal, which had become an independent country under Count Henry and his descendants.

Spain became a great Catholic country producing many saints and missionaries. Portugal became a nation of great traders and explorers, who led the way to the New World.

FOR BETTER UNDERSTANDING

Checking Up

1. Describe the natural boundaries of the Iberian Peninsula.

2. Who were the early inhabitants of Spain?

3. What were some of the important effects of the Roman conquest of Spain?

4. Did the Goths establish a strong government in Spain?

5. Tell how the Spaniards gradually drove the Moors from Spain.

6. Why was the marriage of Ferdinand and Isabella important?

7. Why was 1492 an important date for Spain?

8. How did Ferdinand and Isabella curb the power of the nobles?

9. Tell how Portugal became a separate kingdom.

10. What two modern languages are spoken on the Iberian Peninsula?

11. Identify and tell the importance of each of the following dates: 711, 1139, 1262, 1469, 1492.

Yesterday and Today

1. Make a list of the countries in the Western Hemisphere where the Spanish and Portuguese languages are spoken.

2. Find the names of several cities, rivers, and mountain ranges in our country that are of Spanish origin.

3. Use your classroom or library encyclopedia to find out what kind of governments Spain and Portugal have today. Who are the leaders of the governments and how do these governments differ from the type of government in the time of Ferdinand and Isabella and Alfonso I?

Persons, Places, and Terms

Identify: Ferdinand, Isabella, St. Dominic, St. Ignatius Loyola, St. Francis Xavier, Christopher Columbus, Henry of Burgundy, Theresa of León, Alfonso I.

Locate: Castile, Portugal, Pyrenees Mountains, Gibraltar, Andalusia, León, Cordova, Navarre, Aragon, Granada.

Define: Moors, Andalusia, Cortes, Castile.

Interesting Things to Do

1. Collect some pictures of Spain and Portugal for a bulletin board display. Be sure you use pictures that will show the various influences on the peninsula.

2. Although the Moors were in Spain and Portugal for only a few hundred years, they had a great influence on the culture of the two countries. Using reference books for further facts, make a list of contributions the Moors made to these countries.

20

Other Lands Become Nations

THE HOLY ROMAN EMPIRE

A Catholic Community. During the Middle Ages all the people of Europe belonged to one universal Church, the same Catholic Church to which you belong. The word *Catholic*, as you know, means *universal*. The people of the Middle Ages thought that they would have peace and order if everyone also belonged to one universal country, or empire.

The title of Roman Emperor had never entirely died out. You will remember that on Christmas Day in the year 800, the pope had placed a crown on the head of Charlemagne and hailed him as *Emperor of the Romans*. Charlemagne had united Western Europe into one empire and brought order out of the lawlessness that had disturbed Europe since the beginning of the barbarian invasions.

After the death of Charlemagne, his empire was divided among his three grandsons—Charles, Louis, and Lothair. Yet, the ideal of a single church and a single empire remained in the minds of many Europeans. This ideal was especially strong in the areas of Europe that now comprise modern Germany and Italy.

Louis of Germany. Of the three grandsons of Charlemagne, Louis II was the most capable. The brother of Charles and Lothair, he was the ruler of that section of Charlemagne's empire that we today call Germany. Louis's problems were similar to those of Charles the Bald in France. The fierce Vikings were a constant danger on the north. On the east and southeast were the Slavs and the Hungarians, who were continually trying to conquer Germany.

THE HOLY ROMAN EMPIRE
—— AT THE END OF THE ELEVENTH CENTURY

Louis also had difficulty with the great feudal lords in Germany. The people of Germany had for centuries given their loyalty to tribal leaders instead of to one central king. When threatened by invaders, they naturally looked to their local leaders for protection. At the time of Louis II, there were five great semi-independent states in Germany— *Bavaria* (bȧ·vâr'ĭ·ȧ), *Franconia* (frăng·kō'nĭ·ȧ), *Lorraine* (lǒ·rān'), *Saxony* (sak's'n·ĭ), and *Swabia* (swā'bĭ·ȧ). The dukes, as the lords of these duchies, or states, were called, were often at war with one another and with the king.

Henry the Emperor. After the last of the family of Charlemagne died in Germany, the great dukes de-

cided to elect one of their own number as king. In this matter the German dukes were like the French nobles who elected Odo. They had no intention of obeying any king.

Nevertheless, in the year 919, *Henry* the duke of Saxony was elected king by the other German dukes. When the messengers went to tell Henry of his election they found him riding out to hunt. On his arm he had his falcon. The falcon, which is a bird of prey, was used in the hunting of birds, or *fowl* as they were called. For this reason and because he liked to hunt, the new king of Germany became known as *Henry the Fowler*.

Henry the Fowler did not attempt to weaken the power of the

other dukes. He needed their help against the Northmen and against the Slavs and the Hungarians. While Henry did not succeed in establishing himself as absolute king in Germany, his wisdom and courage caused the dukes to look with more respect upon the office of king. Thus, Henry prepared the way for his successors to build a strong united kingdom.

Henry's Son. In the year 936, Henry the Fowler was succeeded as king by his son, *Otto*. Otto was determined to rid Germany of invaders. He defeated the Hungarians, who then settled down in their own lands and developed the kingdom of Hungary.

Otto also defeated the Slavs. Then he organized the entire border of Germany in such a way that the country was freed from the threat of invasion. He adopted a policy that had been used by Charlemagne. He established a series of marches, or marks. These were military districts that served as a defense against any possible invader. Some of these marches became the foundation of countries. For instance, the *East Mark* became the modern country of *Austria*.

Otto was determined to unite his kingdom and to make all Germany obey his rule. He was untiring in his efforts to accomplish this purpose. By one means or another, but mostly through warfare, Otto succeeded in taking the duchies away from the noble families who ruled them. He gave these duchies to nobles of his own choosing. These new dukes were his friends and relatives.

* * * * *

Was Otto's policy of appointing his friends and relatives to high positions a good one? Explain why or why not.

* * * * *

If Otto had given all his attention to ruling Germany, perhaps Germany would have developed into a strong nation before France or England or Spain did. Events in Italy, however, caused Otto to turn his attention to that land, which was on the southern border of Germany.

Italian Rivalries. During this period, in the central part of Italy, rival Roman families struggled for power in the states near Rome. Mohammedans controlled Sicily and southern Italy. On the whole, there was great confusion and disorder throughout the entire peninsula.

In Italy, the king had been killed and a rival had set himself up on the throne. *Adelaide* (ăd'ĕ·lād), the widow of the king, fled to Otto for protection. Otto took up Adelaide's cause and led an army across the Alps. In 951, he deposed the man who had seized the throne, and then Otto married Adelaide. As a result of this marriage, Otto was crowned king of Italy.

During Otto's campaign in Italy, affairs did not go so well in Germany. Otto's son by his first wife tried to make himself king, so Otto was forced to rush home from Italy. Once home Otto defeated his rebellious son and restored order.

Emperor of the Romans. In 961, trouble again broke out in Italy. Otto once again led an army across the Alps and restored peace and order. The next year, *Pope John XII* crowned Otto *Emperor of the Romans* using the same crown with which Charlemagne had once been crowned.

The crowning of Otto as emperor in 962 revived the hope that the old Roman Empire and the empire of Charlemagne could actually be restored. Otto resolved to be emperor in fact as well as in name. He promised to protect the pope. The pope in turn acknowledged that he was Otto's subject and swore to be loyal to the emperor. Otto's empire began to be called the *Holy Roman Empire* because it seemed to fulfill the hope of One Church and One Empire.

Otto and his successors were never able to unite the peoples of Germany and Italy. The Romans had never conquered the lands east of the Rhine River. As a result, the Germans had a language and customs which were very different from those in the Romanized parts of Europe. In appearance, in manner, and in interests, the German and Latin peoples were also different.

Ruling over two such different

Otto, crowned emperor by the pope, ruled over a Holy Roman Empire which turned out to be "neither holy, nor Roman, nor an empire." It was a group of rulers in central Europe that quarreled continually with Otto and with each other over religious and political affairs.

peoples would at best be difficult. The high Alps separating the two parts of the empire made it an impossible task. While the emperor was trying to keep order on one side of this high mountain barrier, his enemies on the other side were sure to take advantage of his absence.

THE STRUGGLE BETWEEN POPES AND EMPERORS

Two Rulers. The Holy Roman Empire supposedly had two rulers —the emperor and the pope. Everyone was supposed to be loyal to both of these rulers. The pope was the head of the Church and was to rule over all Church matters. The emperor was to control all the affairs of government. This arrangement did not always work well. It was often very hard to decide whether a matter was the business of the pope or the emperor. The appointment of bishops came to be a continual cause of conflict between the pope and the emperor.

The bishops of the Church, as the successors of the apostles, are subject to the spiritual authority of the pope, who is the successor of St. Peter and the Vicar of Christ on earth. Their powers are the spiritual powers given to them by Christ. Their duties as leaders are to administer to the spiritual needs of the faithful in their dioceses.

As you have already read, the kings and emperors of the Middle Ages constantly sought the advice and assistance of churchmen. The churchmen were usually the best educated men in the various kingdoms. A king could rely on their loyalty to him.

The kings and emperors bestowed large areas of land upon the archbishops and bishops. Otto the Great, like the kings of England and France and Spain, tried to weaken the power of the dukes by giving more and more land to the bishops. The bishops were expected to rule their lands like feudal nobles. They even had to supply military support for the rulers. In Germany, some of the bishops acted as representatives of the emperor. They collected taxes, coined money, saw to it that the emperor's laws were enforced, and performed other duties as imperial officers.

This situation was not good for the Church. Many of the bishops were so busy governing their lands that they had little time for the spiritual needs of their people. Many excellent men held high positions in Church and State. However, unworthy men were often attracted to Churchly positions by the wealth and honors of the bishopric. These men sometimes bribed the king in order to secure an appointment. These people were guilty of the sin of *simony*, that is, the buying or selling of a sacred office.

In Germany, it was the custom when a bishop died that his successor be elected by the priests of his cathedral. Sometimes, an emperor would force the priests to elect the candidate of his choice. If the man elected was unworthy, great harm could be done to the Church.

Before a bishop took office, he took part in the ceremony of investiture. He was *invested*, or installed ceremonially with the symbols of his sacred office—the *crosier* (krō′zhĕr), *miter* (mī′tĕr), and the bishop's

ring. The emperor began to use the occasion to invest the bishop with a *sword* and *scepter* (sĕp′tĕr). These were the symbols of the civil power of the bishop over the lands given to him by the emperor.

The emperors began to combine both parts of the investiture ceremony. They insisted on presenting both sets of symbols to the new bishop. The popes and the Church did not like this practice, since it appeared as if the emperors were able to confer spiritual power and authority. Since the emperors were laymen, this practice came to be called *lay investiture*.

Gregory VII. The problem of lay investiture came to a real crisis when *Cardinal Hildebrand* (hĭl′dĕ·brănd) became *Pope Gregory VII* in the year 1073. Pope Gregory was a

Because they gave church officials large grants of land and sought their advice in secular affairs, emperors felt that the privilege of choosing and installing new bishops in office should be theirs. Below, a bishop goes through lay investiture at the hands of an emperor.

small man with a weak voice, but he had an iron will and tremendous courage.

As a young man, Hildebrand had become a Benedictine monk. He spent some time at the great Abbey of *Cluny* (klōō′nĭ) in eastern France. The monks of Cluny had dedicated themselves to the task of improving the spiritual lives of the people of Europe. They worked and prayed and preached to eliminate any evils that threatened the Church. These monks considered lay investiture to be the chief evil of their time.

Hildebrand determined to put the Cluny reforms into effect throughout the entire Church. Two years after his election as pope, he notified the Holy Roman Emperor and the kings of England and France that lay investiture was forbidden.

Henry IV. The greatest opposition to the pope's reforms came from the Holy Roman Emperor, who at that time was *Henry IV*. Henry ignored Pope Gregory's decree, which forbade anyone except the pope to appoint bishops. In other matters, Henry also refused to recognize the authority of the pope.

After a long disagreement, Pope Gregory excommunicated Henry in 1076 A.D. This meant that Henry was expelled from the Church and that no Catholic could have anything to do with him.

Henry saw that he was in danger of losing not only the imperial crown but also his kingdom in Germany. Even though it was midwinter, Henry hurried across the Alps into northern Italy. Hearing that the emperor was approaching, the pope fearing an attack went to a castle at *Canossa* (kä·nŏs′sá) for protection.

Henry went directly to Canossa. He did not come as an emperor with a large army. Henry arrived at the castle of Canossa clothed as a repentant sinner. For three days the emperor waited in the snow outside the castle, imploring the pope to forgive him. Then Gregory admitted Henry to his presence. Henry asked forgiveness and promised not to interfere with the election of bishops. The pope pardoned Henry and removed the ban of excommunication in the year 1077.

As soon as Henry felt that he had sufficient support among his people in Germany, he again ignored the pope's decrees. In 1080, the pope again excommunicated Henry. This time, however, Henry took a large army and marched into Italy. There he forced Gregory to flee, and soon afterward Gregory died.

The dispute over lay investiture reached a partial solution under *Pope Calixtus* (kȧ·lĭks′tŭs) *II* and *Emperor Henry V*, son of Henry IV. An agreement was drawn up in 1122 that was called the *Concordat of Worms* (kŏn·kôr′dät ŏv wûrmz). In the concordat, the emperor promised to permit free elections of bishops. He also promised to give up the practice of investing the new bishop with the ring and crosier. At the same time he was permitted to be present at the election of a bishop in order to make certain that the new bishop would be a loyal vassal. The emperor was also permitted to invest a bishop with the scepter.

* * * * *

How does the First Amendment of our Constitution affect relations between our government and religious groups?

* * * * *

THE EMPIRE DECLINES

Emperor with a Red Beard. About thirty years after the Concordat of Worms, a man named *Frederick* became emperor. The most remarkable thing about this emperor's appearance was his red beard. So he was nicknamed *Barbarossa* (bär′bȧ·rŏs′ȧ), which means *red beard*.

Frederick Barbarossa was a soldier and a knight who loved battle. He was also a capable ruler, strict with himself, and just to others. He brought peace and order to Germany. He destroyed the power of the great duchies by breaking them up into smaller fiefs. Land which never before had been tilled was cleared and made into farms. Frederick was very popular with the

Frederick Barbarossa, the red-bearded soldier, was one of the most brilliant of the Holy Roman emperors. He brought peace and order as well as agricultural advances to Germany.

people of Germany. On his way to the Third Crusade, with Richard the Lionhearted of England and Philip Augustus of France, he was drowned in a river in the year 1190. He was so popular in Germany that the people could not believe that he was dead. A legend grew up that he was only asleep in a cave and that his red beard continued to grow.

Failure in Italy. By Frederick Barbarossa's time, there had grown up in northern Italy a number of towns like *Milan* and *Genoa*. They had become prosperous by engaging in trade, and they were determined to be independent of the emperor. Frederick tried to force them to acknowledge him as their ruler and to pay tribute to him. The towns resisted so stubbornly that he was forced to give up his attempt to subdue them.

The central part of Italy was ruled by the pope and was called the *Papal States*. Frederick Barbarossa and his successors wanted to make Rome, in central Italy, the capital of the empire. Because of this, new quarrels broke out between the popes and emperors.

Southern Italy was no longer in the hands of the Mohammedans. A group of Norman knights had driven the Moslems out of that area and had set up a new Norman king-dom of Sicily and Naples around the year 1091. The area was known as the *Kingdom of Sicily* or the *Kingdom of Naples*. Naples was its capital city.

Before Frederick Barbarossa went on the Third Crusade, he thought of a plan which would bind the German and Italian sections of the empire together. It would also give the emperor a personal stronghold in southern Italy. Frederick arranged for his son to marry an Italian princess, the heiress to the kingdom of Sicily. But the marriage accomplished little. Frederick Barbarossa's son *Henry VI* died after a very short reign. Henry VI left as his heir a little son only three years old. This little son was named *Frederick* in honor of his grandfather, Frederick Barbarossa.

Frederick II. When he was two years old, Frederick was crowned king of Germany. At the age of four, he became king of Sicily and southern Italy. In Sicily, he established a splendid court to which he welcomed scholars of all nations. The boy-king learned to speak many languages—Italian, German, Latin, Arabic, Greek, and Hebrew. He liked to read and to write poetry, and he enjoyed carrying on discussions with scholars who visited him.

When Frederick reached manhood, he was invited to claim his heritage. He went north and was proclaimed Emperor Frederick II of the Holy Roman Empire.

Frederick returned to Sicily with the idea of making Italy and not Germany the leading state in the empire. In order to hold the loyalty of the German nobles, he granted them many privileges. In doing this he gave up many of his powers as emperor in Germany. No other emperor ever gained the power and authority which his grandfather, Frederick Barbarossa, had held in Germany.

Frederick II was not successful in Italy either. He engaged in a series of wars with the Papal States and the northern cities, which had formed the *Lombard League*. After

his death in 1250, Frederick's sons attempted to carry on his policies. They had very little power and even their possessions in Sicily were taken from them.

The Holy Roman Empire had never been a strong empire. After the death of Frederick II, it was even less an empire than it had been before. The title of emperor was still held by the German kings, who had little power. None of them seriously attempted to again make themselves real rulers in Italy.

After Frederick II. After the emperors withdrew from the Italian peninsula, the peoples of Italy did not unite into one nation. The northern part of Italy was dominated by the great cities of *Milan*, *Venice*, and *Florence.* In the south, the kingdom of Sicily, or Naples, was in the hands of the French and later the Spaniards. The popes continued to rule the Papal States in central Italy. The popes always wanted to be independent of any other government, and because the Church is universal, it does not wish to be part of a particular nation. Even today the pope is an independent sovereign who rules over a section of Rome that is an independent state called Vatican City.

The position of the emperors in Germany was also weakened. For

MEDIEVAL ITALY

St. Gall
The Alps
Milan
Bobbio
Genoa
Venice
Bologna
Florence
Sienna
ITALY
PAPAL STATES
Adriatic Sea
CORSICA (To Genoa)
Rome
Monte Cassino
KINGDOM OF NAPLES
Naples
SARDINIA
Tyrrhenian Sea
Palermo
SICILY
Mediterranean Sea

twenty years there was no emperor at all. Then, the imperial title was taken over by the *Hapsburg* (hăps′bûrg) family. These nobles, from an area that today is part of southern Germany, Switzerland, and Austria, came to dominate the empire. Their descendants, many of whom you will read about, came to dominate many kingdoms in Europe. The empire itself became a loose confederation divided into about three hundred small states— duchies, marks, and free cities.

OTHER NATIONS DEVELOP

The Swiss Nation. The region that was the Roman province of *Helvetia* (hĕl·vē′shĭ·à) for over four centuries was composed of small city-states and villages set in the valleys of the Alps and *Jura* (jo͞or′à) Mountains.

The Swiss city-states became part of feudal Germany under the Holy Roman Empire. The German emperor, however, was far away, and the Swiss villages were so isolated that the people lived much as they chose. All this was changed when *Count Rudolph* of Hapsburg, a ruler in nearby Austria, became Holy Roman Emperor in 1273. As a result, three little *cantons*, as the Swiss city-states are called, near *Lake Luzerne* (lŭ·sûrn′) were afraid that they would lose what independence they had. So they joined together in 1291 to defend themselves against the emperor. The emperor did not want these cantons to be free since they had control of the mountain passes through which passed the trade between Germany and Italy.

Thus, began a long war of independence in which the Swiss won great renown for their heroism and fighting qualities. Other cantons joined the fight for freedom.

* * * * *

Do you believe that mountains encourage an independent spirit in the people who live among them? Explain why or why not.

* * * * *

During this time, many stories grew up about such heroes as *William Tell*, who had to shoot an apple from his son's head when ordered to do so by a cruel Austrian.

By 1499, the Swiss had won their freedom from the Holy Roman Empire. These people, in whose country three different languages were spoken—German, French, and

Italian—proved that their love of liberty could win out over the differences of language. They then formed a strong and united nation.

Scandinavia. The peninsulas of northern Europe had developed a hardy race of Northmen, or Vikings. You have read of their courage and daring in sailing across the Atlantic to North America. You have studied about their exploits in England and France. You may remember how some of them settled in those two countries.

During the Middle Ages, the Northmen who remained in Scandinavia warred among themselves. Three separate kingdoms—*Norway, Sweden,* and *Denmark*—then began to emerge. A remarkable woman, *Queen Margaret* of Norway, thought that a union of the three kingdoms might bring peace to the region. In 1397, she persuaded the three kingdoms to sign an agreement at *Kalmar* in Sweden. This treaty was called the *Union of Kalmar.* It united the Scandinavian people into one large country that also included Greenland and Finland.

However, feudal warfare continued until the kings broke the power of the nobles by taking their land. The common people were then given a more important place in the government. By the end of the Middle Ages, the Union of Kalmar had broken up into the separate kingdoms of Denmark and Sweden, which have continued as such down to this day. It was not until the early part of this century that Norway, which had long been under Danish then Swedish influence, became an independent country again.

Eastern Europe. The Slavic peoples to the east of the boundaries of Charlemagne's old empire began to resist German settlement in the Middle Ages. Independent kingdoms like *Bohemia* appeared in this area, but Bohemia soon became part of the Holy Roman Empire. It did not regain its independence until modern times.

Poland. *Poland* and *Lithuania* were important powers in eastern Europe in the late Middle Ages. At different times Lithuania and Poland controlled vast territories from the Baltic Sea on the north to the Black Sea on the south. These two countries were united when, in 1386, *Grand Duke Jagelo* (yä·gĕl'ō) of Lithuania married *Princess Jadwiga* (yäd·vē'gä) of Poland. Jagelo ruled both countries as *Ladislas* (lăd'ĭs·lôs) *II* and introduced Christianity to Lithuania.

Other Slavic Nations. Early in the Christian age many Slavs lived between the *Oder River* that flows through modern Germany and Poland and the *Dnieper River* in what is now modern Russia. Most of these people were farmers and herdsmen. The time came when the Slavs spread in all directions. The map on this page will help you see in what directions they went. The Slavs founded *Bulgaria* and *Serbia*, but these nations were swallowed up by the Turks before the year 1500.

Russia. The Russian nation began while the Vikings were still powerful and controlled much of what is now northern and western Russia. About 862 the Slavs who lived near *Novgorod* (nŏv′gô·rŏd), an important trading center in northern Russia, asked a Viking leader named *Rurik* (rŏŏr′ĭk) to become their ruler. He and his descendants gradually expanded their territory and united the Slavic tribes into the large nation of Russia. Vladimir, who brought Christianity to Russia, was a descendant of Rurik.

Just when the Russian nation was beginning to develop, many thousands of *Mongols* poured out of central Asia. In the eleventh century they pushed across Europe, robbing, burning, and murdering the people. They laid waste to much of western Russia, destroying al-

most every city. The Russian princes fought many years to evict the Mongols. It was not until 1480 that the Mongol power in Russia was finally overthrown.

* * * * *

What kind of government does Russia have today?

* * * * *

Summing Up. All of the leaders after Otto, who was crowned Holy Roman Emperor by the pope, tried to unify Germany. These emperors also tried to unite Italy with the Holy Roman Empire, but the popes and emperors became involved in a long struggle over the rights of the Church. As a result, the empire declined and Germany and Italy remained divided and confused. Meanwhile, Switzerland, Denmark, Sweden, Poland and Lithuania, and Russia all became nations by the year 1500.

MOVEMENT OF THE SLAVS

FOR BETTER UNDERSTANDING

Checking Up

1. Why did the idea of a single empire appeal to the people of central Europe during the Middle Ages?

2. Discuss the chief problems of Louis II in Germany.

3. What was the importance of Otto's coronation as emperor?

4. What were the difficulties of uniting Germany and Italy into one empire?

5. How did some of the bishops become great feudal lords? Why was this harmful to the Church?

6. Explain what is meant by the investiture of a bishop.

7. What reforms did Pope Gregory VII put into effect?

8. How did the empire come to an end in Italy?

9. How did the Swiss become independent?

10. Name the Scandinavian countries that were independent nations by 1500.

11. What did the Mongols do to Russia?

12. Identify and tell the importance of each of the following dates: 936, 962, 1273 1397, 1480.

Yesterday and Today

1. Make a list of the countries mentioned in this chapter that are now behind the Iron Curtain.

2. After you do some detective work, see if you can draw a map that shows the main parts of the Holy Roman Empire. Then compare this with maps of modern Germany and Italy. Have the boundaries of these two countries been changed greatly since the early days of the Holy Roman Empire?

Persons, Places, and Terms

Identify: Louis II of Germany, Lothair, Henry the Fowler, Otto, Adelaide, Pope Gregory VII, Henry IV, Pope Calixtus II, Henry V, Frederick Barbarossa, Frederick II, Rudolph of Hapsburg, Queen Margaret, Ladislas II, Rurik.

Locate: Bavaria, Franconia, Lorraine, Swabia, Milan, Papal States, Sicily, Naples, Venice, Florence, Bohemia, Poland, Russia, Bulgaria, Serbia, Black Sea, Oder River, Dnieper River.

Define: East Mark, simony, crosier, miter, scepter, lay investiture, Concordat of Worms, Lombard League, Union of Kalmar, canton.

Interesting Things to Do

1. For your scrapbook, look up and prepare a report on the present-day countries of Germany and Italy. In your report be sure to name their important leaders, what type of food they raise, and what their most important industries are.

2. For your bulletin board, make a display of the various national costumes of Poland, Lithuania, Russia, Bohemia, and Bulgaria.

21

Wars to Rescue the Holy Land

THE EASTERN EMPIRE

Center of Culture. If you will look at the map on page 276, you will see the area occupied by the Eastern Roman Empire in the year 1000 A.D. The Eastern Empire, with its capital at Constantinople, existed for a thousand years after the last Roman Emperor of the West was deposed in 476.

All during the time of the barbarian invasions, during the time of Charlemagne's empire, and during the period when the modern nations of Western Europe began to develop, the empire of the East remained a center of culture and civilization. With its official language of Greek, the Eastern Empire preserved much of the earlier civilization of the Greeks and Romans.

The Church Divides. The emperors at Constantinople were absolute rulers. They wanted the Church in their empire to be subject to them. So they encouraged the bishops within the empire to become independent of Rome. The patriarchs at Constantinople refused to acknowledge that the pope, the Bishop of Rome, was the Vicar of Christ on earth and the visible head of the Church.

This split, or *schism* (sĭz'm) in the Church, was a matter of long struggles with the popes on one side and the emperors and patriarchs of Constantinople on the other. In the year 1054, the break, or schism, became complete. The Church in the Eastern Empire became known as the *Greek Orthodox Church.* This Church, which exists today, teaches practically the same doctrines as the Roman Catholic Church. Its sacraments are real sacraments and its bishops and priests have re-

THE EASTERN ROMAN EMPIRE
ABOUT THE YEAR 1000

THE EASTERN ROMAN EMPIRE
ABOUT THE YEAR 1000

Danube River

Black Sea

Adriatic Sea

ITALY

Constantinople

GREECE

Aegean Sea

Athens

ASIA MINOR

CRETE

CYPRUS

Mediterranean Sea

UNDER MOSLEM CONTROL

new conquests. Soon these Turks were in control of much of the land between China and Constantinople. The eastern emperor lost much of his empire and was afraid that the city of Constantinople could not hold out against the onrush of the Turks. In this crisis, the emperor at Constantinople requested the pope to send aid.

The pope was interested in stopping the conquests of the Turks since many pilgrims returning from visits to the Holy Land had told of the tortures and hardships they had suffered at the hands of the Turks.

Pilgrimages. A pilgrimage is a trip by a group of the faithful to a shrine sacred to the memory of Our Lord, His Blessed Mother, or a saint. The pilgrims are often led by their bishop or a priest. At the shrine, the people go to confession and perform various acts of penance. A solemn procession usually precedes High Mass, and the people receive the Blessed Sacrament.

From the very early days of the Church, Catholics were especially anxious to make pilgrimages to the Holy Land. They wanted to visit Bethlehem, where Christ was born. They wanted to visit Nazareth, where He lived as a boy and young man. They wanted to visit Jerusalem and follow His journey to

ceived valid Holy Orders. Although the Greek Orthodox Church has been separated from the Roman Catholic Church for many centuries, the pope wants us to pray for its return to the true Church.

Mohammedan Conquerors. Constantinople was a city with strong fortifications and a mighty navy. Even the Mohammedans, under the leadership of the desert Arabs, were not able to take Constantinople. You will remember reading that the emperors of the Eastern Empire had checked the advance of the Moslems toward Europe.

A new threat to the empire came out of eastern Asia. Fierce, warlike tribes of Turks had moved into Persia, where they adopted the Moslem religion and then set out on

Calvary. More than anything else they wanted to pray at the tomb of Christ, the *Holy Sepulchre* (sĕp′ŭl·kẽr), where Christ arose from the dead. The Emperor Constantine had erected a church over the Holy Sepulchre.

*   *   *   *   *

Pilgrimages are very exciting. Would you like to make a pilgrimage to the Holy Land? If so, tell why.

*   *   *   *   *

After the Arabs had adopted the religion of Mohammed and set out on their campaign of conquest, the Holy Land came under their control by the year 637 A.D. The Arabs did not stop the Christian pilgrims from coming to Jerusalem. Christians in the Holy Land could not, however, erect a cross on their buildings, and they had to pay special taxes to the Arabs. These conditions did not discourage the pilgrims. During the four hundred years after the Arabs conquered the Holy Land, the number of pilgrimages continued to increase.

THE CRUSADES BEGIN

Cruel Turks. This situation was changed when the tribes of eastern Turks defeated the Arabs and conquered Jerusalem in the year 1071. These Turks were cruel and barbaric. They killed many pilgrims and sold others as slaves. Then as the Turks went on to threaten Constantinople and all Europe, the pope took action.

Pope Urban II. *Pope Urban II* called together a council of the Church at *Clermont* in France during the year 1095. Nearly seven hundred archbishops, bishops, and abbots, as well as many priests and laymen attended the meeting.

At Clermont, the pope called on all Western Christians to rescue the Holy Land from the Turks and to give aid to the Christians of the Eastern Empire. He said that all men going on this holy pilgrimage should wear a cross on their forehead or breast. As they returned home, they would wear the cross on their back as a sign they had fulfilled their holy vow. The holy pilgrimage to rescue the Holy Land was called a *Crusade*. The word Crusade means *to take the cross.*

The plea of Pope Urban was so eloquent and so earnest that his listeners were filled with great enthusiasm. As the pope finished his speech, it is reported that the

The enthusiasm of the pilgrims in the Crusades was so high that many left their homes unprepared for more than a few days' journey. Food was scarce and clothes became tattered.

whole assembly shouted, "God wills it!" This became the battle cry of the Crusaders and was echoed in every country of Europe.

* * * * *

Can you explain why Pope Urban made the type of appeal that he did?

* * * * *

The People's Crusade. Enthusiasm for the Crusade spread throughout Europe like a raging fire. Many people were so anxious to rescue the Holy Land that they would not wait for the regular expedition that had been planned. One man, *Peter the Hermit*, rode far and wide, preaching to the poorer people and asking their help. Many people left their

homes immediately, and soon thousands had gathered together.

Taking up the cry, "God wills it!" these pilgrims set out overland on the long and dangerous journey to Palestine. Some groups were led by Peter the Hermit. Some were under the guidance of a poor knight called *Walter the Penniless.*

Most of these pilgrims were unarmed and untrained in fighting. Among them were many women and children. Without food or money, the pilgrims were soon hungry and weary. Some took to robbing and pillaging the countryside through which they were passing. Many of them died before they reached Constantinople.

Those who lived to reach Constantinople united under Peter the Hermit and started the march to the Holy Land. The Turks attacked and massacred them when they had gone but a short distance.

The Knights Prepare. Meanwhile, the lords and knights were making ready for a Crusade. Many of the nobles, answering the call of Pope Urban, had agreed to go and take their fighting men with them. The lords and knights knew that the Turks were fierce enemies. Accordingly, they repaired their armor and provided themselves with shields, swords, lances, and battle-axes. They also provided themselves with provisions and money. To do this many were forced to sell their lands and other possessions.

In spite of the strong faith of the people of the Middle Ages who went on the Crusades, some of the Crusaders were influenced by other motives. The love of adventure and the fighting spirit of the knights prompted many to go to the Holy Land. Under the feudal system only the oldest son received the inheritance of his father. Many younger sons saw in the Crusades a chance to gain lands for themselves in the East. The merchants in the cities of Italy and southern France gave support to the Crusades because they realized that there would be an increase of trade and commerce with the East. Yet, the desire for fame or land or trade was not the principal motive behind the Crusades. The chief reason for the Crusades was the desire to be of service to God and to His Church. This desire united all Christendom in the effort to rescue the places which had been made holy and sacred by the presence of Our Lord on earth.

Some of the chief leaders of the First Crusade were *Robert of Normandy*, a brother of the king of England; *Hugh*, a brother of the king of France; *Bohemund* (bō′ĕ·mŭd), the son of the Norman ruler of Sicily; and *Tancred* (tăng′krĕd), a cousin of Bohemund. *Godfrey of Bouillon* (bōō′yôn′) and his brother *Baldwin* led a large company of French and German knights, while *Raymond of Toulouse* (tōō·lōōz′), the most powerful noble in southern France, collected a large army from his domain.

The First Crusade. This large army of Crusaders was well equipped. The various groups of knights had very little trouble on their march to Constantinople. However, as soon as the Crusaders crossed from Europe into Asia Minor in 1097, their troubles began. The heat, the lack of food and water, sickness and fever, as well as constant skirmishes

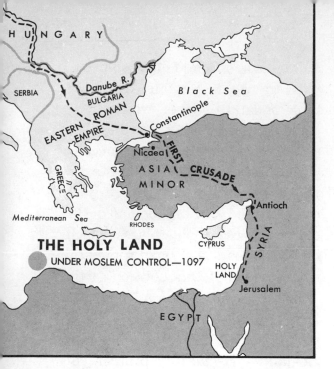

HUNGARY

SERBIA

Danube R.

BULGARIA

Black Sea

EASTERN ROMAN EMPIRE

Constantinople

GREECE

Nicaea

ASIA MINOR

FIRST CRUSADE

Antioch

Mediterranean Sea

RHODES

CYPRUS

SYRIA

THE HOLY LAND

UNDER MOSLEM CONTROL—1097

HOLY LAND

Jerusalem

EGYPT

month the gates were opened. The first of the Crusades ended with the capture of Jerusalem on July 15, 1099.

*   *   *   *   *

Can you think of any other ventures for which men were willing to make such great sacrifices?

*   *   *   *   *

Kingdom of Jerusalem. To hold the newly won land, the Crusaders chose a ruler for the city of Jerusalem. Godfrey of Bouillon was selected because he had shown the most unselfish devotion to the holy cause. He took the title *Defender of the Holy Sepulchre,* but he refused to wear a crown of gold in the city where Our Lord had worn a crown of thorns.

The following year Godfrey died, and his brother Baldwin became king of Jerusalem. The little state of the Crusaders became known as the *Latin Kingdom of Jerusalem.* A set of feudal laws was drawn up to govern the kingdom, and the Latin Kingdom of Jerusalem lasted for about two hundred years.

Orders of Monk-Knights. Most of the Crusaders had returned home as soon as their goal had been achieved. The Latin Kingdom had only a small army for its defense. To meet the need for a defending

with the Turks made their path a difficult one. However, they were successful. They captured Nicaea and restored a large part of Asia Minor to the emperor at Constantinople. Then, after a long siege, the city of Antioch was taken.

In May of 1099, the Crusaders approached the sacred city of Jerusalem after nearly two years of fighting. Jerusalem was a walled city, and a siege had to be made. The Crusaders built high towers of wood, which could be rolled up against the walls. After marching around the city barefoot, praying at all the holy places outside the walls, the Crusaders then rolled their towers up to the city walls. From these towers, the top of the walls could be reached and within a force in the Holy Land, a new type of warrior appeared, the warrior-monk.

Three new orders of monks were founded. They took the three religious vows of poverty, chastity, and obedience like all other monks. Another vow was added—a vow to protect the pilgrims coming to the Holy Land and to fight against the infidels. Thus, the members were both monks and knights.

The *Knights Hospitalers of St. John* originated at the Hospital of St. John in Jerusalem. This hospital had been founded to take care of pilgrims before the Crusades began. After the Crusades were over, the Knights Hospitalers continued to defend the Mediterranean islands of *Cyprus*, *Rhodes*, and *Malta* against the Turks. This order still survives in the Church as the *Knights of Malta*. It is now devoted mainly to works of charity.

A second order, the *Knights Templars*, was founded. Their headquarters was close to the site of Solomon's Temple in Jerusalem. They became powerful defenders of the Holy Land.

Encouraged by the Holy Roman Emperor, Frederick Barbarossa, a third order, the *Teutonic Knights*, was founded about a century after the other two. This order later transferred its efforts from the Holy Land to the eastern border of Germany. Here they waged a Crusade against the pagan peoples who lived along the shores of the Baltic Sea. Their Crusade ended when Poland and Lithuania were united, and the people of Lithuania were converted to Christianity.

THE LATER CRUSADES

Saint Bernard. The Latin Kingdom of Jerusalem was free from strong attack for about fifty years, but finally the Moslems united and drove the Christians from the city of *Edessa* (ĕ·dĕs′à). The Christians in Jerusalem hurriedly sent a messenger to the pope asking aid.

The pope called on *St. Bernard*, a French monk famous for his piety and his eloquence, to preach a Second Crusade. Wherever St. Bernard preached, nobles and common people became enthusiastic about the new Crusade. He even persuaded the king of France, *Louis VII*, and the king of Germany, *Conrad III*, to lead the Crusaders' army.

This Crusade met with complete disaster. The emperor at Constantinople gave no help to the Crusaders. There was an unsuccessful

Since the Crusaders could not travel with much more than their provisions and ready lances and spears, they had to make rock throwers and other heavy weapons by hand before each battle.

siege of Antioch, and the Crusaders were vigorously attacked by the Turks. So great were the losses that only the remnants of the great army reached Jerusalem. Weary and discouraged, the survivors of the second Crusade returned home in 1148 and 1149.

The Third Crusade. Forty years later a new Mohammedan leader arose in the East. This was *Saladin* (săl'*a*·dĭn), the sultan who united all the Moslems of Egypt and Asia Minor under his command. In 1187, he captured the city of Jerusalem. All Europe was alarmed.

The pope called for a Third Crusade. Thousands responded to the challenge. The greatest monarchs of Europe became the leaders of this Crusade. These were Fred-

erick Barbarossa, the Holy Roman Emperor; Philip Augustus, king of France; and Richard the Lionhearted, king of England. Preparations were carefully made for the crusading expedition.

The emperor, Frederick Barbarossa, who was nearly seventy years old, and his German followers were the first to start. They took the overland route through Hungary, Bulgaria, and Constantinople. You have read how Frederick Barbarossa was drowned in Asia Minor. His army was then disbanded. Some knights joined the other Crusaders, but many returned home.

Both Richard and Philip took the water route across the Mediterranean. In the year 1191, they landed near the port of *Acre* (ä'kẽr), which was not far from Jerusalem. The Latin Kingdom Christians were besieging the city of Acre, which was held by the Turks, when Richard and Philip arrived.

Richard directed the building of more rock-throwing machines. These machines could hurl large stones, and by constant bombardment a strong wall could be weakened. When the wall was sufficiently weakened, the besiegers would try to pull out loose stones. To protect themselves while doing this, the Crusaders were covered by a shed made of wickerwork overlaid with hides. In this fashion, holes were made in the walls of Acre, and the city was forced to surrender.

Quarrels soon broke out between Richard and Philip. As a result, Philip returned to France leaving Richard to carry on the fight for Jerusalem. During the next year, Richard distinguished himself by the courage and skill with which he led his army. The Crusaders, because of the might of Saladin, were unable to make any progress in their effort to capture Jerusalem.

Richard was also worried about affairs in England, where his unpopular brother John was ruling in his place. So, Richard arranged a truce with Saladin in 1192. According to this truce the Turks were to keep Jerusalem, but they were to allow Christian pilgrims in small groups to visit without paying tribute. Then Richard returned to England, and the Third Crusade was brought to an end.

The results of the Crusade were that the Christians had Acre as a friendly headquarters when their pilgrims arrived in the Holy Land, and the pilgrims had been granted the right to visit the sacred places of Jerusalem.

The Fourth Crusade. The people of Europe were not satisfied with the results of the Third Crusade. A few years after Richard returned to England, *Pope Innocent III* called on all Christians to form a Fourth Crusade. The response to a new Crusade came chiefly from the French knights.

The Fourth Crusade went by land to the city of Venice. In 1202, the Venetians had agreed to transport the knights by water to the Holy Land. In order to pay for the voyage, the Crusaders were forced to capture the port of *Zara*, which was a rival of Venice for the trade of the Adriatic Sea. Then the Crusaders became involved in a quarrel between the rivals for the emperor's throne at Constantinople. As a result, the Fourth Crusade never reached the Holy Land.

Children's Crusade. A few years later, the children of Europe gave a remarkable demonstration of their zeal for the Crusaders' cause. In the year 1212, *Stephen*, a young shepherd boy of France, became convinced that a Crusade of boys and girls would be successful even though men had failed. He gathered together thousands of children, and they started the march to the Holy Land in order to capture Jerusalem from the Turks. Hunger finally forced the children to return home.

The same year, a German boy named *Nicholas* began to lead over twenty thousand children on a Crusade. Most of these were boys under twelve years of age. No one seemed to be able to restrain their enthusiasm. They marched south across the Alps into Italy. Many perished from hunger, cold, sickness, and exhaustion. When the remaining children reached Rome, Pope Innocent III asked them to return home. He suggested that they wait until they grew to manhood before undertaking a Crusade. But many children continued, still determined to reach and conquer the Holy Land. Some returned in time, some were sold into slavery, and some died of hunger and exposure.

* * * * *

What ways do the boys and girls of today have of helping spread the Faith of Christ?

* * * * *

Other Crusades. More Crusades followed, but there was no major

The Children's Crusade was representative of the deep religious faith of the common people, but the failure of this expedition in effect put an end to the Crusades.

victory gained in the Holy Land. The king of Hungary led the Fifth Crusade, which lasted from 1218 to 1221. The emperor of the Holy Roman Empire, Frederick II, was the leader of the Sixth Crusade, which took place during 1228 and 1229. St. Louis, king of France, and his three brothers led the Seventh Crusade in 1248. Twenty years later, St. Louis and his three sons led the Eighth Crusade. During this expedition St. Louis died. This was the last Crusade to the Holy Land.

However, the crusading spirit did not die out. The Knights Hospitalers and the Knights Templars and many other knights from all parts of Europe helped to drive the Moslems from Spain. The warrior-monks also kept many Christian strongholds, such as the islands of Malta and Cyprus, for a number of centuries more.

AFTER THE CRUSADES

The Results. One might consider the Crusades to be a great failure. They did not succeed in their main goal. They were unable to drive the Moslems from the Holy Land.

During the two centuries—the twelfth and thirteenth—that the Crusades lasted, Western Europe was united in a common cause. The Catholic Church had provided a common goal for all her people. Nobles and freemen from every part of Europe met together. They realized that they had common interests and a common culture even though they came from different nations. This type of unifying force was valuable for Europe. During the Crusades, the Truce of God had put a stop to the feuds and petty wars that had kept Europe in a disturbed condition for so many years.

Feudalism Declines. Perhaps, it was the feudal nobles who made the greatest sacrifices in order to take part in the Crusades. They were the warrior-knights who bore the brunt of the battles. They also had to bear a very large part of the expense of the Crusades. Each noble had to pay for the equipment, food, and travel expenses of his followers. Since most of their wealth was in land, the nobles were obliged to sell or mortgage their estates.

The hardships of the nobles permitted the kings to increase their power. Many nobles died on the Crusades and left no heirs. Their lands often went to the king. Those who did return were, on the whole, too poor to oppose the king. In order to raise money for the Crusades, the nobles frequently had to give greater liberties to their vassals and to the towns. Thus, were the feudal customs and practices weakened, and in their place came new ways brought about by strong kings and emerging towns.

Trade and Travel. One of the chief problems of the crusading armies was to transport their supplies over so great a distance. Some of the seaport towns of the Mediterranean area solved the problem. These cities were Venice, Genoa, and Pisa in Italy; Marseilles in France; and Barcelona in Spain. These city-states agreed to supply ships for the voyage and often the needed supplies—weapons, horses, and food.

In return, these cities were allowed to establish market districts, in Asia Minor and the Holy Land, in the areas captured by the Crusaders. From these market districts in the Holy Land there began to be sent back to Europe many new products from the East. From the city of *Mosul* (mȯ·sool′), in Persia, the merchants obtained *muslin* cloth. *Damascus* (dȧ·măs′kŭs), in the area of the Fertile Crescent not far from the Holy Land, supplied the Italian merchants with the cloth

that is called *damask*. Other types of cloth like *calico*, *satin*, and *silk*, which were made in the East, were also sent back to Europe, along with perfumes, gems, and other luxuries. The Crusaders and the merchants who aided them brought back many new food items, such as sugar and spices, oranges and lemons, rice, apricots, and dates. These foods helped to improve the diet of the European people.

A New Vision. The millions of Europeans who traveled to the Holy Land as pilgrims, or as Crusaders, met people from the other nations of Europe. They came in contact with the older civilization of the Roman Empire of the East. They also came in contact with the differing way of life, the ideas, and the civilization of the Moslems in the Near East. For example, the Crusaders saw windmills for the first time. Soon many windmills were built in Europe. Think what an effect that had on low countries such as Holland. Wind could be used to pump water and to grind grain into flour.

The many thousands of Crusaders and pilgrims brought back to Europe new ideas about architecture, medicine, and geography. These ideas helped develop a great Catholic civilization in Europe.

*   *   *   *   *

Do you think that you would have enjoyed being alive during the period of the Crusades? Tell why or why not.

*   *   *   *   *

Summing Up. During the eleventh century, fierce Turks captured Palestine, even Jerusalem, from the more friendly Arabs. Then the Turks began to overthrow the Eastern Roman Empire. When they got near to Constantinople, the emperor asked the pope to send soldiers. So the pope called upon the European nobles and knights to free the holy places.

The two hundred years between 1095 and 1295 were filled with the Crusades to the Holy Land. The Crusaders won Jerusalem and parts of Palestine, and even held them for a while, but in the end the Mohammedans were triumphant. Even though the holy places remained under Mohammedan control, Western Europe was enriched by the flow of trade and new ideas. All the peoples of Europe benefited from the decline of feudalism, the stopping of petty wars, and the resulting growth of Christian nations in a new Catholic civilization.

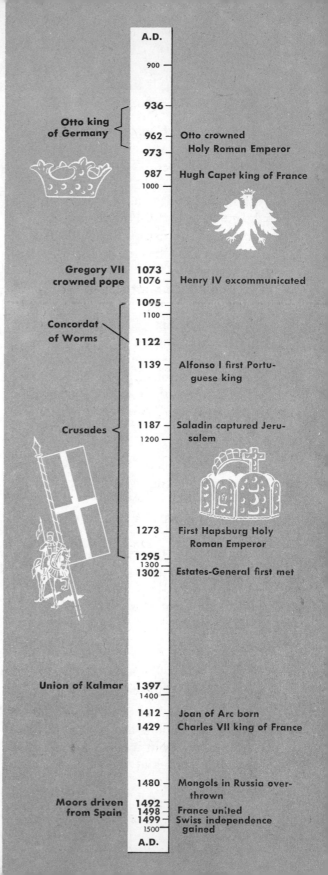

A.D.

900

Otto king of Germany {
936

962 — Otto crowned Holy Roman Emperor
973

987 — Hugh Capet king of France
1000

Gregory VII crowned pope 1073
1076 — Henry IV excommunicated

Concordat of Worms {
1095
1100

1122

1139 — Alfonso I first Portuguese king

Crusades {
1187 — Saladin captured Jerusalem
1200

1273 — First Hapsburg Holy Roman Emperor

1295
1300
1302 — Estates-General first met

Union of Kalmar 1397
1400

1412 — Joan of Arc born
1429 — Charles VII king of France

1480 — Mongols in Russia overthrown

Moors driven from Spain 1492
1498 — France united
1499 — Swiss independence gained
1500

A.D.

FOR BETTER UNDERSTANDING

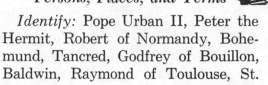

Checking Up

1. Why did Constantinople remain such an important city for 1,000 years after the collapse of the Western Empire?

2. Explain why the Christians made pilgrimages to the Holy Land.

3. What hardships did the Turks impose on the Christian pilgrims to the Holy Land?

4. Explain the purpose of the Council of Clermont.

5. Was the First Crusade successful? Explain your answer.

6. What type of government did the Christians establish in the Holy Land?

7. Describe the religious orders of warrior-monks.

8. What were the chief events of the Second Crusade?

9. Name the leaders of the Third Crusade and tell what happened to each.

10. Why was the Fourth Crusade a failure?

11. Explain the overall results of the Crusades upon Western Europe.

12. Identify the following dates and tell the importance of each: 1054, 1071, 1095, 1099, 1191, 1202.

Yesterday and Today

1. Have you ever made a pilgrimage either to a religious or patriotic shrine? If so, tell how your mode of travel, your living quarters, and the services available differ from those of the medieval pilgrims in the Holy Land.

2. Do you know of any movements or worthy causes of today that are sometimes called crusades? If so, why are they different or like the Holy Crusades of the Middle Ages?

Persons, Places, and Terms

Identify: Pope Urban II, Peter the Hermit, Robert of Normandy, Bohemund, Tancred, Godfrey of Bouillon, Baldwin, Raymond of Toulouse, St. Bernard, Louis VII, Conrad III, Saladin, Pope Innocent III, Frederick II, St. Louis IX.

Locate: Constantinople, Holy Land, Jerusalem, Clermont, Asia Minor, Nicaea, Antioch, Cyprus, Rhodes, Acre, Venice, Genoa.

Define: schism, pilgrimage, Knights Hospitalers of St. John, Teutonic Knights, Holy Sepulchre, Crusade.

Interesting Things to Do

1. Make a chart for your scrapbook that shows the dates, leaders, and results of the various Crusades.

2. Find pictures and make drawings of the Christian knights, the Turkish soldiers, and the castles and fortifications that were in the Holy Land during the Crusades.

3. For your history class or a school assembly, have your teacher help you secure a speaker who has visited the sacred shrines in the Holy Land.

UNDERSTANDING THE UNIT

For Discussion

1. Why do wars help to increase the power of a king, or central government?

2. Why were the kings of France able to become absolute rulers?

3. Why did the idea of a Holy Roman Empire appeal to so many of the people in central Europe?

4. Why did Frederick Barbarossa find it difficult to hold Italy in close union with Germany?

5. What were the chief motives prompting men to join the Crusades?

For You to Answer

1. Explain the differences between the way in which the English Parliament and the French Estates-General developed.

2. What were the results of the Hundred Years' War for France and England?

3. Describe the policies and accomplishments of Ferdinand and Isabella.

4. Explain how the investiture quarrel developed.

5. What were the circumstances leading to the Eastern Schism?

6. What happened in Palestine in 1071 that upset the Christians of Western Europe?

7. What were the chief events of the Third Crusade?

Linking Geography and History

1. Do you think that the natural features of the several peninsulas that are part of the continent of Europe had any influence on the way national states developed? Explain why or why not.

2. Why would you expect the history of Spain to be closely connected with that of North Africa?

3. Show how mountain ranges helped to create national boundaries in Europe. Use the nations studied about in this unit to illustrate your answer.

Interesting Things to Do

1. As a class, plan a period which will be devoted to the songs and music of the countries that you have studied in this unit. Ask your teacher to help you find this music and to help you rehearse it.

2. Tell the story of St. Joan of Arc in pictures. Make a list of scenes which should be included. Class members who like to draw could do many of the pictures you need. When you are finished put the display on the class bulletin board.

Books to Read

Anderson, Paul, *The High Crusade.*
Best, Herbert, *The Sea Warriors.*
Bragdon, Lillian, *Land of Joan of Arc.*
Buff, Mary, *The Apple and the Arrow.*
Coe, Frederick, *Knight of the Cross.*
Hubbard, Margaret A., *St. Louis and the Last Crusade.*
Lownsberry, Eloise, *Boy Knight of Rheims.*
Magoon, Marion, *Little Dusty Foot.*
Paine, Albert B., *Girl in White Armor.*
West, Anthony, *The Crusades.*

UNIT 8
The Late Middle Ages

(1000 A.D. — 1500 A.D.)

CHAPTER

22. Monks and Cathedrals
23. Schools and Culture in the Middle Ages
24. The Growth of Towns and Trade

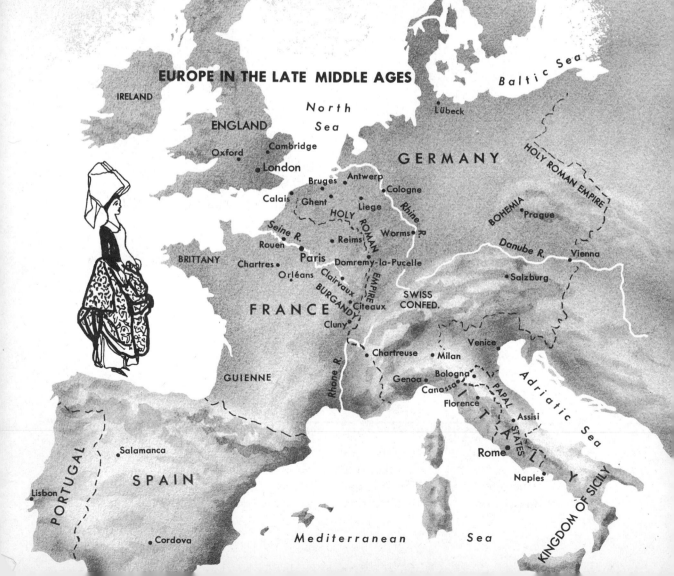

EUROPE IN THE LATE MIDDLE AGES

IRELAND

North Sea

Baltic Sea

Lübeck

ENGLAND

Oxford · Cambridge
· London

GERMANY

HOLY ROMAN EMPIRE

Bruges · Antwerp
Calais · Ghent · Cologne
· Liège · *Rhine R.*

HOLY ROMAN EMPIRE

Worms · R.

BOHEMIA · Prague

Seine R.
Rouen · Reims

Danube R. · Vienna

BRITTANY
Chartres · Paris
Orléans · Domremy-la-Pucelle

· Salzburg

Clairvaux
BURGUNDY · Cîteaux

SWISS CONFED.

FRANCE

Cluny

Venice

Rhône R.
· Chartreuse · Milan

Genoa · Bologna

Adriatic Sea

GUIENNE

Canossa
· Florence

ITALY

PAPAL STATES

· Assisi

Salamanca

PORTUGAL

SPAIN

Rome

Lisbon

Naples

Córdova

KINGDOM OF SICILY

Mediterranean Sea

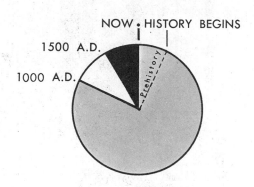

NOW • HISTORY BEGINS

1500 A.D.

1000 A.D.

Prehistory

INTRODUCTION

In the new civilization that developed in Europe during the Middle Ages, men applied Christian principles to every part of their lives. As you read this unit you will learn that the influence of the Catholic Church could be seen everywhere in medieval Europe. Schools and universities were established to help men gain knowledge, and to come to know and understand God and the teachings of Christ. New religious orders were founded. Many men and women dedicated themselves to a religious life of prayer, study, and service.

During the Middle Ages nations of Europe developed everyday languages of their own, which gradually replaced Latin. These languages became the means by which people were able to appreciate the truths of their religion. New and important works of literature also appeared in these languages.

As towns in Europe grew, they attracted people from rural villages. There was a sense of security to be had within the high walls of a medieval town. People were able to find employment and live as freemen.

As wealth from trade and commerce came to the towns, the townspeople constructed guild and town halls, churches, and great cathedrals. We can still see examples of this medieval architecture in Europe today.

The merchants and craftsmen of the towns formed organizations called *guilds*. The guilds attempted to improve the quality of the goods the members produced. They helped boys and young men learn the skills needed to become master craftsmen. They also put into practice the principles of justice, charity, and fair dealing taught by the Church.

Monks and Cathedrals

THE SPIRITUAL LIFE OF THE MIDDLE AGES

A New Fervor. After the conversion of Europe in the eleventh century, the Church set out to build a thoroughly Christian society. You have read how the Church curbed the fighting impulse of the war-like peoples who had destroyed the Western Roman Empire and how the Church had turned this enthusiasm for fighting to good use in the Crusades.

As time passed, the people became more deeply devoted to the Catholic Faith. One example of this religious vigor was the founding during the twelfth and thirteenth centuries of a number of new religious orders. You have already read how new orders of warrior-monks were formed to aid the Crusades. Other men, however, preferred a purely religious order that would have no worldly distractions.

It was their desire to withdraw as much as possible from the world in order to be nearer to God.

St. Bruno of Cologne was a man who wished to adapt the Rule of St. Benedict to the ideal life of withdrawal from the world. St. Bruno founded a monastery at *Chartreuse* (shàr′trûz′), in southern France, in the year 1084. The monks of this monastery and those who accepted the new rule were called *Carthusians* (kär·thū′zhănz).

At Chartreuse, each monk had his own cottage, or cell. There he prayed, read, ate, slept, worked, and kept a small garden. The entire monastery met together only for Mass and periods of prayer. Occasionally, the monks met for recreation or a common meal. Their entire life was spent in prayer, fasting, and in works of penance.

The monastery of Clairvaux became the center of the Cistercian order under St. Bernard.

A few years after the founding of the Carthusians, another group of Benedictine monks under the leadership of *St. Robert* founded a new monastery at *Cîteaux* (sē'tō'), also in southern France. The monks of Cîteaux strictly followed the Rule of St. Benedict. They did not eat meat, fish, eggs, cheese, butter, or white bread. Their meals consisted of coarse dark bread and vegetables. Water was their only drink. They kept a constant silence. They permitted themselves only six hours sleep at night. The monks of Cîteaux slept on rude cots that were often only hard boards. Even their short period of sleep was broken by a period of prayer in the chapel.

* * * * *

Why did the monks want to live such a hard life?

* * * * *

St. Bernard. For the first fifteen years, the monastery of Cîteaux attracted only a few men who were willing to follow its very strict rule. In the year 1113, a young nobleman, who was destined to become the most outstanding leader in Europe for the next forty years, entered the monastery at Cîteaux. *Bernard*, whom we call St. Bernard, not only entered Cîteaux but convinced thirty other young nobles to enter the monastery with him. St. Bernard seemed to breathe a new life into the monks of Cîteaux, or the *Cistercians* (sĭs·tûr'shănz) as they came to be called. New monasteries of the order were soon founded. St. Bernard became abbot at the monastery of *Clairvaux* (klĕr'vō'), in northeastern France. His father and his six brothers also became monks.

St. Bernard was not permitted to spend all his time at his monastery. He was such an outstanding preacher that he was in much demand. He was, for example, asked by the pope to preach the Second Crusade.

St. Bernard founded one hundred and sixty Cistercian monasteries before he died in 1153. Before the end of the twelfth century, there were over five hundred Cistercian monasteries. Even today, the Cistercian spirit flourishes in our own country. The first abbey in the United States was established during the time George Washington was president.

In addition to the long periods of prayer and spiritual reading, the Cistercian monks spent several hours daily in manual labor. This time was usually spent in farming. The monks became experts in agriculture. They performed a very valuable service to the rest of Europe by their continual improvements in the methods of farming and forestry.

New Orders. Early in the thirteenth century a new type of religious order came into existence. The new religious groups were known as *friars*, which is from the Latin word for *brothers*. These monks were both priests and lay brothers. They prepared themselves to become active missionaries for the Church.

The Franciscans. One of the best loved saints of the Church is *St. Francis*. His father was a wealthy merchant in the Italian town of *Assisi* (*ȧ·sē′zē̇*), but Francis was not interested in becoming a businessman. He preferred the carefree life of his wealthy young friends.

One time while he was recovering from an illness, Francis began to think of Our Lord's invitation, given in the gospel, to give up all things and follow Him. Francis made a great decision. He vowed that he would imitate Our Lord by a life of poverty, prayer, and preaching.

At first, Francis met with opposition from his family. His former companions made fun of him. Soon, however, a group of young men joined Francis in his Christlike way of life. Francis gave his band of followers the humble title of *Friars Minor*, or the *little brothers*. They are usually called *Franciscans*. The pope approved this order in 1209.

Francis never lost the cheerful disposition that made him so popular with his companions as a young man. He had chosen a life of poverty and hardship, but in this way he was happy to serve God. In his last years, St. Francis was rewarded with a sign from God. He was marked on his hands, feet, and side with the same wounds that Christ suffered at His crucifixion. These marks are called the *stigmata* (*stĭg′mȧ·tȧ*).

St. Francis was eager to convert the Mohammedans to Christianity. He made a visit to the Holy Land during the Fifth Crusade. As a result of his interest, the Franciscans

Franciscan and Dominican friars preached out of doors to the poor in their own languages.

in the world. The members of the Third Order say extra prayers daily, have extra periods of fasting, perform special works of penance and charity, and take part in other special religious works.

* * * * *

Do you know someone who belongs to a Third Order? If so, tell about some of their good works.

* * * * *

Order of Preachers. *St. Dominic* came from a noble and very religious Spanish family. He was a great scholar who became alarmed at the success that many false believers, or heretics, were having in spreading their doctrines. He decided to found a religious order that would be devoted to the work of preaching and teaching the true doctrine of Christ. Accordingly he founded the *Order of Preachers*, whom we usually call the *Dominicans*. St. Dominic received the approval for this order from the pope in 1216. While he was in Rome, St. Dominic met St. Francis. They told each other of their plans to win souls for God. They each prayed for the success of the other's order.

St. Dominic founded the Dominican nuns as a second order in the battle to defend the Church against heresy. He also founded a Third

have since been the guardians of the holy places in and around Jerusalem.

Saint Clare. One day a young girl named *Clare* came to see St. Francis. Her mother and father were of noble birth and lived in Assisi. Clare wanted to live the same life of poverty, chastity, and prayer as the Friars Minor. So, St. Francis founded a second order for St. Clare and her companions. These nuns are usually called the *Poor Clares*, because of their great poverty.

Another Order. St. Francis also founded the *Third Order*. Men and women who joined this order were permitted to share some of the religious exercises of the friars and nuns and still continue their duties

Order for men and women who could become apostles of the true Church in their homes and at their work.

St. Dominic was very devoted to Our Lady. As a result, the Dominican friars, nuns, and members of the Dominican Third Order spread the devotion of the rosary throughout Europe and later throughout the world.

The Thirteenth Century. By the thirteenth century, many large towns had attracted thousands of people from their rural homes. During the time of the Crusades, a great many serfs had bought their freedom and had gone to live in the towns. When these people had lived in the country districts, they had been close to the village priest or to some monastery. The towns had grown so large and so rapidly that there were not enough parishes to take care of all the people. Here was an opportunity for the friars.

Shortly after they were founded, the gray-robed Franciscans and the Dominicans in their white robes began to be seen in every section of Europe. They preached out-of-doors in the market places, in the public squares, or on the steps of the churches. They did not preach in Latin but in the new popular languages that were growing up in Europe. In this way, they were able to teach the truths of the Catholic religion even to the uneducated. The pope gave the friars permission to hear confessions anywhere.

The friars lived in the strictest poverty. They had to beg for their food. The wealthy began to shower them with gifts, which they shared with the poor who lived near them. Rich and poor alike were influenced by the friars to lead holier lives.

The friars began to teach at the great universities. They fought against false teachings by becoming the best teachers themselves. Three of these friars earned the title *Doctor of the Church.* They were *St. Bonaventure* (bŏn'a·vĕn'tụr), a Franciscan, and *St. Thomas Aquinas* and *St. Albertus Magnus* (ăl·bûr'tŭs măg'nŭs), both Dominicans. St. Bonaventure is known as the *Seraphic Doctor.*

St. Thomas has influenced all Catholic teaching since his time. The *Angelic Doctor*, as St. Thomas is called, lived about seven hundred years ago, but the education of Catholic boys and girls is still influenced by his lectures and writings.

Usually, a monk never left the monastery where he took his vows. The friars, however, could be sent great distances by their superiors.

297

Because merchants, seamen, and soldiers were long-distance travelers, the friars often joined them to reach foreign lands. It was considered good fortune to have a friar on the voyage.

This made them valuable in carrying out the missionary work of the Church, especially in the new lands which the explorers were soon to discover. In less than a hundred years, friars were found all the way from Greenland to China. Friars accompanied Columbus and the other Catholic explorers on their voyages.

These friars played an important part in the exploration and settlement of our own southwestern United States. There are many towns and cities in California which bear the names of saints of the Church. These cities have developed from the mission churches founded there by the friars.

THE AGE OF THE CATHEDRALS

Basilicas. After 395 A.D., when Christians became free of Roman persecution, they looked for places where they might worship God with proper reverence. The basilicas, or the buildings which the Romans used for law courts, seemed to be suitable for the celebration of the Mass and the other ceremonies of the Church. A basilica was usually a great hall with large interior columns holding up a heavy roof.

One end of the building was shaped like a semicircle and was called the *apse* (ăps). There the Christians placed the altar and the bishop's throne. The early churches and cathedrals were of this type.

Later, the Christians began to make changes in this style. They added two wings, or *transepts*, in order to give the cathedral the shape of a cross. They used the Roman type of arch in many places—in the dome, the doors, the windows, and in the decorations. For this reason, this style of church building was called *Romanesque* (rō′măn·ĕsk′). For centuries, the cathedrals in Europe were built in this style. You can see the chief features of the Romanesque architecture by studying the picture on this page.

Cathedrals in the Middle Ages. During the Middle Ages, builders were able to make improvements on the Romanesque style of church architecture. In fact, they made so many changes that they developed a new type of architecture called *Gothic*.

In the Romanesque churches, the heavy roofs were supported by thick walls, which had very few windows. The builders of the Gothic cathedrals tried new methods for supporting the roof. On the top of each pillar was a group of stone ribs. These ribs extended in all directions just as the branches of a tree grow out from the main trunk. In this way the great pillars with their stone ribs were able to bear the weight of all sections of the roof.

The walls of the Gothic cathedrals were given additional support on the outside. These supports were called *buttresses*. You can see an

The Church of St. Francis at Assisi, Italy, shows the solidarity of Romanesque architecture. A long series of Roman arches supports portions of the roof and provides a covered walkway.

The ornate buttresses of the Notre Dame Cathedral in Paris are called *flying buttresses* because they stand out from the building. In later churches they were enclosed or built in.

example of these buttresses in the picture on this page. Notice that these features are both useful and beautiful. Every feature of a Gothic cathedral had these two qualities, usefulness and beauty.

The walls of the Gothic cathedrals could be built higher than those of the earlier churches. Because of the buttresses, the walls did not have to be very thick. This permitted the builders to include more windows.

Church Windows. Windows became one of the chief glories of the Gothic cathedrals. Scenes from the life of Our Lord or the saints were shown in the beautifully colored windows. The picture was not painted on the glass, because the color would have lasted only a few years. Instead, the glassmakers put the color into the glass at the time the glass was made. They had to make hundreds of pieces of glass of different colors in order to arrange a picture for a single window. The color of these stained glass windows is just as brilliant today as it was seven hundred years ago. Over the main entrance of the cathedral there was usually a beautiful *rose* *window,* so called because it had the shape and coloring of an open rose.

* * * * *

Does your parish church, or do any neighboring parishes, have a rose window?

* * * * *

The tall, graceful spires and the pointed arches of the Gothic cathedrals elevated the eyes, the minds, and the hearts of the people towards heaven. Today, these Gothic cathedrals serve as a lasting example of the deep religious spirit of the Middle Ages.

Everyone Helped. The Gothic cathedrals are remarkable for more than their beauty. They also show the wonderful spirit of the people who built them. Each city wanted to have as beautiful a cathedral as possible. The people thought that only the best building was suitable for the celebration of Mass and the other ceremonies of the Church.

Usually, some great bishop inspired the building of a cathedral, and every person in the town helped to construct this church. The architects, the stone masons, the glassmakers, the wood carvers, and all the skilled craftsmen tried to make the building a worthy temple in which to celebrate the Divine Sacrifice of the Mass. Those who

were wealthy gave money and precious jewels. Ordinary men, who were neither wealthy nor skilled in the arts, gave their time and labor.

Gothic cathedrals of great beauty were built in all the countries of Western Europe. Some of the most famous are those at *Chartres* (shär'tr'), Reims, and Paris—all in France; Salisbury and York in England; Cologne in Germany; Milan in Italy; and Burgos in Spain.

Delicate stone carving often outlines areas in rose windows which are fitted with glass.

Ornamentation. Every item of decoration in a cathedral was reverently and beautifully made. The vestments, the tapestries, the candlesticks, the sacred altar vessels, and the wood carvings all showed the same careful workmanship as did the cathedral itself. The skilled craftsmen used their best efforts in preparing these objects for the service and worship of God.

Blank spaces on the walls, and even on the ceilings, were often filled in with paintings. Like the windows, they showed scenes of the life of Our Lord, the Blessed Mother, or the saints. These paintings served a double purpose. They formed a beautiful decoration for the cathedral, and they helped to instruct the people at a time when books were scarce.

Sculptors made statues from the same type of stone that was used in the construction of the cathedral. The statues also helped to acquaint the people with the life of Our Lord and the lives of the saints. There are four thousand statues on the inside of the Cathedral of Chartres.

Frequently, on the outside of the cathedral, the stonemasons would place statues of persons who were living at that time. At various corners of the building, the rainspouts were made in the shape of grotesque, ugly figures called *gargoyles* (gär′goilz).

Church Music. In the Middle Ages, music was also used to beautify

The life-like figures at the left, and the grotesque gargoyles below, all carved out of stone, appear on Notre Dame Cathedral.

the Divine Service. Pope Gregory the Great prompted the development of a type of choral singing, or chant, which accompanied the sacred words of Church ceremonies. The singing is called *Gregorian Chant*, or plain chant, and is used in Church services today. When you sing the plain chant at the Mass, you are able to join with the Catholics of centuries ago in singing the praises of God.

Some of our most important hymns were written in the Middle Ages. St. Bernard of Clairvaux composed several. St. Thomas Aquinas wrote the two hymns which we use at Benediction—*O Salutaris Hostia* (O Saving Victim) and *Tantum Ergo* (Lo, We before Him bending). The hymn *Stabat Mater* (Sorrowful Mother), which we sing at the Stations of the Cross, was also written in the thirteenth century. Another celebrated hymn written in the thirteenth century is the *Dies Irae* (Day of Wrath), which is sung at Masses for the dead.

* * * * *

Do you know the English words to any of the hymns mentioned above?

* * * * *

The pipe organ had come into use by the time the great Gothic cathedrals were being built. The music of the organ gave beauty and reverence to the cathedral ceremonies and introduced a whole new era in Church music.

Summing Up. After the conversion of Europe, the Church set out to build a thoroughly Catholic civilization. As evidence of the medieval peoples' deep faith and their love of God, a great society built on the principles that Jesus had taught came into being.

Great new religious orders such as the Carthusians, and Cistercians were founded. And, in response to the growing need to serve the expanding population in the towns, the Franciscans and Dominicans were formed.

From these orders came not only a great religious appeal directed to the people, but some of the great minds of the Church devoted to bringing man more understanding about God.

One of the greatest evidences of Catholic civilization was the spirit of many towns where the great cathedrals were built. Often, inspired by a great bishop, almost every person in a community would give of his time, labor, and talent to show his love and reverence for God by helping to erect a beautiful temple in His honor.

FOR BETTER UNDERSTANDING

Checking Up

1. Describe the origin and work of the Carthusians.

2. Who was St. Bernard of Clairvaux?

3. How did the friars differ from other monks?

4. Tell briefly about the life of St. Francis of Assisi.

5. Describe the work of the orders founded by St. Dominic.

6. What was the origin of the Romanesque style of architecture?

7. What are the chief features of Romanesque architecture?

8. What are the chief features of the Gothic style of architecture?

9. What means were used by medieval men to beautify the Divine Service as well as their cathedrals?

10. Identify and tell the importance of each of the following dates: 1084, 1113, 1209, 1216.

Yesterday and Today

1. Do you know of any religious orders that have been founded in recent years in order to meet some special need of today?

2. Compare the architecture and decoration of your parish church with that of the Romanesque and Gothic churches. How is your parish church like or different from them in style?

Persons, Places, and Terms

Identify: St. Bruno of Cologne, St. Robert, St. Bernard, St. Francis, St. Clare, St. Dominic, St. Bonaventure, St. Thomas Aquinas, St. Albertus Magnus.

Locate: Chartreuse, Cîteaux, Clairvaux, Assisi, Chartres, Reims, Paris, Cologne, Milan.

Define: Carthusian, Cistercian, friars, friary, stigmata, Poor Clares, Third Order, Seraphic Doctor, Angelic Doctor, basilica, apse, transept, Romanesque, Gothic, buttress, rose window, gargoyle, plain chant.

Interesting Things to Do

1. If there is a Gothic cathedral or church in your community, ask your teacher to plan a class visit to it so you can study its features.

2. Perhaps your class could make a model of a stained glass window as an art project. Ask your teacher to suggest various materials that will help you in your project.

3. Prepare a program for a music period in which your class sings the hymns of St. Bernard, St. Thomas Aquinas, and other monks and nuns of the Middle Ages.

4. Prepare for your scrapbook a report on the life of one of the following:
  a. St. Thomas Aquinas
  b. St. Dominic
  c. St. Bernard of Clairvaux
  d. St. Clare

23

Schools and Culture in the Middle Ages

CATHOLIC EDUCATION

Higher Education Begins. The Catholic Church was faced with a gigantic task as the barbarian tribes settled down in permanent homes and began to develop as nations. The Church had begun to convert and civilize these people and had established schools to help with this work. Soon the popes required that every cathedral and every monastery should have a school. Rulers like Charlemagne gave sums of money to support these schools. In time, most parish churches, in the country districts as well as in the towns, had their own schools. The only schools in the Middle Ages were those conducted by the Church.

By the early thirteenth century, the Crusades had awakened the curiosity of the European people about many different subjects.

From Constantinople, some of the Crusaders had brought books written by the ancient Greeks. Yet, more than anything else the people of the Middle Ages wanted to know more about God, the teachings of Christ, and of the Church.

In order to satisfy this thirst for knowledge, the bishops invited famous scholars to lecture at the cathedral schools. Soon, crowds of young men began to attend these lectures. In time, students who wanted to become teachers studied a variety of subjects until they earned a *degree*. This was like a license to teach.

The First Universities. In the ancient world there had been many great teachers. Each one of them had large numbers of students. However, when a teacher died, his school came to an end. On the

Founded in 1441, King's College of Cambridge University is considered to be an excellent example of English medieval architecture.

dents of the Middle Ages were organized into groups with certain rights and duties. This organization of professors and students came to be called a *university*.

The popes of the Middle Ages encouraged an interest in learning. They granted charters to thirty-three universities. The charter stated the rights and duties of the professors and students. There were about forty other universities. Most of these had received their charters from emperors or kings. Every section of Catholic Europe had a university. The oldest universities were at *Bologna* (bȯ·lōn′yȧ) in Italy and at Paris in France. Other famous universities were at Salerno in Italy, Salamanca in Spain,

other hand, the great teachers of the Middle Ages trained others to take their places. The teachers and stu-

MEDIEVAL UNIVERSITIES

Prague in Czechoslovakia, Vienna in Austria, and Oxford and Cambridge in England.

At A Medieval University. In the Middle Ages, a single university would have throngs of students who had come from every country in Europe. These students had two things in common. They all had the same Catholic Faith, and they all spoke a common language, Latin, besides their own native tongue.

The universities had very little equipment. Books were very scarce because they had to be copied by hand. The students sat on rude benches and took notes while the professor lectured. All the lectures were in Latin. Students everywhere wore a special cap and gown. At our American colleges and high schools the same type of cap and gown is still worn at graduation time.

The students were interested in learning and discussing new ideas. They studied a variety of subjects—language, mathematics, science, history, geography, and music. These subjects formed a background for the most important study, the knowledge of God and His relationship with men. This was the subject that we call *theology* (thē·ŏl'ō·jĭ), and it was known as the *queen of sciences*. St. Thomas Aquinas was a great theology professor.

A
MEDIEVAL
STUDENT'S
DAY

5 A.M. STUDENTS AWAKE AND PREPARE FOR LECTURES

7 A.M.– 10 A.M. LECTURE

10 A.M.– 11 A.M. STUDY OF LECTURE NOTES

11 A.M. FIRST MEAL OF THE DAY, AND PREPARATION FOR AFTERNOON LECTURE

1 P.M.– 4 P.M. LECTURE

4 P.M.–5 P.M. STUDY OF LECTURE NOTES

5 P.M. SUPPER

7 P.M. EVENING STUDY HOURS

As early as the 1200's Roger Bacon predicted that one day men would drive horseless carriages and would fly through the air. He urged scientists to seek the truth through experimentation.

*   *   *   *   *

Why do you suppose theology was called the queen of sciences?

*   *   *   *   *

The teachers, or schoolmen, of the Middle Ages followed the ancient Greek philosopher Aristotle in their teaching of philosophy. However, they added many Christian ideas and developed a new system of philosophy. This system was taught at all the schools and universities of the Middle Ages, and it was called *scholastic* (skŏ·lăs′tĭc) *philosophy*. This philosophy is still taught at numerous colleges all over the world today.

A Great Scientist. The greatest scientist of the thirteenth century was *Roger Bacon*. He was an Englishman who became a Franciscan friar. He taught at two universities, Oxford and Paris, and he wrote many books for the pope. In these books, Bacon suggested that men could learn much more about nature and science by conducting experiments and watching the results. Thus, he can be considered a founder of the modern scientific method.

THE RISE OF MODERN LANGUAGES

Latin. For centuries, Latin, the language spoken by the Romans, remained the chief language of Europe. It was the language that the Church used to speak to all the peoples of the West—through ceremonies, sermons, hymns, and books. It was the language used in the law courts, in the classrooms, and in treaties between nations. Merchants trading with distant cities made use of Latin, which everyone could understand. The Bible was also studied in a Latin version.

Romance Languages. The Normans in France and the Lombards in Italy spoke and read the same Latin language, but they spoke it differently as did the men of each country. These variations of the Latin language eventually developed into the separate Romance languages — French, Italian, Spanish, Portuguese, and Rumanian.

For a long time, these popular languages were not written down. All books continued to be written in Latin, which all educated people could read. Yet, the people who were not educated talked to one another in their local language. Latin therefore became a dead language used only by the educated and only in certain times and places.

Language in the British Isles. Perhaps, in reading, you have noticed that the Romance languages—such as French, Spanish, and Italian—developed within the boundaries of the old Roman Empire. In those sections of Europe that had not been conquered or completely controlled by the Romans, other languages were spoken.

The people of Ireland, Scotland, Wales, and the Brittany district of France continued to speak Celtic languages.

You have already read that our own tongue, the English language, is very mixed. The Celts, the Romans, the Anglo-Saxons, and the Norman-French have all contributed words and expressions to the language that we speak today.

Other Languages. East and north of the Rhine River, the Teutonic peoples developed their own Germanic languages. The Slavic nations in the east of Europe had still another set of languages. At Constantinople and throughout the Eastern Roman Empire, the official language was Greek.

Folk Literature and Songs. During the early Middle Ages, no stories or books were written in the popular languages. However, people began

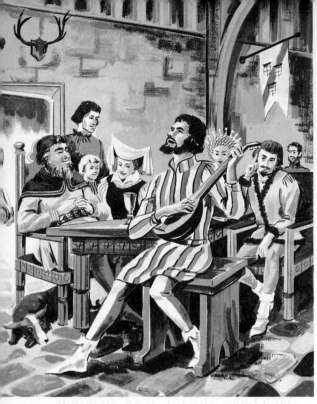

to develop a literature that was spoken. This was not a new practice as many of the ancient peoples had done the same. You may remember reading how the stories that Homer had told in ancient Greece were not written down until many years after his death.

You will remember reading about the songs that were sung in the castles of France about Charlemagne and Roland and in England about King Arthur and the Knights of the Round Table. These songs and tales, like those about Robin Hood, were sung or told in the popular languages.

Troubadours. In southern Europe, wandering poets, called troubadours or minstrels, began to appear during the early part of the Middle Ages. They journeyed from castle to castle where they entertained the people by telling wonderful stories of courage and valor. These stories were not recited, but were sung. To add to the entertainment, the singer usually accompanied himself on a lute.

In Germany these minstrels were called minnesingers, and in Ireland they were called bards. In Ireland,

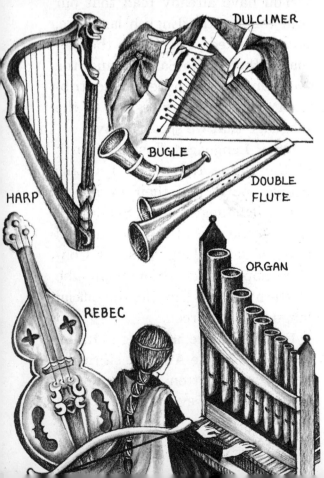

DULCIMER

BUGLE

DOUBLE FLUTE

HARP

ORGAN

REBEC

A scene from the Divine Comedy shows Dante being guided in heaven by the "divine Beatrice." Although some of Dante's characters were imaginary, most of them were actual historical figures.

the minstrels used the harp instead of the lute for accompaniment.

A Great Poet. By the beginning of the thirteenth century, most of the stories and songs in the popular languages had been written down in books. Printing, however, had not yet been invented.

The thirteenth century produced one of the greatest poets the world has ever known. This was *Dante* (dǎn'tė), who lived in the city of Florence in Tuscany, a section of Italy. When he began to write, Dante used the language that was spoken in his native Tuscany. Dante's writing was so beautiful and powerful that later writers imitated him, and in time the Tuscan dialect became the official Italian language.

In his greatest poem, the *Divine Comedy*, Dante leads his readers on an imaginary pilgrimage through hell, purgatory, and heaven. He describes the frightful results of sin and the terrible torments of hell. He tells how human beings may atone in purgatory for their offenses against God. In his book on paradise, Dante tells of the peace and happiness of the blessed souls in heaven as they enjoy the eternal vision of God.

This very long poem contains many vivid descriptions and interesting stories. The real meaning of the *Divine Comedy* concerns the struggle of each human being to gain a place in heaven. Thus, in the beautiful language of poetry, Dante expresses the deep religious fervor of the people of the Middle Ages.

Canterbury Tales. The first great poet to use the English language was Geoffrey Chaucer, who lived in the fourteenth century. Like Dante, he helped to form a modern language.

You may remember reading about Chaucer's *Canterbury Tales*. This is a story of a group of pilgrims traveling together to the shrine of St. Thomas à Becket at Canterbury. Instead of riding "dumb as a stone," they each agree to tell two tales to amuse the others. In telling these stories, Chaucer also shows us how the people of England lived six hundred years ago.

Books in the Middle Ages. In the Middle Ages, all books had to be written by hand. To make a copy of a book was a long, slow process. Some books were so valuable that they were chained to the reading stands in the libraries to prevent theft.

You will remember reading how the monks were the chief copyists. By long hours of careful labor, they made possible the great libraries attached to the monasteries and universities.

Many of the books copied by the monks were religious books, such as the Bible and the Missal, which contains the prayers of the Mass. The monks wanted every book used in the service of God to be as beauti-

The pilgrims below, from the Canterbury Tales, are traveling to the shrine of St. Thomas à Becket at Canterbury. Pilgrimages to the shrines of various saints were among the favorite holiday excursions for people of fourteenth-century England. Notice their dress.

When ancient libraries were destroyed, the books were salvaged and sent to medieval monasteries to be copied. Much classical literature has been preserved through the ages by this means.

ful as possible. They decorated or illuminated the pages with beautiful designs, pictures, and symbols of Our Lord and the saints. The initial letter in each chapter became a magnificent work of great beauty. In many of these books, the colors are just as vivid now as when the book was first made centuries ago.

Each one of these illuminated books is considered a great treasure today. They are given careful protection in our libraries in order that future generations may also see their beauty and workmanship.

* * * * *

Why should we protect and care for the books we use?

* * * * *

Summing Up. Even before all Europe was converted, the Church was building schools. Out of these schools grew the great universities that are still in existence today. Among the great teachers who were called schoolmen and who gave us scholastic philosophy—which still influences education today—was St. Thomas Aquinas.

The popular languages, such as English—which you speak—and the other modern languages, grew up during this same period. Some of the great works of literature were written in these languages. This literature includes Dante's *Divine Comedy* and Chaucer's *Canterbury Tales*.

Among the great masterpieces of the Middle Ages are the books that the monks wrote and copied. These beautiful manuscripts exist even today to inform and inspire us.

FOR BETTER UNDERSTANDING

Checking Up

1. Tell how the cathedral schools of the Middle Ages developed into great universities.

2. What were the chief studies at a medieval university?

3. Why is the friar, Roger Bacon, considered to be a founder of modern science?

4. How and where did the Romance languages develop?

5. What were some of the other popular languages that developed in Europe?

6. In what poem did Dante express the religious spirit of the medieval people?

7. What setting did Chaucer use to provide a basis for the different stories in the *Canterbury Tales?*

8. How did the monks of the Middle Ages beautify the books they were copying?

Yesterday and Today

1. List some of the ways that the books you use in school differ from Medieval manuscripts.

2. How is modern college life different from life at a medieval university?

3. What are some of the items in science that you have studied about this year which were not known in Roger Bacon's day?

Persons, Places, and Terms

Identify: Roger Bacon, Dante, Chaucer, St. Thomas Aquinas.

Locate: Bologna, Paris, Salerno, Salamanca, Prague, Vienna, Cambridge, Oxford, Florence.

Define: university, degree, theology, troubadour, minnesinger, bard, *Divine Comedy, Canterbury Tales.*

Interesting Things to Do

1. Plan a troubadour hour in which the members of your class present a program of songs or poems that tell stories.

2. By reading your library or classroom encyclopedias and books, find out all you can about the friar, Roger Bacon. Then the class can make a picture display showing some of the interesting things he discovered.

3. For your scrapbook, make sample pages of illuminated manuscripts. You can begin by choosing a poem, a passage from the Bible, or a selection from the Missal to copy and illustrate. Plan how you want your page to look. Then print your selection on good paper. Next, illustrate, or illuminate, the page with crayon or paint drawings and decorated capital letters.

24

The Growth of Towns and Trade

EUROPEAN TOWNS

New Towns. Late in the Middle Ages, many new towns came into existence. The names of many of these towns give us clues that explain their origin. In England, for example, town names having the suffix *bury* or *borough*, such as *Canterbury*, indicated a fortified place. In the same way, the suffix *caster* or *chester*, as in *Winchester*, meant that the town was originally a Roman camp. These towns were used as places of refuge by the people of the countryside when some danger threatened.

Some towns grew up at places that were favorable to trade. A good harbor, or a port at the mouth of a river—for example, *Plymouth*—attacted traders. Other towns were located where two roads met, or where a river could be forded, for example, *Stratford*, or where there

was a bridge across the river, as at *Cambridge*.

* * * * *

Can you find other examples, in the English language, of place names that show the origin of the towns?

* * * * *

Another group of towns grew up near castles and monasteries. These places offered both protection and employment to large numbers of people.

How the Towns Became Free. At first, most of the towns were part of the feudal system. Each town was subject to the lord upon whose estate it had developed. The lords demanded military service of the men; imposed heavy taxes; and charged the merchants heavy fees, or tolls, for passing through their territory. This was most unsatisfactory.

*   *   *   *   *

Can you tell why the lords' behavior towards the towns and merchants was unsatisfactory?

*   *   *   *   *

The towns tried to gain their independence, and many succeeded. In countries like England, France, and Spain, where a king was trying to decrease the power of the nobles, he frequently took the side of the towns against the nobles. The king would grant favors to the towns and help them gain their freedom from the nobles. The towns then paid taxes and were subject only to the king.

Most nobles who went to the Holy Land took their knights and soldiers with them. The nobles had plenty of land but very little money. To get the equipment and gold that they needed, they were willing to sell certain rights or even complete freedom to the towns on their land.

These rights were carefully writ-

ten down in a charter that a nobleman gave to a town in exchange for the funds he needed. A charter usually explained what taxes had to be paid and what privileges the townsmen were to enjoy. In most cases, the townsmen could elect a mayor and other officers to rule the city.

Usually, a charter freed the town from allegiance to a lord. Thereafter, the people of a town owed their loyalty directly to the king. As the towns continued to grow in importance in England, France, and Spain, the kings invited them to send representatives to the parliaments to sit with the nobles and bishops.

In Germany and Italy, where there was no strong king, many of the towns won complete freedom and became known as free cities. Like the city-states of ancient Greece, they became independent republics. As you will read later in this chapter, many of these free

The walls surrounding a medieval town offered protection to the inhabitants, but they limited the growth of the town.

cities became very prosperous and powerful.

Within the Walls of a Town. As a traveler during the later Middle Ages approached a town, he was met with a very impressive sight. At first, he saw the town as a fortress with high walls, great watchtowers, and heavily guarded gates. Beyond the walls, he could see the spires of the churches and cathedral, the belfry of the town hall, and the roofs of some of the larger houses.

Once inside the walls, the town might not seem so attractive. So many people wanted to live inside the protective walls of the towns that the towns were overcrowded.

The houses were often four or five stories high, with the upper floors extending out over the street in order to provide more apartments. At first, the roofs were made of thatch, but these caught fire so easily that tiles came to be used. A fire was a very serious matter in such crowded towns. If one house caught fire, the whole town might burn, and frequently did. A hand brigade passing buckets of water from wells or a river was not much help in controlling a fire.

*   *   *   *   *

Can you describe the many modern methods that are used to fight fires in our towns and cities today?

*   *   *   *   *

A visit from the king was the occasion for a holiday in medieval towns.

The streets in the towns of the Middle Ages were narrow and unpaved. In rainy weather walking was very difficult because of the mud. The sunlight hardly ever reached the streets because of the overhanging stories of the houses. Refuse was thrown into the streets, as the towns had no sewers and no street cleaners, garbage collectors, or sanitary departments.

Since there were no street lights, anyone going out at night carried a lantern with him. The wealthy traveler might also need a couple of armed servants to protect him from robbers. As you might guess, very few people ventured out at night.

Amusements. No one in the towns worked from Saturday noon until Monday morning. The holydays of the Church provided many holidays for the people. The children played many of the same games that we enjoy today. Boys and men played at wrestling, tilting, and various games of ball. The games, however, were likely to be interrupted by the procession of a bishop, or perhaps a noble with a troop of knights and soldiers in gleaming armor and bright livery. When the king rode through the city, the streets were covered with straw, and the houses were decked with colorful rugs, and bright silks hung from the windows. Everyone stopped what he was doing to enjoy the sight of these gay festivities.

One of the most attractive features of medieval town life was a religious procession. On several holydays during the year, great processions were held in honor of Our Lord, the Blessed Virgin, or some patron saint. The colorful procession began after Mass. Large numbers of men, women, and children dressed in their best clothes and carrying beautiful banners took part in the procession. Various groups of men carried floats which showed scenes from the life of Our Lord or the saints. After the procession, the people continued the festival in the great square in front of the cathedral. The rest of the day would be spent in games, contests, singing, and dancing.

Fairs in the Middle Ages. A fair ordinarily began on the feast of some patron saint, and the people attended Mass before the business of the fair began. Usually, a fair was held just outside the walls of the town.

The local people brought their wares or crops to sell. Some brought in sheep, pigs, cows, or chickens; and others brought farm produce. The chief attraction for people was the variety of goods brought by merchants from far-off places. Many of these items could be bought only when the merchants came.

If you had been at a fair in a German town of the Middle Ages, you might have seen men from England with strong woolen cloth, and merchants who had brought linens and laces and other fine cloth from the part of France called *Flanders*. Other merchants would have brought furs from Russia, and still others wines and iron from Spain. The merchants from the Italian cities would have displayed goods from the Eastern lands like Persia and India.

* * * * *

How does the medieval fair compare with the state fairs in this country?

* * * * *

Fairs were important to the commerce of the Middle Ages. They often lasted a week or longer and served as a clearinghouse not only for merchandise but also for ideas.

MERCHANT AND CRAFT GUILDS

Merchants Join Together. The growth of towns brought with it an increased need for more permanent stores and shops. More and more traders set themselves up as merchants in busy towns. To protect themselves from strange traders and unfair taxes, merchants formed societies called *merchant guilds.*

These guilds set standards of quality. No member could sell goods of poor quality or cheat his customers. As trade increased and the members grew wealthy, the guilds became very powerful. They took over more and more of the political offices of the towns until in most cities the government was entirely in their hands.

The activities and influence of these merchant guilds were not limited to their towns. They did many things for the comfort and security of their members in other countries. In foreign lands, some of the guilds kept homes where their members could live. Warehouses where merchandise could be stored were also maintained. The merchant guilds arranged with foreign guild officials for members to buy merchandise in foreign lands or to ship it through other territories.

You can see how the merchant guilds were largely responsible for the growth of towns and trade.

Craftsmen Join Together. At first, weavers, shoemakers, and such people not only made the cloth or shoes, but they also sold them. Many craftsmen made their articles in their own homes and had a shop in the front of the house to sell their goods. Because they were traders, they could join the merchant guilds. With the growth of towns and the increase in trade, the men who actually made an article organized societies called *craft guilds.*

All the men who were engaged in the same craft belonged to the same guild. There were guilds of carpenters, blacksmiths, weavers, saddlers, tailors, and every other type of craft, or skilled occupation. All members of a craft usually lived in the same street, or neighborhood, and many of the streets of the towns took their names from the local craft. If a person wanted leather for shoes, he went to the Street of the Tanners. It was about this time also that people began to adopt family names, and many took the name of their craft. This was the origin of names like Smith, Baker, or Cooper.

* * * * *

Can you guess what kind of craftsmen lived on Threadneedle Street in London?

* * * * *

Training of Craftsmen. If a man was a craftsman, his sons usually followed in his footsteps, but other boys could also be trained. The training took several years and could be just as difficult for a young boy as going to a regular school.

Usually, a boy between the ages of seven and ten who was to learn a craft would be sent to live as an *apprentice* with a master craftsman. There the boy made himself useful and in time learned the fine points of the craft. He received no pay, but the master gave him his board and room as well as his training.

After about seven years, the young man became a *journeyman*. Then he could receive daily wages for his work. He might also journey to other cities, or to other countries, studying the methods used by the members of his craft in different places.

In order to be admitted to the guild as a *master* craftsman, a young artisan had to pass a very strict examination. He had to prepare a *masterpiece* and present it to the guild masters for their inspection. If the other masters felt that his work was up to the high standard of

Members of the guilds paraded on the feast days of their patron saints and on other festival days. From the banners shown, can you identify the guilds represented?

CHAIN MAIL

A journeyman submits his masterpiece, a chain mail suit, to a guild master for inspection.

the craft, he was permitted to set himself up as a master craftsman.

The Guilds and the Church. The members of merchant and craft guilds were deeply religious. Each guild had a patron saint, whose name it took. For instance, the carpenters might belong to the Guild of St. Joseph. On the feast of the patron saint, all of the members of the guild and their families went to Mass, received Holy Communion, and then held a religious procession in honor of the saint.

Guilds also engaged in many works of charity. If a member became ill and could not work, the guild took care of him and his family. A guild usually supported aged members and the widows and orphans of its members. If a member who was the father of a family died, the guild paid for the training of the boys as apprentices or for their education at regular schools. In the later Middle Ages, the guilds built many schools to educate their own members' children and the children of the poor.

Some guilds maintained hospitals for the sick, and others loaned money to the needy. They also gave valuable help to their pastors in a variety of ways.

*   *   *   *   *

Do you or your parents belong to any groups, or societies, that engage in religious activities similar to those of the medieval guilds?

*   *   *   *   *

The guild members of the Middle Ages were inspired by the teachings of the Catholic Church concerning justice and charity. No man could charge more for his work than the just price. This was determined by the cost of the material plus a fair and reasonable return for the craftsman's labor. Each craftsman took great pride in his workmanship and would not make articles of poor quality. The guilds also supervised weights and measures so that the

322

buyer was always certain of an honest weight or measure.

Religious Plays. The guilds had a prominent part in the religious festivities of a town. The guild members would act out important scenes in the life of Christ. In this way, they helped to teach the people the great mysteries of the Faith, such as the birth, death, and resurrection of Our Lord. For this reason, the plays were called *mystery* or *miracle* plays. Even though the guild system has disappeared, this type of religious drama is still presented in the Catholic parts of Europe, and attracts visitors from all over the world.

Sometimes, guild members presented plays in which each actor represented either a virtue or a vice. These were called *morality* plays. Out of these plays developed our modern drama and many of its traditions. For example, from the morality plays, we get character parts for actors who represent either good or bad people.

MEDITERRANEAN TRADE

Venice. Two of the most important cities during the Middle Ages were *Venice* and *Genoa*. If you look at the map on page 290, you will see that Venice lies at the head of the Adriatic Sea. It is one of the few cities in Italy that was not founded by the early Etruscans, Greeks, or Romans. It was founded when the Huns invaded northern Italy, and some of the people fled to a group of islands a few miles from the mainland. After the danger of the Huns had passed, the people continued to live on these islands. They engaged in fishing and in making salt from the sea water. The Venetians became prosperous traders.

In time, they built the great and beautiful city of Venice on this group of islands. The main street of the city is the *Grand Canal* and other streets are also canals. The islands are connected by nearly four hundred bridges. Early in its history the city was placed under the protection of St. Mark, and a magnificent cathedral was built in his honor.

Genoa. As the map on page 290 shows, *Genoa* has a favored position on the western side of the Italian peninsula. The galleys of Genoa sailed to all sections of the Mediterranean and out into the Atlantic. When the trade of Genoa with the

East was finally cut off by the Turks, the sailors of Genoa began to look for a western route to the far Indies. One of the sailors of Genoa, *Christopher Columbus*, discovered America while searching for a new route to the East.

The Crusades gave Venice and Genoa their greatest prosperity and power. Most of the Crusaders had marched overland, but many of them went by sea from Italian ports. The Venetian and Genoese fleets carried many of these Crusaders to eastern ports. Later, they carried food and supplies to the Christians who remained in the Holy Land.

For its assistance to the Crusaders, one or the other of these cities was granted a section in every conquered port. There either Genoa or Venice built warehouses and wharves. Ships sent out from Italy with supplies returned laden with sugar, spices, silks, rugs, and perfumes from the East.

Florence. If you will look at the map on page 290, you will see the location of Florence, which was on the land route from Rome to the north. Florence had some of the best craftsmen of Europe. They made fine woolen and silk goods. They were also skilled in the making of metalwork and jewelry.

You have already read that the great poet Dante came from Florence and that the dialect of that

Italian ships returned from the East heavily laden with exotic goods. The ports of Venice and Genoa became prosperous and were known as centers of trade and culture.

section became the official language of the Italian people. Florence, in addition, has given us some of the most famous painters, sculptors, and architects that the world has ever known. America received its name from an explorer who was born in Florence—*Amerigo Vespucci* (ä′mȧ·rē′gȯ vĕs·pōō′chĕ).

The First Banks. One of the handicaps to trading in early medieval days was lack of money or any sort of bank. From trading in the East, the Italians learned much from the Arabs, and these Italian merchants built up the first banking system in Europe. Italian bankers did business all over Europe and throughout the East.

A merchant going to Egypt, for example, no longer had to carry sacks of gold with him. He gave his gold to a banker and was given a letter to the banker's agent in Egypt. This was a great help—no pirate or robber would be interested in such a letter.

* * * * *

Why wouldn't a robber be interested in a letter to a banker's agent?

* * * * *

NORTHERN EUROPEAN TRADE

Great Trade League. If you look on page 290, you will see the location of the Baltic Sea, which became a great highway of commerce for northern Europe.

In Germany there were many merchants. The first German *hanses* (hăns′ĕz), or guilds, were unions of merchants trading abroad. These merchants were trading in England as early as the tenth century. They had won from the English king the same trading rights as Englishmen.

These merchants also needed rights and protection at home. Robbers and feudal wars among the nobles made life miserable for the people. So the merchants of the German cities made agreements among themselves.

First, they granted each other's merchants the full rights of citizenship. Then, led by *Lübeck* (lōō′bĕk), a city on the Baltic Sea, several neighboring cities agreed to assist one another in fighting robbers and pirates. Under such agreements, the cities grew in size and wealth. Other cities joined, and the union eventually became a powerful guild, or hanse, of cities called the *Hanseatic* (hăn′sė̇·ăt′ĭk) *League.*

Hanseatic League. The Hanseatic League established trading posts along the shores of the Baltic and in other regions. The League had a post in London and one as far east as the city of Novgorod in Russia. These trading posts in distant lands served as market places, as storehouses for merchandise, and as fortresses for the members of the League.

For three hundred years the Hanseatic League had enormous power. It did not hesitate to use it for the benefit of its members. The League even had a very large navy and was strong enough to enforce its will against cities and even kings.

English Trade. England remained an agricultural country long after the Germans and Italians had become busy traders. The people of England exchanged their wool, skins, leather, tallow, salt meat, copper, lead, and tin for cloth, silks, and spices brought in by German and Italian merchants and traders.

When Danish kings ruled England, they encouraged trade between England and their homeland. When the Normans came to England, they too encouraged trade, but they favored foreign merchants for a long time. At the end of the fourteenth century there were probably not more than six towns with a population of more than five thousand people in the whole of England.

London was by far the largest and most important town. It had received a charter granting it certain rights and privileges, and it was a wealthy and prosperous city. Some of the best shops of the city were located on the famous London Bridge.

The first Englishmen to trade abroad were wool merchants. They had the sole right to buy English wool and sell it to foreign merchants. It was from English wool that the Italian weavers and the weavers in Flanders made cloth.

Flanders. The territory of Flanders covered very much the same area as the modern country of Belgium. The people of Flanders were engaged chiefly in the weaving of English wool into fine cloth. Some of the towns began to specialize in particular types of cloth. For instance, *cambric* cloth was made at *Cambrai* (kăm·brā′), and *lisle* was the chief product of *Lille* (lēl).

Merchants came from all parts of Europe to buy the woolen cloth of the towns of Flanders. The guild of merchants in Flanders formed its own hanse, which had members in nearly sixty towns. *Bruges* (brōōzh) and *Ghent* (gĕnt) became the leading towns of Flanders in the

326

early days. *Antwerp* (ănt'wûrp), now in modern Holland, became the leading town of Flanders in later times.

Summing Up. The growth of towns in the Middle Ages, brought on by the Crusades, resulted in an increase in the number of craftsmen. They traded their extra goods for farm products in a public place. Finally, the craftsmen opened little shops in their homes. Eventually, some of them traveled from town to town exchanging and trading goods.

Medieval towns were dusty and unhealthy places in which to live. So many people wanted to live inside its protective walls that the medieval town was usually extremely overcrowded.

Many towns became great centers of trade such as Venice, Genoa, and Florence in Italy.

In the towns, merchants and craftsmen came to form groups called guilds. Guild members paid dues and made rules that all had to obey. The guilds helped keep the quality of goods high, the prices fair, and members happy. The guilds also contributed to the social life of the Middle Ages and encouraged trade through the formation of such enterprises as the Hanseatic League.

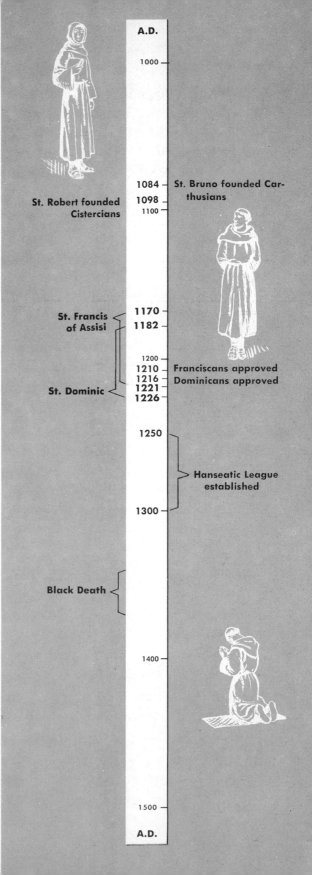

A.D.

1000

1084 — St. Bruno founded Carthusians
St. Robert founded 1098
Cistercians 1100

St. Francis 1170
of Assisi 1182

1200
1210 — Franciscans approved
1216 — Dominicans approved
St. Dominic 1221
1226

1250

Hanseatic League
established

1300

Black Death

1400

1500

A.D.

FOR BETTER UNDERSTANDING

 Checking Up

1. Describe the appearance of a medieval town.

2. Why were the holydays of the Church welcomed by the medieval people?

3. Describe a medieval fair.

4. What was the chief purpose of the merchant guilds?

5. Tell how the craft guilds were organized.

6. Explain how a boy of the Middle Ages prepared to become a master craftsman.

7. How did the guilds reflect the religious spirit of the people?

8. How did the teachings of the Church influence the medieval guilds?

9. What were the mystery and morality plays?

10. What was the Hanseatic League?

 Yesterday and Today

1. Have you ever been to a county, state, or other large fair? If so, compare and contrast it with what you know about a medieval fair.

2. Compare a medieval town with your town or city. How do they differ in appearance, recreational facilities, and public services?

 Places and Terms

Locate: Venice, Genoa, Adriatic Sea, Baltic Sea, North Sea, Florence, Lübeck, London, Ghent, Antwerp. Bruges.

Define: borough, charter, merchant guild, craft guild, apprentice, journeyman, master craftsman, mystery play, morality play, Grand Canal.

Interesting Things to Do

1. As a class, prepare a large picture map of Europe that will show the location of the chief towns and cities. On the map, place pictures or photographs of the chief products of each town. Consult your geography book and encyclopedias for suggestions.

2. For your scrapbook, make a list of important towns and cities close to your school. See what you can find about the origin of each town and the origin of its name.

3. Use your classroom or library encyclopedias to look up the history of the medieval guilds. Then make a report to your class about these guilds. Be sure you include the names of the patron saints of the various guilds as well as telling about the guilds' charitable and religious activities.

UNDERSTANDING THE UNIT

For Discussion

1. Tell why the friars were important in meeting the religious needs of the townspeople in the thirteenth century.

2. Describe the conditions that hindered trade in the early Middle Ages.

3. How did the Crusades help to increase trade?

4. Why were friars more important to the people of the Middle Ages than they are to us?

5. How were the towns able to gain self-government and other special privileges?

6. Tell why the trading towns of northern Europe formed the Hanseatic League.

For You to Answer

1. Describe the chief features of the Romanesque and Gothic styles of architecture.

2. Describe the chief work done in the Middle Ages by the religious orders founded by St. Dominic and St. Francis of Assisi.

3. Explain how the universities of the Middle Ages grew in size and importance.

4. Name two of the most important books written during the Middle Ages, and tell how each book influenced the development of a modern popular language.

5. What special services, or help, did a guild give to its members?

Linking Geography and History

1. Tell the special reasons why each of the following towns became important as a center of trade:

Venice — Constantinople
Marseilles — Genoa
Lübeck — Antwerp

2. Give examples of how a city or a nation of the Middle Ages was made rich by the seafaring activities of its people.

Interesting Things to Do

1. For your scrapbook, prepare a list of the many ways in which the Church influenced the lives of the people in the Middle Ages.

2. The merchants of Florence were the first European bankers. Use your encyclopedia, and then make a report to your class concerning the growth of banking during the Middle Ages. Be sure you tell how banking today differs from that of medieval times.

Books to Read

Boardman, Fon Wyman, *Castles.*
Chubb, Thomas C., *The Byzantines.*
Francis of Assisi, Saint, *Song of the Sun.*
Harnett, Cynthia, *Caxton's Challenge.*
Hewes, Agnes, *Spice Ho!*
Keiderstadt, Dorothy, *Knights and Champions.*
Lamprey, Louise, *In the Days of the Guilds.*
Larnen and Lomask, *St. Thomas Aquinas and the Preaching Beggars.*
Ormondroyd, Edward, *The Tale of Alain.*
Ritchie, Rita, *Golden Hawks of Genghis Khan.*

UNIT 9
The Age of Change

(1300 A.D. — 1600 A.D.)

CHAPTER
25. A New Age of the Arts and Learning
26. Protestant Revolution and Catholic Reformation
27. Europeans Begin to Explore the World

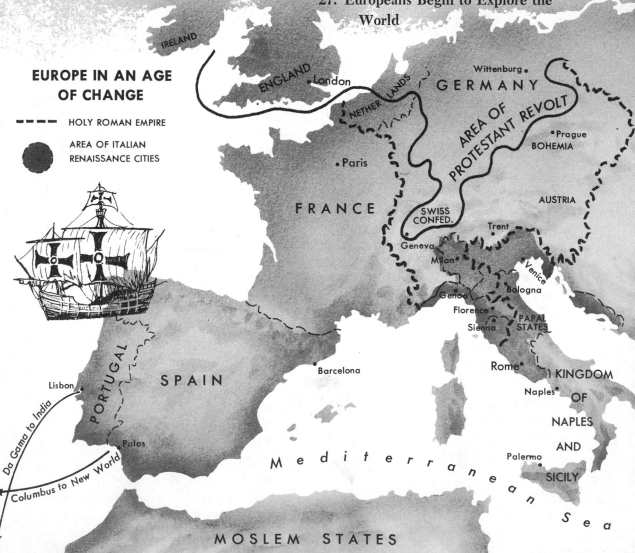

EUROPE IN AN AGE OF CHANGE

- - - - HOLY ROMAN EMPIRE

● AREA OF ITALIAN RENAISSANCE CITIES

IRELAND

ENGLAND

London

NETHERLANDS

GERMANY

Wittenburg

AREA OF PROTESTANT REVOLT

Prague
BOHEMIA

Paris

FRANCE

SWISS CONFED.

AUSTRIA

Geneva

Trent

Milan

Venice

Genoa

Bologna

Florence

Sienna

PAPAL STATES

PORTUGAL

Lisbon

Da Gama to India

Palos

Columbus to New World

SPAIN

Barcelona

Rome

KINGDOM

OF

Naples

NAPLES

AND

Palermo

SICILY

M e d i t e r r a n e a n   S e a

MOSLEM   STATES

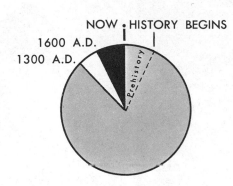

NOW • HISTORY BEGINS
1600 A.D.
1300 A.D.
Prehistory

INTRODUCTION

The life and ideas of man never stand still or remain the same. They are always changing. We live in an age that is witnessing many rapid and exciting changes. In this unit you will learn that such a period of rapid change was experienced toward the close of the Middle Ages. It was an age of intellectual energy in Western Europe during which medieval men began to seek new knowledge about God's world and to have new ideas about art, literature, and science.

During this period, some men refused to accept the teachings of the Catholic Church. As a result, many people left the Church and joined new Protestant sects. Popes and bishops then set out to find new methods of bringing the truths of Christ to those who accepted false beliefs. The Catholic Reformation, as this movement came to be called, resulted in a strengthening of the Church and in the establishment of new religious orders.

The interest of the people who lived in this era was not confined to books and art and inventions. There were daring voyages and explorations that opened new trade routes to the Far East and led to the discovery of the New World. The exploration of lands then unknown was just as exciting and as important as the exploration of outer space is today.

The discovery of the New World led thousands of Europeans to cross the Atlantic to the Western Hemisphere. There they founded colonies which, in time, became great nations. These people brought with them the ideas and ideals of Western Civilization, whose origin and development you have read about in this book.

_____ 25

A New Age of the Arts and Learning

A REBIRTH OF INTEREST IN THE ANCIENT WORLD

The Crusades and Learning. The scholars of the Middle Ages had never lost their interest in the knowledge acquired by the ancient Greeks and Romans. For instance, St. Thomas Aquinas followed many of the teachings of the Greek philosopher, Aristotle, and the poet Dante was a follower of the Roman poet, Virgil. Latin was the official language of the Church and the universities in the West, while Greek continued to be the official language in the Eastern Roman Empire.

Impressed by the survival of Greek learning at Constantinople, returning Crusaders brought copies of Greek books back to Europe. Many of these books had not been seen by scholars in Western Europe since before the barbarian invasions. Often these books were donated to the universities and were valued as priceless treasures. After the Crusades, popes, kings, and scholars began a real treasure hunt to find more of these ancient manuscripts. These ancient books began to be called _classics_.

The Merchants Support the Arts. The wealth from trade that was flowing into the towns also helped to produce this great revival of learning that we call the _Renaissance_ (rĕn′ĕ·zäns′). Renaissance is a French word which means _rebirth_ or _to be born again_. The age, or the period, of the Renaissance is generally considered to be the two hundred years after the Crusades (1300 to 1500).

A number of the wealthy merchants were anxious to have copies of ancient Greek or Roman art

Lorenzo de' Medici, a Renaissance prince, patronized the arts and learning in Italy.

works, or works in the ancient style. So the merchants were willing to support sculptors and artists. In fact, many wealthy merchants began to compete with one another as patrons of the arts.

When the Turks conquered the Eastern Empire, a number of the scholars from Constantinople fled to Italy where they became professors at the various universities.

These two factors, revival of interest in the classics and the merchants' patronage of artists, were among the most important influences that were responsible for the Renaissance.

Italy. The Renaissance began in the cities of Italy. During the late Middle Ages, the people of the city of Florence began to show a great interest in art and literature. It was Florence that first invited a Greek scholar to give lectures to its citizens. Florence was also the birthplace of many of the most renowned artists of the Renaissance and of the great poet Dante. Its cathedral, palaces, and public buildings are among the most beautiful in the world, and they reflect the spirit of the Renaissance.

Rome also became an important center of Renaissance study—ancient history, literature, and science—that was called the *new learning*. The popes of the Renaissance period were outstanding students of the ancient classics as well as patrons of the revival in art. Pope *Nicholas V* founded the Vatican library, which has one of the largest collections of books in the world. He sent scholars to search for the manuscripts of ancient books. He kept hundreds of persons busy recopying the old manuscripts. By his encouragement he helped to spread the new learning to other sections of Europe.

St. Peter's. The most magnificent monument of the Renaissance in Italy is the *Basilica of St. Peter* in Rome. It is the largest church in the entire world. It was built on the spot where St. Peter, the first pope, was martyred. The building of the present St. Peter's was begun in the year

1506, not many years after Columbus made his first voyage to America. The work was not completed until 1626, six years after our Pilgrim Fathers landed at Plymouth Rock. Hundreds of thousands of people make trips to Rome each year to visit this basilica, to pray at the tomb of St. Peter, and to receive the blessing of the Holy Father.

RENAISSANCE ART

Architecture. Architects of the Renaissance began to use Greek columns and Roman arches in their buildings. They thought that the great cathedrals built during the Middle Ages were barbaric. They used the name *Gothic*, after the barbarian Goths, to show their contempt for the style of architecture that was so different from the ancient classical style.

If you look at the picture of St. Peter's Church in Rome on this page, you can see how the architects used the Greek columns and the Roman arch throughout the building. You will notice that the most prominent part of the church is its

St. Peter's Church in Rome, the largest Christian Church in the world, was begun in 1506 but was not completed until more than one hundred years later. The original part of the church was built over what was believed to be the tomb of St. Peter.

Raphael's *Sistine Madonna* (above) and Michelangelo's *Delphic Sibyl* (below) are outstanding examples of Renaissance painting.

magnificent dome, which is a development of the arch. You will find many of the same features in St. Paul's Cathedral at London.

* * * * *

Are there any famous public buildings in the United States that have copied this Renaissance style? If so, can you name some of them?

* * * * *

Paintings. During the Middle Ages, artists painted pictures of Our Lord, His Blessed Mother, and the saints. At first the artists tried to imagine what Christ and His Blessed Mother looked like, but their pictures had no life or expression. Then the artists tried to make the Christ Child and Our Lady look like children and mothers that they knew. Everyone liked these new pictures so well that the artists of the Renaissance began to paint pictures of ordinary people.

Many of the great paintings of the Renaissance were painted on the walls, and sometimes the ceilings, of churches and palaces. These paintings are called *frescoes* (frĕs′kōz). To paint a fresco the artist mixed his colors with water and then painted on a newly plastered surface. The artists later learned to mix oil with their colors and to paint on wood or on canvas.

With each artist making some improvement, pictures gradually improved. Then at the end of the fifteenth century came three outstanding Italian painters— *Michelangelo* (mī′kĕl·ăn′jĕ·lō), *Leonardo da Vinci* (lä·ō·när′dŏ dä vĕn′chĕ), and *Raphael* (răf′ȧ·ĕl).

Michelangelo. The pope asked Michelangelo (1475-1564) to decorate the Sistine Chapel. This is the private chapel of the pope, and it is located in the Vatican Palace. For four and a half years Michelangelo lay on his back, painting the ceiling of this chapel. No painting in the world equals this fresco for boldness and grandeur. This great painting tells the story of the Creation from the Old Testament and many other Biblical stories as well. There are more than three hundred figures in it.

Michelangelo was gifted in many ways. In addition to being a painter and sculptor, he was a poet, a scientist, an architect, and an engineer. When he was about seventy years of age, he designed the great dome of St. Peter's Church in Rome.

Leonardo da Vinci. One of the most remarkable men in history was Leonardo da Vinci (1452-1519). His interest in almost all of the arts and sciences was characteristic of the Renaissance man.

In his pictures, Leonardo tried to show people as they appeared when they were sad or happy or angry. Among his greatest pictures is *The Last Supper*. In this great painting, he pictures Christ and the twelve apostles. Christ has just announced that one of them would betray Him. The painting shows that the apostles were startled and dismayed at the statement. The faces of the apostles express their feelings. You can see the guilt of Judas, although he tries to hide it.

Leonardo was interested in nature. He experimented with many things. Modern scholars who read his notebooks are amazed at his understanding of scientific truths. From his study of birds and their flight, he designed an airplane that needed only a motor to fly. Leonardo was also a writer, a musician, and an engineer. He even built fortifications for the city of Milan.

Raphael. Raphael (1483-1520) was a Renaissance artist noted for his paintings of *Madonnas*. A Madonna is a picture representing the Blessed Mother and the Christ Child. Raphael's Madonnas were admired for their soft colors and for their tranquility. *The Sistine Madonna*, on page 336, is one of Raphael's most famous paintings. In this picture, the painter included *St. Bar-*

The ancient *Apollo of the Belvedere* (above) from the 4th century, and Michelangelo's *David* (below) from the Renaissance, are sometimes compared. Can you see any similarities?

bara and *Pope Sixtus*, who are adoring the Christ Child. At the bottom of the picture, Raphael painted two *cherubs*, or little angels.

Madonnas were a favorite subject of the Renaissance painters. Hundreds of beautiful Madonnas were painted during this period.

Leonardo and Michelangelo were natives of Florence. Raphael was born in another section of Italy, but went to Florence to study art when he was about twenty years old. In spite of his youth, Raphael was soon accepted as an equal of the other great artists of Renaissance Florence.

The pope invited Raphael to live in Rome and to decorate several rooms in the Vatican Palace. Both Raphael and Michelangelo were working at the Vatican at the same time. It is no wonder that every visitor to Europe wants to see the Vatican Palace and the great Church of St. Peter, which adjoins it.

Sculpture. The wealthy merchants of Florence and other Italian cities brought many of the fine old statues from Greece. These statues were set up in outdoor gardens or in the merchants' and nobles' palaces. Many young artists and sculptors came to study these statues because they seemed so natural and lifelike.

These two scenes from Ghiberti's famous doors depict Christ driving the money changers from the temple and Christ walking on the water. The gold used to cover the doors is almost intact.

Michelangelo was also one of the sculptors of Florence. Once the citizens of Florence asked young Michelangelo to see what he could do with a great piece of marble that another sculptor had started to carve but had never finished. After working for many months, Michelangelo completed one of the most beautiful statues in the world, the statue of *David*. From a cold block of marble, Michelangelo was able to create a statue showing the strength and character of the boy who killed Goliath and went on to become king of Israel.

Not all the sculptors used marble in making their statues. Some of the skilled craftsmen of Florence made figures of gold or silver or bronze. A famous sculptor that used bronze was *Lorenzo Ghiberti* (gḗ·bĕr′tḗ). He lived from 1378 to 1455. Ghiberti fashioned a pair of bronze doors for the *baptistry* (băp′tĭs·trĭ) opposite the cathedral in Florence. Each door had several panels on which were carved scenes from the Bible. The people of Florence thought these doors were beautiful enough to be placed at the entrance of heaven.

Northern Painters. The early German and Flemish artists liked to paint on wooden panels. These panels were used to decorate church altars. The greatest of these altar pieces were painted by two brothers,

Hubert and Jan van Eyck (vän īk′). The Van Eycks were the most famous of the Flemish artists.

Hubert van Eyck (1366?-1426) perfected the art of oil painting. This was of great importance. Pictures painted by earlier methods were easily damaged by dampness and the colors did not always last. Hubert's techniques made it possible for paintings to remain bright and beautiful for centuries.

Many of the pictures painted by Jan van Eyck (1370?-1440) were portraits, that is, lifelike pictures of individual people. Portrait painting was a type of painting for which the Flemish and German artists became famous. Besides contributing to the art of painting in oil, the Van Eycks had an immense influence on the artists who followed them.

Another Flemish Painter. Of the great Flemish painters who followed the Van Eycks, *Peter Paul Rubens* (rōo′bĕnz),) is perhaps the most outstanding. Rubens (1577-1640) spent many years in Italy studying the Italian masters. He added some of the color and richness of the Italians to the rather severe Flemish style.

Wealthy merchants as well as nobles were eager to have their portraits painted. Rubens was flooded with orders for portraits and church pictures. Two of his greatest religious pictures are *The Descent from the Cross* and *The Assumption of the Blessed Virgin.*

The Pagan Renaissance. In the beginning of the Renaissance period, men were as pious and devoted as the men of the Middle Ages. The great painters, sculptors, and architects of the Renaissance used their talents for the service of God. Later, men began to use pagan subjects for their books and paintings and statues. Some people of the Renaissance period even began to try to live and think like the pagans of ancient Greece and Rome.

The ancient pagans had no knowledge of the true God. The gods whom they worshiped were more like men. Since some of the people of the Renaissance imitated the ancient pagans, they exalted man and ignored God.

The men of the Middle Ages had created a society where all people worked for the common good, and all were inspired by a zeal for Christian charity. Some men of the Renaissance tended to make the individual man so important that charity and justice were forgotten. Instead, men began to exalt fame and wealth, pleasure and power. Thus, many men became selfish, greedy, and godless.

340

Modern methods of printing that we take for granted today began in Gutenberg's shop. The printing of books made them more accurate and helped to standardize grammar and spelling.

NEW DISCOVERIES

The Printing Press. Perhaps no other invention has meant more to the world than the invention of the printing press. This happened midway in the Renaissance period. From about the ninth century on, people had known how to make a single print on a page. A single letter, or an entire word, or sometimes a paragraph would be cut into a small block of hard wood. Frequently, a picture was carved on the block with an explanation in printed words carved below the picture. Then the block was inked, and an impression was made on parchment. This system of engraved blocks, however, never could produce books rapidly.

Movable type was developed in Germany by a man named *Johann Gutenberg* (yō'hän gōō't'n·bûrg). He made a great many sets of individual metal letters, or type. Then he fitted the letters together into a shallow tray. After inking this tray of type, he was able to stamp, or print, a whole paper sheet, or page, at a time. You can see how easy it would be to make up and print many pages, as well as make changes in any of the pages of type already made up.

The Bible. The largest book that came from Gutenberg's press was the Latin version of the Bible. This was printed in the year 1454. You may see a copy of this famous book in the Library of Congress at Washington, D.C., where it is one of the chief treasures.

Soon after Gutenberg's invention of movable type, other printers set up presses in various parts of Europe. It is estimated that about twenty million volumes were printed before 1500. A book was then no longer a priceless work that took several years of copying by hand to complete. With more books available, books became reasonable in price. More and more people owned books. The libraries of the schools and universities could then make even larger collections of good books.

* * * * *

In what ways did the invention of the printing press benefit mankind?

* * * * *

New Materials. You may remember reading how the ancient Egyptians had invented a kind of paper made from the papyrus reeds that grew along the Nile. During the Middle Ages the monks used parchment for their manuscripts. Parchment was made from the skins of animals, especially sheep. Both the papyrus and parchment were very strong and durable. They were also too scarce and expensive to supply enough paper for the new printing presses.

The Arabs, however, had learned from the Chinese how to make paper from silk. The merchants of southern Europe learned this process from the Arabs. Then, the Spaniards learned how to make the hemp and flax, which grow in their country, into a fine linen paper. This paper was much cheaper than the parchment, and it took the ink impression from the type much better.

Water Travel Improved. The Crusades had helped to improve travel by water. Bigger ships were built to carry large armies to the Holy Land. Merchants then found the larger ships to be valuable because they could carry heavier cargoes.

The perfection of the *magnetic compass* helped more than anything else to make the science of navigation more exact. Men had known for a long time that a needlelike piece of magnetized iron, floating on top of a piece of wood in a container of water, would always point north and south. During the Renaissance, the magnetic needle, as it came to be called, was taken out of water and mounted on a pivot over a compass card that showed variations and gradations in direction. This made the magnetic compass really useful for ships. With such a guide, ships could cross the seas without fear. No longer need ships hug the seacoast where they were always in danger of pirate attacks.

* * * * *

Why was it possible for men to sail their ships across the seas without fear by using the improved magnetic compass?

* * * * *

Modern Astronomy. Before the improvement in the magnetic compass, sailors at sea charted the position of their ship in relation to the stars each night. Then they could compute how far they had traveled in a day. Among the scientists who studied the stars was a canon of the cathedral in *Frauenburg* (frou′ĕn·bŏŏrk), Poland. His name was *Nicolous Copernicus* (nĭk′ṓ·lā′ŭs kṓ·pûr′nĭ·kŭs) and he lived from 1473 to 1543. Copernicus made an important discovery. The ancient Greeks had taught that the sun and the stars moved around the earth. For two thousand years all students were taught this same idea. Copernicus studied the movements of the stars for many years. He decided that the earth was a planet, or celestial satellite, and that it moves in a regular order around the sun. He wrote a book explaining these ideas and dedicated the book to *Pope Paul III*.

It took a long time to make people change their ideas about the earth, stars, and sun. They wanted more proof. The proof came about fifty years later when an Italian astronomer named *Galileo Galilei* (găl′ĭ·lē′ṓ gä′lĕ·lâ′ĕ), who lived from 1564 to 1642, improved the telescope. With this instrument, Galileo could see the stars and planets more

Scientists did not pay much attention to Copernicus's theory because he was unable to support it with evidence.

clearly. He saw that some of them moved as Copernicus thought they did. Galileo, however, was jailed for his advanced beliefs. You can see that it took a long time before most people would accept these new ideas.

Calendar Reform. You may remember from studying your science that the calendar is a measure of days, weeks, months, and seasons, all of which go to make up a year. This calendar measure is based on the position of the earth in relation to the sun. The measurement of a day is easy—sunrise to sunrise, or sunset to sunset. However, the measurement of the sun's position on one particular day to the same

343

position 365 days (one year) later is much more difficult. It was particularly hard for men of earlier ages because they knew little of the true movement of the earth. Therefore, their calendars were incorrect. Yet, this was not always obvious to them. It, however, became apparent to the men of the Renaissance period.

The calendar being used during the Renaissance was that which had been drawn up under Julius Caesar and was called the *Julian Calendar*. By the late sixteenth century, the astronomers saw that the Julian Calendar differed from the sun's time about ten days. For example, the calendar said that it was sum-mer ten days before the day when the sun's direct rays reached the Tropic of Cancer, which is the first day of summer.

Pope Gregory XIII made the necessary calendar changes in 1582. He omitted ten days from that year. That brought the calendar into agreement with the sun time. Then, the pope ordered an extra leap-year day to be added every four years. This was done because the earth does not move around the sun in exactly 365 days, but 365 days and a fraction of a day. Thus with a leap-year day added, the calendar is kept right with the sun's time. This addition has kept the calendar cor-

RENAISSANCE ADVANCES

NEW WEAPONS

MOVABLE TYPE

DISCOVERY AND TRADE

rect since that time. Today we still use the *Gregorian Calendar*.

* * * * *

How do scientific discoveries and inventions of the Renaissance affect our lives today?

* * * * *

Summing Up. As a result of the Crusades and the increase of trade, Western Europe became very aware of the ancient culture of the East and of the great heritage that this culture carried on from ancient Rome and Greece.

As a result of this acquaintance with the glories of the past, a new era in history came about in Western Europe. This period of history saw a rebirth of interest in the contributions of the Greeks and Romans. This historical period is called the Renaissance.

Out of this Renaissance period came a new interest in art, in literature, in language, in architecture, in science, and in inventions.

Many of the wonderful things we have in the modern world had their beginnings during the Renaissance. However, many people of the Renaissance forgot about Catholic principles and tried to imitate the pagan ideals of the Greeks and Romans. From this came much suffering and evil in later European history.

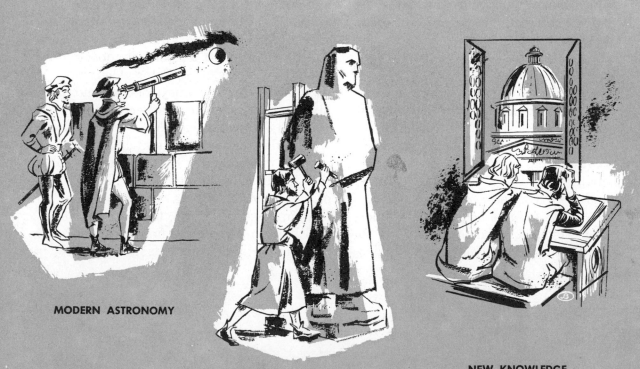

MODERN ASTRONOMY

REVIVAL OF THE ARTS

NEW KNOWLEDGE

FOR BETTER UNDERSTANDING

Checking Up

1. How did the popes encourage the new learning?

2. What were some of the changes made in the style of architecture during the Renaissance period?

3. List some of the chief accomplishments of Leonardo da Vinci.

4. Why was Michelangelo considered a great artist?

5. Name some of the chief paintings of Raphael.

6. In what way did men of the Renaissance turn to pagan ideas?

7. From whom did the Europeans learn how to make paper?

8. What invention made navigation much safer?

9. What changes were made in the calendar by Pope Gregory XIII?

10. Identify each of the following dates and tell the importance of each: 1454, 1506, 1582.

Yesterday and Today

1. How much of your learning at school depends on the invention of the printing press? Could recent inventions like television become adequate substitutes for the printed materials you now use?

2. Are you familiar with some important examples of modern art? If so, compare them with some of the paintings of the Renaissance about which you have studied.

Persons, Places, and Terms

Identify: Pope Nicholas V, Michelangelo, Ghiberti, Leonardo da Vinci, Raphael, Hubert van Eyck, Rubens, Gutenberg, Copernicus, Galileo, Pope Gregory XIII.

Locate: Florence, Rome, Venice, London.

Define: Renaissance, classics, dome, sculptor, baptistry, Madonna, fresco, Sistine Chapel, parchment, magnetic compass, telescope.

Interesting Things to Do

1. As a class prepare an arts festival that will show examples (photographs and drawings) of painting, sculpture, and architecture typical of the Renaissance. Use your encyclopedias and check your local library for help.

2. Write a report for your scrapbook about the beauty of St. Peter's Church in Rome. Use your encyclopedia and library, and ask your teacher to help you find other information.

3. Today we are still searching for ancient manuscripts. You will be interested in learning about the finding of the *Dead Sea Scrolls* and what they contain. Ask your teacher, or your parish priest, to help you find out about these important documents.

26

Protestant Revolution and Catholic Reformation

CAUSES OF THE REVOLT

False Beliefs. You know that most of the truths that we as Catholics believe are found in the Apostles' and Nicene Creeds. When we say these Creeds, we are showing our belief in the truths that Christ taught. In order to preserve these truths, Christ founded the Church with the apostles as its bishops and St. Peter as its head.

*   *   *   *   *

In what ways do the bishops and pope help us today to better understand the truths of the Catholic Church?

*   *   *   *   *

Through the centuries, certain men have denied some of these Catholic truths. Other men have taught ideas different from the real teachings of Christ. These false teachings are called *heresies*, and

the false teachers are called *heretics*.

The leaders of the Church have always had the duty to point out the errors of false teachers, or heretics. Sometimes these heretics have given up their heresies and returned to the Catholic Church. Others have refused to accept the true teachings and are not counted as members of the Church.

Bad Leaders. You have read how, during the Middle Ages, kings and emperors had bestowed great areas of land on the Church. These leaders knew that these lands would be well governed. Naturally, these lands became a source of great wealth for the Church.

Power-loving rulers and nobles often wanted to gain control of the Church lands. To accomplish this purpose, they sometimes persuaded greedy relatives and friends to enter religious life, and then they helped these relatives to become bishops and abbots. Then, these unworthy leaders used the Church's offices to enrich themselves and their relatives and friends who had helped them. The unworthy leaders often failed to carry out the religious duties of their positions and more often neglected to teach the faithful the truths of Christ's religion. As a result, there was a great danger when the heretics began to preach their doctrines, because many persons were not able to tell the difference between the true teachings of the Church and the false teachings of the heretics. Likewise, the idle life of these unworthy leaders gave scandal to the faithful and caused many to have doubts about the sincerity of the Church's mission.

National Unity. All through the Middle Ages there had been disputes between the popes and the rulers of the various countries concerning the rights of the Church. Emperors, kings, and nobles wanted to decrease the influence of the popes in order to increase their own power. As the feeling of national unity and false local pride grew stronger in each of the European nations, the people often sided with their king, who was close by, and against the pope, who was far away.

* * * * *

Should patriotism, or love of country, affect religious belief? Explain why or why not.

* * * * *

These three reasons—heresy, unworthy men in high positions in the Church, and national pride—gave rise to a revolt against the teachings and authority of the Church. This revolt is sometimes called the *Protestant Reformation.* However, it was a separation and revolt from the Church and is more properly called a *revolution.* The Church's efforts to combat both the evils that caused this revolution, as well as the bad effects of the revolution itself, is what we call the *Catholic Reformation,* or the *Counter-Reformation.*

THE REVOLT

German Protestantism. In the year 1517, *Martin Luther*, an Augustinian monk and a professor at the University in *Wittenberg* (wĭt″n·bûrg), Germany, attacked some of the practices in the Church that had grown up with regard to indulgences. These practices were not approved by the officials of the Church, and Luther had a right to criticize them. However, he soon went on to deny some of the chief teachings of the Church.

Luther, who lived from 1483 to 1546, began to teach that a man could attain salvation merely by having strong faith in God. The Catholic Church has always taught that man must express faith by performing good deeds in order to merit salvation. In addition, the Church has always urged the faithful to receive the sacraments in order to obtain sanctifying grace. Luther said that faith alone was necessary. He rejected five sacraments and the need for sanctifying grace. He also rejected the teachings on Purgatory and the need for an ordained priesthood.

The invention of the printing press and the great increase in the number of presses became one of Luther's chief weapons in his war on the Church. He wrote and printed many fiery pamphlets and distributed them far and wide. Many people believed what Luther wrote and supported him.

Luther also gained support from some of the German princes, especially *Frederick*, the Elector of Saxony. Some of the nobles saw an opportunity to seize the lands of the Church. Others wanted to weaken the power of the Holy Roman Emperor, *Charles V* of Spain, the grandson of Ferdinand and Isabella. Charles was loyal to the teachings of the Church.

Switzerland. *John Calvin* (1509-1564), who was of French background, studied to be a priest, but later decided to study law at Paris.

Luther used the invention of the printing press to spread his ideas to other people. Here, he examines a copy of a pamphlet he has written before it is distributed.

When he was twenty years old, he began to preach doctrines that were similar to Luther's. The French king, *Francis I*, was opposed to heresy in his kingdom, so Calvin went to Switzerland where he later made Geneva his headquarters.

Calvin thought that men no longer needed the Church as a guide to the teachings of Christ. Calvin said that everyone could take his own meaning and understanding from the Bible, but he persecuted those who did not believe as he did about the Bible.

Calvin taught that from the beginning of time God had destined certain men to be saved and all other men to be damned. Under this system it was not necessary for anyone to perform good deeds in order to merit salvation. Calvin rejected all the sacraments except baptism, and he accepted a commemoration of the Last Supper, which was very different from the Mass.

Scotland. Calvin gained many supporters among the merchants and bankers of France and Holland. One of his chief disciples, *John Knox*, went to Scotland where he founded the *Presbyterian Church*. Calvinism spread into England, where it was opposed by the government. Later, a group of English Calvinists went to Holland and then

came to America seeking religious freedom. These were the Pilgrims who landed at Plymouth in 1620.

Protestantism in England. You may remember reading that England had engaged in the Hundred Years' War with France. This was followed by a civil war in England known as the *Wars of the Roses* (each side had a different colored rose as its symbol). For thirty years (1455-1485) two rival families, the House of York and the House of Lancaster, fought bitterly for the throne of England. In 1485, when all England was exhausted by the long and terrible war, *Henry Tudor* (tū′dẽr) was recognized as *King Henry VII*. He married the heiress of the rival family, *Elizabeth of York*, who was the daughter of Edward IV. This brought peace and order to the kingdom.

One result of this war was to increase the power of the king beyond anything that had ever been known in England. Because most of the great nobles had been killed during the civil war, there was little opposition to the king, either in the Parliament or on the field of battle.

When *Henry VIII* (1491-1547) succeeded his father, Henry VII, as king of England, he was a staunch Catholic. In fact, Henry VIII wrote a book which condemned the teachings of Luther. Because of this, in 1521, the pope conferred on Henry the title *Defender of the Faith*.

Later, however, King Henry asked the pope to grant him a divorce from Queen Catherine, who was the daughter of Ferdinand and Isabella of Spain. The pope refused to grant the divorce because it was against the law of God.

Henry became enraged. He went to Parliament and asked them to make him head of the Church in England. There were very few in Parliament who dared oppose the king. In 1534, Parliament declared that the king was the head of the Church in England. They also granted him a divorce. Henry was later married five more times. The pope excommunicated Henry VIII in 1538.

In order to further increase his power and to weaken the position of the loyal Catholics, Henry closed hundreds of monasteries, colleges, hospitals, and shrines. He distributed, or sold, the Church lands to his own followers.

Opponents of Henry. There was much popular opposition to the changes that King Henry was making in the Church. There were also people in high places who defied the king. One of these was *John Fisher*, bishop of Rochester, a saint-

Sir Thomas More was popular with the common people as Chancellor of England.

ly and learned man. The pope made Bishop Fisher a cardinal for his loyalty to the true Church. However, St. John Fisher was beheaded at the king's order before he received the red hat, which is the symbol of the cardinal's position.

Another prominent martyr was *St. Thomas More*. He was a distinguished Catholic author, gentleman, and lawyer, who was one of the outstanding leaders of the Renaissance in England. He wrote a book, called *Utopia* (ŭ·tō′pĭ·à), in which he gave his ideas on what a perfect government would be like.

St. Thomas More was such an outstanding man that the king had made him Chancellor of England. However, St. Thomas More would not recognize the king as the head of the Church, and he did not approve the king's divorce from Queen Catherine. As a result, St. Thomas was arrested, separated from his wife and children, and beheaded in the year 1535.

These two famous martyrs were canonized by *Pope Pius XI* in 1935.

England after Henry VIII. It took a long time to break England away from the Catholic Faith. The people did not want a new religion. Under *Edward VI*, the son and successor of Henry VIII, the government outlawed the Mass, the sacraments, and Catholic priests and nuns. A generation then grew up that barely knew what the Catholic Church was like.

Edward VI died in 1553 and was succeeded by *Queen Mary*, the daughter of Henry and Queen Catherine. Mary was a devout Catholic, and it looked for a while as if England would remain a Catholic country. Mary's reign was only a short one: she died in 1558. Her sister *Elizabeth* then became queen, and she chose as her advisers men who were opposed to the Catholic Church. Elizabeth accepted the title head of the Church of England. The *Church of England*, or the *Anglican Church* as it is sometimes called, has remained the official church in England ever since. In the United States, it is known as the *Episcopal Church.*

Later Developments. When Luther and his followers protested against the laws that the emperor, Charles V, made to protect the Catholic Church, they became known as *Protestants.* The term soon came to be applied to all those who broke away from the Catholic Church.

The Protestants by no means agreed with one another. Some wanted three sacraments, some wanted two, and some even did away with baptism. Some wanted their church governed by bishops, while others thought that each parish should be ruled by its congregation. The Protestants rejected the Catholic Church as the teacher of the truths of Christianity, yet, they could not agree on what the Bible taught.

Persecution for religious beliefs was a common practice of the times and was not confined to any one religious denomination. When physical persecution was involved, it was usually inflicted by the civil authorities who were trying to protect a particular denomination. As a result of the religious persecution in England, many refugees fled to North America where they settled in English colonies.

THE CHURCH REFORMS

Worthy Men. There were many loyal Catholics who did not like to see unworthy men holding Church offices. They were distressed to see some bishops living like warrior nobles. These loyal men thought that whatever abuses had crept into the Church should be abolished. They wanted to make reforms in the Church; yet, they had no intention of breaking away from the Catholic Church.

A great movement of reform spread through the Church. A series of popes took strong measures to correct abuses wherever they were found. Further, only those priests who had proved their worthiness were appointed as cardinals and bishops by the popes.

A Threefold Attack. This *Catholic Reformation* had three phases, or aspects. First, succeeding popes, cardinals, and bishops worked to prevent heresies from gaining further ground. Then these churchmen began a campaign to win back some of the districts where the Protestant leaders had been successful. Third, the Church sent missionaries to America and to other areas that were discovered during the fifteenth and sixteenth centuries.

The Great Council. The pope called together a great council of the cardinals and bishops of the Church. It met at *Trent*, on the border of Italy and Germany, beginning in 1545. It was the longest council ever held by the Church.

The Council of Trent met to define Catholic beliefs and to re-examine Church laws.

The council's work, which was done in three separate sessions, was not completed until 1563.

The *Council of Trent*, as it is called, stated its belief in all the articles of the Creed. Then each article of the Creed was explained. This was done in such a way that there would be no possibility that a Catholic might be confused between the truth and heresy. These truths were placed in a catechism so that Catholics all over the world might know and understand their religion.

There were no changes made in the beliefs of Catholics by the Council of Trent. The truths of the religion have remained unchanged since the time of Christ. The bishops of the Council of Trent did make several changes in the rules and laws of the Church. Many rules were made stricter. Seminaries were established to give future priests careful training. By this method unworthy men would be prevented from holding offices in the Church.

New Enthusiasm. A new zeal for the Faith became evident during the Catholic Reformation. It was partly due to the leadership of the popes and partly due to the inspiration of the Council of Trent.

Many people in Europe had never lost the religious fervor that was so common during the Middle Ages.

One example of this strong religious spirit was contained in a little book written by *Thomas a Kempis* (*à kĕm′pĭs*) not many years before the revolt of Luther. The book, called *The Imitation of Christ*, showed every man how to lead a better life.

The Catholic Reformation of the sixteenth century was aided by many men and women of outstanding holiness and sanctity. Most of them were also renowned for their ability and activity in carrying out the work of the Church.

The Church has canonized many of these persons, such as *Pope St. Pius V*, who enforced the reforms of the Council of Trent. *St. Charles Borromeo* (*bōr′rṓ·mâ′ȯ*) was another of the great men of the period. He helped with the preparation for the Council of Trent and made his diocese of Milan a model for the rest of the world. *St. Philip Neri* (*nā′rḕ*) set an example of personal holiness for priests and laymen.

St. Francis of Sales was the Catholic bishop in Geneva, which was the headquarters of the Calvinists. His sermons were remarkable for their clear explanation of the truths of the Catholic Chuch. He also wrote a book called *Introduction to the Devout Life*. This book has helped laymen to a greater love of God.

St. Vincent de Paul came from a peasant farm family in France. His father sold livestock to pay for his education. St. Vincent was known as a friend of the poor. He worked hard to help fill the physical as well as the religious needs of the destitute.

St. Vincent de Paul was known for his charity and work among the poor and the destitute in Paris. *St. Teresa of Ávila* (ä'vĕ·lä) restored her own convent of the Carmelites to its previous strict rule. With her great vigor and sanctity, she succeeded in reforming many other Carmelite convents in Spain and in founding several new ones. She is also famous for her writings.

New Orders. Another prominent feature of the Catholic Reformation was the renewed zeal of the older religious orders and the appearance of several new ones. The Franciscans and Dominicans doubled their efforts to win souls for God. They carried their work overseas to the newly discovered lands.

The new orders for men founded during the Catholic Reformation were all planned to work closely with the people and thus to prevent the further spread of heresy.

This was also true of the new orders for women. Previously all orders of nuns were restricted to the various types of work which could be done inside their convents. In 1537, *St. Angela Merici* (mȧ·rē'chĕ) founded the *Ursulines* (ûr'sù·lĭnz) for the purpose of establishing schools for girls. The *Visitation Order* of nuns was founded for a similar purpose by St. Francis of Sales and *St. Joan Frances de Chantal.* St. Vincent de Paul founded the *Sisters of Charity* to work among the sick and the needy.

355

THE SOCIETY OF JESUS

The Founder. The most influential of the great saints of the Catholic Reformation was *St. Ignatius Loyola* (loi·ō′là). He was the founder of the *Society of Jesus*, whose members are usually called *Jesuits* (jĕz′u·ĭtz).

St. Ignatius was born at the castle of Loyola in northern Spain during the year 1491. A few months after his birth, the monarchs of Spain, Ferdinand and Isabella, captured Granada, the last Mohammedan stronghold on the peninsula. In another few months Columbus had set out on his first great voyage into the western ocean.

* * * * *

Do you believe that the great and stirring events of the times could have inspired Ignatius to do great deeds? If so, why?

* * * * *

At the age of thirteen, Ignatius was sent as a page to the household of a great noble who was Lord Treasurer for King Ferdinand. Ignatius received the usual training of a page. He had very little schooling, but he was taught to read and write. With his lord, he visited the court of the king many times. When Ignatius came of age, he was knighted. He then began a career as a soldier of Spain. In a few years, his career was cut short by a cannon ball that severely wounded his left leg.

His recovery was slow. He was confined to bed for many weeks. As he began to recover, he asked for

EVENTS IN THE LIFE OF IGNATIUS LOYOLA

KNIGHTHOOD

CONVALESCING

IN BATTLE

some books to read. There were only two books available. One was *The Life of Christ*, and the other was a collection of the lives of the saints.

A Great Decision. As he read, Ignatius began to realize that many of the saints were remarkable heroes. He was very much impressed with the lives of St. Francis of Assisi and St. Dominic. In 1521, Ignatius decided to give up his career as a soldier and to devote his life to the service of the Church. This was the same year that Martin Luther left the Catholic Church.

It took Ignatius some time to decide what form this service would actually take. He spent many weeks in prayer and in meditation. Ignatius then began to write a book, which is called *Spiritual Exercises*. Next, he made a pilgrimage to the Holy Land, and as a result, he became interested in converting the Mohammedans.

On his return to Spain, he deter-

mined to improve his education. Although he was thirty-three years old, he entered a school and worked very diligently. After two years he was ready for the university. He studied at several Spanish universities. Later he went to the University of Paris where he entered the same college at which Calvin had studied.

While Ignatius was in Paris, he met some other students who wanted to devote their lives to the service of God and His Church. Together they formed a religious society, or order. Ignatius requested the pope to approve the new order. Within a short time, the approval of the Holy Father was granted to this

RESUMES HIS STUDIES

GIVES UP WORLDLY PLEASURES TO SERVE THE CHURCH

PILGRIMAGE TO HOLY LAND

AIDS IN FORMING THE SOCIETY OF JESUS

order that was called the Society of Jesus.

Special Work. It had not yet been decided what the special work of the new Society would be. In their motto the Jesuits had pledged themselves to work *ad majorem Dei gloriam* (to the greater glory of God). They also placed themselves at the service of the Holy Father.

*   *   *   *   *

Was placing the Jesuit order at the service of the pope particularly important? Explain why or why not.

*   *   *   *   *

It soon became clear that the Jesuits could be used to check the religious revolt. Each member of the Society of Jesus went through a very long period of training before he was ordained to the priesthood. By virtue of this, the Jesuits became renowned for their piety, virtue, and learning.

The Jesuits, although they were men of outstanding virtue and ability, refused to accept high honors in the Church. A Jesuit would accept the position of bishop or cardinal only when he was given a special command by the pope. People were pleased to see such devotion to duty without hope of reward. A new respect for the priesthood became evident.

Counterattack. One of the chief methods used by the Jesuits to combat this revolt was the training of children and young people. The Jesuits opened schools and colleges in many countries of Europe. They improved the methods of teaching children, and their classrooms became filled with eager and interested pupils. The Jesuit schools and colleges became so famous that many Protestants sent their sons to be educated by the Jesuits.

The Society of Jesus also undertook the difficult task of winning back some of the sections of Europe that had become Protestant. Despite strong opposition, the Jesuits began their work of preaching and teaching. They brought the sacraments and the Mass to people who for years had been deprived of these instruments of grace. They opened colleges that became known as *fortresses of the Faith*. They were so successful that Belgium, Poland, Czechoslovakia, Hungary, and a large part of Germany were won back to the Catholic Faith.

In England. Under Queen Elizabeth I of England, a priest would be put to death if he were found in the kingdom. However, some of the Jesuits who were Englishmen returned to their homeland in disguise. Going from house to house, they said Mass for a few people at a time. They brought the sacraments to the English Catholics.

Overseas Missions. Jesuits, Dominicans, and Franciscans helped to win souls for God in the far-off regions. Frequently they themselves became explorers.

Perhaps the most famous of the missionaries of this period was *St. Francis Xavier* (zā'vĭ·ẽr). He was a brilliant young Spanish noble who had won a remarkable reputation as a scholar and lecturer at the University of Paris. St. Ignatius Loyola met Francis Xavier at the university and had many long talks with his fellow countryman. As a result, Xavier became one of the first members of the Society of Jesus.

You probably know about the great work of St. Francis Xavier in India, the East Indian Islands, and Japan. He died just as he was preparing to enter China.

Summing Up. Because the Church had come to be plagued with unworthy men, heresy, and the false pride of the new European nations, the so-called Protestant Reformation took place. Of course, this was not a reformation, but a revolt from the teachings and authority of Christ's Church.

Martin Luther, a former German monk, John Calvin, a Frenchman,

St. Francis Xavier's missionary work took him across the greater part of the Far East.

and Henry VIII, king of England, led the revolt in Europe that caused many people to leave the Church.

The Church fought back quickly, reforming the abuses that gave rise to scandal and giving exact definition to the Catholic Faith through the Council of Trent. New religious orders were organized to fight heresy and convert souls to Christ both in Europe and in foreign lands. Among the most famous of the leaders of the new orders were St. Ignatius Loyola, St. Francis of Sales, St. Vincent de Paul, St. Angela Merici, and St. Francis Xavier.

FOR BETTER UNDERSTANDING

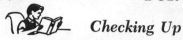 *Checking Up*

1. What is meant by heresy?

2. List the main causes of the Protestant Revolt.

3. Briefly describe the life and teachings of Martin Luther.

4. What were the chief religious ideas of John Calvin?

5. Why did King Henry VIII break away from the Catholic Church?

6. What were the names and the locations of the chief Protestant groups in Europe?

7. What important steps did the Catholic Church take to stop the spread of heresy?

8. What were the important results of the Council of Trent?

9. Give a brief account of the life of St. Ignatius Loyola.

10. Describe the early work of the Society of Jesus.

11. Identify and tell the importance of each of the following dates: 1485, 1517, 1521, 1538, 1545, 1563.

 Yesterday and Today

1. Are there any Catholic colleges in your state? Name some of them and tell what religious orders conduct these colleges.

2. Can you tell some of the ways in which religious leaders have influence in the secular world of today?

3. How many different Protestant religious groups have churches in your neighborhood or community?

4. How was the Ecumenical Council held in Rome, beginning October 1962, like and different from the Council of Trent?

Persons, Places, and Terms

Identify: Frederick of Saxony, Charles V, John Calvin, Francis I, John Knox, Henry VIII, Queen Catherine, St. John Fisher, St. Thomas More, Edward VI, Queen Mary, Queen Elizabeth I, Thomas a Kempis, Pope St. Pius V, St. Charles Borromeo, St. Philip Neri, St. Francis of Sales, St. Vincent de Paul, St. Teresa of Avila, St. Angela Merici, St. Joan Frances de Chantal, St. Francis Xavier.

Locate: Trent, Wittenberg, Geneva.

Define: heresy, Reformation, Counter-Reformation, Protestant, Wars of the Roses, *Utopia*, Anglican Church, Jesuit, *Spiritual Exercises, Introduction to the Devout Life.*

Interesting Things to Do

1. The saints of the Reformation period led active and interesting lives. For your scrapbook, each member of the class could look up the life of one of these saints and write a report.

2. Each member of your class might like to write his own *Utopia,* in which he or she could explain his own ideas for a perfect world.

3. Your class might like to spend five minutes each day in considering and discussing some of the ideas which Thomas a Kempis included in his book, *The Imitation of Christ.* Be sure you ask your teacher to help the class.

27

Europeans Begin to Explore the World

THE PATHS OF TRADE

Routes to the East. After the Crusades, the trade between Europe and Asia became very important. The prosperity of cities like Genoa depended on cargoes of silks, spices, and other materials from the East.

The merchants of Europe followed three main trade routes to the East. You can see how these trade routes connected East and West by studying the map on page 362.

The northern route, usually taken by the merchants of Genoa, brought European merchants through the Mediterranean Sea to Constantinople. Then they sailed on to the ports of the Black Sea. At these ports the merchants met caravans that had come overland from Persia and India.

By following the central route, the European merchants sailed their ships to one of the ports in Asia Minor like Antioch or the harbors near Damascus. Then they could take the short land journey with a caravan to the great trading center of Baghdad. There the merchants met traders who had come from India by way of the Persian Gulf and the Tigris River.

The merchants of Venice favored the southern route that brought them to Alexandria or Cairo in Egypt. Ships coming from India sailed up the Red Sea. The goods on the Indian ships were then sent a short distance overland to the Nile River and then up the river to the Mediterranean ports.

Ancient China. *Marco Polo*, who lived from about 1254 to 1324, was born in Venice. His father was a wealthy merchant, who also had a home at Constantinople and trading posts in various parts of the

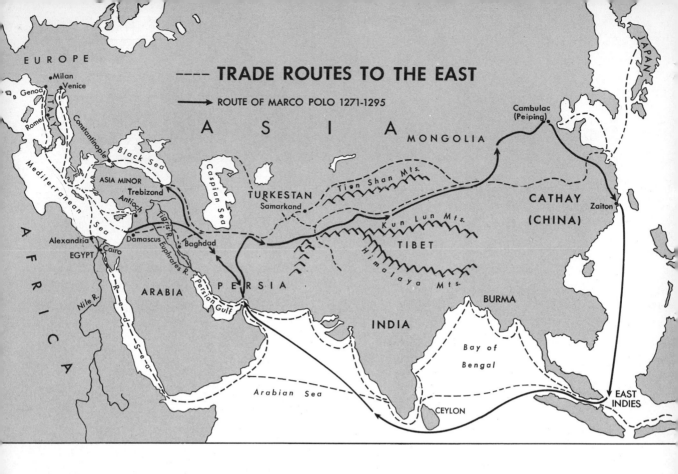

TRADE ROUTES TO THE EAST

---- TRADE ROUTES TO THE EAST

→ ROUTE OF MARCO POLO 1271-1295

East. When Marco was about fifteen years old, his father and uncle returned from a trip to *Cathay* (kă·thā′), which we know as China. They had visited the great *Kublai Khan* (kū′blĭ kän′) in his capital at *Cambulac* (City of the Khan), which we now call Peiping (bā′pĭng′). The Khan had asked the Polos to return and to bring with them some Catholic missionaries to instruct the people of China in the Faith.

When the Polo brothers returned to Cathay, young Marco went with them. They remained in Cathay for seventeen years. During that time Marco Polo was often sent as a special messenger of the Khan to other lands in the Far East.

The Polos finally left China. They returned to Europe on a ship, coming by way of the East Indies, Ceylon, India, and through the Persian Gulf. Hardly anyone in Venice knew them after their absence of so many years.

Later, Marco Polo took part in a war between Venice and Genoa. He was captured by the Genoese and was kept prisoner for a year. A fellow prisoner was a writer. This man began to write down the wonderful stories that Marco Polo told of his travels and adventures in the Far East.

In this way *The Book of Marco Polo* was written. Many people in Europe read the book, and it was translated into several languages. Nearly two hundred years later, Christopher Columbus read *The Book of Marco Polo* and learned about the wealth and splendor of the Indies and Cathay.

*   *   *   *   *

What are the names of some books of adventure and exploration that you have read, which make you want to go out and discover new worlds?

*   *   *   *   *

During the thirteenth and fourteenth centuries, many Franciscan monks made the long trip to Cathay. They were successful in converting many of the Chinese people to the Catholic religion.

However, a revolution at Cathay in 1368 changed the situation. The descendants of Kublai Khan who were favorable to Europeans were overthrown. The new rulers cut off all direct contact with the missionaries and merchants of Europe.

Moslem Conquerors. In the year 1453, the Turks succeeded in capturing the city of Constantinople. This event brought to an end the Eastern Roman Empire, and the Turks became masters of the entire eastern section of the Mediterranean Sea. All the trade routes to

Today's missionaries can attend fine schools to learn foreign languages and cultures. There are numerous reference books and language records available. How would you imagine a fifteenth-century missionary prepared himself for travel to a far-off country like Cathay?

the East passed through the territory conquered by the Turks. The Turks placed heavy taxes on the western merchants, and Turkish pirates roamed the sea.

As a result of the Turkish conquests, the great ships remained idle in European harbors because it was too dangerous to send them to the East by the old routes. Yet, the people of Europe needed the products of India and the other Eastern countries. The mariners of Genoa and the other trading cities began to wonder about finding new routes to the East.

PORTUGAL LEADS THE WAY

Royal Sailor. Portugal was at peace when many of the other nations of Europe were busy with wars during the fourteenth and fifteenth centuries. For example, in Spain the people were trying to expel the Mohammedans. France and England were engaged in the Hundred Years' War. Also, the Turks controlled the Near Eastern lands and had cut off all Mediterranean trade. The Portuguese had time to explore.

Prince Henry (1394-1460) was the son of the king of Portugal. Henry, as a result of his interest in trade and navigation, founded a school for mariners. He brought some of the best sea captains from Genoa and Venice to train his sailors.

At the school, the sailors were shown how to use the compass and other instruments which had recently been invented. They also learned how to find their position by the stars.

Prince Henry collected maps and navigation charts from various parts of Europe. Better maps were then made at Prince Henry's school, as a result of the information that had been collected. Prince Henry sent his seamen on voyages along the coast of Africa. He believed that an all-water route to the East could be found by sailing around the southern end of Africa.

One Portuguese ship after another sailed south along the African coast. Each ship sailed a little farther than the one before. It took great courage to set out on such voyages, for no one had ever sailed far to the south and no one knew what lay beyond.

Some years after Prince Henry's death, and about six years before the discovery of America, a seaman named *Bartholomeu Dias* (dē′*a*sh) succeeded in reaching the southern end of Africa. Finding the weather there stormy, he called the tip of

Africa the *Cape of Storms*. He reported his success to the king of Portugal. The king was delighted when he learned that the southern end of Africa had been reached. So, he renamed the tip the *Cape of Good Hope*.

Thrilled by the success of Dias, other Portuguese captains set out hoping to sail to India and China by going around the Cape of Good Hope. At length, *Vasco da Gama* (gǎ′má) made the dream of Prince Henry come true. Da Gama reached India in 1498 and proved that an all-water route around Africa to India could be used.

The Portuguese later took possession of the islands of *Ceylon, Sumatra, Java,* and the *Spice Islands*. They reached China and Japan and opened up the entire Far East to missionary priests and to merchants.

* * * * *

Did Portugal's new route to India and its possession of many lands in the Far East give it an advantage in trade over other European countries and cities? If so, how?

* * * * *

Christopher Columbus. There was another mariner in the employ of Portugal who thought that a different all-water route to India was possible. This was *Christopher Columbus* (1451-1506).

Columbus had been born in Genoa. As a child, he was interested in the activities of the harbor and in becoming a mariner. With eager ears, he listened to the stories of seamen. He studied everything he could find about geography.

Later Columbus, the sailor, entered the service of Portugal. He studied the maps and charts of the famous navigation school of Prince Henry. From his study of geography, from his conversations with other mariners, and from his own thinking, Columbus became convinced that the shortest route to the Indies was westward across the Atlantic.

To earn his living while studying navigation, the young Columbus became a chart maker.

Getting Help. Columbus needed ships and money and men to undertake such a daring voyage. The king of Portugal was satisfied with the southern route around Africa and refused him aid. When Columbus approached the Spanish king and queen, Ferdinand and Isabella, they were busy with the war against the Moslems. The Spanish monarchs, therefore, refused to help him, and then Columbus asked the aid of the French king, who also refused.

Suddenly, the Spanish victory over the Moslems in Granada changed the situation. Spain was ready to embark on a new adventure. Father *Juan Pérez*, a Franciscan monk, persuaded Queen Isabella to support the plans of Columbus.

Although Columbus was mistaken in his discovery, he still ranks as a great explorer.

Even after he received Isabella's support, Columbus found it very difficult to secure a crew to go with him. Most sailors of the time were afraid to sail out into the unknown seas. Yet, on August 3, 1492, Columbus (after attending Mass and receiving Holy Communion) set sail from *Palos* (pä'lŏs), a seaport in southern Spain. He sailed with three ships—the *Santa Maria* (sän'tȧ mä·rē'ȧ), the *Nina* (nē'nyä), and the *Pinta* (pēn'tä).

A Long Voyage. After a long, dangerous, and exhausting voyage, Columbus sighted land on October 12, 1492. Columbus and his men looked with joy upon the shore of one of the Bahama Islands off the coast of what we today call *Florida*. They landed and with prayers of thanksgiving named the island *San Salvador* (săn săl'vȧ·dôr), which means *Holy Saviour*. Columbus thought he had reached an island off the coast of *India*. So he called the natives of the island *Indians*.

Columbus joyfully returned to

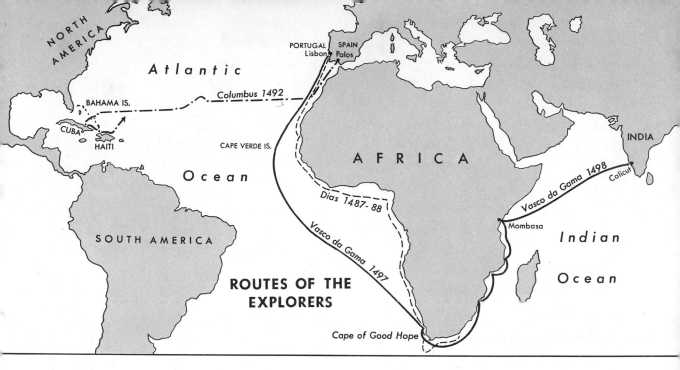

Atlantic

NORTH
AMERICA

PORTUGAL   SPAIN
Lisbon   Palos

BAHAMA IS.

Columbus 1492

CUBA

HAITI

CAPE VERDE IS.

Ocean

AFRICA

INDIA

Dias 1487-88

Vasco da Gama 1498

Calicut

SOUTH AMERICA

Vasco da Gama 1497

Mombasa

Indian

Ocean

**ROUTES OF THE
EXPLORERS**

Cape of Good Hope

Spain. There he was hailed as the world's greatest seaman. Isabella and Ferdinand thought that he had found a new route to the East.

With a well-equipped fleet, Columbus made another voyage the next year. This time he landed on the island that we today call *Haiti*. When he returned to Spain without spices or other eastern products, the Spanish began to lose interest in him.

Twice more Columbus sailed to the west. On one of his voyages he touched the northern part of South America, and on another he saw the coast of Central America. He found no spices and no gold. Broken in spirit, Columbus died, little realizing that he had discovered a *New World*.

Most students of geography at that time thought that the world was much smaller than it actually is. That is why Columbus thought he had reached some outlying part of Asia. However, his voyage and the voyages of Dias and Vasco da Gama caused men to have less fear of the sea. Many adventurous men then eagerly set out across the Atlantic.

*   *   *   *   *

Name some of the major explorations which man has made since the beginning of the twentieth century. What areas are likely to be explored in the future?

*   *   *   *   *

Priests and nuns not only brought the Faith of Christ to the Indian peoples of the Americas, they also brought European, or Old World, culture, learning, and civilization.

EUROPEANS COME TO AMERICA

Settling the Americas. The ships of Portugal and Spain, France and England brought men and women and children to the lands of North and South America. The Portuguese settled in what is now the great country of *Brazil*. Spanish America included the rest of South America, all of Central America, and much of what is now the western United States. The French explored deep into the heart of North America by way of the St. Lawrence River, the Great Lakes, and the Mississippi River. England sent thousands of colonists to the eastern shores of North America.

Each of these groups brought to the American wilderness their language, their customs, and their laws.

They also brought their religion. In the case of the people from Spain, Portugal, and France, this was the Catholic religion.

Catholic priests, brothers, and nuns came in considerable numbers to the Americas. They performed many heroic tasks. They converted and civilized many of the Indians. They built churches, schools, and hospitals. Some of them suffered the death of martyrs because they taught the doctrines of Christ. These peoples struggled and labored, worked and prayed to make America much as it is today.

* * * * *

The Church still carries out missionary work in our country today. How is this work like and how is it different from the work of the earliest missionaries?

* * * * *

Our Heritage. In previous chapters of this book, you have read how the influence of Rome lasted in Europe even though the Roman Empire passed out of existence fifteen hundred years ago. Because of the venturesome explorations of men like Columbus, Dias, and Vasco da

The Old World influence is still seen in many parts of the United States today. Above, the Spanish influence is pictured in California; below, the French influence in New Orleans.

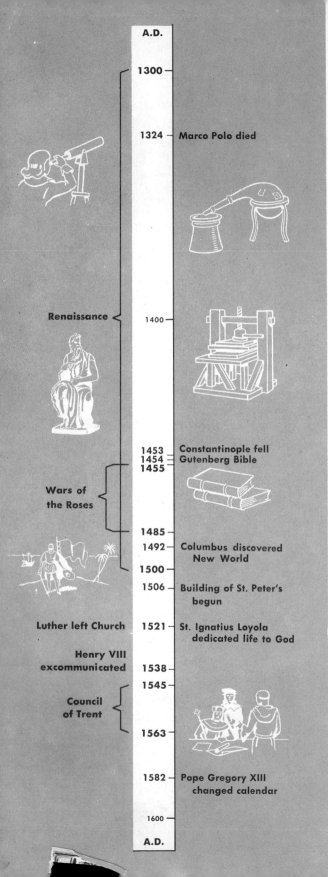

A.D.

1300

1324 — Marco Polo died

Renaissance

1400

1453 — Constantinople fell
1454 — Gutenberg Bible
1455

Wars of
the Roses

1485
1492 — Columbus discovered
New World
1500
1506 — Building of St. Peter's
begun
Luther left Church   1521 — St. Ignatius Loyola
dedicated life to God
Henry VIII
excommunicated   1538
1545
Council
of Trent   1563

1582 — Pope Gregory XIII
changed calendar

1600

A.D.

Gama, a New World was found. In this New World, the influence of Portugal and Spain, France and England has endured throughout the Americas even to this day.

Everywhere that we turn in the United States, we are reminded of our Old World background. We meet it in the names of our streets, our towns, our rivers, and our lakes. It can be clearly seen in our public buildings, our homes, our schools, and our churches. This is the heritage we have to preserve, protect, improve, and pass on to those who follow us.

Summing Up. During the last years of the Middle Ages and at the beginning of the Renaissance period, men of many backgrounds began to explore new lands and seas. Inspired by the example set by Marco Polo and by the Moslem conquest of the Near East, the Portuguese led the way under Prince Henry.

Columbus discovered a New World and claimed it for Spain. Da Gama opened up new all-water routes to the East.

Settlers and missionaries traveled to the new lands to build, to civilize, to convert, and to plant firmly on the shores of the Americas a new civilization that was the outgrowth of the old.

FOR BETTER UNDERSTANDING

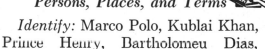 *Checking Up*

1. Briefly tell of the travels of Marco Polo.

2. What happened in China that stopped the work of Catholic missionaries?

3. Tell how the capture of Constantinople by the Turks affected the trade of Europe.

4. Why was Portugal interested in a new route to the East?

5. What was the importance of Prince Henry's school for navigators?

6. Why was Vasco da Gama's voyage of 1497 important?

7. Tell briefly about the chief events in the life of Christopher Columbus.

8. Explain how the civilization of Europe was brought to America.

9. Identify and tell the importance of each of the following dates: 1368, 1453, 1492, 1498.

Yesterday and Today

1. In this chapter you have read about the beginning of the colonial empires of the nations of Western Europe. Today you are living in an era when these same colonial empires are being disbanded. Make a list of the African and Asian nations that have become independent since 1945, and list under what country's control they were before independence.

2. Find out the size and power of such modern telescopes as the one at the observatory on *Mt. Palomar* (păl'ȯ·mär) in California. Compare this with what you can find out about the telescope used by Galileo.

3. Compare what you have read about the exploratory ocean voyages of the fifteenth and sixteenth centuries with the modern-day voyages into space and beneath the sea. Do you believe that the modern explorers are more daring than the early day navigators? Tell why or why not.

Persons, Places, and Terms

Identify: Marco Polo, Kublai Khan, Prince Henry, Bartholomeu Dias, Vasco da Gama, Father Pérez.

Locate: Cathay, Peiping, Ceylon, Cape of Good Hope, Sumatra, Java, Spice Islands, Japan, Bahama Islands, Haiti, Brazil, St. Lawrence River, Great Lakes, Mississippi River.

Define: The Book of Marco Polo, Nina, Pinta, Santa Maria.

Interesting Things to Do

1. Prepare a classroom exhibit showing the work of present-day Catholic missionaries in the Far East.

2. For your scrapbook, draw a color map showing the chief trade routes from Europe to the East during the fifteenth century (1400-1500). As a guide, use the maps in this book as well as your encyclopedias or the historical atlas in your library.

3. Present a play about the main events in the life of Christopher Columbus. Some members of your class might read books and stories about Columbus in order to get ideas for writing the various scenes. Other class members might look up the types of costumes worn in the fifteenth century.

UNDERSTANDING THE UNIT

For Discussion

1. Tell why Italy was the place where the Renaissance began.

2. Why was *The Book of Marco Polo* important?

3. Why do you think that the invention of movable type was one of the greatest inventions in history?

4. Why was the year 1453 an important turning point in the history of Europe?

5. Was the voyage of Vasco da Gama as important as that of Columbus? Tell why or why not.

6. Why was the Council of Trent one of the most important councils in the history of the Church?

For You to Answer

1. Briefly tell how Florence and Rome became centers of the Renaissance.

2. What was the famous invention of Gutenberg?

3. Name two men of the Renaissance who made great advances in the science of astronomy.

4. List three main causes of the Protestant revolt.

5. What were the three phases of the Catholic Reformation?

6. Briefly list and explain the most important actions of the Council of Trent.

7. In a few words tell about the exploits of the Portuguese navigator, Bartholomeu Dias.

8. What lands did the Portuguese explore?

9. What was the most important result of the voyages of Columbus?

Linking Geography and History

1. You may have noticed that most of the countries you have studied about during this year were close to the Mediterranean Sea. Explain why the Mediterranean began to lose its former importance during the fifteenth century.

2. Recall what you have read about the colonizing activities of the Greeks. Compare the motives of the Greeks with those of European colonizers in the New World. How were their motives similar, how were they different?

Interesting Things to Do

The boys in your class may be interested in preparing an exhibit that will show changes and improvements in sea-going vessels from the earliest times. You will want to draw pictures or make models of an Egyptian galley (1500 B.C.); a Roman trireme (100 B.C.); a Viking ship (1000 A.D.); and a Spanish ship (1500 A.D.). You may want to add models of modern ships and submarines.

Books to Read

Bothwell, Jean, *First Book of Roads.*
Clemens, Samuel L. (Mark Twain), *Prince and the Pauper.*
Derleth, August, *St. Ignatius and the Company of Jesus.*
Holme, Bryan, *Pictures to Live With.*
Lauber, Patricia, *The Quest of Galileo.*
Ripley, Elizabeth, *Michelangelo.*
Syme, Ronald, *Vasco da Gama.*
Walsh, Richard J., *Adventures and Discoveries of Marco Polo.*

Quia defecerunt sicut fumus dies mei:
z ossa mea sicut cremium aruerunt.
Percussus sum ut fenū z aruit cor meū:
qa oblitus sum comedere panem meū.
A uoce gemitus mei: adhesit os meum

Glossary

The following system of indicating pronunciation is used by permission of the publishers of the Merriam-Webster Dictionaries, from Webster's New International Dictionary, Second Edition, copyright 1959 by G. & C. Merriam Co.

ā āte	ä ärm	ê êvent	ĭ ĭll	ŏ tŏp	th then
ȧ vȧcation	a ȧsk	ĕ ĕnd	i famĭly	ǒ cǒnnect	ū ūse
â câre	a̍ sofa̍	ē silĕnt	ō ōld	oi oil	ů ůnite
ă ădd	ē bē	ē makẽr	ȯ ȯbey	ᴐᴐ fᴐᴐd	ŭ ŭp
ă ărrive	ę hęre	ī īce	ô ôrder	ᴐᴐ fᴐᴐt	u circŭs

Abbess (ăb'ĕs), the superior of a convent, or religious community of women.

Abbey (ăb'ĭ), the building or buildings that form the residence, chapel, and workrooms of a community of monks; a monastery.

Abbot (ăb'ŭt), the superior of an abbey, or monastery.

Acropolis (a̍·krŏp'ȯ·lĭs), the highest part of a Greek city, usually fortified; especially the beautiful one at Athens.

Aeneid (ė·nē'ĭd), a long epic poem of the Romans, written by Virgil.

Angelic Doctor (ăn·jĕl'ĭk dŏk'tẽr), title given to St. Thomas Aquinas.

Apprentice (a̍·prĕn'tĭs), in the Middle Ages, one who learned a trade by on-the-job training under a master craftsman.

Apse (ăps), the recessed area at one end of a church, usually having a semicircular back wall, where the altar is placed.

Aqueduct (ăk'wė·dŭkt), a large pipe or channel used to bring water great distances overland, often supported by arches and columns.

Archaeologist (är'kė·ŏl'ō·jĭst), a scientist who studies the lives of ancient peoples by examining the remains of their caves, cities, and graves.

Archbishop (ärch'bĭsh'ŭp), a bishop who rules over an archdiocese, often with some jurisdiction over a group of dioceses.

Architect (är'kĭ·tĕkt), one who designs structures such as bridges, churches, or other buildings.

Asia Minor (ā'zha̍ mī'nẽr), smaller Asia; that section of Asia that lies between the Black Sea and the Mediterranean Sea.

Astrology (a̍s·trŏl'ȯ·jĭ), a false science claiming stars influence human affairs.

Astronomy (a̍s·trŏn'ȯ·mĭ), the science that studies the stars and planets.

Baptistry (băp′tĭs·trĭ), the part of a church building where the sacrament of Baptism is performed.

Basilica (ba·sĭl′ĭ·ka), an oblong-shaped building with interior columns, used as a law court by the Romans; style was used by early Christians for important churches.

Bible (bī′b'l), the sacred writings of the Christian Religion; the Old Testament (forty-six books) and the New Testament (twenty-seven books).

Bishop (bĭsh′ŭp), a successor of the Apostles, the head of a diocese.

Black Death (blăk dĕth), the bubonic plague that spread over Europe in the fourteenth century.

Britannia (brĭ·tăn′ĭ·a), Roman name for island of Great Britain; Roman province in Great Britain.

Canterbury (kăn′tẽr·bẽr′ĭ), chief center of the Catholic Church in England, established by St. Augustine.

Capetian Kings (ka·pē′shăn kĭngz), the kings of France who were descendants of Hugh Capet.

Catacombs (kăt′a·kōmz), underground burial chambers and passageways used by the early Christians at Rome for religious exercises.

Cell (sĕl), a small room where a monk prays, reads, and sleeps.

Charter (chär′tẽr), a written document issued by a king (or other authority), listing rights promised to a person or a particular group.

Chivalry (shĭv′ăl·rĭ), the rules and ideals governing knighthood in the Middle Ages.

City-state (sĭt′ĭ-stāt), the unit of government, comprising a city and the surrounding countryside.

Classical (klăs′ĭ·kăl), pertaining to or following the standards set by the artists and authors of ancient Greece and Rome.

Colony (kŏl′ò·nĭ), a group of people who settle in another country, but who remain citizens of the mother country.

Colosseum (kŏl′ŏ·sē′ŭm), a large open-air amphitheater in Rome.

Common law (kŏm′ŭn lô), the ordinary law of a country. In England it includes the unwritten laws that were followed for centuries.

Commons (kŏm′ŭnz), those sections of a feudal village (pasture, woodland, etc.) in which all the people had common rights.

Compass (kŭm′pàs), an instrument used to find direction by the use of a needle, which points to the magnetic north pole.

Concordat of Worms (kŏn·kôr′dăt ŏv wûrmz), an agreement with the pope signed at Worms in 1122, in which the Holy Roman Emperor promised to permit the free election of bishops.

Confessor (kŏn·fĕs′ẽr), name used for Christian saints who witnessed strongly for the Faith, but did not suffer martyrdom.

Consul (kŏn′sŭl), either of the two chief officials of the Roman Republic.

Council of Trent (koun′sĭl ŏv trĕnt), a council of the Church (1545-1563) that corrected certain abuses in the Church and defined more exactly the doctrines attacked by the Protestants.

Crozier (krō′zhẽr), the staff used by a bishop, or abbot; symbol of his position as a shepherd of souls.

Crusade (krōo·sād′), one of the series of expeditions by Western Christians to capture the Holy Land from the Moslems.

Culture (kŭl′tũr), the civilization of a people at a particular time, including its arts, customs, education, religious beliefs, etc.

Cuneiform (kû·nē′ĭ·fôrm), the wedge-shaped characters used by the Babylonians when writing.

Danelaw (dān′lô′), the northeastern part of England once held by the Danes, and where the Danish law was in force.

Dauphin (dô′fĭn), the title given to the eldest son of the king of France.

Deacon (dē′kŭn), a Churchman in Holy Orders who ranks just below a priest and has certain duties that have come down from Apostolic times.

Degree (dĕ·grē′), a title and certificate, given by a college or university in recognition of work accomplished.

Deity (dē′ĭ·tĭ), another name for God; sometimes used for pagan gods.

Democracy (dĕ·mŏk′rȧ·sĭ), a state or country where the people make the laws and run the government.

Despot (dĕs′pŏt), one who rules without regard for the rights of the people.

Dictator (dĭk·tā′tēr), an official of ancient Rome granted supreme powers for a limited time; modern-day despot.

Domesday Book (do͞omz′dā′ bo͝ok), the records of the census taken in England in the reign of William the Conqueror.

Domesticated (dȯ·mĕs′tĭ·kāt·ĕd), animals or plants tamed or cultivated for the use of man.

Druid (dro͞o′ĭd), a priest of the pagan Celtic tribes.

Ealdorman (ôl′dēr·mȧn), or alderman, in England, the chief official of a county.

Eastern Schism (ēs′tērn sĭz′m), a break in the unity of Christendom, by which most of the Catholics of the Eastern Roman Empire were removed from the spiritual authority of the pope.

Emperor (ĕm′pēr·ēr), a ruler who governs several states, or nations.

Estates-General (ĕs·tātz′ jĕn′ēr·ȧl), name of the French parliament, or legislature.

Excommunication (ĕks′kŏ·mū′nĭ·kā′shŭn), a punishment which deprives a person of the sacraments of the Church.

Far East (fär ēst), eastern Asia including India, China, Japan, and the East Indies.

Feudalism (fū′dȧl·ĭz′m), a way of life that developed in the Middle Ages. Under it a man gave to an overlord certain services and a share of the crops or goods he produced. In return the man received protection and land for his use.

Fief (fēf), land held by a vassal.

Flying Buttress (flī′ĭng bŭt′rĕs), the stone arch and column on the outside of Gothic churches, used as a support for the main wall.

Forum (fō′rŭm), the market place in ancient Rome.

Fresco (frĕs′kō), the method of painting, or a painting done, with water colors on a freshly plastered wall or ceiling.

Friar (frī′ēr), a priest or brother who is a member of certain religious orders, such as the Franciscans.

Gargoyle (gär′goil), a waterspout on a medieval building humorously, or grotesquely, shaped like a man or animal.

Gothic (gŏth′ĭk), a style of architecture using pointed arches and steep roofs.

Guild (gĭld), a type of organization in the Middle Ages by which skilled workers or merchants protected themselves and their interests.

Hanseatic League (hăn′sė·ăt′ĭk lēg), a league of the cities of Northern Germany and the Baltic Sea area for the protection of their trade.

Hastings (hās′tĭngz), the site of the battle in 1066 when William, Duke of Normandy, defeated the English.

Hegira (hė·jī′rȧ), the flight of Mohammed from Mecca to Medina in the year 622 A. D., which marks the beginning of the Moslem calendar.

Hellespont (hĕl′ĕs·pŏnt), the strait connecting the Black Sea and the Mediterranean Sea; known as the Dardanelles.

Heretic (hĕr′ĕ·tĭk), a baptized person who rejects one or more revealed truths of the Catholic Faith.

Hieroglyphics (hī′ĕr·ȯ·glĭf′ĭks), a form of writing used by the ancient Egyptians in which pictures were used instead of the characters of an alphabet.

Hospice (hŏs′pĭs), an inn, usually run by a religious order for the use of pilgrims.

Hundred Years' War (hŭn′drĕd yẽrz wôr), a series of wars between France and England from 1337 to 1453.

Iliad (ĭl′ĭ·ăd), a long epic poem of the Greeks written by Homer.

Illuminated manuscript (ĭ·lū′mĭ·nāt′ĕd măn′ū·skrĭpt), handwritten pages or books in which first letters and sometimes borders are made beautiful with gold or colored drawings.

Indulgence (ĭn·dŭl′jĕns), a remission by the Church of the temporal punishment due to sin, after the sin has been forgiven.

Interdict (ĭn′tẽr·dĭkt), a punishment that cuts off a person, group, or nation from the rites of the Church.

Investiture (ĭn·vĕs′tĭ·tûr), the ceremony by which an official of the Church or State is installed in office.

Islam (ĭs′lȧm), the religion of the followers of Mohammed; Mohammedanism.

Journeyman (jûr′nĭ·măn), a medieval workman who learned a craft or trade, but who worked for others because he was not yet a mastercraftsman.

Joust (jŭst), a contest between two knights at a tournament.

Jury (jŏŏr′ĭ), twelve men chosen to decide in a law court if a person is guilty or not guilty; in early England twelve men chosen to tell about local crime.

Justinian Code (jŭs·tĭn′ĭ·ăn kōd), collection of Roman laws ordered by the Emperor Justinian that became the law for the entire Empire; it is the basis of law for much of Europe today.

Knight (nīt), a horse-mounted noble of medieval times who took a solemn promise to do good deeds.

Knights Hospitalers (nītz hŏs′pĭt·'l·ẽrz), a religious order of warrior-monks devoted to works of charity.

Koran (kȯ·răn′), the book containing the sacred writings of the Mohammedans.

Madonna (mȧ·dŏn′ȧ), a picture or carving of Our Lady.

Magna Carta (măg′nȧ kär′tȧ), the Great Charter of liberties for certain Englishmen signed by King John in 1215.

Manor (măn′ẽr), a large estate in the Middle Ages, part of which was used by the lord, and part for the use of the serfs.

March (märch), or mark, a military district organized by Charlemagne as a protective area on the frontiers of his empire.

Martyr (mär′tẽr), a person who gives up his life for the Faith of Christ.

Matins (măt′ĭnz), prayers and psalms usually recited or sung at midnight; part of the Divine Office.

May-field (mā-fēld), an outdoor meeting conducted each spring by Charlemagne to discuss the laws with his people.

Minnesinger (mĭn′ė·sĭng′ẽr), name of German wandering minstrels during the Middle Ages.

Minstrel (mĭn′strĕl), a wandering poet, singer, or musician of the Middle Ages.

Missionary (mĭsh′ŭn·ĕr′ĭ), one who journeys to a distant land for the purpose of winning new souls for Christ.

Miter (mī′tẽr), or mitre, a tall headdress (or hat) worn by bishops at public ceremonies.

Moat (mōt), a large ditch usually filled with water that surrounds a castle.

Monastery (mŏn′ȧs·tẽr′ĭ), the buildings that house a community of monks.

Monk (mŭngk), a member of a religious community of men who live apart from the world in work and prayer.

Morality Play (mŏ·răl'ĭ·tĭ plā), a religious drama of the Middle Ages in which each actor represents a virtue or a vice.

Mosaic (mŏ·zā'ĭk), a picture or design made by setting small pieces of colored glass or stones in definite patterns.

Moslem (mŏz'lĕm), one who believes in the teachings of Mohammed.

Mosque (mŏsk), a Moslem place of worship.

Mummy (mŭm'ĭ), in ancient Egypt, a body preserved with spices, wrapped in linen, and enclosed in a mummy case.

Mystery Play (mĭs'tēr·ĭ plā), a religious drama of the Middle Ages dealing with the great mysteries of the Faith.

Near East (nēr ēst), the regions close to the eastern end of the Mediterranean Sea.

Nicene Creed (nī·sēn' krēd), a prayer constituting the chief truths of the Catholic Church drawn up at the Council of Nicaea in 325 A. D.

Oath (ōth), a calling upon God to witness the truth of what we say.

Odyssey (ŏd'ĭ·sĭ), a long epic poem of the Greeks that deals with the wanderings of Odysseus after the Trojan War.

Open-field system (ō'pĕn-fēld sĭs'tĕm), unfenced fields used by the peasants of the Middle Ages for growing their crops.

Pagan (pā'găn), one who practices a primitive, non-Christian religion.

Page (pāj), a boy of the Middle Ages who trained for knighthood.

Palisade (păl'ĭ·sād'), a protective fence of heavy posts driven into the ground.

Pantheon (păn'thė·ŏn), temple in ancient Rome dedicated to all the gods; noted for its dome.

Parchment (pärch'mĕnt), a writing material made from the skin of a sheep or another animal.

Parliament (pär'lĭ·mĕnt), the assembly that makes the laws in England.

Parthenon (pär'thė·nŏn), the chief temple on the Athenian acropolis.

Patriarch (pā'trĭ·ärk), a leader of the early Hebrews; later, the title given to certain bishops.

Patrician (pả·trĭsh'ăn), a noble in ancient Rome.

Peace of God (pēs ŏv gŏd), a custom that kept warfare away from sacred places during the Middle Ages.

Pentathlon (pĕn·tăth'lŏn), an athletic contest of five events at the Olympic Games.

Pentecost (pĕn'tė·kŏst), the fiftieth day after Easter, when the Holy Ghost descended upon the Apostles.

Persecution (pûr'sė·kū'shŭn), a campaign of injury and attack usually directed against a religious group.

Pharaoh (fâr'ȯ), the ruler, or king, of ancient Egypt.

Philosopher (fĭ·lŏs'ȯ·fẽr), a lover of wisdom; one who strives for wisdom by study.

Plantagenet (plăn·tăj'ē·nĕt), a line of English kings, which received its name from a sprig of broom plant worn in the cap of its founder.

Plebeian (plė·bē'yăn), a common man in ancient Rome.

Pope (pōp), the Holy Father, the Bishop of Rome; successor of St. Peter, head of the Roman Catholic Church.

Protestant (prŏt'ĕs·tănt), a member of those Christian sects that broke away from the Catholic Church.

Province (prŏv'ĭns), one of the major divisions of the Roman Empire.

Punic Wars (pū'nĭk wôrz), three wars waged by Rome against Carthage.

Refectory (rė·fĕk'tȯ·rĭ), the dining hall of a monastery.

Renaissance (rĕn′ĕ·zäns′), a rebirth of interest in art, literature, learning, and exploration that began in the last half of the fifteenth century.

Republic (rē·pŭb′lĭk), a country in which the people elect their officials.

Revelation (rĕv′ĕ·lā′shŭn), the revealing of truths by God to man.

Romance Language (rō·măns′ lăng′ gwĭj), a modern language derived from Latin.

Romanesque (rō′măn·ĕsk′), a style of architecture borrowed from the Romans.

Rosetta Stone (rō·zĕt′ȧ stōn), a stone with three inscriptions, which made it possible to decipher ancient Egyptian hieroglyphic writing.

Rose Window (rōz wĭn′dō), a circular window, with the shape and coloring of an open rose, in the east end of Gothic cathedrals.

Rostrum (rŏs′trŭm), the speaker's platform in the Roman Forum.

Scholastic Philosophy (skō·lăs′tĭk fĭ·lŏs′ ō·fĭ), a system of Christian philosophy developed in the medieval universities.

Serf (sûrf), a peasant of the Middle Ages who could not be sold but passed to a new owner of the land when it was captured or sold.

Sheriff (shĕr′ĭf), or shire reeve, the chief official in an English shire, or county.

Simony (sĭm′ō·nĭ), the selling of sacred objects or offices.

Squire (skwīr), a boy, already a page, being trained for knighthood.

Stigmata (stĭg′mȧ·tȧ), marks resembling the wounds on the Body of Christ.

Stylus (stī′lŭs), a pointed instrument, or tool, used for writing on a clay or wax tablet.

Theology (thē·ŏl′ō·jĭ), the study of God and His attributes; called the "queen of sciences."

Third Order (thûrd ôr′dēr), an association of the laity, under the sponsorship of a religious order; the members live in the world and strive for Christian perfection by prayer and good works.

Toga (tō′gȧ), the loose outer garment the Romans wore in public.

Tournament (tŏor′nȧ·mĕnt), an armed contest in which knights on horseback showed their bravery and skill for a prize.

Tribune (trĭb′ūn), a Roman official who protected the rights of the plebeians.

Trireme (trī′rēm), an ancient warship with three sets of oars on each side.

Troubadour (trōo′bȧ·dŏor), a wandering singer and story-teller in France of the Middle Ages.

Truce of God (trōos ŏv gŏd), a custom by which men refrained from warfare during certain seasons of the year.

Tyrant (tī′rănt), one who rules in a cruel manner; a despot.

University (ū′nĭ·vûr′sĭ·tĭ), a school for the teaching of the higher branches of learning, usually comprising several colleges.

Utopia (ū·tō′pĭ·ȧ), an imaginary and perfect land.

Vassal (văs′ȧl), in feudal times one who promised loyalty and services to a lord in return for protection.

Vespers (vĕs′pērz), part of the Divine Office; prayers and psalms recited or sung in the late afternoon or early evening.

Villein (vĭl′ĭn), a common man or a serf.

Wars of the Roses (wŏrz ŏv thē rōz′ĕz), civil war in England (1455-1485) between rivals for the throne.

Witan (wĭt′ăn), an early council of bishops and nobles to advise the king in England.

Witchcraft (wĭch′krȧft′), acting with the help of the devil and evil spirits.

Index

A

Acropolis (*à·krŏp'ò·lĭs*), defined, 45; in Athens, 60-61, *ill.* 42, 45

A.D., meaning of, 38

Alexander the Great, 63-67, *ill.* 66

Alfred the Great, 207-210, *ill.* 198, 207

Alphabet: Babylonian, 27; Egyptian, 23, *ill.* 23; Greek, 44, *ill.* 44; Phoenician, 33, *ill.* 44; Roman, 76

America, settlement of, 368-370

Angles (*ăng'g'lz*), 121

Anglo-Saxons, defined, 204; tribes, 203-205

Apostles. *See* Bishops.

Apprentice, 321

Arabia, 125-126, *m.* 127

Arabs, 276

Arch, 96, 335-336, *ill.* 72, 255

Archaeologist, 11, 96

Architecture: Babylonian, 26-27, *ill.* 27; in cathedrals, 299-303, *ill.* 292; Egyptian, 21-22, *ill.* 21; Gothic, 299-302, *ill.* 300; Grecian, 45, *ill.* 42; Persian, 32, *ill.* 31; Renaissance, 335; Roman, 96, *ill.* 72, 82; Romanesque, 299, *ill.* 299

Aristotle, 64-65

Armor and weapons: Anglo-Saxon and Norman, 215; Assyrian, 29; Athenian, 50; cannon invented, 246; of castle defenders, 163; Celtic, 200; during Crusades, 283; Huns', *ill.* 119; of knights, 171-172, *ill.* 173; New Stone Age, 13; Old Stone Age, 11; Teutonic, 119

Art: under Alexander, 66; Assyrian, *ill.* 29; Babylonian, 26; of early man, 12; Egyptian, 23, *ill.* 22; Etruscan, 75; Grecian, 60-61; manuscript, 312-313, *ill.* 373; medieval, 299-303, *ill.* 302; Roman, 94; Renaissance, 335-340, *ill.* 332, 335, 336, 338, 339

Arthur, king, *ill.* 203

Astronomy, 24, 95; modern, 343-345, *ill.* 345

Assyria, 29-30, *m.* 26

Athens: Golden Age of, 60-63; history of, 48-50, 60-64; location of, 48-49, *m.* 40; Parthenon in, 60-61; and Persian wars, 57-59

Attila, 120

Augustus Caesar, 93-94

Austria: conversion of, 141; in Charlemagne's time, 151; and Teutonic tribes, 117

B

Babylonia: Hanging Gardens, 27; history of area, 25-32; written laws in, 28-29; great rivers of, 25-26, *m.* 26

Bacon, Roger, 308, *ill.* 308

Baghdad, 129

Banking: in Babylon, 27; Renaissance, 325

Barbarians: Burgundians, 121; and Charlemagne, 151-152, *ill.* 153; Huns, 119; Lombards, 121, 150-151, *ill.* 153; migrations of, *m.* 116; Picts, 201; and Roman Empire, 117-123; in Spain, 254; Vandals, 121. *See also* Angles, Anglo-Saxons, Celts, Franks, Gothic tribes, Saxons, Teutonic tribes, Vikings.

Battles: Acre (*ä'kẽr*), 282; Adrianople, 120; Bannockburn, 232; Clontarf, 232; Granada, 257; Hastings, 215; Jerusalem, 280, 282; Marathon, 57-58; Milvian Bridge, 111; Orleans, 247, *ill.* 248; Salamis, 59; Thermopylae, 58-59; Tours, 128, 150; Troy, 53, *ill.* 52

B.C., meaning of, 38

Bible, Old Testament, 17, 33-34

Bishops: as Apostles, 112; and conversion of Europe, 135-143, and investiture struggle, 265-268; in Middle Ages, 181-183, *ill.* 182, 183; and Protestant Revolt, 347-348, 353-354; in Roman Empire, 112-113

Black Death, 250

Blessed Virgin Mary, 105, 110, *ill.* 336

Bohemia, 272, *m.* 262

Books: Babylonian, 27; Egyptian, 23; Grecian, 52-53; medieval, 312-313, *ill.* 313; and modern printing, 341-342; Roman, 98

British Isles, 199, *m.* 196

Bronze Age, 16, *ill.* 16

C

Caesar, (*sē'zẽr*), Julius, in Britain, 201; history of, 90-93, *ill.* 91, 92; 344

Calendar: Babylonian, 28; Egyptian, 24; Julian, 92, 344; Gregorian, 343-345

Calvin, John, 349-350

Canterbury Tales, 224, 311-312, *ill.* 312

Canute, 210-211, *ill.* 211

Capet, Hugh, 240

Carthage, 83-85

Carthusians (kär·thū′zhănz), 293-294

Castle: description of, 163-166, *ill.* 165; entertainment in, 166, *ill.* 310; during Hundred Years' War, 246; knight's training in, 169-171; meals in, 164-166; life of women in, 167

Catacombs, 108-109, *ill.* 110

Catholic: defined, 107; Reformation, 353-359. *See also* Church.

Celts, 118, 199-201, 231-233

Chaldea, 30, *m.* 26

Charlemagne: history of, 151-157, *ill.* 148, 152, 156; *m.* 146, 157; empire after death of, 159-160, 239-240, 261-262

Charles VII, 247-249

Charles VIII, 251

Charles Martel (the Hammer), 128, 150

Chaucer, Geoffrey, 224, 311-312

China, 361-363

Chivalry, 184-185

Christianity. *See* Church, Greek Orthodox Church, Jesus Christ, Protestant Revolt.

Church: and Alfred the Great, 209-210; survives Barbarian invasions, 123; and Calendar reform, 344-345; in China, 363; and a Catholic community, 261; and Charlemagne, 155-156, *ill.* 148; during Crusades, 277-285; and Eastern Schism, 275-277; in early England, 204-205, *ill.* 205; education, schools, and learning in, 186-193, 305-308, 312-313, 333-334; and conversion of Europe, 135-143; founding of, 106; early growth of, 106-113; and guilds, 322-323; and Henry II, 224; and Holy Roman Emperors, 265-268, *ill.* 264; and King John, 226-227; in Middle Ages, 181-193, 293-303; monasticism in, 131-135; music in, 302-303; persecutions of, 108-111, *ill.* 108-109; and Philip Augustus, 241; revolt from and reformation in, 347-359; in Spain, 254, 257

Church of England (Anglican), 352

Cincinnatus, 78-79, *ill.* 78

Cistercians (sĭs·tûr′shănz), 294-295, *ill.* 294

City-state, 45, 63-65

Clovis, 135-136, 149-150, *ill.* 104

Colonies: Carthaginian, 83; European in America, 368-370; English, 228, 352; Greek, 46, 57, 75-76; Phoenician, 83; Portuguese, 368; Spanish, 366-367

Columbus, Christopher, 365-367, *ill.* 365, 366; *m.* 367

Constantine, 111, 112

Constantinople, 115, 275, 334, 363, *ill.* 122

Copernicus, Nicolous, 343, *ill.* 343

Council: of Nicaea, 113; of Trent, 353-354; of Whitby, 205.

Crusade: defined, 277; history of, 275-287; *ill.* 238, 282, 284; *m.* 236

D

Da Gama (gä′mȧ), Vasco, 365, *m.* 367

Danes, in England, 206-211

Dante, 311, *ill.* 311

Darius the Great, 31

David, 34, *ill.* 338

Da Vinci, Leonardo, 337-338

Demosthenes, 63

Dias (dē′ȧsh), Bartholomeu, 364-365, *m.* 367

Diocletian (dī′ȯ·klē′shăn), 111

Draco, 49

E

Eastern Roman Empire, 115, 121-122, 275-277, 333-334, 363, *m.* 276

Edgar, king, 210

Edict of Milan, 111

Education: and Alfred the Great, 209; in Athens, 50-51; under Charlemagne, 154-155; in medieval convents, 191; in feudal times, 169-171; and guilds, 322; in Prince Henry's school, 364, *ill.* 365; by the Jesuits, 358; in Middle Ages, 305-308, *ill.* 306; and new learning, 334; in Persia, 31; in Sparta, 47-48, *ill.* 47

Edward I, 230-232

Edward II, 231-232

Edward III, 231, 245

Egypt: history of, 19-25; science in, 24; *ill.* 24; trade in, 25

England: under the Conqueror, 216-219; conversion of, 138-139; in France, 245-250, *m.* 245; early history of, 199-211; later medieval history of, 221-233; Protestant revolt in, 350-352; trade in, 326; *m.* 139, 196

Ericson, Leif, 206, *m.* 206

Estates-General, 244, *ill.* 244

Etruscans (ê·trŭs′kănz), 75-77, *ill.* 75, 77

Euphrates (ù·frā·tēz) River, 25, *m.* 26

F

Fairs, medieval, 319, *ill.* 319

Farming: in Babylon, 25-26, *ill.* 32; discovery of, 14-15; in Egypt, 19-20; in feudal times, 177-179; in Greece, 44; at medieval monasteries, 192; in Roman Empire, 116-117

Ferdinand, 256-257, 366

Fertile Crescent, defined, 32, *m.* 26

Feudalism, 160-167

Fief, 161-162

Fire, discovery of, 15

Florence, 270, 324-325, 338, *m.* 138, 290

France: Church in, 184-185; history of, 239-251; Romans in, 91; *m.* 245. *See also* Franks.

Francis I, 350

Franks: history of, 121, 149-152; conversion of, 135-136

Frederick II, 269-270, 285

Frederick Barbarossa, 268-269, 281

Friars, 295-299

G

Galilei (gä′lê·lâ′ê), Galileo, 343

Genoa, 324, *m.* 290

Germany: and Charlemagne, 151-155; after Charlemagne, 156-157; conversion of, 140; and Crusades, 281; Holy Roman Empire in, 261-270, *m.* 262; Protestant Revolt in, 348-349; Teutonic tribes in, 117; trade in, 325

Godwin, 214-215

Gothic tribes, 119-120

Government: under Alfred the Great, 210; in Athens, 49-50, *ill.* 49; under Charlemagne, 151-157; under Conqueror, 216-219; in Egypt, 20-21; under Henry II, 221-223; under King John, 225-229; in Persia, 31; under Philip IV, 243-244; in prehistoric times, 16; under Roman Empire, 98; in Roman

Government (*continued*) Republic, 77-82, *ill.* 79; in Spain, 257-258; in Sparta, 48; among the Teutons, 118-119, *ill.* 117

Gracchus, Gaius and Tiberius, 90

Greece: colonies in Italy, 73, 75; Golden Age of, 60-63; history of, 43-67; influence of, 66, 95; *m.* 40

Greek Orthodox Church, 275-276

Gregory VII, pope, 266-268

Gregory XIII, pope, 344-345

Guilds, craft and merchant, 321-323

Gutenberg, Johann, 341, *ill.* 341

H

Hammurabi (häm′ōō·rä′bê), 28-29, *ill.* 28

Hannibal, 84-85, *ill.* 84

Hanseatic League, 325-326

Hapsburg Family, 270, 271

Harold, king, 214

Hebrew: nation, 33-36, *m.* 26; religion, 35-36

Henry II, 221-224

Henry III, 229

Henry IV, Holy Roman Emperor, 267-268

Henry VII, 350-351

Henry VIII, 351-352

Henry of Burgandy, 258-259

Henry of Portugal, 364, 365

Henry the Fowler, 262-263

Hieroglyphics, 23-24, *ill.* 23

Historians: under Alfred the Great, 209, *ill.* 198; under Charlemagne, 155; Greek, 62; Julius Caesar as, 98, 199; monks as, 191; Roman, 118

Holy Roman Empire, 261-270, 272, *m.* 262

Homage ceremony, 162

Homer, 52

Hundred Years' War, 245-250

Hungary, 141-142

I

Iliad, 52-53

Illuminated manuscripts, 312-313, *ill.* 373

Innocent III, 226-227, 284

Inquest, 222

Investiture struggle, 265-268, *ill.* 266

Ireland, 136-137, 199, 232-233, *m.* 196

Iron Age, 16

Irrigation, discovery of, 19-20

Isabella, 256-257, 366

Israel, 34

Italy: and Holy Roman Empire, 261-270, *m.* 262; land of, 73-74, *m.* 70; Papal States in, 150-151, *m.* 262; Renaissance in, 334-339; towns in, 323-325; and trade, 263-269, *m.* 362. *See also* Rome.

J

Jerusalem: 34-35, 277, 280, 282; *m.* 112, 236; Kingdom of, 280-281
Jesus Christ: life of, 105-107, *ill.* 106; shrines of in Holy Land, 276-277; teachings of, 109-110
Joan of Arc, 247-249, *ill.* 248, 249
John, king, 225-228, *ill.* 227
John XII, pope, 264, *ill.* 264
Journeyman, 321
Judea, 34-35
Jury, 222-223
Justinian Code, 98

K

Knight, 169-173, *ill.* 173
Knox, John, 350
Koran, 126-127
Kublai Khan, 362

L

Language: Anglo-Saxon, 218-219; Aramaic, 134; Celtic (Gaelic), 199; English, 218-219, 309, *ill.* 218-219; French, 149, 218, 271, 309; Greek, 51, 309; Latin, 76, 96-97; Romance, *ill.* 97; Spanish, 97, 254; Portuguese, 97, 254
Law: and Alfred the Great, 208-209; in Athens, 49; in Babylon, 28-29, *ill.* 28; and Charlemagne, 154; of the Church in England, 205; first collected, 28; under Henry II, 222-223; and Justinian Code, 98; under Louis IX, 243; and Magna Carta, 227-228, *ill.* 227, 228; in Middle Ages, 184; in Rome, 81; among the Teutons, 118-119
Leo III, pope, 153
Libraries: in Babylon, 27; in the Middle Ages, 312
Longbow, 246, *ill.* 246
Lothair (lȯ·thâr′), 156
Louis VII, 174, 281
Louis VIII, 242
Louis XI, 250-251, *ill.* 251
Louis XII, 251
Luther, Martin, 348-349, *ill.* 349

M

Magna Carta, 227-228, *ill.* 227, 228
Manorialism, defined, 159
Martyrs, early Christian, 108-109
Mary, queen, 352
Mecca, 125-126, *m.* 127
Mesopotamia, 25-33, *m.* 8
Metals, Age of, 16-17
Michelangelo, 337-339, *ill.* 336
Middle Ages: castle life in, 163-167; Church in, 181-193; Crusades in, 275-287; defined, 162; knights in, 169-173; monasticism in, 134-143, 186-193; serfs in, 173-179; schools and culture in, 305-313; towns and trade in, 315-327
Milan, 270, *m.* 262, 362
Miltiades, 58
Minstrel. *See* Troubadour.
Mohammed, 125-128
Mohammedanism: 125-129; defined, 126; in Spain, 254-256; *m.* 127
Mongols, 273
Monks: as book copyists, 312-313, *ill.* 190; defined, 131; in the East, 131-132; in feudal times, 174; as friars, 295-297; in later Middle Ages, 293-298; life of in medieval times, 188-189, *ill.* 187, 188; schools of, 134, 305-306; vows of, 134; in West, 132-135
Moors, 255-256
Moses, 34, *ill.* 36

N

Nebuchadnezzar, 30, 35
New Stone Age, 13-16
Nicene Creed, 113
Nicholas V, pope, 334
Nile River, 19-20, *m.* 8, 20
Northumbria, 138-139, *m.* 139
Numbers: Arabic, 128-129; Roman, 76
Nuns: in Germany, 140; in Middle Ages, 191-192, *ill.* 191; Reformation orders of, 355; in Rome, 134; in Spain, 257

O

Odo, 240
Odyssey, 52-53
Old Stone Age, 11-13
Olympic Games, 54-55, *ill.* 54
Order of Friars Minor, 295-296, 297-298, *ill.* 296
Order of Preachers, 296-297
Otto, 263-265

P

Palestine: birthplace of Christ (Holy Land), 105-106; Crusades to rescue, 275-287; home of Hebrews and Phoenicians, 32-37; *m.* 26

Papal States, 150-151, 269, *m.* 262

Papyrus (pȧ·pī′rŭs), 23

Parthenon, 60-61, *ill.* 61

Parliament: Cortes, 258; in England, 229-231; Estates-General, 244; Model, 230-231

Patricians, 79-80

Pepin, 150-151

Pericles, 60-61

Persia: history of, 30-32; wars with Grece, 57-59; *m.* 26

Philip Augustus, 240-242, 282-283

Philip of Macedonia, 64

Philip IV (the Fair), 243-244

Philip VI, 245

Philosophers, Greek, 62-63

Phoenicia: colonies of, 83; Greeks learn from, 44, 46; nation and traders, 32-33

Pius XI, pope, 352

Plato, 62

Plebeians, 80-81

Poland, 272, 281

Polo, Marco, 361-363

Pope: and Eastern Empire and Crusades, 275-278; and education and learning, 306; and England, 204-205, 226-227; and Franks, 149-153; as head of the Church, 107, 112; and Holy Roman Emperors, 265-268

Portugal, 258-259, 364, *m.* 254

Prehistoric man, 11-17, *ill.* 12, 14, 15, 17

Presbyterian Church, 350

Protestant Revolt, causes and history of, 347-352

Provinces, Roman, 87

Publicans, 87

Punic Wars, 83-85

Pyramids, 21-22, *ill.* 10, 21

R

Raphael (răf′ȧ·ĕl), 337-338, *ill.* 336

Reformation. *See* Protestant Revolt.

Religion: Arabian, 125; Athenian, 60-62; Babylonian, 28; Celtic, 200; Hebrew, 35-36; Grecian, 54-55; Mohammedan, 125-129; Roman, 76; Teutonic, 118

Renaissance, 333-345

Rome: in Great Britain, 201-203; heritage of, 95-99; history of, 77-85, *ill.* 77; 87-99, 116; early Church in, 108-113. *See also* Eastern Roman Empire, Western Roman Empire.

Rosetta Stone, 23-24, *ill.* 23

Rubens, Peter Paul, 340

Russia, 142-143, 273, *m.* 102

S

Saint: Adalbert, 141; Aidan, 139; Albertus Magnus, 297; Angela Merici, 355; Ansgar, 141; Anthony of Egypt, 131-132; Augustine of Canterbury, 138, 204-205; Augustine of Hippo, 63; Basil, 132; Benedict, 132-134; Bernard, 281, 294-295; Bonaventure, 297; Boniface, 140-141; Brendan, 199; Bruno of Cologne, 293; Catherine, 247; Charles Borromeo, 354; Clare, 296; Clotilda, 135-136; Columba, 137, *ill.* 137; Columban, 137-138; Cyril and Methodius, 142; Dominic, 257, 296-297, *ill.* 257; Edward the Confessor, 213-214, *ill.* 214; Francis of Sales, 355; Francis of Assisi, 295-297, *ill.* 296; Francis Xavier, 257, 359; Gall, 138; Gregory the Great, pope, 134-135; Helena, 111; Ignatius, Loyola, 257, 356-358, *ill.* 357; Joan Frances de Chantal, 355; Joan of Arc. *See* Joan of Arc; John Fisher, 351; Joseph, 105; Leo, pope, 121; Louis of France, 242-243, 285; Margaret, 247; Michael the Archangel, 247; Olga, 142; Patrick, 136-137; Paul, 107; Peter, 106-107; Philip Neri, 354; Pius V, pope, 354; Remigius, 136, *ill.* 104; Robert, 294; Scholastica, 134; Stephen of Hungary, 141-142; Teresa of Avila, 257, 355, *ill.* 257; Thomas à Becket, 224; Thomas Aquinas, 63, 297, 307; Thomas More, 351-352; Vincent de Paul, 355; Virgil, 141; Vladimir the Great, 142-143

St. Peter's in Rome, 334-335, *ill.* 335

Saladin, 282-283

Saxons, 151, 203

Scandinavia, 141, 206, 272, *m.* 102

Scholastic Philosophy, 308

Science: of astronomy, 24, 95, 343-345; Babylonian, 28; Egyptian, 24-25;

Science (*continued*)
Greek, 62-63; inventions of, 341-344; in medieval universities, 307
Scotland, 137, 201, 232, 350, *m.* 196
Serfs: defined, 160; life of, 173-179; *ill.* 175, 176, 178
Sicily, 73-74, 269, *m.* 70, 262
Slavs, 118, 141, *m.* 273
Society of Jesus, 356-359
Socrates, 62
Spain: Barbarians in, 121; explorations for, 365-367, *m.* 367; history of, 253-257, *m.* 254; Moors in, 128; Rome and Carthage in, 84, *m.* 93
Sparta: and war with Athens, 63-64; government and life in, 47-48; at Marathon, 57-58; at Thermopylae, 58-59; *m.* 40
Squire, 170, *ill.* 170
Sweden, 272, *m.* 102
Switzerland, 138, 271-272, 350
Sylvester II, pope, 142, 174

T

Ten Commandments, 36
Teutonic tribes, 117-119, *ill.* 117
Themistocles, 59
Theology, defined, 307
Theresa of León, 258-259
Third Orders, 297
Thucydides (thû·sĭd′ĭ·dēz), 62
Tiber River, 75, *m.* 70
Tigris River, 25, *m.* 26
Tower of London, 216, *ill.* 216
Towns: in France, 241; in Italy, 269; life in Middle Ages, 315-320, *ill.* 316-317; in Spain, 258; trade of, 323-327
Trade: Babylonian, 27-28; after Cru-

Trade (*continued*)
sades, 286; with East, 361-363, *m.* 362; Egyptian, 25; northern European, 325-327; Grecian, 46; at medieval fairs, 319; Mediterranean, 323-325; Phoenician, 32-33; Portuguese, 259
Tribune, 81
Troubadour, 166, 309-310, *ill.* 310
Troy, 53, *m.* 40
Turks, 277-281
Type, movable, 341, *ill.* 341

U

Union of Kalmar, 272
Universities. *See* Education, in Middle Ages.
Urban II, 277

V

Van Eyck (vän īk′), Hubert and Jan, 340
Vassal, 160-162
Vatican City, 270, 338, *ill.* 335
Venice, 270, 323-324
Vestal Virgins, 76, *ill.* 76
Vikings, 206, 272

W

Wales, 231-232, *m.* 196
Wallace, William, 232
Wars of the Roses, 350
Western Roman Empire, 115-117, 119-122, *m.* 93. *See also* Rome.
William the Conqueror, 214-219
Witan, 216, 229
Writing: Babylonian, 27; Egyptian, 23; invention of, 16-17; manuscript, 190-191, *ill.* 373. *See also* Alphabet.

X

Xerxes (zûrk′sēz), 32

Y

Yugoslavia, conversion of, 141

Acknowledgments

Alinari: 36, 338 *both*
Artext Prints Inc.: 336 *both*
Bettmann Archive: 75, 294, 299, 302 *left*
British Information Service: 13, 201, 209, 216, 229, 306
British Museum: 23
British Travel Association: 231
Brown Brothers: 300, 302 *right*, 334, 359
Charles Phelps Cushing: 45

Chicago Natural History Museum: 12
Culver Pictures, Inc.: 122, 204, 244
Ewing Galloway: 61, 82, 255
Historical Pictures Service: 228
Oriental Institute, University of Chicago: 28, 29, 44
Paul's Photos: 74, 339
United Press International: 351
Wide World Photos: 21, 22, 31, 133